FEMALE ENTREPRENEURS
IN NINETEENTH-CENTURY RUSSIA

T0330528

Perspectives in Economic and Social History

Series Editors: Andreas Gestrich
                               Steven King
                               Robert E. Wright

Titles in this Series

1 Migrants and Urban Change: Newcomers to Antwerp, 1760–1860
Anne Winter

Forthcoming Titles

Barriers to Competition: The Evolution of the Debate
Ana Rosado Cubero

Rural Unwed Mothers: An American Experience 1870–1950
Mazie Hough

The World of Carolus Clusius: Natural History in the Making, 1550–1610
Florike Egmond

FEMALE ENTREPRENEURS IN NINETEENTH-CENTURY RUSSIA

BY

Galina Ulianova

Routledge
Taylor & Francis Group

LONDON AND NEW YORK

First published 2009 by Pickering & Chatto (Publishers) Limited

Published 2016 by Routledge
2 Park Square, Milton Park, Abingdon, Oxfordshire OX14 4RN
711 Third Avenue, New York, NY 10017, USA

First issued in paperback 2015

Routledge is an imprint of the Taylor & Francis Group, an informa business

© Taylor & Francis 2009
© Galina Ulianova 2009
Translated by Anna and Aleksey Yurasovsky

BRITISH LIBRARY CATALOGUING IN PUBLICATION DATA

Ulianova, Galina.
Female entrepreneurs in nineteenth-century Russia. – (Perspectives in economic and social history)
1. Businesswomen – Russia – History – 19th century. 2. Women-owned business enterprises – Russia – History – 19th century. 3. Women – Legal status, laws, etc. – Russia – History – 19th century.
I. Title II. Series
338'.04'082'0947-dc22

ISBN-13: 978-1-138-66372-5 (pbk)
ISBN-13: 978-1-85196-967-8 (hbk)

Typeset by Pickering & Chatto (Publishers) Limited

CONTENTS

Acknowledgements   vii
List of Figures, Tables and Images   ix

Introduction   1
1 Female Entrepreneurship in the 1800s–20s: Business and the Issue of
    Property   9
2 Female Entrepreneurship in the 1830s–40s: A Hidden Success   33
3 Female Entrepreneurship in the 1850s–60s: An Unstable Rise: The
    Moscow and St Petersburg cases   73
4 Female Entrepreneurship in the 1870s: Family Levers in Business Regu-
    lation   111
5 Female Entrepreneurship in the 1880s: The Dictate of Money Inside the
    Family Circle   135
6 Female Entrepreneurship in the 1890s: A Breakthrough Towards Inde-
    pendence   165
Conclusion   193

Notes   201
Works Cited   227
Index   239

ACKNOWLEDGEMENTS

A number of my colleagues in Russia, Europe and the USA helped me with this work, and I am much indebted to them for this help and comments. First, I must thank the American historian David L. Ransel (Indiana University) for the time he spent in discussing with me the prospects of developing the subject. Adele Lindenmeyr (Villanova University) and Bianka Pietrow-Ennker (Konstanz University) shared with me their knowledge of Russian women in the context of social history. I am especially grateful to Steven King (Oxford Brookes University), who was the first reader of the manuscript and who gave me valuable advice concerning its structure. In the course of writing individual chapters and the book, I benefited from the aid and counsel of the following eminent historians: Boris Anan'ich (Institute of History, St Petersburg); Yuri Petrov (Institute of Russian History, Moscow; he presently works for the Central Bank of Russia); Liudmila Bulgakova (Institute of History, St Petersburg); Guido Hausmann (Freiburg University); Catherine Evtuhov (Georgetown University); Alastair Owens (Queen Mary, University of London); Tamara Kondratieva (Paris, Centre d'études du monde russe, soviétique et post-soviétique, EHESS); Joseph Bradley (University of Tulsa); Christine Ruane (University of Tulsa); Leonid Borodkin (Moscow State University); Roger Bartlett (Birmingham University); Wendy Rosslyn (Nottingham University); Sergey Antonov (Columbia University); Michelle Marrese (New York City); Michael Middeke (London); Rustam Shukurov (Moscow State University); Nailia Tagirova (Samara State Economic University). I am deeply grateful to my friends, Anvar and Natasha Shukurov (Newcastle University), and Liza and Alex Fridman (London) for their hospitality and for having been enormously supportive at all times.

My thanks are especially due to the translators of my book, Anna and Aleksey Yurasovsky, for their meticulous work and indispensable professional advice concerning the finalization of the text.

I also owe a great debt to Roger Bartlett (Birmingham University) for his invaluable advice and the excellent translation of my first article on the issue of female entrepreneurship to be published in the UK (Palgrave Macmillan Publishers). It was later reworked into Chapter 1 of the present monograph.

I received some very useful information from Michael Zolotarev, and it is already the third time that I borrow material from his collection of historical photographs to serve as illustrations for my books.

Finally, I can only inadequately express my gratitude to my mother, Liudmila Ulianova, my sister Marina Ulianova, my son, Oyat Shukurov (he helped me to draw the map and to compose the bibliography for the book), and my aunt, Natalia Bolikhovskaia, for so much family support while this monograph was being written. It is most regretful that my father Nikolai Ulianov (who passed away in early June 2008) will not see this book, for it is thanks to his belief in my creative abilities that my work on the project could have been started and brought to conclusion.

And I am deeply thankful to my faithful friend Leonid Radzikhovsky, who has played an exceptional role in the destiny of the book, and whose emotional and intellectual assistance was of crucial importance for me during the past decade and especially in 2008, when the work on the text was in its final stage.

LIST OF FIGURES, TABLES AND IMAGES

Figure 3.1. The ethnic composition of businesswomen in St Petersburg
and Moscow (1869)   95
Figure 3.2. The age of St Petersburg and Moscow businesswomen (1869,
per cent)   96
Figure 3.3. The distribution of St Petersburg and Moscow businesswomen
by business specialization (1869)   100
Figure 4.1. The distribution of proprietresses of industrial enterprises by
estate group (1879)   121
Figure 4.2. The ethnic composition of proprietresses of industrial enterprises (1879)   122
Figure 7.1. The share of female-owned enterprises. 1814–97   195

Table 1.1. Number of enterprises owned by women by branch of indus-
trial activity (1814)   17
Table 1.2. Soap-Boiling Enterprises in Kazan' (1814)   22
Table 1.3. Data on Women of the Merchant Estate and the Value of their Property Lost in Consequence of the Burning of Moscow during the 1812 War   26
Table 2.1. The number of enterprises owned by women, by branch of
industry (1832)   34
Table 2.2. The provinces with the largest number of female entrepreneurs
(1832)   41
Table 2.3. The by-branch composition of Moscow commercial establish-
ments belonging to female entrepreneurs (1838)   55
Table 2.4. The types of business management (1838)   59
Table 2.5. The per-person distribution of enterprises belonging to women
(1838)   64
Table 3.1. number of enterprises owned by women by branch of indus-
trial activity (Moscow, 1853)   76
Table 3.2. Moscow enterprises owned by women, by number of workers
employed (1853)   80

Table 3.3. Women-owned enterprises with more than 100 workers (Moscow, 1853)   82

Table 3.4. Number of Enterprises Owned by Women by Branch of Industrial Activity (St Petersburg, 1862)   89

Table 3.5. The age of proprietresses of Moscow enterprises (1869)   100

Table 3.6. The specialization of the proprietresses of commercial enterprises in St Petersburg and Moscow, belonging to the First and the Second Guilds (1869)   103

Table 4.1. Number of Enterprises Owned by Women, by Branch of Industrial Activity (Russian Empire, 1879)   115

Table 4.2. Female-owned textile enterprises with annual output in excess of 0.5 million roubles (Russian Empirs, 1879)   117

Table 5.1. Number of Enterprises Owned by Women, by Branch of Industrial Activity (Russian Empire, 1884)   139

Table 6.1. Number of Enterprises Owned by Women, by Branch of Industrial Activity (Russian Empire, 1897)   168

Table 6.2. The specialization of the proprietresses of commercial enterprises in St Petersburg and Moscow, belonging to the First and Second Guilds (1895)   182

1. Portrait of Avdot'ia Rakhmanova, a wealthy Moscow female merchant. 1826. Courtesy of Mikhail Zolotarev, Moscow.   9

2. Portrait of an unknown female merchant. 1840s. Courtesy of Mikhail Zolotarev, Moscow.   40

3. The Alekseev family. Widow Vera Alekseeva, owner of a gold-cloth factory for 26 years (1823–49) and of 64 shops in Kitai-Gorod, is seated on the right. Vera was the great-grandmother of Constantine Stanislavsky, theatre innovator and creator of the Stanislavsky system of acting (later Method acting). Source: The Chetverikovs – N. A. Dobrynina Family Archive.   57

4. Autograph signature of Natalia Nosova, head (in 1829–52) of a wool-weaving mill in Moscow. 1849. Courtesy of Mikhail Zolotarev, Moscow   87

5. View of the biggest cloth mill 'The Babkin Brothers', which was owned for 40 years (1842–83) by the Moscow female merchant Maria Matveeva. 1840s. Source: L. Samoilov, Atlas promyshlennosti Moskovskoi gubernii (1845).   124

6. Portrait of Maria Morozova, head (in 1889–1911) of Russia's largest textile enterprise – the Partnership of the Nikolskaia Manufactory of 'Savva Morozov's Son and Co'. Courtesy of Mikhail Zolotarev, Moscow.   146

7. View of the Nikolskaia manufactory. 1890s. Courtesy of Mikhail
　　Zolotarev, Moscow.　　　　　　　　　　　　　　　　　147
8. The inner yard of the Sandunov Bath House in Moscow, owned by
　　Vera Firsanova. Late 1890s. Courtesy of Mikhail Zolotarev, Moscow.　188

The distribution of female entrepreneurship in the European part
of Russian Empire.

INTRODUCTION

In 1832, a 'moral narrative' novel (as it was stated on its title page) was published in Moscow. Its author was Aleksandr Orlov, its title – *Anna, a Merchant's Daughter, or a Velvet Reticule from the Haberdashery Row*. The hero of this novel was a young trader in haberdashery from Kitai-Gorod, Valerian, whose way of doing business was to cut the price of his goods – in exchange for his female customers' smiles and attention – to the lowest possible level, and this brought him to the brink of ruin.

However, Valerian was saved from this ruinous outcome by a letter sent to him by his beautiful customer Anna, a merchant's daughter. In this letter, Anna demonstrated her liking and sympathy for the young merchant by offering the following rational piece of advice:

> 'Valerian! I am a merchant's daughter, and my name is Anna. I have heard from my father and brother that you are reduced to resorting to credit by selling your goods for a song to women, and so you will have nothing to buy any [more] goods with for your shop, and you cannot have them any more on credit. At least so I have heard my father and brother say – who, knowing all merchants' turnovers, and having large-scale speculations of their own, seldom make mistakes either in their calculations or in their judgment of trading people. I sympathize with you sincerely, and wish with a pure heart that you may set right your affairs. Anna'.[1]

Then Anna, without disclosing her surname, sent Valerian 1,000 roubles, to enable him to repay the credit and once again make his trade profitable. The plot develops further: the young people made personal acquaintance when Anna, under the pretence of being a customer, once again visited Valerian's shop. They gradually developed romantic feelings for each other, and their story had a happy ending: they got married.

This is a fictional illustration of a situation when a young merchant's daughter's tender feelings become intertwined with her pragmatic outlook and her ideas of 'the right way' to transact business – based on her ability to count money and to rationally invest available financial resources in the development of an enterprise.

Orlov's novel depicts a fairly typical social situation. In the nineteenth century, Russian women were brought up with the notion that a female had to be as competent as her male counterpart in tackling financial issues and carrying out trade and real estate transactions. This was also true of women belonging to all economically active classes: noblewomen, female merchants, *meshchanki* and to a certain degree, peasant women who settled in towns. Michelle Marrese, in her in-depth study on the noblewomen's control of property in Russia, noted that

> by the nineteenth century noblewomen featured in roughly 40 percent of real estate transfers, as sellers and investors, throughout Russia – a figure, as far as we know, that greatly exceeded female property holding in other European countries.[2]

Marrese's statistical analysis demonstrates that noblewomen owned no less than one-third of all privately held land in the decades before the Emancipation of the Serfs in 1861.

1. The Issue of Separate Property

The major difference between Russian and west-European legislation consisted in the fact that, according to Russian law, women enjoyed the same property rights as men.[3] By a law adopted in 1753, wives were permitted to 'sell their own property without the consent of [their] husbands'.[4] Each of the spouses could own and independently acquire new and separate property (through purchase, gifts, inheritance or by any other legal means). Moreover, spouses could enter into certain legal relationships with each other involving transfer of property under a deed of gift, purchase-and-sale, etc., as if they were unrelated persons. In 1825 this right was confirmed by a special legal provision entitled 'Explanation that the Sale of an Estate from One Spouse to the Other is Not Contrary to the Law'.[5]

In the *Corpus of Laws of the Russian Empire*, first published in 1832, the principle of separate property in marriage was definitely consolidated in the following legal formula: that the property of a wife shall not become the husband's property, moreover, irrespective of the way and time of its acquisition (be it during or before marriage), the husband even shall not acquire, through marriage, the right to use his wife's property.[6] This legislative landmark made it possible for a woman to become independent in property matters. Adele Lindenmeyr characterized this dichotomy – expressed in a situation when

> Russia's patriarchal family law imposed severe restrictions on women's autonomy', while at the same time 'its property and inheritance law protected the rights of women' – as 'one of the most intriguing paradoxes in Russian history.[7]

In the eighteenth and nineteenth centuries, the right of independent owner-ship of property was a very important factor that definitely shaped the Russian woman's gender role in management and household structures. A detailed expla-nation of this phenomenon is offered by Barbara A. Engel:

> Although the 'domestic' was defined as women's proper sphere, as it was in Europe and the United States, in Russia the domestic extended well beyond the confines of home and housework. Women's subordinate status in life and law coexisted, some-times uneasily, with their legal rights to own and manage immovable property, which Russian wives, as well as single women and widows, enjoyed. Even married women could buy and sell and enter contracts, a status that was unique in Europe.[8]

William G. Wagner was the first contemporary historian to address the issue of separate property on the basis on Russian material.[9] Due to the availability of published studies where this issue is tackled in the context of European countries and the United States,[10] Wagner, by applying comparative analysis, came to the conclusion that

> the most important legal advantage enjoyed by married women in Imperial Russia in comparison with their Western European and American counterparts, however, was their right to control their own property, including their dowries ... Such proprietary power could provide wives with a counterweight to their complete personal subor-dination to their husbands. Except in limited circumstances, by contrast, married women in most Western European countries and American states did not acquire comparable proprietary independence until the mid-nineteenth century or later.[11]

Still more progress in our understanding of the nature of women's property rights, as reflected both in legislation and everyday practice, became possible owing to pioneering monographs by Michelle Lamarche Marrese[12] and Lee Far-row,[13] which appeared two years later.

This independence in property matters was the key factor in the develop-ment of female entrepreneurship because of the 'patterns of ownership being closely related to patterns of control'.[14] According to one Russian lawyer of the late nineteenth century,

> the separateness of spouses' property, which is in no way compatible with the nature and idea of marriage, did its historical service to the Russian woman in a much better and more feasible way than the currently existing systems of Germanic community property and Roman dowry.[15]

(However, researchers should by no means absolutize the principle of independ-ent female property ownership, thus overlooking the paradoxical nature of the situation when the principle of separate property of spouses coexisted with the legally consolidated subordination of a wife to her husband and of daughters to their father in the context of personal legal relations.)

As early as the dawn of industrial development, in the mid-eighteenth century, some women were already owners of big enterprises. Thus, for example, in 1748, the Kadashevskaia Linen Manufactory in Moscow belonged to 'a merchant's widow' Natal'ia Babkina; another two cloth manufactories (established in 1763 and 1769) were owned by noblewomen – an admiral's wife, Miatleva, and Princess Yusupova.[16]

Throughout the nineteenth century female entrepreneurship was continually expanding to encompass various new spheres of commercial activity. At the same time, legislation regulating trade and industry did not treat female entrepreneurs as a special group, distinct from their male counterparts.

2. The Historiographical Situation and the Beginning of Studies on the History of Russian Female Entrepreneurship

The history of women in Russia, within the framework of general discourse on women's history and gender studies, has become an important segment of humanities research. In the last twenty-five years there have appeared a number of works shedding light on various aspects of this segment of Russian history. Valuable contributions to recent bibliography in this field were made by L. H. Edmondson, R. Stites, G. A. Tishkin, D. L Ransel, B. A. Engel, D. B. Clements, N. L. Pushkareva, C. Worobec, B. Pietrow-Ennker, O. A. Khasbulatova, C. Ruane, W. Rosslyn and other authors of note.[17]

However, despite the existing interest in the problem of female entrepreneurship in Western historiography, the study of Russian women entrepreneurs in retrospect is still in its initial phase. In the article by Catriona Kelly, published more than ten years ago, it was aptly noted that,

> whilst trading and factory owning made the fortunes of few women, they appear to have provided a number with a reasonable living; and though the proportion of women traders ... in city populations was far lower than that of factory workers or servants, the mercantile elite no less deserves description than those other elites (for example, women writers or women revolutionaries).[18]

It is also true that since then the situation with regard to historiography has improved only slightly.

Adele Lindenmeyr and Muriel Joffe analysed for the first time a group of the Moscow merchant elite women and noted:

> merchant wives and daughters who owned the required amount of capital were registered in the merchant guilds, owned stock in family corporations, and attended meetings of corporate shareholders.[19]

The issue of female entrepreneurs is essentially outlined in the monograph by M. L. Marrese.[20] The greatest analytical contribution to this problem so far has been made by N. Kozlova, in a series of her articles on the economic status and entrepreneurial activity of Moscow female merchants in the eighteenth century.[21] It is Kozlova who put in circulation archival documents illustrating the thesis that the economic independence of merchants' wives was a widespread phenomenon (which, by the way, is also confirmed by our materials dating to the nineteenth century). Kozlova's views are shared by O. Fomina, whose research addresses the issues of women's property status within the merchant family during the last third of the eighteenth century.[22]

As for the nineteenth century, there have been no extensive studies of this period as yet – all that is published is several articles and a section in a book written by I. Potkina, M. Tikhomirova, and the present author.[23]

We should also mention that in our study of female entrepreneurship we also used as sources the works by our predecessors, who have greatly increased our understanding of the history of the Russian bourgeoisie – B. Anan'ich, A. Rieber, Yu. Petrov, M. Hildermeier, A. Aksenov, J.A. Ruckman, J. West, D. L. Ransel, A. Bokhanov and T. C. Owen.[24]

3. The Prospective Approaches Developed in Western Historiography: 'to Render Businesswomen Visible'

The study of the history of female entrepreneurship in Russia is still young, although for the past fifteen years the issue of women's economic role in the nineteenth century has been attracting increasing interest from historians from both Europe and the USA.[25]

It appears desirable that in our brief historiographical overview we should pay tribute to the research approaches developed by Western historians, which create promising prospects for the study of female entrepreneurship in Russia.

Since the 1960s, historians' attention to the roles of women in history has been steadily growing. An important milestone was reached in 1987 with the publication of *Family Fortunes* by Leonore Davidoff and Catherine Hall. Immediately recognized as a 'classic in its field', the book deals with such fundamental issues as the 'separate spheres' and gender system in the English middle strata.[26] The authors' conceptual approaches to the history of property relationships between men and women attracted many followers and provided a strong impetus to further discussion of the issues raised in their work. The most notable contribution to this discourse was made by Amanda Vickery in her eloquently titled article 'Golden Age to separate spheres? A review of the categories and chronology of English Women history', where the excessive use of the separate spheres pattern was justly criticized.[27]

From the early 1990s historians, in their attempts to understand precisely where the boundaries between these separate spheres lay, have begun to study the issue of the property rights enjoyed by women belonging to the middle urban strata.

Maxine Berg, by analysing the wills of women from entrepreneurial families in Birmingham and Sheffield, demonstrated that this source of historical information could somewhat alter our understanding of the woman's property status as being restricted by legislative acts. Thus, within the family women could indeed control property while not being exactly its owners: '...Women set up a good proportion of trusts themselves and played a significant role as executors'.[28] Arguing against the assumption put forth by Davidoff and Hall, that after the death of their husbands women received only income in trust, Berg put forth the following objection: 'of women leaving wills in the Birmingham and Sheffield samples, 46.8 per cent in both towns owned real property, that is, land or houses', and, furthermore, 'approximately 33 per cent of men's property bequests were made to wives, and another 14 per cent to daughters'.[29]

Therefore, it is logical that the discourse on the property rights of women gave rise to interest in the sources of their incomes and wealth, and particularly those specific to the group of female entrepreneurs whose personal estates were created as a result of their activities outside of their domestic circle. While characterizing the study of female entrepreneurs as a gap in contemporary historiography, Wendy Gamber concluded her article (1998) with a meaningful statement:

> Much work, empirical and theoretical, remains to be done. Only then will we be able to render businesswomen visible, to see them not as exceptions to preconceived rules, but as part of the gendered history of economic life.[30]

However, three years later it was already obvious that several dozen researchers were simultaneously developing this theme in different countries, with the results beginning to be published, and so Angel Kwolek-Folland wrote as follows in her analytical article:

> In the last few years, many books, articles, and dissertations have raised important questions about gender in the history of business, suggesting that the topic is one of the fastest growing and most intellectually innovative areas of historical study.[31]

The outcome of the development of this 'innovative area' was several important publications that appeared in the last decade. In monographs by W. Gamber, A. Kwolek-Folland, H. Barker, N. Phillips and a number of other authors, various regional and national female entrepreneurship models were presented. The product of the participation of a broader circle of researchers in the studies aimed at adequately assessing the role of female entrepreneurship in the economic development of European countries was the book 'Women, Business, and Finance in

Nineteenth-century Europe. Rethinking Separate Spheres' (2005), where one can find a variety of scientific approaches and research aspects. Its introduction offers an analytical review of the currently existing areas of research with regard to female entrepreneurship. It is suggested that one should be guided by the basic principle that

> the separate spheres ideology was but one among many forms of gender identity co-existing and overlapping in nineteenth-century Europe.[32]

In the future, studies across different countries and regions – as well as those aimed at correlating the development of female entrepreneurship in the nineteenth century with that of the Industrial Revolution – could provide a sound grounding for generalization, if based on careful empirical research.

4. A Note on Sources and Our Approach to Research

First, this study examines the history of female entrepreneurship in the Russian Empire in the course of its industrial development in the nineteenth century. Our goal was not only to describe female entrepreneurship *per se*, but also to discuss it in the general context of the development of Russian business. We wanted to find out in which sectors of industry and trade it was possible for women to achieve greatest success, and also which economic and social factors determined their victories and defeats in various business spheres. Wherever possible, we tried to achieve integration of quantitative and qualitative analysis. Much of this investigation is based on primary sources previously untapped, including archival documents, which contain statistical information on female entrepreneurs from 1814 to 1900. Besides, we made an attempt to analyze, from a sociological point of view, the relevant statistics with regard to wide range of enterprises, from the smallest to the biggest. (Regretfully, it was impossible to draw any comprehensive comparison, because there are no uniform data for the entire nineteenth century in the available sources. Thus, the book also lacks data on the dynamics of trade in the 1830s-40s and the 1850s-60s, for absence of relevant sources).

The second focus of this book is the examination of legal materials. The purpose of these materials was to define the driving forces of female entrepreneurship and to see how legal challenges were shaping women's business strategies. Thus, property disputes were increasingly frequently submitted to the consideration by the Commercial Court and other supreme instances (for example, after submitting an appeal to the governor-general of a given province).

Thirdly, the work concentrates on the correlation of economic parameters with the available data on the social world of female entrepreneurs. In each of the chapters, we provided some lively case-histories in order to illustrate the 'dry' statistics. Their incorporation in the text helped to reveal the background of a number of fortunes, including the instances of bankruptcy and property litigations which involved close relatives and criminal proceedings initiated against sales personnel. The unwavering desire of certain individuals to increase their wealth was influencing their family life and thus gave rise to some rather bizarre situations. Three examples: a merchant's widow, who married a merchant, transacts business independently of her second husband, so that the factory can be inherited by her son from a previous marriage; a husband changes his family name for that of his wife in order to preserve their firm's brand and retain clients; a husband is expelled from the matrimonial bedroom for his failure in business.

The case-studies presented in the book are reconstructions of the biographies of women who were directly involved as leading entrepreneurs or partners in family-run businesses. Our main sources were the rich documentary collections kept in Moscow archives, which contain materials pertaining to Moscow as the Empire's most important commercial and industrial centre and to some other cities of European Russia as well. Our emphasis on Moscow documents enabled us to trace the lives of several generations of merchant dynasties and to depict female entrepreneurship in the context of urban industrial transformation. Regretfully, we have yet failed to find in the archives, in sufficient quantities, certain valuable sources like the wills or insurance policies of female entrepreneurs. However, even occasional documents of this type have made it possible for us to define the size of capital owned by women entrepreneurs, and thus to obtain comprehensive information on female entrepreneurship.

By using the symbiosis of the statistical and biographical approaches, we are going to show how the patterns of ownership and the social composition of the strata of female entrepreneurs were changing over the course of the century.

It is our hope that, once this goal is achieved, our results may shed some light on the question of whether (and to what extent) Russia was unique in the way its female entrepreneurship was developing – or, conversely, shared, in this respect, many common features with European countries.

I hope that this book may become a starting point for reviving the long-forgotten histories of Russian women who, while evidently putting much at stake when engaging in business, were, nevertheless, ready to take this risk in order to fulfil their mission, viewed primarily as sustaining the economic viability of their families.

1 FEMALE ENTREPRENEURSHIP IN THE 1800s–20s: BUSINESS AND THE ISSUE OF PROPERTY

Portrait of Avdot'ia Rakhmanova, a wealthy Moscow female merchant. 1826.
Courtesy of Mikhail Zolotarev, Moscow.

In the contemporary historiography, the nineteenth century in Russian history is often called 'the European Century'.[1] Over this period, Europe provided the model for economic, social and administrative improvements. These improvements were imperative because, in the words of historian Vasily Kliuchevskii, at the turn of the eighteenth century Russia was a country with 'an unsightly past and present'.[2] Some of the borrowings were fruitful, other were ill-fitted for the Russian social environment. Nevertheless, by the end of the nineteenth century Russia had been included in the economic and political space of the European continent.

One of the elements of the transformation of economic mechanisms taking place at that time was the legally unrestricted participation of women in commerce and industry.

In the early nineteenth century commercial activity by women was provided for in the legislation of the Russian Empire: according to the laws concerning persons of the merchant class, on the death of an owner the management of his business was to pass to his widow. Frequently, even when the son or sons were commercially very experienced and active, family businesses were formally and in actual fact headed by the widow. Another, slightly less frequent, practice was to bequeath the management of a firm to daughters (both married and unmarried) if there were no male heirs. (These provisions were contained in a decree of 25 May 1775, and were confirmed in 1809, 1824 and 1865).[3] The examples below of how women acquired merchant status will illustrate the various legal procedures for their entering the sphere of entrepreneurship.

This chapter also examines female entrepreneurship in industry and the structure of immovable and movable property owned by businesswomen. The latter aspect will be studied on the basis of a specific source: petitions submitted to the Moscow Governor-General written by women.

However, let us first turn to legislative acts regulating women's participation in entrepreneurship. It should be noted that the principle of equal rights of men and women to engage in commerce and industry, enunciated in the late eighteenth and early nineteenth centuries, was fully valid until the 1917 Revolution.

1. Female Entrepreneurship in the Legislation of the Late Eighteenth and Early Nineteenth Centuries

According to the laws of the Russian Empire, women had equal rights to those of men when engaging in commerce. In the reign of Catherine II, on 25 May 1775, the Senate issued a decree 'Concerning the levy from merchants of one per cent of declared capital, instead of the soul tax, and concerning their division into guilds'.[4] This stated among other things:

Persons of the female sex are assigned to guilds on exactly the same basis as men: unmarried women according to the estate into which they were born, married and widowed women according to the status acquired through their marriage.

The same document repeated this proposition in different words:

The regulations concerning [male] merchants are also to be applied to widows who carry on the trade of deceased merchants, their husbands, or who conduct commerce independently with their own capital.

In this way the legislation reflected the actual situation in the sphere of female entrepreneurship, in which in Russia (as indeed in other countries too) three groups of persons of female sex, defined by their marital status, carried on their activities. These were merchants' widows (the most numerous group both in Russia and in other European countries), married female merchants, and unmarried daughters of merchants.

The division of merchants into guilds had first taken place in Russia in 1720, under Peter I. A clear definition of the rights of the so-called 'town inhabitants' (*gorodovye obyvateli*), of whom the merchantry constituted the highest social stratum, was given in the Charter to the Towns of 1785.[5] Thus freedom of entrepreneurship was enshrined in law. The Charter divided the merchantry into three guilds in accordance with the amount of the individual's declared capital and the extent of his or her commercial activity. In the first guild were registered persons with a declared capital of 10,000–50,000 roubles. According to the Urban Statute (part of the Charter to the Towns) they were

not only allowed, but also encouraged to conduct all sorts of trade both within and outside the Empire, to import and export goods, to sell, exchange and purchase them both wholesale and retail.

Members of the second guild, with declared capital of 5,000–10,000 roubles, were permitted to

conduct all sorts of trade within the Empire, and to convey goods both by land and by water, to towns and fairs, and there to sell, exchange and purchase items necessary for their trade both wholesale and retail.

Third-guild merchants, with capital of 1,000–5,000 roubles, were permitted to conduct

petty trade in towns and districts, to sell small articles in the town and its surroundings, and to convey that petty trade by land and water to villages, settlements and rural trading points, and there to sell, exchange and purchase items necessary for their petty trade wholesale or separate'.[6]

Besides members of the merchantry, townspeople (members of the *meshchanstvo*, the lowest stratum of the urban population in Russia)[7] were also allowed to engage in entrepreneurial activity on a small scale:

> A townsman is free to set up looms and workbenches of all sorts and to produce on them all sorts of handicrafts.[8]

Evidence for the wide extent of female entrepreneurship by the time of Alexander I can be found in another document, the draft Commercial Code of the Russian Empire drawn up in 1814 by the Commission for the Compilation of Laws. The draft Code contained a separate, if brief, chapter entitled 'Concerning persons of the female sex engaged in merchant activities'. It included two important clauses, the first of which stated that a woman, on reaching her majority, 'acquires the right to engage in commerce'; the second declared that 'on receipt of permission from the appropriate government office to engage in commerce, she [the woman] is endowed with all merchant prerogatives, according to the branch of commerce she pursues'.[9] Although, as is well known, the draft Commercial Code was not passed into law, its significance in the historical context is that the inclusion in it of a special chapter on women reflected already existing phenomena and demonstrates the presence of female entrepreneurship in the period studied.

Now we are going to consider by what means women entered the merchant estate.

2. How Women Acquired Merchant Status

In terms of social mobility, women had several possible ways of entering the merchantry. As already noted, the most common variant was through inheritance: merchant widows inherited the business on their husband's death, or unmarried daughters on the death of their father. Transfer to the merchant estate from the peasantry or petty townsfolk (*meshchanstvo*) was more complicated.[10] It was regulated by the provisions of the Urban Statute included in the 1785 Charter. Thus, Article 79 of the Charter, citing Catherine's Manifesto of 17 March 1775, Article 46, declared that serfs manumitted by their masters had the right to settle in towns. At the tax-census they were to declare

> what branch of Our service, either the townspeople's or the merchant estate, they wish to enter into in the towns; and whichever they voluntarily select for themselves, they must be granted equality in that estate with other as concerns state requisitions, or freed from the latter.[11]

The bureaucratic procedure of transfer from one estate to another involved, firstly, obtaining the agreement of the merchant corporation of the town in which the female 'candidate merchant' wished to settle, and secondly, getting the transfer duly registered in the Fiscal Chamber (the office responsible for financial matters) of the province in question – the Chamber was obliged to report the transfer to the Senate.[12] Should transfer from the peasantry to an urban estate meet obstacles which could not be resolved 'by means of the general law', the Fiscal Chamber had to seek a review by means of 'representations through the Minister of Finances to the Governing Senate'.[13]

Representatives of all the basic subdivisions of the peasantry (servile landlords' peasants, treasury or state peasants, appanage peasants) were recruited into the merchant estate.[14] State peasants were allowed to transfer into the merchantry if they were already actively engaged in commercial enterprise and had moved to a town. The official procedure required them to submit the following documents to the Fiscal Chamber: a declaration of desire to join the merchantry, details of family and property, certification from the village commune that the would-be merchant had 'no arrears outstanding in either taxes or service obligations', and that when he moved to the town his land allocation in the village would revert to the commune ('after his departure his land, which previously he farmed, will not be left waste') and an undertaking to pay in to the merchant corporation which he was joining a monetary deposit equal to three years' taxes due from him in his new station.[15] Appanage peasants wishing to transfer had to receive a 'certificate of release' from the Appanage Department: for this they were to present evidence of the possession of suitable capital. The law stated:

> Peasants (*poseliane*) who on inspection of their property are found to be capable of presenting significant (*znatnye*) capital in the merchant calling shall be released on payment.

Under the terms of the 1798 decree cited above, the amount of the 'release payment' was to be determined by a resolution of the applicant's native commune, confirmed by the Appanage Department. Under this arrangement 7/8 of the payment went to 'Appanage revenues' and 1/8 to the charitable needs of the commune ('assistance to peasants in a distressed condition').[16] The 'Appanage Department Statute' promulgated on 15 May 1808 confirmed the right of appanage peasants to be released into the merchantry.[17]

The state sought to maximise its fiscal advantage in such cases. Despite having formally moved from one estate to another, merchants of recent peasant origin were obliged under article 139 of the Urban Statute to pay taxes in both estates until the next tax census, which finally confirmed their new social status.[18] The procedure of transfer into the merchantry became the same for landlords' serfs and appanage peasants in 1821.[19]

To illustrate these legislative prescriptions we will examine several cases whose records have come to light in the Central Historical Archive of the City of Moscow. Thus, in 1814 the 'peasant woman widow' (*krest'ianskaia zhenka vdova*) Dar'ia Andreeva, from the village of Belkovo in Moscow Province, declared her wish to enter the third guild of the Moscow merchantry. Dari'a's family consisted of twelve persons in addition to herself, including three sons (Karp, Ivan and Ignatii) and their wives (respectively Irina, Akulina and Tat'iana) and six grand-children, two by each son (Akulina, Dar'ia, Andrei, Fedor, Domna and Luker'ia). The Moscow Fiscal Chamber enquired of the Ministry of Finances in Petersburg about registering such a large number of people in the merchantry, and the question went further, to the Senate. The latter gave permission on condition that all peasant dues had been paid. Thereupon Dar'ia Andreeva gave the Fiscal Chamber a signed undertaking, promising to pay all required state taxes and to observe the law ('not to do anything unworthy or contrary to the laws').[20] 'Because of her illiteracy', at Dar'ia Andreeva's request the undertaking was signed by her son Karp. Her sureties were three members of the Moscow merchantry: second-guild merchant Osip Goriunov, a 'fish trader' and member of the third guild, Semen Safronov, who dealt in horses, and silk-merchant Egor Il'in, also of the third guild. Information from census returns shows that all three sureties were former neighbours of Andreeva from her previous place of residence, all originating from neighbouring villages of Vokhna volost' in Bogorodsk district of Moscow province. The population of Vokhna volost' were Old Believers, among whom mutual support was particularly strongly developed. It is not impossible that Dar'ia was related to one or more of her sureties.

Our second case is similar to the first, but the 'candidate-merchant' came not from the metropolitan Moscow area, but from the more distant Vladimir province. The widow Avdot'ia Matveeva was admitted to the Moscow merchantry in 1814 from the economic-peasant 'settlement (*sel'tso*) of Krasnoe, also called Boroviki Chervlenye', together with her three sons Dmitrii, Koz'ma and Vasilii, her daughters-in-law Dar'ia and Natal'ia and grandsons Afanasii and Efim.[21] Her son Dmitrii signed the transfer application for his illiterate mother. Avdot'ia Matveeva's sureties were second-guild merchant Petr Silin, member of the third guild Filipp Shatrov and Moscow third-guild merchant Nikita Ukhanov; all three specialized in trade in 'iron goods'.

Other information found in the archive concerning admission to the merchantry shows that women recruits to the merchant estate came from various social groups. Thus, in 1814 the Moscow third guild received into membership the economic peasant Akulina Burmakina of Bol'shoe Besovo village in Yaroslavl' province. Burmakina, a 60-year-old widow, brought with her two adult sons and their wives (Paramon, aged 35, with Mavra, and Evstrat, 32, with Fedora), daughter Pelageia and grandson Arsenii. Burmakina was illiterate; Paramon signed her documents. Uniquely among the known petitions for admission to the merchantry, Burmakina's file includes a statement of her physical features: she was 'of middle height, with hazel eyes and dark brown hair'.[22] In the same year, 1814, the following were admitted into the Moscow merchantry: merchant's widow Irina Khlebnikova (illiterate) from the town of Kaluga, with five sons; the young woman (*devka*) Mar'ia Podobedova, a literate manumitted household serf of landowner Miasoedova (place of residence unknown); a merchant's widow from the town of Toropets in Tver' province, Anna Aksenova, literate, with two children; the Moscow artisan-guild member Maria Diulu [Marie Dulout], literate; economic peasant widow Avdot'ia Gornostaeva, illiterate, from the village of Denisovo in Kaluga province, with three sons, five daughters and their families, in all nine persons; and the unmarried Varvara Gracheva, daughter of a Moscow First Guild merchant.[23]

The case of Gracheva is particularly interesting, and somewhat atypical. As a rule unmarried daughters entered the merchantry after the death of their parents. But Gracheva decided to apply for merchant status during the lifetime of her father, who had his own separate certificate as a member of the first guild – he died two years later, in 1816. In 1814 Varvara's father Efim Grachev was 73; his wife Praskov'ia, daughter of Kornoukhov, a major merchant from Suzdal' (Vladimir Province),[24] was aged 77. At the end of the eighteenth century the Grachev family belonged among the first-rank (*pervostateinoe*) merchantry, the highest category of richest entrepreneurs. It is known that in the early eighteenth century the Grachevs' forebears were serfs of Count N. P. Sheremetev in the industrial village of Ivanovo in Vladimir Province which in the nineteenth century grew into the textile centre of Ivanovo-Voznesensk, and they conducted considerable trade in Novgorod.[25] The Grachevs joined the First Guild of Moscow merchants in 1795, on their release from servile status. Father Efim and son Dmitrii Grachev possessed 'a particularly powerful grasp of business' and together with two merchant members of the Kornoukhov family they owned a major cotton textile factory in Moscow (the production of which, for example, was worth 244,190 roubles in 1799).[26] In 1814 the Grachev factory in Moscow had 648 hired and 318 purchased workers.[27] Dmitrii Grachev died in 1808 at the age of 43, leaving two young sons. In 1814 Varvara was 41 and never married.[28] Explaining her reasons for entering the merchantry, she wrote in her application:

> Through a certain conjuncture I have obtained on my own account the sum of twenty thousand roubles, and therefore humbly request that this my petition be accepted, since I have capital to declare sufficient for the second guild.[29]

Varvara was illiterate; at her request, her petition was signed for her by Moscow merchant of the second guild Lavrentii Osipov.

The acquisition of merchant status made it possible for women to participate in retail trade and manufacturing. The ownership of industrial enterprises was one of the major indicators of female entrepreneurship, which will be addressed in the next section of this chapter.

3. The Statistics of Female Industrial Entrepreneurship

Unfortunately, there is no accurate statistical information on women entrepreneurs for the end of the eighteenth century, although it is known that already in the early stages of industrial development, in the mid-eighteenth century, a number of major enterprises belonged to women. But the earliest full set of data available relates to 1814. It was published by the Ministry of Finances in the 'Register of Factories in Russia for the Years 1813 and 1814'.[30] According to the Register, in 1814 business-women owned 165 light and heavy industrial enterprises out of a total of 3,731 undertakings: 4.4 per cent. However, in some branches of industry the proportion of 'female business' was relatively high – 13.5 per cent in paper-making, 12.3 per cent in cloth manufacture, 12.0 per cent in metalworking (iron and steel). The leading branch in terms of the actual number of female-owned enterprises was tanning: women owned 31 tanneries out of a total of 1,530, or 2.03 per cent. Women owned 29 cloth mills and 22 linen mills (10.23 per cent), 19 soap-boiling and candle-making works (5.01 per cent) and 15 glass and crystal manufactures (9.68 per cent). Aggregate figures for the number of female-owned enterprises, the social status of the owners and the labour force are given in Table 1.1.

The data in Table 1.1 show that the number of female merchants among 165 female factory owners was 63 (38 per cent); noblewomen numbered 76 (46 per cent), townswomen – 20 (12 per cent). The remaining six (4 per cent) included peasant women, a soldier's wife[31] and a Cossack w-oman. Female industrial enterprise was characterised by socially mixed ownership. Therefore our further discussion, while focused on female merchants, will of necessity (though to a lesser degree) also deal with noblewomen, townswomen, peasant and Cossack women who owned industrial enterprises.

We will now examine more closely those branches where women owners were numerous, beginning with cloth-making, which had the oldest enterprises and was also subject to official protectionism. In cloth-making women were the owners of 12.34 per cent of all enterprises, 29 out of 235. As regards geographical distribution, the largest number of female-owned enterprises was to be found in Moscow and Simbirsk provinces (five in each). These two provinces were leaders in the whole Russian Empire in terms of numbers of cloth mills: Moscow province had 28 and Simbirsk 25, together 53 or nearly one quarter of the Russian total. The social composition of female ownership was heavily weighted towards noblewomen – 89.6 per cent of female owners (26 out of 29 persons), whereas only 10.4 per cent belonged to the merchantry. A large pro-

Table 1.1. Number of Enterprises Owned by Women by Branch of Industrial Activity (1814)

The branches are placed in the Table in descending order of the number of 'female' enterprises

Branch	Total enter-prises	Number of enterprises owned by women	As a percent-tage of the total	Social estate of owner (no. of persons/ per cent)	Composition of workforce by estate (persons/ per cent)
Tanning	1,530	31	2.03 per cent	Noblewomen – 4 (12.9 per cent), female merchants –16 (51.6 per cent), *meshchanki* – 11 (35.5 per cent)	Serfs (2.8 per cent), purchased and ascribed 51 (15.8 per cent), free 263 (81.4 per cent)
Cloth-making (woollens)	235	29	12.34 per cent	Noblewomen – 26 (89.6 per cent), female merchants –3 (10.4 per cent)	Serfs 1,487 (12.4 per cent), purchased and ascribedn –9,510 (79.2 per cent), free – 1,009 (8.4 per cent)
Linen	215	22	10.23 per cent	Noblewomen – 15 (68.2 per cent), female merchants – 7 (31.8 per cent)	Serfs 110 (5.9 per cent), purchased and ascribed 118 (6.3 per cent) free 1,640 (87.8 per cent). No data for 4 enterprises.
Soap boiling, tallow candle-making, wax production.	379	19	5.01 per cent	Female merchants 12 (63.1 per cent), *meshchank* 5 (26.3 per cent), soldier's wife 1 (5.3 per cent), cossack woman (5.3 per cent)	Free 108 at 18 enterprises (100 per cent)
Glass and crystal production	155	15	9.68 per cent	Noblewomen 13 (86.6 per cent), female merchants 1 (6.8 per cent), peasant woman 1 (6.8 per cent)	Serfs 206 (57.4 per cent), purchased and ascribed 18 (5.0 per cent), free 135 (37.6 per cent)

Branch	Total enterprises	Number of enterprises owned by women	As a percentage of the total	Social estate of owner (no. of persons/ per cent)	Composition of workforce by estate (persons/ per cent)
Paper	79	10	13.51 per cent	Noblewomen 8 (80 per cent), female merchants 2 (20 per cent)	Serfs 269 (26.1 per cent), purchased and ascribed 709 (68.8 per cent), free 53 (5.1 per cent)
Cotton	423	10	2.36 per cent	Noblewoman 1 (10 per cent), female merchants 8 (80 per cent), peasant woman 1 (10 per cent)	Serfs 3 (0.6 per cent), free 529 (99.4 per cent)
Iron and steel goods	75	9	12.0 per cent	Noblewomen 5 (55.5 per cent), female merchants 3 (33.3 per cent), *meshchanka* 1 (10.2 per cent)	Serfs 293 (19.5 per cent), purchased and ascribed 1,155 (76.9 per cent), free 54 (3.6 per cent)
Silk	158	5	3.16 per cent	Female merchants 2, *meshchanka* 1, peasant women 2	Free 46 at 4 factories (100 per cent)
Rope-making	102	3	2.94 per cent	Female merchants 2, *meshchanka* 1	Free 159 (100 per cent)
Potash	31	3	9.68 per cent	Noblewomen 2 *meshchanka* 1	Serfs 18 (100 per cent)
China and pottery	30	2	6.7 per cent	Female merchants 2	Serfs 22 (5.6 per cent), ascribed 47 (12.1 per cent) free 321 (82.3 per cent)
Copper (brass) and button-making	59	2	3.4 per cent	Noblewoman 1 female merchant 1	Free 61 (100 per cent)
Hats	41	1	2.4 per cent	Female merchant 1	Free 2

Branch	Total enter-prises	Number of enterprises owned by women	As a percent-tage of the total	Social estate of owner (no. of persons/ per cent)	Composition of workforce by estate (persons/ per cent)
Lacquering	5	1	20 per cent	Noblewoman 1	Free 3
Sugar	51	1	2.0 per cent	Female merchant 1	Free 11
Paint production	27	1	3.7 per cent	Female merchant 1	Free 6
Vitriol and sulphur produc-tion	22	1	4.5 per cent	Female merchant 1	Free 6
Total	3,731	165	4.4 per cent		

portion of noblewomens' mills operated on their owners' estates. Noblewoman owners included Princess (*kniazhna*, unmarried) Varvara Shakhovskaia (mill in Moscow province), Countess Stepanida Tolstoy (Nizhnii-Novgorod Province), Princess (*kniaginia,* married) Varvara Dolgorukova (Penza Province), Countess Aleksandra la Valle' (Penza province), Princess (*kniazhna*) Aleksandra Volkonskaia (Saratov Province), Countess Natal'ia Zubova (Simbirsk Province), Countess Praskov'ia Potemkina (Kursk Province). As a rule, noble factories used serf labour. This very significant predominance of noblewoman-owners is to be explained by the historical development of the Russian cloth industry. From the outset this branch of industry was developed to meet the army's need of cloth for uniforms. For this purpose laws of 1721 and 1744 allowed nobles and merchants to purchase peasants for their factories by whole villages.[32] (From 1797 this category of labour received the special title of 'possessional' peasants.) But since merchants rarely possessed the large capital which would have allowed such purchases, it was mainly nobles who took advantage of this opportunity. Together with such purchased peasants nobles used so-called 'ascribed' peasants: state peasants who could be 'ascribed' to work out their state quit-rent in the enterprises of private owners if the latter were fulfilling state contracts. Under Catherine II a law was passed in 1769 which allowed all those so wishing to establish looms (on payment of one rouble per loom),[33] an indication of a trend towards greater freedom of enterprise. Merchant enterprises began to appear, producing cloth for sale on the open market. However a shortage of army cloth in the 1790s compelled the authorities to return to the system of production for the government. Consequently the number of 'old' noble cloth-mills was still considerable even in 1814.

The largest of the female-owned enterprises was the mill producing army cloth belonging to Countess Praskov'ia Potemkina, situated in the village of Glushkovo in Kursk Province. The labour force consisted of 9,413 purchased and ascribed workers servicing 553 looms, and in 1814 cloth production totalled 552,731 *arshins* (392,439m), of which 76 per cent was soldier cloth.[34] Apart from such large operations, the majority were smaller enterprises with a workforce of from ten to sixty serfs. Of the twenty-nine female-owned cloth-mills only six used free (hired) labour: four with exclusively free labour and two with mixed – free and servile. Exclusively free labour was to be found in the enterprises belonging to the above-mentioned Countess Stepanida Tolstoy, to *starostina*[35] Agata Linkiewicz (a mill in the village of Gushcha in Volhynia Province, with sixty-six workers and four looms), to the 'merchant wife' (*kupetskaia zhena*) Anna Kumanina (mill in Moscow, twenty-six workers on three looms), and to the 'merchant wife' Bulgakova (an enterprise in Moscow jointly owned with Bulgakova's brother, the townsman Kaletin, fifty-nine workers on seventeen looms).[36] The two operations using mixed free and servile labour were the soldier-cloth factory of Lt.-General's wife (or widow, *generalleitenantsha*) Anna Panova in Krotovka in Simbirsk Province, and the factory of *shliakhtianka* Güb-ner near the village of Ksaverovo in Volhynia Province. In the cloth industry the correlation between owners' merchant status and the use of free labour is very evident. The merchant enterprises were exceptional islands of free-market activity in the ocean of mills working in accordance with the rules of state-regulated cloth production.

In tanning, the proportion of women entrepreneurs was also high: thirty-one enterprises in 1814. Unlike the cloth industry, tanning was not subject to state protectionism. This is reflected in the incidence of free labour: 28 enterprises employed hired workers and only three tanneries used unfree workers (purchased and ascribed) – these belonged to the female heirs of Count Salty-kov in Simbirsk Province, to landowner Shostakova of Mogilev Province, and to Princess Golitsyna of Orel Province.[37]

The question of the social status of the owners is of particular interest here. In this respect the tanning industry was very different from cloth-making. Only four enterprises (12.9 per cent) belonged to noblewomen: Princess (*kniaginia*) Elizaveta Glebova-Streshneva in Moscow Province, and Saltykov's heirs mentioned above, Shostakova and Golitsyna. Thus the great majority of tanning enterprises (twenty-seven out of thirty-one, or 87 per cent) belonged to women of unprivileged status, from the merchantry and townsfolk (*meshchanstvo*). Merchant wives and widows and independent women merchants owned 16 enterprises (51.5 per cent) and townswomen owned eleven (35.5 per cent). While tanneries belonging to merchant women had workforces of from two to twenty-three workers (the average for all sixteen tanneries was 9.2), the figures for townswomen's enterprises were between two and ten, average 4.8. A similar correlation obtained in regard to volume of production: the merchant enterprises had an annual production of 500–7,000 hides (average 2,971) and the townswomen produced 70–3,200 hides with an average 1,073.

In terms of geographical distribution, the high density of tanneries in Pskov Province (six enterprises) and Kazan' Province (four enterprises) is notable. Three tanneries, all owned by merchants, were located in Saransk in Penza Province, where leather production became such a popular business that one of the merchant families owned two tanneries simultaneously, one belonging to the husband, Safon Korovin, the other to his wife, Domna Korovina. The formation of such 'nests' of industry was evidently connected with the availability of necessary raw materials, and also with the 'imitation principle', when one woman's business success became a stimulus to other local women who had capital and wished to go into commerce. The tanning industry also attracted some non-Russian women: two Tatars from Kazan' Province and a German in Volhynia Province. The tannery of merchant's wife Ziuliukha (probably: Zuleikha)

Abdulova, which produced soft leather (*iuft'*) in the village of Novye Mengery in Kazan' Province, employed twelve hired workers. Townswoman Vakhrama Sabimova used ten hired workers to produce goats' hides in Kazan' itself. And in Zhitomir in Volhynia Province, four hired workers laboured for the German female merchant Anna Albrecht, producing shoe-sole and soft leathers.[38]

A high proportion of female merchant enterprises was also to be found in the soap and candle trade, producing soap and tallow and wax candles. Here twelve enterprises out of nineteen (63.1 per cent) belonged to female merchants and five (26.3 per cent) to townswomen.[39] There were no noblewomen among the owners. One enterprise was owned by the Cossack woman Praskov'ia Shirabardina in Saratov, another by the soldier's wife Tat'iana Fedotova in Kursk. The latter two businesses should more accurately be termed workshops: for the boiling of Fedotova's soap, which the mistress evidently undertook herself, one worker had been hired and production amounted to 15 *poods* (240kg)[40] per annum. Shirabardina likewise had one worker and her workshop produced 30 *poods* (480kg) of tallow candles annually. The largest number of workers in this group was to be found in four soap-boiling enterprises in Kazan'. Two of these belonged to female merchants of Russian descent, two to Tatars (see Table 1.2).

Table 1.2. Soap-Boiling Enterprises in Kazan' (1814)

Name and social status of female owner	Ethnic origin	Number of workers (all hired)	Number of cauldrons for boiling soap	Volume of soap production in 1814 (*poods*/kg.)
Aleksandra Koniukhova, merchant	Russian	12	3	6,600 / 105,600
Gadiba Kitaeva, merchant	Tatar	11	6	10,000 / 160,000
Katerina Ivoilova, merchant	Russian	7	4	11,000 / 176,000
Zuleikha Iskakova, merchant	Tatar	7	2	3,000 / 48,000

In paper-making, ten enterprises out of seventy-four (13.5 per cent) belonged to women. Of the nine owners (State Counsellor's wife Anna Poltoratskaia had two enterprises in St Petersburg Province) only two came from the merchant estate: Maria Kopteva, whose wallpaper factory was located in Moscow, and the Tatar Sagida Mamatova, who produced writing-paper in the village of Paranga in Viatka Province. Kopteva's factory had four hired workers and produced 10,000 sheets of wall-paper in the year 1814; Mamatova's employed 39 hired workers and turned out 3,175 reams of writing paper in the same period.[41] The remaining eight paper mills belonged to noblewomen and employed serf labour.

The highest proportion of female merchant owners was concentrated in the cotton textile industry (80 per cent). The two remaining female owners were a noblewoman and a peasant. This branch of industry also had an extremely high level of hired labour – 99.4 per cent, while serfs made up a mere 0.6 per cent. Three of the ten merchant enterprises were located in Moscow, and we will say a little about the biographies of the owners of these mills, Avdot'ia Medvedeva, Nastas'ia Sichkova and Avdot'ia Vlas'eva. Avdot'ia Medvedeva's mill employed 76 weavers working 50 looms; in 1814 production was 62,750 pieces of cloth for headscarves.[42] According to the census returns for 1811 and 1815, Avdot'ia had come to Moscow with her husband Mikhail Nikolaev on 30 March 1800; they were former treasury peasants from the village of Afin'evo in Vladimir Province. The husband entered the third guild of Moscow merchants. On her arrival Avdot'ia was 44; a year later, aged 45, she gave birth to her only son, Fedor. Her husband died in 1803, and Avdot'ia took out a guild certificate in her own name. In 1814 she owned a house in Khamovniki, a district of Moscow. On 12 February 1817 Avdot'ia and her son received permission to take the family name of Medvedev.[43] Nastas'ia Sichkova employed 104 workers on 96 looms; in 1814 they produced 54,075 *arshins* (38,340 m) of nankeen (thick cotton fabric) and 5,000 headscarves. According to the 1811 Census returns, the 23-year-old Nastas'ia was the second wife of the merchant of the Second Guild Koz'ma Ivanov, aged 44, who on 9 November 1798 had gained the right to use the family name Sichkov. Koz'ma had entered the Moscow merchantry in 1787 together with his parents and brother from the economic-peasant village of Prokunino in Vokhna volost' in Moscow Province. Koz'ma Sichkov had a son Ivan and daughter Elena from his first marriage, and from the second with Nastas'ia he had a son, Mikhail, born in 1810. The Sichkovs lived in their own house in the Taganka district of Moscow.[44] Nastas'ia became owner of the mill on the death of her husband. Avdot'ia Vlas'eva's operation had a workforce of 18 weavers servicing 15 looms, who in 1814 produced 15,500 *arshins* (11,000 m) of calico. (Further biographical details on Vlas'eva are given in the section below concerning property.)

In conclusion, we can say that there was a clear predominance of the merchant element among women owners of industrial enterprises in such branches as cotton textiles (80 per cent), soap, tallow and candle production (63.1 per cent), and tanning (51.6 per cent). These enterprises produced goods for mass consumption and thus stimulated the development of production in their particular field as well as widening the circle of persons who wished to engage in it, including women.

Female entrepreneurs were not just producers – they were consumers. The reflection of their victories and defeats in entrepreneurial activity was the structure of the personal property of businesswomen. It is precisely this issue that we are now going to turn our attention to.

4. The Structure of Immovable and Movable Property

The material culture of the merchantry not only testified to the character of consumer demand and personal preferences, but also reflected the position of an owner in the social hierarchy.[45]

Study of the question of immovable property belonging to women of the merchant stratum is greatly complicated by lack of suitable data. For our study information has been derived from two basic sources. The first is documentary evidence on contracts for the sale and purchase of houses, shops and plots of land, which provide information about immovable property and its mobilization. Secondly, we have a very valuable source, connected with the events of the war against Napoleon in 1812. As is well known, the Russian commander Kutuzov surrendered Moscow to the French. On the eve of the enemy's entry into the city, the majority of its inhabitants left for Russia's eastern provinces, taking with them only a minimum of essentials. During the French occupation a fierce fire destroyed 6,500 houses and churches, two-thirds of the total.[46] After the war a Commission was set up by the order of the tsar 'for the consideration of petitions from the inhabitants of Moscow City and Province who have suffered ruin from the enemy'. The petitions submitted to this Commission, addressed to the Governor-General of Moscow, Count Saltykov, and requesting financial compensation for losses sustained, contain information on movable and immovable property.

The contracts of property transactions preserved in the archives show women from merchant families engaged in deals of three sorts: sales, purchases, and deeds of gift (*peredacha po darstvennoi*). By way of example, some contracts preserved for the year 1805 are presented here. Thus on 2 January 1805 a purchase agreement was registered between the 'merchant wife' Praskov'ia Ignat'eva and Second Lt's wife Elizaveta Purgusova, whereby Ignat'eva bought from Purgusova a house and land (*dvor*) in the parish of the Church of the Ascension in the Serpukhovskaia district of Moscow for 1,000 roubles.[47] On the same day another transaction was registered: merchant's wife Anna Kozlova sold to Registrar (*registrator*) Timofei Prikaznyi a house and land with wooden outbuildings in the parish of the Church of Khariton the Confessor in the Yauza district of Moscow, also for 1,000 roubles. Kozlova had previously bought the property (*domovladenie*) from the nobleman Aleksandr Iakovlev on 13 November 1802.[48] On 11 November 1803 the merchant's wife Feodora Kondrat'eva sold to Avdot'ia Stepanova, wife of a College Secretary, a house and land in the parish of the Church of Nicholas the Miracleworker in the Prechistenka district of Moscow. The purchase price is not shown, but it is known that fourteen months later Stepanova sold ownership of the house for 14,000 roubles.[49] On 9 January 1805 the merchant's wife Praskov'ia Egorova sold for 5,000 roubles to the Moscow merchant Mikhail Moskvenkov a masonry shop in the Fresh Fish Trade Row (*Zhivorybnyi riad*) 'on the banks of the Moscow river at the Moskvoretskii Gates'[50]; she had bought it in 1804 from the townsman Fedor Ivanov. The plot of land on which the shop stood measured approximately nine *sazhens* square.[51] As Praskov'ia could not write, the purchase agreement was signed 'at her request' by her husband Stepan Egorov. Nine merchants appended their signatures to the document as witnesses. On 25 January 1805 Elizaveta Arakelova, 'wife of an Armenian merchant', bought from College Assessor Fedor Ardalionov 'a masonry house with land and all kind of brick and wooden buildings, in Moscow, between Pokrovka and Miasnitskaia Streets' in the parish of the Church of Nicholas the Miracleworker, for 9,000 roubles. Arakelova was literate and signed the contract herself.[52] On 31 January 1805 Moscow merchant Prokofii Chilikin registered his transfer by deed of gift to his daughter Nastas'ia of five masonry shops in the Moskatel'nyi (dry chemicals and dyes) and Old Needle Rows. Chilikin had previously bought the shops from the merchants Mikhail Moskvenkov and Mikhail Zabelin. Four of them stood together forming a terrace, above which a single 'tent' (canvas awning) had been erected. The fifth shop, which was detached, had a cellar. The value of all five shops, declared 'according to conscience', was 200 roubles, but it is likely that Chilikin deliberately declared a low value in order to pay the minimum duty on the transaction (immovable property transactions attracted a duty of 5 per cent). The plot on which each shop stood was of standard size, the façade 4.2 m wide and the depth of the building about 12 m.[53]

The information gleaned from female merchants' petitions for compensation for property destroyed in the 1812 fire adds a different perspective. The archive contains seven files containing merchant wives' petitions. However only three files include a detailed list of property – items of personal use and goods intended for sale. Table 1.3 provides aggregated data concerning persons who suffered loss of property.

In some cases, the combination of archival material with census returns makes it possible to reconstruct the biographies of women entrepreneurs. Anis'ia Blokhina was the only daughter of the merchant of the Third Guild Tikhon Borisov. She was a late child, born when her father was 43 and her mother 39.[55] She married the son of merchant Blokhin (first name unknown) and bore three children. Anis'ia characterized her husband's situation with regard to property as follows: 'As to my husband, he is a son who has not separated from his father and has nothing whatsoever that is his own property'.[56] The basic source of income for Anis'ia's family was probably the letting of their big masonry house. It was built on a plot of land (60m long by 55m wide), which Anis'ia had inherited on the death of her father. In her petition for compensation Anis'ia declared that 'at the time of the universal fire caused by the enemy in Moscow' the house

Table 1.3. Data on Women of the Merchant Estate and the Value of their Property Lost in Consequence of the Burning of Moscow during the 1812 War[54]

Name of female owner, her social status and literacy	Composition and ages of family in 1814	Commercial specialisation	Ownership of immovable property and place of residence before the fire	Valuation of loss suffered (roubles)	Amount of compensation received, place of residence after fire
Anis'ia Blokhina, wife of the son of a Moscow merchant, daughter of Moscow merchant of the Third Guild Tikhon Borisov; literate	Five persons: Blokhina, aged 33, her husband and three young children	Renting out of house. Her father, who died in 1797, served 'as a watchman in the Butter and Caftan Row'	Her own stone house worth 40,000 roubles in the Piatnitskaia district, inherited from her father, and which was rented out. The Blokhin family rented accommodation in the house of *meshchanin* Shavardin in the Yauza district	87,711 roubles 80 kopecks	8,000 roubles; temporary accommodation in Moscow, with relatives in the Yauza district
Elena Bartel's, widow of a Moscow merchant of the Third Guild who originally came from Narva; literate	Two persons: Bartel's herself (age unknown) and her young daughter; husband died in 1812	Trade in various goods (fabrics, clothing, china and glassware from Britain, Austria, and Poland)	No immovable property of her own, rented accommodation and a shop in the house of Countess Razumovskaia in the Miasnitskaia district	26,980 roubles	Amount of compensation unknown; rented accommodation in the same place as before
Avdot'ia Vlas'eva, female merchant of the Third Guild, widow, daughter of Moscow merchant Fedor Gorskii; illiterate	Six persons: Vlas'eva herself, aged 49, two sons Aleksei (28) and Andrei (21), three daughters Elisaveta (26), Maria (23), Anna (19); husband died in 1793	Calico-printing factory in her own house	Own wooden house on a stone foundation, with wings (*s fligeliami*), value 18,000 roubles, in Piatnitskaia district	20,967 roubles 90 kopecks	4,000 roubles; temporarily rented accommodation in house of *meshchanin* Mamyrdov in Serpukhovskaia district
Matrena Zezina, widow of a Moscow merchant of the Third Guild; illiterate	Four persons: Zezina herself (38), her son Nikolai (14) and two daughters, Tat'iana (16), Natal'ia (14); husband died in 1805	No information found	Own house (ground floor masonry, first floor wooden) with five wings on masonry foundations, at a value of 20,000 roubles, in the Yauza district	25,897 roubles	4,000 roubles. Place of residence after fire unknown

Name of female owner, her social status and literacy	Composition and ages of family in 1814	Commercial specialisation	Ownership of immovable property and place of residence before the fire	Valuation of loss suffered (roubles)	Amount of compensation received, place of residence after fire
Matrena Protopopova, widow of a Moscow merchant of the Third Guild; illiterate	Five persons: Protopopova herself (51), five sons – Nikolai, Ivan, Iakov, Mikhail, Pavel; husband died in 1802.	Trade in textile goods in a rented booth in the Gostinyi Dvor	No immovable property of her own, rented accommodation in the house of a priest in the Serpukhovskaia district	9,527 roubles 74 kopecks	2,000 roubles; in the Znamenskii Convent in Ostashkov, Tver' Province
Akulina Strukova, widow of a Moscow merchant of the Third Guild ; illiterate	Four persons: Strukova herself (33), two sons – Ivan (9), Aleksandr (7) – daughter Anna (13); husband died in 1812	Trade in iron goods	Own wooden house in the Yauza district, inherited from her husband; rented a shop in the Tverskaia district from merchant Pashkov	69,086 roubles	8,000 roubles; rented temporary accommodation in Moscow
Varvara Shelepova, wife of a Tula merchant of the Third Guild; literate	Four persons: Shelepova herself and three sons – Sergey, Petr and Gavriil	Trade in textile goods	Own wooden house in the Iakimanskaia district, bought in 1797 for 1,000 roubles and a masonry house built on this plot in 1808 valued at 12,000 roubles. Son rented a storage facility in the Gostinyi Dvor to keep goods	23,965 roubles	2,000 roubles; rented temporary accommodation in Moscow

had burned down, 'so that I suffered total ruin to the cost of 87,711 roubles and 80 kopecks'. She presented confirmation, signed by the Moscow Chief of Police (*ober-politsmeister*), that the house had indeed been 'totally consumed by fire'.

Three of the seven files containing petitions for compensation include registers of lost property, for the merchant women Protopopova, Zezina and Vlas'eva. The 'Register of Property and Goods Burnt and Looted' presented by Matrena Protopopova lists only movable property: items of personal use and the goods in which Matrena traded.[57] Matrena had no immovable property of her own: she rented both the accommodation in which her family lived and the shop in which she conducted her business together with her son. After her husband's death in 1802 Matrena Protopopova's family had dropped for three years (1803–5) into the townsman's estate (*meshchanstvo*); they returned to the merchantry in 1806.[58] While they were townspeople the Protopopov family lost the right to immunity from the recruit levy, and consequently in 1806 17-year-old Iakov was 'surrendered to military service'. On the eve of the French occupation Matrena and her children left Moscow for the town of Murom in Vladimir Province, 300 km to the north-east of the old capital. Matrena left her furniture and tableware in the apartment which they rented, but took her icons for safe-keeping to her acquaintances the merchants Petr Nakhodkin and Stepan Solodovnikov. Her goods were sealed in the shop in Gostinyi Dvor. Among the personal items on Protopopova's list there was a large quantity of furniture which had been in her home before the fire: four tables (two oaken, two ordinary), 17 chairs ('six new ones, covered in leather' and eleven 'oaken ones, somewhat worn'), an oak bed-stead, a 'leather-covered sofa', and 'one worn woollen Turkish carpet'. The total value of the furniture was 73 roubles. Besides that, the apartment had been graced by two portraits ('two painted portraits, one of me, the other of my husband') and 15 'various pictures'. The portraits were valued at 27 roubles the pair, the pictures at 20 roubles. Two liturgical books were mentioned: a 'psalter printed in Moscow' and a 'prayer-book printed in Kiev'. The list also included china crockery valued at 97 roubles, silver tableware (kept in a separate chest) worth 55 roubles, brassware (15 roubles and 50 kopecks) and pewter (46 roubles and 50 kopecks). The most valuable items were the icons: three icons of the Deisis painted 'in the old style' were valued at 250 roubles, a mahogany and bronze iconostasis at 24 roubles, and another four icons with silver covers at 225 roubles 89 kopecks. A further list of goods lost gives an idea of Protopopova's stock. With her middle son Nikolai she traded in Chinese pearls (she had had 2,509 roubles worth in her shop), Chinese silk (450 roubles), Kalmyk sheepskin coats (2,677 roubles 50 kopecks), and textiles (muslin, dimity, chintz, canvas: 1,968 roubles 90 kopecks). Clothes off the peg also made up a considerable part of the trade of mother and son Protopopov: among items for sale was 'one new frock-coat of dark English cloth', 'one new dark-grey greatcoat of Dutch cloth', six waistcoats, eight linen men's shirts, 11 silken neck-cloths, 'one beaver hat with a green velvet crown', and other things. Matrena Protopopova estimated her total loss at 9,527 roubles 74 kopecks.

Another female Moscow merchant, Matrena Zezina, calculated her losses during the war at 25,927 roubles – 20,000 roubles in immovable and 5,927 in movable property.[59] Zezina had become the owner of a two-storey house on the death of her husband. The latter, merchant of the third guild Andrei Zezin, had entered the Moscow merchantry in 1795 from the economic peasantry of the village of Pupki in Vladimir Province. At the age of 29 he had married the 17-year-old Matrena Tolchevskaia, a native of Pupki, and took his young wife to Moscow. Andrei Zezin himself had a business in St Petersburg, but his family – at least four children were born – was resident in Moscow.[60] When Zezin died in 1805 at the age of 42, Matrena became the head of the family and took out a guild certificate in her own name. Her 'Register' indicates the wealthy lifestyle of this merchant family. It lists 38 pieces of expensive furniture (not counting chairs and armchairs), principally mahogany, and including: cupboards worth 500, 150 and 150 roubles, a bureau at 80 roubles, and two mirrors in gold frames at 50 roubles each. Also included were a dozen mahogany chairs 'covered with morocco' (100 roubles); half a dozen armchairs 'covered in black leather, mahogany' (75 roubles); and half a dozen 'simple armchairs' (30 roubles). Zezina claimed to have lost china crockery to the value of 125 roubles, glass tableware worth 30, pottery worth 30 and wooden ware worth 200 roubles. Also listed were two four-wheeled carriages: a 'sprung' *droshky* and a 'simple' *droshky*. Like Protopopova, female merchant Zezina's family had valuable icons, framed in mahogany iconostases, and together worth 625 roubles. Zezina also mentioned in her register 'small pictures' which had adorned her home and which she valued at 2,000 roubles.

Our third female merchant, Avdot'ia Vlas'eva, listed in her register along with her house and personal movable property the trade goods which had been burnt in the fire, so (as with Protopopova) we can form an impression of her commercial activity.[61] Before the war of 1812 Vlas'eva had had a calico-printing factory in her own house, which was 'built of wood on masonry foundations'. The original house had been bought by her husband in 1787 from the Moscow merchant Sergei Skorgin for 1,000 roubles. Left a widow in 1793, with five small children, the 27-year-old Vlas'eva dismantled the old house and in its place erected a new one, with two wings built on to the principal building, together with a carriage shed, cellar and stables in the yard. The area of this urban estate was about 127 square metres. Vlas'eva reckoned the value of the buildings after reconstruction at 18,000 roubles. It is possible that the money for the rebuilding came from Vlas'eva's father, the Moscow merchant Fedor Gorskii, from whom she may also have inherited her business. Vlas'eva's enterprise worked on orders from Moscow textile manufacturers, taking uncoloured calico and carrying out printing and dyeing. Among the clients from whom she received calico and cloth for headscarves for processing (to a total value of 8,241 roubles 90 kopecks) were the Moscow merchants Pavel and Ivan Torochkov, Nikolai Kaftannikov, Vasilii Abramov, Nikolai Remezov, Petr Miakishev and Grigorii Alekseev. Besides taking orders, Vlas'eva also printed calico on her own account for resale (production worth 8,000 roubles). The value of equipment and materials at her enterprise ('various items for the factory – colours [dyes], tables, vessels') was placed at 3,850 roubles. The list of personal movable items shows that Vlas'eva's home did not enjoy such luxury as Zezina's. Furniture mentioned includes two mahogany commodes (50 roubles), a mahogany cupboard (40), two mahogany tables (together, 40), eighteen 'oaken chairs with leather seats' (together, 20), three oaken bedsteads (together, 34), two mirrors in mahogany frames (together, 30 roubles) etc. The register includes some items not found in the possession of others: gusli (a sort of small harp) made of alder wood (25 roubles) and 'a Norton silver pocket watch' (150 roubles). Unlike our other cases, the fate of Avdot'ia Vlas'eva can be followed beyond 1814. She succeeded in restoring her enterprise to working order after the destruction of the war. Its profile changed: instead of calico printing, she turned to making cotton textiles, employing eighteen hired workers on eighteen looms.[62]

These three cases demonstrate that the example of the nobility, the elite of which, starting from the eighteenth century, widely used clothes, tableware, furniture and interior items (including luxury goods) crafted in European fashion, was followed by female merchants and merchants' wives, whose tastes and financial capabilities in the first third of the nineteenth century bore witness to Russia's developing step by step into a 'modern' consumer society.

Conclusion

We see that, in the period from 1800 to the end of the 1820s, at least several hundred women managed to materialize their right to handle business on equal terms with men, as it was stipulated by legislation of the Russian Empire, and to join the ranks of the economically active population. The major precondition for this was women's control over property. It can be said with confidence that there existed a high correlation between proprietorship and household headship. Control over property either made women independent in disposing of their possessions and in managing businesses or made it possible for them to be in active partnership with family members, for the most part with adult sons. Women, especially widows, were actual heads of the households. In this case, women had the bridging function in the context of the long entrepreneurial history of a dynasty.

Although the complete official industrial statistics of the Russian Empire exist only for the year 1814, and the data are missing until the year 1832, some conclusions can be made nonetheless. According to the data from the year 1814, there were 165 women who owned industrial enterprises. These enterprises accounted for 4.4 per cent of the total number. Typical of female entrepreneurship in industry was that the owners belonged to various estates, with noble women being most numerous (76 persons, or 46 per cent), and merchant women second to them (63 persons, or 38 per cent). Merchant women, as a rule, represented the first or the second (and extremely rarely, the third) generation in the families who had chosen business as their occupation. Having originated from the peasant or merchant milieu, they could rely on their own capital only. On average, the capital of those merchant women was smaller than that of their noble counterparts. Also, the noble women had an advantage in resources such as land, real estate and, frequently, serf labour force. In the branches of industry where noble proprietresses were most numerous (cloth manufacture, glass- and crystal-making, paper production, and ferrous metallurgy), between 62.4 and 96.4 per cent of the workers were serfs, either 'ascribed' or bought. By contrast, the branches of industry where the majority of proprietresses belonged to the merchant estate for the most part used the labour of personally free hired workers, whose proportion was highest in the cotton industry (where 99.4 per cent of workers were hired and only 0.6 per cent were serfs) and in the branch which combined soap-boiling, tallow-boiling, candle-making enterprises and wax-foundries (where 100 per cent of workers were hired).

So far as the issue of property ownership is concerned, the legislatively stipulated right of women to disposition of property was actively realized in daily practice. Women were active agents in transactions of three sorts: sales, purchases and deeds of gift, and they demonstrated a perpetual desire to increase their property.

All this testifies to the fact that, despite all the complexity of the bureaucratic procedure for the merchant estate to be joined by representatives of lower social strata (the peasantry and the *meshchanstvo*), some women were persistent in their attempts to elevate their social and property status. Thereby they were realizing their own individual aspirations but were also making it possible for their families to move upward in the social structure. However, in the first decades of the nineteenth-century business was frequently unstable, and beside some success stories of female entrepreneurship we often come across cases when business ventures were shortlived and ended in a return into a lower social stratum.

2 FEMALE ENTREPRENEURSHIP IN THE 1830s–40s: A HIDDEN SUCCESS

During the period under consideration, the economic situation was characterized by the predominance, among female entrepreneurs, of widows who had inherited property and businesses from their husbands.

The surviving sources containing information on entrepreneurship in the 1830s–40s are far from numerous. The published sources are limited to the all-Russia roster 'The List of Factory-Owners and Manufacturers of the Russian Empire for the Year 1832' (hereinafter *the 1832 List*) and 'The Atlas of Industry of Moscow Province';[1] the archival sources – to 'The List of Names of All Persons Who Carry Out Trade and Craftsmanship in Moscow and Own Factories and Works, for the Year 1838' (hereinafter *the 1838 List*)[2]. A combination of the information from the 1832 List with the data of the censuses for poll-tax revision and the genealogical information of noble female entrepreneurs reveals a picture of the independent economic activity of female entrepreneurs in the 1830s and 40s. The 1832 List is a basic source for analysing the sphere of industrial entrepreneurship in the Russian Empire on the whole, while the 1838 List is a similar source for examining female industrial entrepreneurship and commercial activity in Moscow, the most industrially developed city of the Russian Empire.

The chapter shows a steady rise in the numbers of women entrepreneurs. We analyse the statistics of female entrepreneurship in industry and trade, and examine two patterns of management, conventionally named as 'noble' and 'merchant'.

1. The Structure of Female Entrepreneurship in Industry According to the 1832 List

Our analysis of the 1832 List to reconstruct the distribution of enterprises by estate status of their female owners shows that noblewomen owned 241 enterprises out of 484 (or 49.8 per cent); female merchants – 172 (or 35.6 per cent); forty-eight women from the *meshchanstvo* estate (*meshchanki*)[3] (or 9.9 per cent);

sixteen peasant women (or 3.3 per cent); six women inscribed in artisans' corporations (*tsekhovye*) (or 1.2 per cent); and one soldier's wife (or 0.2 per cent). By comparison with 1814, the total number of nobles' enterprises increased by 3.2 times (while their share grew from 46 to almost 50 per cent) and merchants' ones by 2.7 times (their share dropped from 38 to 36 per cent); while the overall share of enterprises owned by women of low social status (*meshchanki*, peasant women, *tsekhovye*, the soldier's wife) rose by 2.7 times (or from 16 to 18 per cent). Thus, no significant changes in the proportions of the social composition of female ownership took place in the period between 1814 and 1832. This bears witness to a linear development of industrial production during this timespan.

The economy oriented to agriculture corresponded to a low level of urbanization (7.4 per cent of the population lived in towns in 1825).[4] Approximately one half of 'female-owned' enterprises were situated on landowners' estates, the major economic units of the country's economy. In the first half of the nineteenth century, the landowning aristocracy owned nearly 29 per cent of the territory of European Russia.[5]

The 1832 statistics demonstrate that the considerable rise in the number of enterprises owned by women became an important index, because their total number increased by 2.9 times (from 165 to 484). Still more important is an increase in the proportion of women among factory owners – the number of enterprises belonging to them grew to 9.1 per cent (from 4.4 per cent in 1814).

The comprehensive qualitative and quantitative data on this matter are shown in Table 2.1.

Table 2.1. The number of enterprises owned by women, by branch of industry (1832)

The branches are placed in the Table in descending order of the number of 'female' enterprises

Branch	Total number of enterprises	Number of enterprises owned by women	As a percentage of the total	Number of enterprises by estate status of female owners, in percent
Cotton textile industry Including:	868	75	8.6	female merchants – 40 (53.3 per cent),
Cotton-weaving	571	49	8.6	noblewomen – 17 (22.7 per
Cotton-spinning	18	3	16.7	cent),
Cotton dying and printing industry	279	23	8.2	peasant women – 11 (14.7 per cent)
				meshchanki – 5 (6.7 per cent),
				tsekhovye – 2 (2.6 per cent)
Woollen industry	424	69	16.3	noblewomen – 64 (92.75 per cent),
				female merchants – 5 (7.25 per cent)

Branch	Total number of enterprises	Number of enterprises owned by women	As a percentage of the total	Number of enterprises by estate status of female owners, in percent
Soap-boiling, fat-rendering, candle-making, and wax-refining industries	1078	67	6.2	female merchants – 45 (67.1 per cent), *meshchanki* – 16 (23.9 per cent), noblewomen – 3 (4.5 per cent), *tsekhovye* – 2 (3 per cent), soldier wife – 1 (1.5 per cent)
Tanning industry	1463	65	4.4	female merchants – 33 (50.8 per cent), *meshchanki* – 24 (36.9 per cent), noblewomen – 6 (9.2 per cent), peasant women – 2 (3.1 per cent)
Production of metal articles (iron, steel, copper)	300	42	15	noblewomen – 34 (80.95 per cent), female merchants – 8 (19.05 per cent)
Potash industry	209	45	21.5	noblewomen – 36 (80 per cent), female merchants – 7 (15.6 per cent), *meshchanka* – 1 (2.2 per cent), peasant woman – 1 (2.2 per cent),
Saltpetre production	89	28	31.5	noblewomen – 28 (100 per cent)
Glass and crystal industry	182	27	14.8	noblewomen – 22 (81.5 per cent), female merchants – 5 (18,5 per cent)
Writing paper industry	118	20	17	noblewomen – 16 (80 per cent), female merchants – 3 (15 per cent), *tsekhovye* – 1 (5 per cent)
Silk industry	139	14	10.1	female merchants – 10 (71.4 per cent), peasant women – 2 (14.3 per cent) noblewoman – 1 (7,15 per cent), *tsekhovaia* – 1 (7.15 per cent)
Flax and hemp industry	22	7	31.8	noblewomen – 4 (57.1 per cent), female merchants – 3 (42.9 per cent)
Rope industry	85	6	7.1	female merchants – 6 (100 per cent)
Sugar industry	56	5	8.9	noblewomen – 5 (100 per cent)
Vinegar production	18	4	22.2	*meshchanki* – 2, noblewoman – 1, female merchant –1
Chemical industry	55	3	5.5	female merchants – 2, noblewoman – 1
Cosmetics (pomade) production	6	2	33.3	female merchants – 2

Branch	Total number of enterprises	Number of enterprises owned by women	As a percentage of the total	Number of enterprises by estate status of female owners, in percent
Tobacco industry	49	2	4.1	noblewoman – 1, female merchant – 1
Production of dyestuffs	35	1	2.9	noblewoman – 1
Braid production	18	1	5.6	female merchant – 1
Hat industry	83	1	1.2	Noblewoman – 1
Porcelain and pottery industry; production of oilcloth, varnished articles, sealing-wax, and snuff-boxes	52	none	–	–
TOTAL	**5,349**	**484**	**9.1 per cent**	

Ownership of industrial enterprises can be subdivided into two types, conventionally denoted as 'noble' and 'merchant'. In a noble economic unit centred on the manorial estate, industrial enterprises were one of the elements of infrastructure. Incomes from industrial enterprises could, to a certain degree, compensate for the low marketability of agricultural production, especially in bad harvest years. In a merchant business, the factory or the shop (most frequently, the shop was the second, finalizing component, providing a guaranteed income from production activities) were the major sources of income received by the merchant family. Each of these two types offered its own guarantees and risks. In the event of a failure to sell products, the poor performance of noble enterprises would not necessarily result in their owner's bankruptcy. In similar situations, merchant enterprises had a minimum potential for survival and could even end up by closing down. In the case of noble-type ownership the proprietress, more often than not, distanced herself from the process of production, while in that of merchant-type ownership the proprietress had to regularly visit the factory, and to go carefully into details of purchasing raw materials and equipment, recruiting the workers, and selling finished products.

Noble female owners were predominant in the wool (93 per cent), metal-working (81 per cent), glass and crystal (81 per cent), writing-paper (80 per cent), and sugar (100 per cent) industries, as well as in production of potash (80 per cent) and saltpetre (100 per cent). The enterprises in question were situated in rural areas, and were using considerable monetary and manpower resources accumulated by several generations of rich noble dynasties. Female merchant owners were predominant in the cotton (53 per cent) and silk (71 per cent) industries, in the soap-boiling, fat-rendering, candle-making, and wax-refining branch (67 per cent), and in the leather (51 per cent) and rope (100 per cent) industries. Merchant enterprises operating in the second quarter of the nineteenth century were most often set up by the husbands of their proprietresses and then passed to the latter by will. A number of enterprises were established by the proprietresses themselves (widows, spinsters and, less frequently, married women). Merchant enterprises used the labour of free, hired workers. 80 per cent of merchant enterprises were in towns and cities, approximately 20 per cent – in rural areas, in large manufacturing settlements.

It should be noted that close to the merchant type were the enterprises owned by *meshchanki,* who played an important part in the leather industry (37 per cent) and the soap-boiling, fat-rendering, candle-making and wax-refining branches (24 per cent). In those industries, most of the enterprises represented workshops with five to fifteen workers. As their products were in high demand in every season of the year and by every category of the population, selling them within the home district was no problem. *Meshchanki* owners did not have long-term credit relations with wholesale buyers (in contrast to female merchants, who sold their goods wholesale on credit for the term of six, eight, nine or twelve months), which safeguarded them from the risk of investing a large opening capital which they simply did not have.

Let us consider in some detail the indices for certain branches where many enterprises were in female ownership.

In the cotton industry, the share of 'female-owned' enterprises was close to the share of women in the total number of owners of all industrial enterprises (9.1 per cent). Between 1814 and 1832, the total number of cotton-processing enterprises doubled (from 423 to 866). The share of female owners significantly increased – from 10 to 75 (or by 7.5 times); 23 per cent of them were noble-women, while the remaining 77 per cent were merchant and peasant women, *meshchanki,* and *tsekhovye.* This growth in the cotton industry was caused by three factors. First, by the successful distribution of cotton fabrics (which were cheaper than wool, silk and flax); second, by the general favourable context of raw-materials supply (import of raw cotton, cotton yarns, and dyes had never been interrupted since the introduction of the 1822 Customs Tariff; the same was true, since the 1830s, of the situation with spinning machines, mainly imported from England, the country which accounted for approximately one-third of Russia's imports) and manpower supply (in 1825, 94 per cent of the workforce were free hired workers[6]); and third, by a rise in the business activity of women who were not afraid to continue businesses passed to them from their late husbands, or to establish enterprises on their own.

An example of successful female entrepreneurship was the case of the Moscow female merchant Anna Riabinina, who established a cotton factory after she had been widowed. In 1825, the year the factory was opened, she was thirty-nine and had two sons – Mikhail and Ivan, aged seventeen and sixteen respectively. The Riabinins were Old Believers, and as such belonged to a confessional group very active in business matters. For the first three years after the establishment of the factory, Riabinina remained in the *meshchanstvo* estate, and then shifted to the merchant one in 1828. To carry out trade in their products – headscarves, shawls and ribbons - the Riabinins rented two shops in the most prestigious commercial district of Moscow, Kitai-Gorod. The shops were managed by the sons, while the factory – by Riabinina herself. Over the 24 years when Anna headed the factory, the number of workers increased (from 80 to 330 between 1839 and 1849), and the factory was transferred from rented premises to a new building bought by Anna in the name of her elder son, Mikhail. In 1842 it was valued at 8,751 silver roubles, and by 1849, the factory equipment consisted of 170 'simple' looms, 80 Jacquard looms, ten warping machines, and two presses. After the death of Anna's younger son, Ivan, in 1848, and her own death in 1849, the business completely passed to the elder son, Mikhail Riabinin, the success of whose business career was confirmed by his shifting to the Second Guild in 1851, and to the First Guild in 1856. In 1853, Riabinin's factory employed 370 workers, its output was worth 53,700 silver roubles. Riabinin was elected to a number of public offices: in particular, he was deputy-chairman of the Committee for the Supervision of Factories and Plants in Moscow (1850–1), and a member of the Commercial Deputation (1852–5). As Mikhail Riabinin was childless, in the 1870s the enterprise passed to his nephew, Aleksandr. [7]

In the 1830s and 1840s, the wool industry continued to be characterized by the situation described in Chapter 3 – it was dominated by the oldest enterprises, and the profits of most of the owners were ensured by guaranteed purchases of their products by the Treasury for the purpose of providing the Army with uniforms. A correlation between the data for the years 1814 and 1832 shows that over eighteen years, the overall number of enterprises engaged in production of woollen-goods increased from 235 to 424 (or by 2.4 times). Correspondingly the proportion of female owners also grew, from 12.3 per cent to 16.3 per cent. Both in 1814 and 1832, the proportion of noblewomen owners amounted to about 90 per cent; the rest of the enterprises belonged to female merchants.

As far as production of metal items (steel, iron, and copper) is concerned, between 1814 and 1832 the overall number of enterprises increased from 134 to 300 (or by 2.2 times), and the number of those owned by women – from 11 to 42 (or by 3.8 times). In 1814, noblewomen owned 55 per cent of enterprises; in 1832 – 81 per cent. It can be explained by both the fact that metal working required considerable investments in the course of establishing new enterprises (such investments were more readily available to proprietresses of big manorial estates than to female merchants), and by the availability of workers who could be easily recruited from the serfs owned by the noblewomen themselves.

Here are several examples of nobles' enterprises. Countess Alexandra Branitskaia [Branicka], née von Engelhardt, owned four metalworking plants in Kiev province (production of ploughs, harrows, and other agricultural machinery).

An admiral's wife Anna Kravtsova (together with partners) owned four iron-works in Viatka province. Of the existing forty-two enterprises engaged in processing of iron and manufacturing of iron articles (agricultural implements), fifteen works were in Volhynian province. Three of them belonged to Dar'ia Opochinina and were established on the estates inherited by her after her father, the prominent military commander Mikhail Kutuzov, who had become famous in the campaigns of Catherine II and in the 1812 War against Napoleon. The landed estates (with 2,000 serfs) were granted to Kutuzov for his service 'into eternal and hereditary possession' by Empress Catherine the Great in 1793.

The fact that the activity of women was on the rise is exemplified by the frequent instances of entrepreneurship in which married women were engaged independently of their husbands. Thus, in Vologda, the *meshchane* (members of the *meshchanstvo* estate) husband and wife Vera and Vasilii Ponomariov had one rope-manufacturing enterprise each; in Gavrilov Posad, Vladimir province, the wife, Pelageia Kovyliaeva, had a cotton-printing mill which, among other things, manufactured kerchiefs, while her husband, the merchant of the Third Guild Kondratii Kovyliaev, owned a calico mill; in the town of Iur'ev, Vladimir province, the wife, Nadezhda Maslennikova, and the husband, Yegor Maslennikov, had one cotton factory each; in the village of Sluzhivaia Ura, Kazan' province, the wife of a merchant, Zugaira Khoziaseitova, owned a cotton mill and writing-paper factory, while two similar enterprises belonged to her husband, the merchant of the Second Guild Mukmin Khoziaseitov (the philanthropist, renown for building, in 1830, the cathedral mosque in Ufa), both were Tatars; and in the town of Kungur, Perm' province, Natal'ia Shmakova and her husband, the merchant of the Third Guild Fedor Shmakov, had one tannery each.[8]

The greatest density of enterprises owned by women was observed in nine of the fifty-six provinces represented in the 1832 List. In each of these nine provinces there were no less than fifteen enterprises owned by women; on the whole, they had 268 (or 55 per cent) out of Russia's total of 487 such enterprises. As regards the overall number of enterprises in the territory of a province, Moscow, Vladimir, Petersburg, Volhynia, and Kursk provinces were clear leaders among the Russian regions (see Table 2.2).

These nine provinces with 22.5 per cent of Russia's population accounted for 45.4 per cent of the total number of Russian industrial enterprises. Their concentration in these regions can be explained by a number of historical traditions, first of all, by the propensity of the population to get engaged in 'crafts', and also by such geographical and geological factors as the presence of forests and rivers as sources of energy supply (fuel and water power), and the abundance of mineral resources. However, the scenarios of industrial development differed from one province to another. In order to consider the question in detail, we can analyze the situation in the four provinces – Moscow, Slobodsko-Ukrain-

Portrait of an unknown female merchant. 1840s. Courtesy of Mikhail Zolotarev, Moscow.

ian, Vladimir, and Kazan' – which held the first four positions with regard to the number of enterprises.

Among the businesswomen of Moscow province, female merchants were predominant (with 36 out of 57 enterprises in female ownership, or 63 per cent of the latter), followed by noblewomen – 21 per cent, *meshchanki* – 7 per cent, *tsekhovye* – 5 per cent, and peasant women – 4 per cent. This situation reflected the fact that Moscow province was deeply involved in market processes as a place of concentration of enterprises whose products were intended for sale on the open market. Only six out of 57 enterprises (which belonged to five proprietresses) operated to state orders, manufacturing woollen fabrics for army uniforms. All those six woollen mills were situated on manorial estates owned by the wives of high-ranking military officers or top officials (the husbands of proprietresses Princess Elena Khovanskaia and Varvara Balk-Poleva were Privy Councillors, those of yet another two – Elena Pushkina and Praskov'ia Akulova – Actual State Councillors, and one proprietress, Fedos'ia Svechina, was married to a colonel).[10] Thus, high social standing opened the way to obtaining lucrative state orders which guaranteed that the factory owners would receive risk-free profits.

In Slobodsko-Ukrainian province (with Kharkov as its centre), industrial enterprises were situated, in the main, on manorial estates, and were manned by serfs. Of the 32 female owners of thirty-five enterprises, only two were female merchants, while thirty were noblewomen-landowners. Of those thirty-five enterprises, twenty-six were saltpetre works, whose whole output was purchased by the State. The reason for such density of enterprises of this branch was the decision to promote saltpetre production manifested by the Senate Decree of 22 June 1714, which also prescribed that 'both Russians and foreigners should by no means sell this saltpetre either on the side or abroad'.[11] Saltpetre was a compo-

Table 2.2. The provinces with the largest number of female entrepreneurs (1832)

The provinces are presented in descending order of the number of 'female-owned' enterprises

Province	Total number of enterprises	Number of enterprises owned by women	As percent-age of total number	Population (thousands)[9]	Position by popula-tion size among 49 provinces of European Russia (per cent of total population)
Moscow	805	57	7.1	1374.0	14 (2.5 per cent)
Slobodsko-Ukrainian	128	35	27.3	1467.4	11 (2.7 per cent)
Vladimir	371	34	9.2	1246.5	18 (2.3 per cent)
Kazan'	163	24	14.7	1342.9	16 (2.5 per cent)
Volhynian	233	23	9.9	1445.5	12 (2.7 per cent)
Orenburg	136	23	16.9	1948.5	1 (3.6 per cent)
Kaluga	167	20	12.0	1006.4	26 (1.9 per cent)
St. Petersburg	229	17	7.4	643.7	42 (1.2 per cent)
Kursk	194	15	7.7	1680.0	6 (3.1 per cent)
TOTAL, in 9 provinces	2,426 (or 45.4 per cent of Russia's total number)	268 (or 55.0 per cent of total number of 'female-owned' enterprises)	11.05 per cent	12,154.9 (out of 54,092.3)	22.5 per cent

nent of black powder, and its production was necessary in order to provide the Army with this propellant.

By the total number of enterprises, Vladimir province ranked second (after Moscow province) among the provinces of the Empire. In 1832, it had 371 enterprises, including thirty-four (or 9.2 per cent) owned by thirty-two women. The most numerous among proprietresses were female merchants (twenty-one, or 66 per cent). In second place were peasant women (eight, or 25 per cent). 6 per cent of proprietresses of enterprises were noblewomen (i.e., two persons) who owned three businesses, and there was also one *meshchanka* (or 3 per cent). Of thirty-four factories, twenty-five were weaving mills. Thirteen of those were situated in Shuia district (*uezd*), mostly in the big manufacturing village of Ivanovo, so abundant of textile establishments that it was called 'the Russian Manchester'. It is noteworthy that all the proprietresses who were inscribed in the peasant estate hailed from this region – the local landowners (most of the land belonged to the Counts Sheremetev) were reluctant to free their serfs, and preferred to have regular income from the business activities of the latter.

Kazan' province had only 163 enterprises, twenty-four of which (including fifteen potash plants) belonged to 18 women. 61 per cent of them were female merchants, 33 per cent - noblewomen, while *meshchanki* in the person of one woman accounted for 6 per cent. There were eleven female merchants who owned twelve enterprises, six noblewomen who owned twelve enterprises (including the four potash plants belonging to Praskov'ia Kandalintseva, wife of a Court Councillor, and the two potash plants owned by Countess Natal'ia Zubova). One potash plant belonged to the *meshchanka* Maria Bogdanova.

A typological comparison between these four provinces has led us to the following conclusions. Two economic patterns can be discerned. Widespread in Moscow and Vladimir provinces was the market type of production, predominantly based on the functioning of the textile industry. Most of the entrepreneurs (both male and female) were merchants. Slobodsko-Ukrainian province was characterized by the predominance of nobles-owned enterprises, most of which operated in the raw materials sector. Kazan' province was an interface between these 'pure' types because of the existence there of both merchant textile enterprises and nobles-owned material-producing (potash) businesses.

Now we will turn to the issue of noble women's activity in industry.

2. Noble Female Entrepreneurs from the 1832 List

According to the 1832 List, noblewomen owned 241 enterprises, including sixty-four woollen factories, thirty-six and twenty-eight enterprises producing potash and saltpetre respectively, thirty-four plants producing metals and metal articles, twenty-two glass and crystal works, and sixteen writing-paper mills. Especially interesting among the noble female owners was the group of representatives of the high nobility. Unfortunately, the scarcity of information makes it impossible to describe in detail the functioning of their enterprises, or to dwell upon such issues as the sales, the demand for and the prices of their products.

However, the prosopography of the female owners makes it possible to analyse the parameters of their properties, influence, and style of management. Of the general list containing information on 241 enterprises in female property, the author analyses a sample of 26 persons selected for this purpose. They (either by birth or by marriage) belonged to such princely families as the Apraksins, Bariatinskys, Volkonskys, Viazemskys, Gagarins, Golitsyns, Dolgorukovs, Meshcherskys, Radziwills, Repnins, Tolstoys and Khovanskys, or to the families of the Counts Branitskys [Branicki], Zakrevskys, Zubovs, la Valles, Orlovs, Pototskys [Potocki], Razumovskys, Saltykovs, Uvarovs, Chernysevs and Sheremetevs.

An analysis of the details of the receiving of property in correlation with the genealogical data makes it possible to discern several types of inheritance and possession of enterprises. The most widespread was inheritance after a parent (thirteen cases out of twenty-six, or 50 per cent; ten persons inherited from their fathers, and three persons from their mothers). There were three ways of obtaining property under this scenario: by gift, as a dowry, or, most frequently, by will. Five persons received property from their husbands (as a gift or by will). In one case, property was obtained through purchase (Countess la Valle). In seven cases out of twenty-six, the scheme of obtaining property remains unclear. Let us consider the most interesting cases of receiving and possessing property.

Princess Natal'ia Golitsyna (1741–1837), née Countess Chernysheva, received property from her parents. According to a legend, Golitsyna (who died at the age of almost 100 years after having been maid of honour under five reigns, and lady-in-waiting at the courts of Alexander I and Nicholas I) was the prototype of the countess in 'The Queen of Spades' by the poet A. Pushkin. She figures in the 1832 List as the owner of three enterprises in Orel province – a tannery and a glass factory at the village of Kokorevka, and a linen factory in the village of Radogoshch. Golitsyna was fabulously rich. She inherited substantial property after her father, Count Chernyshev (1719–73), a senator, a prominent diplomat, and son of Peter I's batman. Chernyshev spent more than 20 years in Europe in the office of Ambassador to Prussia (1741–6), Great Britain (1746–55), and France (1760–2). In the 1740s, he was awarded, for his service, substantial landed estates with serfs, situated in Orel province. On the Count's death in 1773 they were owned by his widow, and then passed to his daughter, Natal'ia. In 1765, Natal'ia married Prince Golitsyn, whose landed estates were side by side with the Chernyshevs'. Evidence indicates that Natal'ia Golitsyna was personally involved in managing her property – it was in her time that the estate's office building, a distillery, a stud-farm, and a masonry church were built in the village of Radogoshch. The serfs who worked in the fields and at the enterprises were mercilessly exploited. In 1797, they rioted and torched the tannery's office and the distillery. Although we have found no data on the composition and the size of Golitsyna's 'latifundium' in the 1830s and 40s, some later data are available. In 1860, the male population of Radogoshch and of the eighteen lesser settlements, inherited after Natal'ia Golitsyna by her son Vladimir, consisted of 3,768 serfs and 134 household serfs (which implies that the total population, including women, was approximately twice that large); the estate comprised 666 households. The land area of the estate amounted to 21,637 *desiatinas* (or 58,420 acres),[12] 28 per cent of which were used by the peasants, and 72 per cent - by the landowner.[13]

The owner of three enterprises Praskov'ia Miatleva (1772–1858), who was the wife of the Privy Councillor and Senator P. Miatlev, inherited a landed estate, in Simbirsk province, which included the big village of Poretskoe, after her father, Field-Marshal Count Ivan Saltykov (1730–1805), who had inherited it after his father, Field-Marshal Count Peter Saltykov (1698–1772) (having been sent to France by Peter I in order to learn navigation and naval science, he spent more than fifteen years serving in the French Navy; in 1762–72 he was Governor General of Moscow). Miatleva's enterprises included a woollen factory (producing woollen cloth and carpets) and a tannery (established by her father), both in Poretskoe, and also a potash works in the village of Bataevo, Kazan' Province.[14] According to the 1839 data, Praskov'ia also had a stearine chandlery in St Petersburg, which she co-owned with M. von Kelderman.[15] Praskov'ia Miatleva visited Poretskoe almost every year.[16] During her summer visits, she thoroughly investigated all the business matters dealing with the estate. However, as it was customary among most landowners, control over the estate was entrusted to a manager. The existing archival documents on land purchases and sales indicate that these transactions were handled, for both parties, by managers, acting by proxy and in the name of the owners.[17] Praskov'ia Miatleva received a good home education and knew several foreign languages. The memoirist Vigel was delighted by the style of behaviour of Countess Saltykova and her daughter Miatleva: 'I do not know where they could get the excellence of their inimitable manners combining all the grandeur of Russian boyar ladies and the natural politeness which distinguished the duchesses of bygone times'.[18] Her major hobby was performances staged at Marfino, her parents' manorial estate near Moscow, especially those timed for the 23 and 24 July, Field-Marshal Saltykov's birthday and name day respectively: 'Mrs. Miatleva had the great passion for appearing on the stage of the home theatre, naturally in French plays'.[19]

Countess Stephanie Sayn-Wittgenstein-Sayn, née Radziwill (1809–32), daughter of Prince Dominique Radziwill (1786–1813), descended from a family known since the fifteenth century. According to the 1832 List, Stephanie owned two enterprises in Minsk Province – a factory manufacturing silk sashes in Slutsk, and a glass factory in the small town Urech'e.[20] The enterprises were founded by Stephanie's ancestors. The sash factory was established in 1758 (and closed in 1844) by Mikhail Radziwill to manufacture sashes woven of gold, silver and silk thread. The handmade sashes, 50cm wide and up to 4m long, were to be worn with traditional ceremonial dress of the Polish nobility. The annual output of the factory was up to 200 sashes. (The town of Slutsk belonged to Stephanie's son Peter Wittgenstein until 1846, when in was bought by the Treasury for 342,821 roubles.[21]) The Urech'e glass factory produced bottles, carafes, tumblers and wineglasses, including diamond-cut and engraved with floral ornaments. The work was in existence from 1738 until the middle of the nineteenth century. No data on the enterprises' revenues were found. On the death of her father, when she was five, Stephanie was educated at the St Petersburg Catherine Institute, an establishment for daughters of aristocrats, and was personally patronized by Empress Dowager Maria Fedorovna, widow of Paul I. Her education completed, Stephanie became maid of honour to Empress Alexandra Fedorovna, consort of Emperor Nicholas I. Stephanie succeeded to an immense fortune in the form of landed estates with magnificent forests: in 1860 (when an inventory of all landed estates was carried out for the sake of solving the issue of redemption payments) her only son and heir, Peter, owned in Minsk, Vil'na, and Vitebsk provinces 695,176 desiatinas in the owner's use and 99,195 desiatinas in the peasants' use (in total, 794,371 desiatinas, or 2,144,801.7 acres) with 68,677 serfs.[22] The guardians allocated 60,000 roubles annually to Stephanie's financial support – 14,000 to the Institute, and the rest as her pocket money. According to the reminiscences of one of her lady friends, Stephanie generously dispensed money to her classmates, including to those about to marry, in which case the sums amounted to 10,000 and 25,000 roubles; and a lot was gifted in small amounts – 'each day 50, 20 or 10 roubles was given away, depending on what was left in the purse'.[23] When Stephanie's governess reproached her, she answered that as the manager of her estates, Dmitriev, was swindling both her and the guardians, it would be better if the money were given to the poor 'than to this scoundrel'. After the premature death of Stephanie at the age of twenty-two, her two children (her son Peter and her daughter Marie) by Ludwig Wittgenstein, son of the Russian Field-Marshal Peter Wittgenstein, became orphans. The capital and estates were inherited by the son, and on his death, in 1887, they passed to his sister Marie (Princess Marie, of Sayn-Wittgenstein-Sayn, daughter of Ludwig Adolph Friedrich, second Prince of Sayn-Wittgenstein-Sayn and his first wife, Princess Caroline (Stephanie) Radziwill), who married, in 1847, Prince Chlodwig Hohenlohe-Schillingsfürst, Minister-President of Bavaria in 1866–70 and Prime Minister of Prussia and Chancellor of Germany in 1896–1900 (who was a nephew of Princess Feodora of Hohenlohe-Langenburg, half-sister to Queen

Victoria of the United Kingdom). At the end of the nineteenth century, in connection with the Tsar's edict forbidding non-Russian citizens to own land in the North-Western provinces, these estates were sold.[24] In the case of Stephanie Wittgenstein, enterprises were received as part of inheritance. Stephanie did nor participate personally in managing her property.

Countess Maria Razumovskaia, née Princess Viazemskaia (1772–1865), was married, first to Prince A. Golitsyn and then (from 1802) to Major General Lev Razumovsky (1757–1818). She owned a wool mill in the town of Karlovka, Poltava province.[25] The Karlovka estate had been donated from the Treasury to her husband's father, Field-Marshal Count Kirill Razumovsky (1728–1803), Hetman of Little Russia in 1750–64.[26] Razumovskaia owned the estate (which included, apart from the town of Karlovka itself, 3 church villages and 10 villages with approximately 20 thousand peasants and 90.4 thousands desiatinas of land[27]) since 1818, the year of her husband's death, until the late 1840s, when she sold it to Grand Duchess Elena Pavlovna for a life annuity. The emergence of the wool factory was one of the manifestations of Karlovka's being 'rationally managed' in order to increase the revenues from selling the products manufactured on the estate. The raw materials used at the factory were all local – in 1845, the estate had 53 thousand sheep, mainly fine-fleeced.[28] A few words about the owner. Prince P. Viazemsky characterized her in most positive terms: 'She was a truthful and candid person. Society's severe judgement and derisive detraction became disarmed and speechless in her presence'; amply possessed by her were 'the treasures of kindness, goodness and compassion'. For her brother she bought a mansion in Tver'skaia Street in Moscow (later the English Club), repaid a big debt made by a young relative, and helped numerous persons without advertising her good deeds. After becoming widow at the age of 46 (she would die in her 94th year), Countess Razumovskaia spent several years 'immersed in ... true and deep sorrow', and then began to periodically visit Europe and remain there for long spells: 'In her well-known and witty letters, published under the name of Vicomte Delaunay, M-me Girardin mentions Countess Razumovskaia and her Paris salon. The grateful Karlsbad has devoted a monument to her: at the spa, she was the life and soul of the party .... Such power cannot be obtained otherwise than by education, by the experience of refined social life, and by the polite manners and habits which have become one's second nature.'[29] In St. Petersburg, Razumovskaia's salon was famous for being visited by Emperor Nicholas I and Empress Alexandra. Her only weakness was a passion for elegant dresses, which the Countess simply could not resist; thus, on returning back to Moscow from Vienna in 1835, she had to apply for help to an acquaintance who served at the Customs Department in order to have her luggage with 300 dresses transited across the border.

Among the cases under consideration there was one of a landed estate with an enterprise obtained through purchase. This purchase, of the Sably estate in the Crimea from Count Zavadovsky, was made by Countess Alexandra de la Valle (1772–1850). The estate had a factory manufacturing fine woollen cloth. Countess de la Valle, née Kozitskaia (a daughter of the State Secretary to Catherine II) descended, on the maternal side, from the well-known millionaires, mine-owners Miasnikov-Tverdyshevs, mentioned by Pushkin in the notes to his 'History of Pugachev': 'Tverdyshev acquired his immense wealth in the course of seven years. The descendants of his heirs are still among the richest people in Russia'. Alexandra's husband, the Frenchman Jean de la Valle (1761–1846), emigrated to Russia during the French Revolution, where he started as a teacher at the Naval School and made his way up to Chamberlainship and a high post at the Ministry of Foreign Affairs. He was created a count by King Louis XVIII (the title was confirmed in Russia in 1817).[30] After the death of Countess de la Valle, the Sably estate passed to her daughter, Ekaterina Trubetskaia, wife of the Decembrist Sergei Trubetskoy, who was to follow him to Siberia and died in exile at Irkutsk in 1854. Whether or not the Countess personally participated in managing the estate remains unclear.

As a rule, noble proprietresses managed their enormous latifundia through the mediation of managers. This does not mean that they trusted the latter blindly and were not interested in the state of affairs with regard to their estates. After having thoroughly investigated the epistolary sources and memoirs, Michelle Marrese comes to the conclusion that, as a rule, noble proprietresses went deep into business matters and determined economic strategy by coordinating the activities of the managers. Marrese notices that many memoirists 'recounted that estate management occupied their mothers from morning to night'.[31] Frequently 'married couples not only owned but sometimes managed their property independently of one another' and many estate-proprietresses 'were deeply concerned with day-to-day activities on their estate'.[32] It should be added that 'day-by-day coordination was possible from May to September (in the warm season which was spent by the landowners on their estates), while during the rest of the year which they stand in their town residences these ladies exercised the control indirectly, by way of regular correspondence (usually on a weekly basis).

The presence of industrial enterprises on an estate was the indication of its female owner's 'enlightenment' and her desire to set up a 'rational' establishment fashioned to European standards. Perhaps, an important role in the wide proliferation of noble enterprises was played by the 'factor of imitation', when the entrepreneurial successes of relatives, neighbours or acquaintances attracted new adepts to business activity.

Next on the agenda is a group of female merchants engaged in industry, to be analysed on the basis of statistics and facts relating to Moscow province.

3. Moscow Female Merchants-Entrepreneurs from the 1832 List

Moscow province was the most industrially developed region of Russia (where 15 per cent of the country's industrial enterprises and 2.7 per cent of its population were concentrated). Of the 57 industrial enterprises mentioned in the 1832 List, 33 enterprises situated in the territory of Moscow belonged to women inscribed in the merchant estate. This group has been selected for analysis because it is possible to carry out its prosopographic description primarily based on the linkage of the 1832 List's materials to the data of merchant population censuses, the data on possession of real estate, and some later data concerning the enterprises. Unfortunately, data on the proprietresses' households are extremely scarce, although it is apparent that in most cases it was they who were heads of the households in question, assisted in this capacity by their adult sons. Of the thirty-three people mentioned in the 1832 List, the censuses contain no data on one person, while the data available on another two are incomplete.

Of the thirty-three enterprises, twenty-five (or 76 per cent) were textile mills (nine silk mills; eight cotton-printing mills; seven cotton mills; one woollen-goods factory); two were bell foundries, two were tallow chandleries; one was a wax refinery, one was a tannery, one was a chemical plant and one was a gold-cloth mill. This proportion clearly demonstrates that it was in the textile industry (textile enterprises amounted to 65 per cent of the total number of industrial enterprises situated in Moscow) that proprietresses were most confident of success.[33]

One of the indicators of wellbeing in a big city was ownership of real estate.[34] In the first half of the nineteenth century Moscow homesteads, however small they might be, always included an orchard (in 1830, 8 per cent of the city territory of Moscow was occupied by orchards at private houses).[35] Beside the owner's house, there were numerous utilitarian structures such as stables, barns for horse harness and firewood, storerooms, larders and wells. The homestead was surrounded with a high fence; the front gate was kept locked at night with the keys brought to the owner by the yardman.[36] One of the wings or a separate outbuilding could house a factory. In the initial period of industrial development (before the emergence of capitalist economic entities in the form of big factories), it was not infrequent that the workers slept on the floor under the machines, as is mentioned in the memoirs of the Moscow entrepreneur Chetverikov: 'the workers used to sleep in the workrooms'.[37] The establishment of specialized factory premises, which started in the 1830s (in historiography, the epoch of the Industrial Revolution in Russia is dated to the 1850s–90s), became a mass phenomenon only in the second half of the nineteenth century.

In 1830, of the 9,842 houses (both masonry and timber) existing in Moscow, 2,165 (or 22 per cent) belonged to persons inscribed in the merchant estate

(1,540 belonged to male merchants, and 625 – to female merchants). The share of merchants in the Moscow population amounted to 5.3 per cent (16,210 persons out of the total population of 305,631). Nevertheless, merchants were predominant among the owners of masonry houses (which made up one-third of the city's housing stock – 3,127 houses out of the total of 9,842), as 38.4 per cent of the latter (or 1,200 such houses out of the total of 3,127) belonged to them. At the same time, nobles owned 33 per cent of the city's housing, but only 31.9 per cent of masonry houses.[38] That the percentage of women (noblewomen, female merchants and *meshchanki*) was high among the owners of real estate was noted in 1832 by the statistician V. Androssov, who wrote that 'as much as one-third of houses in Moscow are registered in women's names'.[39]

Of the 33 female entrepreneurs entered in the 1832 List, thirty-one had their enterprises situated within their own homesteads. Moreover, the very fact of owning a factory was testimony to the stability of its owner's business. Thus, according to the 1811 and 1815 Censuses, more than 80 per cent of the dynasties the said female factory owners belonged to (either through their fathers or husbands) had their own homesteads, while in three cases the homesteads (belonging to the previous generation of a dynasty) had been registered even earlier, in the course of the 1795 Census. Real estate could be a source of additional income: for example, the owner of a factory which manufactured cotton kerchiefs Maria Khodateleva rented out a wing of her house to the merchant Aleksandr Kirilov, as premises for his cotton mill manned with ninety-five registered workers, and also a shop and an apartment, also in her house, to the *meshchanka* Anna Alekseeva, for 275 roubles per year.[40] Although formally Kirilov was Khodateleva's competitor, this lease of premises indicates that the strategy of obtaining revenues adopted by female entrepreneurs was quite flexible. Thus, the strong correlation between the possession of real estate and the possession of a factory attests to a significant wealth of the Moscow women engaged in industrial entrepreneurship.

We have found the data on the number of workers employed at some of the enterprises in the 1830s and 1840s. At the silk mills their numbers were as follows: 122 at Dunasheva's (1838); 37 at Efimova-Fomina's (1834); 27 at Kuchumova's (1838); 122 at the cotton-printing mills at Medvedeva's (1834) and 115 in 1842; 100 at Petrova's (1838); 72 at Rozanova's (1834); 28 at Shelepova's (1834); and 56 at Chasovnikova's wool mill in 1834 and 140 in 1843. Bogdanova's bell-foundry employed five workers (1838, 1843).[41]

Let us turn to certain demographic parameters, including the age of a proprietress and the number of children she had. The age of female merchants-entrepreneurs (estimated for thirty persons, for the year 1832) was between twenty-seven and sixty-seven, including aged twenty to thirty – one person (or 3.3 per cent), thirty-one to forty – four persons (or 13.3 per cent), forty-one to fifty – nine persons (or 30 per cent), fifty-one to sixty – six persons (or 20 per cent) and sixty-one to seventy – ten persons (or 33.3 per cent). A correlation between the data on the age of these women and the information on their matrimonial status indicate that predominant among the female entrepreneurs were widows aged forty-one to sixty-seven (83 per cent). Of the thirty-three female entrepreneurs, three (two widows and one 35-year-old 'maiden') were childless. The subdivision by number of sons (alive in 1832) is as follow: one son – nine persons; two sons – nine persons; three sons – four persons; four sons – five persons; five sons – one person. Two persons with no sons had daughters. One of the businesswomen most advanced in age, the sixty-seven-year-old Avdot'ia Soboleva, who had shifted from the *meshchanstvo* estate to the merchant one in 1825, had three sons and four daughters (in 1832, they were aged forty-five, forty-two, thirty-nine, forty-seven, forty-three, thirty-six, and thirty-three respectively, and were all unmarried which, apparently, testified to the despotic character of their mother). The owner of a wax refinery Pelageia Tolokonnikova, fifty-three, had five sons and four daughters.

Let us consider the ways by which those women became property-owners. Of the thirty-three persons, seventeen (or 52 per cent) became heads of enterprises after the death of their husbands; 6 married female entrepreneurs inherited their enterprises after their parents (18 per cent); the same was true of one unmarried woman; and one case remains unclear. Another eight cases represent more complex combinations. In two cases, female entrepreneurs had become heads of enterprises during the lifetime of their elderly husbands, to which end the latter had been relegated into the *meshchanstvo* estate, while the wives had remained in the merchant one. It is not clear whether those operations were carried out with the husbands' consent, or simply because the latter were too frail and helpless to resist, but in any case the women in question had been doing their best to energetically seize power and obtain full control over both the business situation and relations within their families. In one case, an enterprise was inherited after a mother-in-law (after the death of an eighteen-year-old husband 'attached to his mother'), and in yet another case – after a deceased son. Four persons established enterprises on their own. A correlation between the marital status and the pattern of obtaining an enterprise is absolutely apparent. The widows who inherited after their husbands (seventeen persons) became the owners of the enterprises which had been family businesses of their deceased husbands' families, and then headed them for a number of years (from two to twenty-eight) before passing the establishments to their sons, the next generation of the family businesses' owners. As a rule, both married and unmarried female entrepreneurs inherited businesses after their parents in the absence of sons in a given family.

Now consideration should be given to an example of a widow inheriting after her husband. The youngest of the widows, the thirty-two-year-old Avdot'ia

Gribova (1800–after 1850), female merchant of the Third Guild, had lost her husband, Grigorii, at the age of twenty-five, and inherited after him a factory manufacturing silk shawls and waistcoat fabrics (with eighteen workers in 1838 and twenty-one in 1843). The factory was situated in her own house in Pokrovskaia district; in 1842 it was valued at 10,000 silver roubles. Avdot'ia stated in the documents that she was managing the factory business 'on her own'. In 1838, she leased a shop in the *Zerkal'nyi Riad* (the Mirrors' Row) in Kitai-Gorod, for the purpose of selling shawls produced by her factory. For managing the shop, she hired a merchant's clerk (*prikazchik*) – the Moscow *meshchanin* Vasilii Stepanov.[42] Avdot'ia had a son, Fedor, who died at the age of twenty-five (1824–49); after his premature death she lived under the same roof as her grandchildren, Mikhail and Mar'ia, and her son's widow, Anna. She also had two daughters, Anna and Alexandra (born in 1831, in the sixth year of Avdot'ia's widowhood, Alexandra was her illegitimate offspring). Gribova personally managed the factory for more than twenty-five years, from 1825 to at least 1850. The selling matters were managed by a hired *prikazchik*.

Next is an example of an enterprise being inherited after a father. Ekaterina Bogdanova (1784–between 1843 and 1850), who figures in the documents as a 'Moscow merchant's wife', owned a bell-foundry. At the time of her succession to the property she was 48 years old and had two sons and two daughters. Aged fifteen or sixteen, Ekaterina had married Mikhail Bogdanov, ten years her senior, who had shifted from the Tver' merchantry to the Moscow one in 1801 (it is unclear whether Ekaterina had also moved to Moscow from Tver' or was a Muscovite). From 1832 to 1843, Ekaterina featured as the owner of the bell-foundry. In 1847, the foundry produced goods to the value of 22,504 silver roubles; five workers were employed. The plant was situated in the homestead owned by Ekaterina (as documented in 1816 and 1842), and was valued at 2,827 silver roubles (1842). Ekaterina Bogdanova died between 1843 and 1850, and it was only after her death that the bell-foundry passed to her husband, Mikhail Bogdanov, and on his death between 1854 and 1858 – to their son Pavel (the younger son, Aleksandr, had died in 1835 aged twenty-three). We can say with a high degree of confidence that the enterprise was inherited by Ekaterina after her parents or was built at their expense.[43]

The unmarried female merchant of the Third Guild Matrena Petrova (1797–after 1850) received a cotton-printing mill from her father. She shifted to the merchant estate from the *meshchanstvo* in 1825. In 1838, the mill employed 100 workers; in 1843, it produced goods to the value of 22,450 silver roubles; the number of workers is unknown. The house where she lived was her own property.[44]

Let us turn our attention to the case of a woman becoming head of an enterprise during her husband's lifetime. Fedos'ia Bol'shaia (1782–after 1850) received her silk mill from her elderly husband Vasilii. Vasilii, originally a peasant of the village of Kapotnia (which was owned by Ugresh Monastery), Moscow province, settled in Moscow and inscribed in the Third Guild in 1774, at the age of fourteen. The mill was known to belong to him as early as 1795; in 1795 it employed twenty-six workers. By the size of revenues, the mill was somewhere in the middling position among the 114 silk mills of Moscow.[45] About 1808, Fedos'ia, then aged twenty-six, married the forty-eight-year-old Vasilii; for both of them it was their first marriage. Their first child, Nikolai, died at the age of three. They had no more sons, but there were two daughters, born in 1813 and 1817. In 1819, Fedos'ia, then aged thirty-seven, took over the business, and her fifty-nine-year-old husband was relegated to the *meshchanstvo* estate. In 1830, the then widowed Fedos'ia 'Bol'shova' (in a number of documents her family name is written this way) featured as a female merchant of the Third Guild, living in her own house in Taganskaia district (in 1842, the house was valued at 3,152 silver roubles).[46]

The establishment of an enterprise as one's own venture can be exemplified by the case of the female merchant of the Second Guild Praskov'ia Poliakova (1767–*c*.1840). She owned a silk mill producing brocade and chasubles. Praskov'ia's husband, Anton Poliakov (1763–1804), died in 1804, and it was already after his death, in 1808, that Praskov'ia, then aged forty-one, together with her sixteen-year-old son, Vasilii, shifted from the *meshchanstvo* estate to the Third Guild. At first they did not have a house of their own and rented apartments from a noblewoman Mikhailova (1811), and then a low-ranking official Fedorov (1816). As Poliakova's factory is not mentioned in '*Register of Factories in Russia for the Years 1813 and 1814*', it must have been established after 1814 by Praskov'ia herself. In 1818, Vasilii married Anna, daughter of the Moscow merchant Zamiatin. In 1830, Praskov'ia and Vasilii owned a house in Kitai-Gorod, in the prestigious Ipat'evskii lane (not far from the Kremlin), and a silk mill at the same address.

In the 1830s, the mill's products were awarded two medals at exhibitions. Praskovi'ia traded in silk in Kitai-Gorod. At the time of the 1834 Census, Vasilii had one son and two daughters. In the 1840s, Vasilii's family continued to live in their two-storey house in Ipat'evskii lane, a reasonably expensive building which was valued, in 1842, at 16,000 silver roubles. In 1843, Vasilii, by that time bearer of the rank of manufacture councillor (*manufaktur-sovetnik*), featured as the owner of a silk mill which was divided into two blocks, one in Presnia district and another in Yauza district, and occupied premises bought especially for this purpose. The mill employed 232 workers. In 1843, the enterprise produced goods to the value of 206,297 silver roubles. The success of the business is attested to not only by the factory's revenues and the number of workers employed, but also by the fact that the Poliakovs continued to purchase real estate. One factory building (the value is not known) was registered in the name of Vasilii, the second one (valued in 1842 at 7,142 silver roubles) – in the name of Praskov'ia. The family bought several shops in Kitai-Gorod, four of which were jointly owned by Praskov'ia and her son, and yet another one was registered in the name of Vasilii. With Praskov'ia at the helm, the enterprise had a good running start. Her successor turned out to be an apt businessman. By the time of the 1850 Census, Vasilii had been elevated to the rank of hereditary honorary citizen (which meant that he had belonged to the First Guild for no less than ten years), and had been awarded an order. His eldest son had died, but he still had three surviving sons (Nikolai, Pavel, and Mikhail, aged fourteen, twelve and eleven respectively) and a sixteen-year-old daughter, Alexandra. In 1853, for some unknown reasons, Vasilii sold the house in Ipat'evskii lane and settled in the house in Yauza district, formerly owned by Praskov'ia. The silk mill with 255 workers, whose revenues in 1853 amounted to 321,810 silver roubles, continued to operate in the Poliakovs' house in Presnia district. In 1858, Poliakov generously contributed to the restoration of the burnt-up church of St Nicholas the Beautiful Chime in Kitai-Gorod. In 1869, already after the death of Vasilii, his eldest surviving son Nikolai was known to be the owner of a factory in Presnia district, which manufactured brocade and velvet (1884 – thirty-five workers). The medium son, Pavel, invested in real estate, and in 1890 was the owner of three houses in the prestigious Arbat district. Thus, the strenuous efforts of Praskov'ia had undoubtedly laid very sound foundations for the stable existence of the family which would continue until the early twentieth century.[47]

An analysis of the group of Moscow female industrialists brings us to the conclusion that most of them had outstanding leadership skills and abilities – in the event of the death or illness of her husband, such a woman would become head of the family and would do her best to strengthen the family business in order to pass it in due course to representatives of the next generation.

We will try to reconstruct a more comprehensive picture of female entrepreneurship by way of analyzing the 1838 data relating to the group of Moscow female entrepreneurs who owned industrial and commercial enterprises (295 persons).

4. The Moscow Female Merchants-Entrepreneurs from the 1838 List

The sphere of commerce was one of the most strictly regulated in the Russian Empire. Along with many other institutions vested with controlling powers (for example, the Chancellery of the Governor General), the conduct of trade was supervised by a special public body, the so-called 'commercial deputations' established under the 1824 Law. Members of these deputations (composed of between three and five persons) were elected from the midst of well-respected merchants in order to ensure that trade was conducted honestly and that the annual guild certificates were timely obtained by the traders. They watched over the condition of yardsticks for cloth measuring as well as weights which were to be replaced once in several years.

According to the Statute on Bankrupts of 19 December 1800 and the Law of 22 April 1807, merchants were required to have commercial books for registering all transactions.[48] Each merchant had to have seven books: 1) a register of outgoing letters; 2) a 'memorial' for daily recording of all business matters; 3) a cash receipts and payments book; 4) a 'journal' for registering in detail, one after another, at the beginning and at the end of each month, all the real estate, movables (silverware was to be entered separately), goods, and transactions; 5) an invoice book for goods bought; 6) an invoice book for goods sold; 7) a general ledger, or 'Grossbuch', which could be used for drawing the balance sheet and for assessing the general state of affairs. (Unfortunately, we have failed to find in the archives any such books for the first half of the nineteenth century). Small traders with a turnover of up to 1,000 roubles per year used simplified 'notebooks' for registering sold and bought goods.

The 1838 List, found at the Central Historical Archive of City of Moscow, was composed by the Moscow Commercial Deputation in the course of auditing the local commercial and industrial enterprises in 1838. The purposes of composing the List were primarily fiscal. Structurally the document represents a table, where the answers to the questions, grouped in columns, contain information not only on the location of commercial and industrial enterprises, the types of goods being produced or sold there, but also on the owners of the 'patrimonies' where one or other enterprise is situated, and on those 'who conduct trade at them, or manage or control them'. The latter parameter makes it possible to determine to what extent women were personally involved in managing business matters.

The list contains information on 3,166 persons who owned industrial and commercial enterprises in Moscow, including 295 women. Included in the list are persons from the merchant estate, who traded on the strength of guild-certificates (2,433 persons or 77 per cent), and peasants who carried out trade on the strength of 'tickets' (733 persons or 23 per cent). (By law, representatives of all the estates excepting the clergy were free to engage in trade, provided that the required documents had been issued to them and the duty had been paid thereby. Peasants had the right to trade in imported or native fruits and vegetables, tea, coffee and sugar.)[49] The guild certificates and tickets had to be received and paid for by traders every year in accordance with the size of their trade turnover. According to our estimates, of the 295 female entrepreneurs, 272 (or 92.2 per cent) belonged to the merchant estate, and twenty-three to the peasant one. The list does not include *meshchanki*, who were predominant in the small-business sector, because they traded on the strength of their belonging to the *meshchanstvo*, and were not obliged to receive special documents.

Of the 272 female merchants, nine were from the topmost First Guild, twenty-three were inscribed in the Second Guild (twenty residents of Moscow and three persons from other towns – Bogorodsk (Moscow province), Iur'ev-Pol'skoi (Vladimir province), and Kishinev), and 240 – in the Third Guild. The 1838 List also contains information on twenty-three peasant women who were engaged in entrepreneurial activities in Moscow. They traded in vegetables (nine persons), small wares (three persons), flour (two persons), harnesses, ironware, tableware, *droshkies* (light equipages), fish and mill-stones (one person in each category). Two peasant women kept inns, and one kept a restaurant. All the premises were rented; the businesses were managed by the female owners. All the peasant women hailed from Moscow province (six persons) and the neighbouring Yaroslavl' province (seventeen persons), that is from the areas situated 100 to 300 kilometres from the capital. Of the seventeen Yaroslavl'l women, fourteen were serfs of Count Sherem-etev. Since the late eighteenth century, the Counts Sheremetev, owners of immense estates, had been always eager to let their serfs go into such towns as Moscow, St. Petersburg, and Yaroslavl' to gain money by work.

It is precisely the sample of 272 women from the merchant estate that will become the main object of our analysis, in the course of which we will consider the by-branch composition of commercial enterprises, as well as the issue of independence of women in business management. It should be pointed out in advance that in this category widows were clearly predominant (about 80 per cent). Then our attention will be concentrated on the following two categories of female entrepreneurs: owners of industrial enterprises, and owners of more than one enterprise.

According to our estimates, the most numerous commercial enterprises in Moscow were shops trading in foodstuffs and tobacco (105 out of the total of 378, or 27 per cent), and textiles (85 out of the total of 378, or 22.4 per cent). They were followed by the services sector, including restaurants, hotels, and bath-houses (39 establishments, or 10.3 per cent), and by trade in readymade clothes and metals (by 31 enterprises, or by 8.2 per cent in each of the categories). The generalized data are presented in Table 2.3.

Table 2.3. The by-branch composition of Moscow commercial establishments belonging to female entrepreneurs (1838)

Type of trade	Number of commercial enterprises	As percentage of total number
Foodstuffs and tobacco	106	28.0
Textiles	85	22.4
Services sector (restaurants, hotels, bathhouses)	39	10.3
Ready-made clothes, footwear, headgear	31	8.2
Metals and metal articles	31	8.2

Type of trade	Number of commercial enterprises	As percentage of total number
Haberdashery	19	5.0
Building materials	9	2.35
Chemicals and cosmetics	25	6.6
Money exchange	6	1.6
Horse harnesses, carts and equipages, wheels, etc.	5	1.3
Tableware	4	1.05
Other	19	5.0
TOTAL:	**379**	**100 per cent**

In the 'Foodstuffs' category there were thirty-five flour and bread shops, thirty-two greengrocers, fifteen wine shops, nine tobacco-shops, seven butcher's shops, three fish-shops, two teashops, two shops trading in vegetable oil and one grocery; this information is very valuable for our understanding of the urban population's structure of consumption in the period under study. The 'Textiles' category was comprised of forty-three shops trading in cotton fabrics, ten shops trading in cotton yarn, nineteen shops trading in silk fabrics, and thirteen shops trading in wool ones. In the 'readymade clothes etc'. category, eighteen out of the thirty-one shops traded in European imports, while the other thirteen shops traded in hats, shawls, bast shoes, sashes, stockings, gloves and furs. The 'Metals and Metal Articles' category consisted of eight shops trading in silver, seven in hardware, etc., five in iron, four in cutlery, four in gold and silver braids and laces, one in church-bells, one in needles and one in buttons. The building materials being sold included timber, bricks, wall-paper, canvases, and parchment; the chemicals and cosmetics on sale were dry chemicals and dyes (fifteen shops), wax candles, vinegar, perfumes, pomades and ointments; tableware was represented by porcelain, crystal, and bottles. Of the nineteen haberdasheries, five traded in ribbons and braids, seven in small wares, while the rest of the shops traded in shoe-strings, threads, and feathers. Placed by us in the 'Other' category are 19 shops which traded in books, musical instruments, prints, optical instruments, writing paper, leather goods, brushes, boxes, etc.

Of the 379 commercial establishments (shops, bathhouses, restaurants, and hotels), only in fifty-seven (or 15 per cent) premises belonged to the entrepreneurs, while 322 shops were on rented premises. Correspondingly, one of the important sources of profits for representatives of the old merchant dynasties was the letting of business premises in Kitai-Gorod – the busiest and most prestigious commercial district of the capital, where the value of shops and all other real estate was highest in Moscow. Thus, the price of one desiatina (2.7 acres) of land with buildings in Kitai-Gorod was 705,861 silver roubles, while in Tverskaia district – the second most expensive (where luxurious detached houses of the nobility were concentrated) – its price was four times lower: 176,305 silver roubles.[50] On the whole, women owned 39.5 per cent of shops in Kitai-Gorod (1.449 out of 3,655).[51] Some of the shop-owners were real magnates, for example, the Alekseev family, who owned in 1846 in addition to their core enterprise, the Alekseevs' gold-cloth factory, 174 shops in Kitai-Gorod. 117 of those shops were situated in the most prestigious Upper Rows of Stalls and another 24 in Gostinyi Dvor (shopping center). 64 shops were registered in the name of the wife, Vera Alekseeva, and 110 in the name of the husband, Semen Alekseev (after his death in 1823 they passed to his heirs - the afore-mentioned Vera and his sons, Vladimir and Peter Alekseev).[52]

The archival documents of the Registration Department of the Civil Court's Moscow Chamber, which registered purchases and sales, provide comprehensive information on the size and value of shops in Kitai-Gorod in the year 1845. Prices varied widely according to the size and the state of premises, and to their proximity to Red Square and the three major streets of Kitai-Gorod – Nikol'skaia, Il'inka, and Varvarka. Let us consider several transactions that involved female entrepreneurs. In 1845, female merchant Klavdia Goneshina bought five shops, all in masonry buildings. Three of them were purchased from the merchant Mikhail Levin (who had bought them in 1824 from Natal'ia Kushashnikova, daughter of a Moscow merchant). Of those three shops, two were in the Sash Row (second from Red Square), and one was in the *Moskatel'nyi* (dry chemicals and dyes) Row (sixth from Red Square). The first shop was 3.1m long and 2.2m

The Alekseev family. Widow Vera Alekseeva, owner of a gold-cloth factory for twenty-six years (1823–49) and of 64 shops in Kitai-Gorod, is seated on the right. Vera was the great-grandmother of Constantine Stanislavsky, theatre innovator and creator of the Stanislavsky system of acting (later Method acting). Source: The Chetverikovs – N.A. Dobrynina Family Archive

wide; the second was 3.1m long and 2.2m wide; and the third was 2m long and 1m wide. Goneshina paid 1,285 silver roubles and 72 kopecks for the first two shops, and 1,000 silver roubles for the third. Two more shops (in masonry buildings) in the Sash Row were bought by Klavdia Goneshina from the three Suslov brother-merchants for 1,857 silver roubles and 12 kopecks. The first of those shops was 3.4m long and 2.8m wide; its price was 357 roubles and 12 kopecks. The second shop was narrow and not very long (1m and 2m respectively), but because of its location – according to the deed of purchase, it faced Red Square – the price was set at 1,500 silver roubles.[53]

If a shop was at the end of a row of shops, nearest to a street, and thus the first one in the way of a potential buyer, its price went up significantly. Thus, when selling to the St. Petersburg merchant Day two shops in the Hardware Row after the death of his mother, the female merchant Natal'ia Gzhel'tsova, Ivan Gzhel'tsov was paid for the shop (3.8m by 4.2m in size), facing Il'inka Street, 17,142 silver roubles and 76 kopecks, and only 3,714 silver roubles and 29 kopecks for the second one (3.4m by 3.5m in size) in the same row but more distant from the street.[54]

As a rule, the fact of shop ownership was an indication that the merchants belonged to the 'old-money' caste, and were representatives of the second or third generation of a Moscow merchant dynasty or of the first generation of a non-Moscow dynasty, resettled in the capital. Female entrepreneurs were not strictly divided into those who owned real estate and those who did not. One and the same female entrepreneur could use her own premises for one shop and then to rent premises for another one in the event of expansion of her business. Thus, the female merchant Anis'ia Koroliova kept three restaurants in Prechistenka district, one of which was on her own premises, and the other two – on rented ones. The restaurant situated in her own house was managed by Anis'ia herself, and the two other establishments – by her son, Ivan ('by proxy, in the name of his mother'), and by a clerk, the serf Mikhail Vasil'ev.[55]

In the 1830s–40s, the cost of renting a shop was between 50 and 1,500 silver roubles per year. In Kitai-Gorod, the cost of renting could reach 2,000 roubles - as, for example, in the case of the foreigner Philippina Kapobus, trader in musical instruments imported from Germany, who paid this amount of money in 1838 to the female merchant Bychkova, for renting her shop in the Haberdashery Row.[56] Some shops were rented out with apartments attached to them. Rental of premises for a hotel could cost up to 4,500 roubles per year – the sum paid to the merchant Kiril'tsev by the female merchant Matrena Karneeva (who managed her business 'herself') for renting a house in Piatnitskaia district.[57] The lessor and the lessee could be close relatives – thus, the female merchant Matrena Krasulina, trader in perfumes and pomades, rented a shop in her son's house in Lefortovo district for 200 roubles per year.[58]

Thus, shops were an important source of income for merchant families, and more often than not their owners belonged to the 'elite' of the merchant corporation.

Not without interest is the question of whether the women who figured in the documents as the owners were just formal possessors or actually managed the businesses. Female merchants frequently stated that they were managing business matters 'themselves'. However, in the event of a female entrepreneur having more than one enterprise (their number varied between two and six), her sons' participation and the hiring of clerks were inevitable. There were 103 businesswomen (or 37.9 per cent) with more than one enterprise. The expansion of a business was not necessarily synonymous to its strengthening. In a number of cases, the establishment of several shops by a family with many children was an attempt to reduce the risk of bankruptcy and to maximally involve all the adult family members in the family business.

All the female entrepreneurs could be divided into nine categories by type of business management (see Table 2.4).

Table 2.4. The types of business management (1838)

Person who manages business	Number of persons	As percentage of total number
Herself	49	18.0
Herself and son (sons) – *if there are two or more enterprises*	44	16.2
Herself and clerk (clerks) – *if there are two or more enterprises*	2	0.7
Herself and son and clerk (clerks) – *if there are three or more enterprises*	5	1.8
Herself and husband – *if there are two enterprises*	1	0.4
Husband	2	0.7
Son (sons)	134	49.3 per cent
Son (sons) and clerk (clerks)	13	4.8
Clerk (clerks)	22	8.1
TOTAL	**272**	**100.0 per cent**

In 18 per cent of the cases, the female owner managed a business 'herself'; in 19.1 per cent, if there were more than one enterprise to handle, the female owner assigned her son(s), husband and clerks to manage the other ones. The data indicate that most of the businesses under consideration were run on family lines – clerks were hired only in 15.4 per cent of cases, when there were not enough family members or if the female entrepreneur did not consider her own business qualification to be sufficiently high to ensure a successful management of her enterprise.

We have found only two cases when a wife-owner assigned her husband to the position of clerk in her own business. Dmitrii Syreishchikov (1800–79), a Muscovite in the fourth generation, served as a clerk to his wife Vera Syreishchikova (1809–56), who traded in cloth. His great-grandfather Mikhail Syreishchikov had a shop in the Cloth Row of Kitai-Gorod as early as 1748, his father traded in various European imports in the 1810s. Vera descended from a prominent family of cloth merchants, the Chetverikovs. Dmitrii and Vera had 6 children.[59] Most likely, Vera had received her business from her father, Ivan Chetverikov-Bol'shoi (1775–1852), originally a *meshchanin* from Peremyshl', Kaluga province, who later settled in Moscow. According to Ivan's grandson, a memoirist, 'by 1812, [he] had already been considered the richest and most eminent cloth merchant of Moscow who traded from a number of shops he kept in the Cloth Row';[60] in 1832 he set up his own cloth mill near Moscow. A coordinated family strategy of trading in goods produced at the father-in-law's mill and the presence of the permanent clients 'won over' by the preceding generations of the Syreishchikovs and the Chetverikovs, made it possible for Dmitrii and Vera to earn substantial capital, as is indicated by at least two facts. First, in 1871, shortly before his death, Dmitrii donated to the Moscow Merchants' Association 15,550 roubles for purposes of charity. Second, Peter, son of Vera and Dmitrii, became not only a generous philanthropist (in 1902, he left by will 29,434 roubles to the Moscow Municipal Government), but also a prominent businessman, owner of the banking house 'P. D. Syreishchikov' (1873–1901) in Nikol'skaia Street of Kitai-Gorod, and member of the board of directors of the oldest Moscow bank – the Moscow Merchant Mutual Loan Society in 1880–6. The family history is an expressive illustration to the Jo Ann Ruckman's thesis that 'Marriage between dynasties was not an usual but was indeed frequently responsible for a mutual expansion of business interests'.[61]

The participation of women in entrepreneurship could be expressed in their service as clerks at commercial establishments. Thus, an Italian merchant, Michele Amuretti, had two cosmetics shops in Moscow, one in Kitai-Gorod and one in Tverskaia district. The former was managed by Amuretti himself, and the latter by a female clerk, the Moscow *meshchanka* Tat'iana Vasil'eva, whom he hired for this purpose.[62] The Moscow merchant of the Third Guild Osip Fedorov had his wine-cellar managed by a clerk – his own wife Maria.[63]

Let us now dwell on the characteristics of the proprietresses of factories from the 1838 List. Of the 272 female merchants, thirty-one owned industrial enterprises. The division by branch of industry shows that of those thirty-three enterprises, twenty-two (or 67 per cent) belonged to the textile branch (nine silk mills, two cotton-printing mills, four cotton-weaving mills and seven cloth mills). As is seen, by comparison with 1832, the proportion of textile enterprises had fallen from 76 to 67 per cent. At the same time, the range of industries represented in the list had increased with regard to the listed enterprises in general and to the enterprises owned by women in particular. The 1838 List includes two brick yards, one iron foundry, one dye mill (producing white) and one plant manufacturing equipment (meshes) for cotton-weaving mills. This clearly points to the existence of demand for new kinds of goods and attests to the introduction of more sophisticated types of mechanized production.

As regards the longevity of enterprises, a comparison between the 1832 List and the 1838 List reveals that only six names figure in both of them. A comparison between the 1838 List and 'The Atlas of the Industry of Moscow Province', which contains the data for 1843, shows that the two documents match with regard to eight female owners.[64] But this does not mean that the enterprises ceased to exist – on the death of their female owners they passed to the next generation of proprietors, usually the sons of the deceased businesswomen.

For the year 1838, we have complete information on the number of workers employed at the enterprises. The total number of persons working at the thirty-three listed enterprises was 2,344. The textile enterprises had the largest labour force: Prokhorova's cotton mill employed 570 persons, her cloth mill – 210 persons, Goneshina's cloth mill – 250 persons, and Dunasheva's silk mill - 156 persons. However, more than one half of the enterprises were medium in size, and the number of workers they employed was between 17 and 70.

Let us consider the biography of Ekaterina Prokhorova (1779–1851), owner of three factories. Daughter of the Moscow merchant Nikifor Mokeev (who was born to a peasant family from Kaluga province), she assumed proprietorship of the family business at the age of thirty-five after the death of her husband, the merchant of the Second Guild Vasilii Prokhorov (1753–1815). Prokhorov's wife, twenty-six years his junior, bore four sons and four daughters (three daughters died in their infancy). According to the 1838 data, Prokhorova had a shop in the Mirrors Row, where she traded in shawls, and three mills: one for cotton-weaving, one for cotton and one for cashmere. The total number of workers employed at the mills was 900. The shop and all of the mills were jointly owned by Prokhorova and her son Iakov. In 1842, 74 per cent of the family's real estate to the value of 44,729 silver roubles belonged to Prokhorova, while the remaining 26 per cent to the value of 15,978 silver roubles – to her son Iakov, the total value of the real estate being 60,707 silver roubles.

It is known from a family legend that after the father falling in 1813, all the factory matters had to be shouldered by his second son, Timofei, then aged sixteen; later, the burden was shared by the eldest son, Ivan, who would accompany Timofei on his visits to the fairs. However, until the very end of the 1840s, the business was officially deemed to be owned by Ekaterina Prokhorova, as was determined in her husband's will which stipulated that all the factory assets and the working capital should constitute family property to be legally ascribed to Ekaterina, and it was in her name that the sons were to manage their industrial and commercial business. Such a will was composed by Vasilii Prokhorov in order to avoid the risk of dispersal of property and capital. On 20 April 1824, with the family business already stabilized and the sons grown up, Ekaterina Prokhorova 'amicably divided' the property, and allotted to her sons unequal shares (from 47,000 to 91,000 roubles) of the family capital. In the 1830s, the Prokhorovs' factory business was the largest in the cotton industry, as reflected by the volume of trade: in the 1830s, the annual turnover of the Prokhorovs' shop in the Mirrors Row rose to 1.5 million silver roubles, and in the early 1840s - to 2.25 million. In 1838, when answering the questionnaire of the Moscow Commercial Deputation, Prokhorova stated that she was managing the shop 'herself with [her] children', while the factories were being managed by the sons, Iakov and Ivan.[65] Another important source of the Prokhorov family's income was the renting out of three shops in Kitai-Gorod (one shop was used by them for their own trade). There are also some additional data on the history of the Prokhorov dynasty, whose enterprises (the first of which was founded in 1799) still exist today, which can shed some light on the degree of Ekaterina's involvement in managing the business, and on her family life as well. Thus, the Prokhorovs' 'court' historiographer describes the married couple of Vasilii and Ekaterina Prokhorov in the terms which would be more appropriate in a life of some saint: 'Close to Vasilii Ivanovich in cleverness and moral principles was his second wife Ekaterina Nikiforovna, whom he had married when being well advanced in age (at that time he was 42 or 43 years old, while she was no older than seventeen ... Much younger than her husband, she readily adopted his convictions and views on life and people. ... She worked from dawn to dusk, and liked to say to those around her that indolence was baneful; her free time she devoted to praying, to reading lives of saints, and to singing psalms'.

The reasons for independently managing a business were not always widowhood or spinsterhood. We have an example of a remarried merchant's widow who managed her business independently of her second husband, also a merchant, in order to enable her son from her first marriage to inherit her enterprise. 'The List of Merchants of the City of Moscow for the Year 1830' includes the female merchant of the Second Guild Avdot'ia 'Shaposhnikova in the first marriage and Shomova in the second'. She traded in cotton goods, had a cotton mill, and lived in her own house in Taganka district. Avdot'ia's story is the example we have referred to above. Her first husband was the merchant of the Third Guild Vikul Shaposhnikov. The data of the 1816 Census indicate that at the age of sixteen or seventeen Avdot'ia married a widower who had a daughter from his first marriage, named Zinaida. Avdot'ia and Vikul had a son, Vasilii. On the death of his father in 1816, Vikul, as the eldest brother, became head of a merchant family which included his five junior brothers and sisters aged between six and nineteen, who were 'ascribed [to him] until they shall have come of age'. During the interval between the 1816 and 1834 Censuses Vikul died, and at the time of the 1834 Census Avdot'ia, then aged thirty-nine, was the wife of the forty-nine-year-old merchant of the Third Guild Savva Shomov, who had previously been widowed and had a son, Mikhail, from his first marriage. Native of the village of Ivanovo, Shomov had been engaged in textile business since the days of his youth. He periodically visited Moscow to trade in cotton goods. Shomov was famous for having been the first Ivanovo entrepreneur to reach an agreement with Count Sheremetev and to redeem himself, which was exactly what he did in 1825.[66] It cannot be completely ruled out that one of his motives to become a free man was his romantic feelings towards a certain Moscow widow who happened to be a factory owner. In 1827, Shomov was inscribed in the Third Guild of the Moscow merchants. He did not own any real estate in the capital. By contrast, Avdot'ia possessed some quite expensive fixed assets, namely two houses to the value of 31,429 silver roubles, and 4 shops in Kitai-Gorod; moreover, there was yet another house to the value of 22,571 silver roubles, owned by her son, Vasilii. After the death of Avdot'ia the whole property passed to her son Vasilii. Savva's son from his first marriage, Mikhail, inherited his business. Mikhail never acquired any real estate in the capital, and documents indicate that he was renting an apartment in the house of his stepmother's son, Vasilii Shaposhnikov.[67]

Mention should be made of female factory owners from the lower estates. *Meshchanki* and *tsekhovye* owned scores of small industrial establishments. Archival sources contain information on the cotton mill of the *meshchanka* Irina Utkina (in her own house; twelve workers), the tobacco factory of the *tsekhovaia* Agaf'ia Loginova (on rented premises; ten workers), the glove factory of the *meshchanka* Avdot'ia Selezneva (in her own house; ten workers), the cotton-weaving mill of the *meshchanka* Marfa Stepanova (in her own house; twelve workers), the cotton-weaving mill of the *tsekhovaia* Dar'ia Pimenova (in the house of her sister Mar'ia Pimenova; ten workers), the sash factory of the *tsekhovaia* Tat'iana Alekseeva (on rented premises; five workers), the muslin mill of the *meshchanka* Alexandra Sokolova (on rented premises; four workers), and on the calico mills of the *tsekhovaia* Mar'ia Fedorova (in the house of the *meshchanin* Fedorov, ten workers), the *meshchanka* Matrena Kirilova (on rented premises; fifteen workers), the *meshchanka* Anna Skorobogatova (in her own house; ten workers), and of the *meshchanka* Nadezhda Borisova (in her own house; 10 workers).[68] Also mentioned are the ribbon workshops belonging to 'the daughter of a Kremlin attendant, maid Praskov'ia Ivanovna Kuniaeva' (eight workers), to 'the *tsekhovaia* of the ribbon-makers' corporation' Dar'ia Maksimova (eight workers), to the *meshchanka* Pelageia Luk'ianchikova (eight workers), and to 'an officer's daughter' Avdot'ia Shirokova (five workers).[69]

Let us now turn to the group of women who owned several enterprises each. About one-third of the female merchants (98 persons or 36 per cent) were in possession of more than one enterprise, including twenty-nine (or 10.7 per cent) who owned three or more establishments. This was permitted by law, if the entrepreneurs paid duty for each of the enterprises. The more active female entrepreneurs kept several enterprises each, and as a result, 10.7 per cent of the listed proprietresses kept 24.3 per cent of enterprises and almost one quarter of market outlets. The figures are presented in Table 2.5.

Table 2.5. The per-person distribution of enterprises belonging to women (1838)

Number of enter-prises kept by one proprietress	Number of proprietresses	As percentage of total number of proprietresses	Total number of enterprises	As percentage of total number of enterprises
1	174	64.0	174	42.2
2	69	25.4	138	33.5
3	19	7.0	57	13.8
4	8	2.9	32	7.8
5	1	0.35	5	1.2
6	1	0.35	6	1.5
Total	272	100 per cent	412	100 per cent

The group of proprietresses of several enterprises is apparently worthy of consideration. In fact, by developing network commerce, the proprietresses must have always been in need of effective management for their enterprises. Prosopographical information makes it possible to reconstruct family histories sometimes two, three or four generations-deep, and to find out how corresponding establishments were being managed. We succeeded in reconstructing the life stories of ten businesswomen who kept four to six enterprises at a time. These ten were Tret'iakova (six enterprises), Sukhanova (five enterprises), Belkina, Prokhorova, Sheternikova, Dubrovina, Zaitseva, Lepeshova, Meshkova, and Chamova (four enterprises each). Following are three of these life stories.

The owner of six enterprises, Praskov'ia Tret'iakova (1782–after 1856) was inscribed in the Third Guild. In 1838, she had five shops, four of which were in Kitai-Gorod and one in Tverskaia district. The three Kitai-Gorodian shops were trading in vegetables, and one in tobacco. The fifth shop, in Tverskaia district, was trading in 'teas'. The Tret'iakovs' business was profitable, which enabled them to set up a small pomade factory in Iakimanka district. Both the industrial enterprise and the shops were not privately owned but rented. By 1838, the Tret'iakov family had been living in Moscow for more than forty years. Praskov'ia's husband, Fedor (1771–after 1810), a merchant from the town of Maloiaroslavets, Kaluga province, had settled in Moscow with his mother, Irina Tret'iakova, and his three younger brothers in 1795; hitherto a Maloiaroslavets merchant, he inscribed in the Moscow merchantry. The family rented an apartment, and the four brothers set up 'a shop in the Vegetables Row'. About 1798, Fedor married Praskov'ia. After the deaths of two brothers in 1800 and 1802 the surviving brothers, Fedor and Ivan, split, as is known from the data of the 1811 Census. At that time, Fedor and Praskov'ia with their three sons and three daughters were living in a rented apartment. In the following decade their business did not prosper, maybe because of the family fortunes having been ruined by the 1812 Fire of Moscow during Napoleon's invasion. The family was forced to shift to the *meshchanstvo*. We meet the Tret'iakovs again only in 1821, when they returned to the Third Guild. Now the family comprised the widowed mother, Praskov'ia, her three sons, Aleksandr (b. 1800), Ivan (1804–77) and Fedor (1810–41), and daughter Varvara (b. 1810). According to the 1830 data, Tret'iakova and her three sons were trading in vegetables and were living in a rented apartment in Tverskaia district.

In 1838, the four shops registered in Praskov'ia's name were managed by her three sons, Aleksandr, Ivan and Fedor, and a hired clerk – the Saratov *meshchanin* Dmitrii Antipin. The shop in Tverskaia district was managed by Praskov'ia herself. 'The pomade establishment' was registered in the names of Tret'iakova and her son Aleksandr. In 1839, its products – 'pomades, perfume, soap, and fumigating candles and powders' – were displayed at an exhibition of Russian manufactured products in St Petersburg. The 1843 data indicate that the pomade factory employed nine workers; the value of its annual output amounted to 36,000 silver roubles. According to the 1850 Census, Praskov'ia Tret'iakova, then aged sixty eight, continued to take out guild certificates in her name; her son, fourty-nine-year-old Aleksandr, 'shared capital with her' (he was married to Elizaveta, a noblewoman; the couple were childless), while her second son Ivan had set up on his own. In 1856, the factory employed six workers, and by comparison with 1850 the volume of production had fallen more than twofold – to the value of 16,200 silver roubles. In summing up the examination of the Tret'iakova case, it should be pointed out that despite the existence of five shops and one industrial enterprise which kept the family afloat, her business developed extensively rather than intensively. The presence of several retail outlets was merely an attempt to preserve a certain social and economic status, and in this case it was like constantly walking a tightrope. There is one strong argument in favour of such a judgement: by the end of the 1840s, neither Tret'iakova nor her children had managed to acquire real estate in the capital and continued to live in rented apartments.[70]

The proprietress of five enterprises Anna Sukhanova (1787–after 1850) was inscribed in the Third Guild. In 1853 she rented five shops in Kitai-Gorod. Two shops were managed by her sons, Andrei and Aleksandr (then aged 31 and 24 respectively), and the other three - by hired clerks, the Moscow *meshchane* Aleksandr Miniaev and Nikolai Nazarov, and the Riazan' *meshchanin* Aleksandr Vasil'ev. Although the guild certificate was issued in the name of Anna's husband Andrei Sukhanov (1779–1847), for some reasons all the family property was registered in the name of Anna. It is not clear why two of her four sons, Mikhail and Petr (in 1838 aged 34 and 38 respectively), were excluded from the business; possibly, they were engaged in wholesale purchasing of the goods. It can be assumed that the mother kept the life of the family under her absolute control: according to the 1855 Census, none of the four brothers was married, and they continued to live under one roof after the deaths of their parents, although at that time they were aged 53, 50, 47 and 43 respectively. The latest information dates to 1869, when Andrei Sukhanov was in the Second Guild and was trading in haberdashery in Kitai-Gorod. In this case, the existence of five shops does not testify to the efficiency of the family business, but was rather an attempt at making the ends meet. After the death of the dynasty's founder Vasilii Sukhanov in 1810, his children (including Sukhanova's husband, Andrei) were forced to sell the family house. During the next 60 years, none of the family members managed to acquire any real estate.[71]

In 1838, the female merchant of the Third Guild Ol'ga Chamova (1781–1856), a widow, had a network of four dry chemicals shops, only one of which was in Kitai-Gorod. All the premises were rented. The Chamovs treaded a thornier path than many of the above merchant families. For quite a long time, despite possessing real estate, the Chamovs failed to rise to merchant status. Ol'ga's husband, a Viaz'ma merchant Savva Chamov, had come to Moscow in 1774, but as his capital was insufficient for him to inscribe in the Moscow merchantry, he inscribed in the Moscow *meshchanstvo*. Before long (about 1776), Savva married Luker'ia Monetchikova, daughter of a watchman of the Moscow Mint, who was two years his senior; as her dowry she brought him a house in the parish of St Nicholas on the Chips (in 1842, it was valued at 4,285 silver roubles; Savva's descendants owned the house as late as 1872). In 1795, Savva was in the Third Guild and kept a shop in the *Moskatel'nyi* (dyes and dry chemicals) Row of Kitai-Gorod. Savva and Luker'ia had an only child, Mar'ia. Apparently, Luker'ia died some time in the late 1790s, and Savva remarried to Ol'ga, thirty-three years his junior. In 1808, with his business in doldrums, Savva had to sink into the *meschanstvo*. It was not until 1825 that Savva, then aged seventy-seven, returned to the Third Guild. He died two years later. After his death, the business was inherited by his widow Ol'ga, aged forty-six, and his nineteen-year-old son, Pavel. Ol'ga turned out to be a very enterprising woman. In 1838, after eleven years at the helm, she was keeping four shops. The business was being managed by her son Pavel (1808–75), who supervised the 'main' shop in Kitai-Gorod, and by three clerks – Andrei Ivanov, a serf of Count Sheremetev, Ivan Ivanov, a peasant, and the Moscow *meshchanin* Pavel Makarov. Ol'ga Chamova was deemed to be head of the business until her death in 1856 at the age of seventy-five. After this, the enterprise passed to Pavel Chamov, then aged forty-eight. Pavel reorganized the trade in dyes and dry chemicals – he closed the existing small shops, and opened instead a large one in Moskvoretskaia Street; he also strengthened the business by setting up his own chemical plant in the town of Pokrov, Vladimir province (100 kilometres from Moscow). Pavel had five sons. The Chamovs' history of trading in dyes and dry chemicals was almost a century-long. The credit for developing and strengthening the family business should be given to Ol'ga Chamova with her ability to minimize the risks by properly organizing the conduct of trade. As a result, she managed to pass to her only son and five grandsons a prosperous and robust business.[72]

Prosopography reveals that it was not untypical for a family keeping several outlets to be quite versatile in its business activities, for example, to combine trading in vegetables, tea and tobacco with production of cosmetics (as in the case of Tret'iakova). One rather peculiar case in point relates to the group of proprietresses of three establishments. Thus, the female merchant of the Third Guild Matrena Lepekhina (1781–1841) had three outlets, quite different in their specialization. The shop rented in Kitai-Gorod traded in cotton fabrics; it was managed by Lepekhina's son, Aleksandr. Also, Lepekhina had a tavern in Rogozhskaia district in the house of the merchant Gromozdkin; that was managed by a clerk, the serf Fedor Alekseev. Matrena herself managed a bleachery (with 30 workers) situated in her own house in Basmannaia district (in 1842, the house was valued at 7,428 roubles). There are some mysteries in Lepekhina's case. The eldest son of Lepekhina, Mikhail, did not participate in the family business; in 1842, soon after her death, he had to shift to the *meshchanstvo*. It is possible that the stern mother had treated her son in accordance with the 1833 legislative norm which envisaged that merchants should have the right 'not to include their sons, for [their] irreverence, into the family guild certificate, and thus to shift them to the *meshchanstvo*'.[73] It was during the time of Lepekhina's management that this family business was in its prime.[74]

Sometimes even the presence of three enterprises could not prevent bankruptcy if the proprietress slackened her personal control. Typical in this respect is the example of Mar'ia Barkova who had had too much trust in her son, and was bankrupted as a result. Mar'ia Barkova (1786–after 1850) was a female merchant of the First Guild and one of the biggest Moscow traders in iron. For her trade, she kept three rented shops. According to the 1838 data, one of the shops was managed by her son, Semen, the second shop – by herself, and the third one – by a clerk, the serf Andrei Artamonov.[75] The Barkovs had come to Moscow from St Petersburg (where they were also inscribed in the merchantry) in 1825. The family head, Nikifor, died in 1831 at the age of forty-four. In his lifetime, on 1 June 1830, the husband and wife had executed a reciprocal will to the effect that all the property of the deceased spouse should be passed to the surviving spouse.[76] On becoming a widow with five children (the sons: sixteen-year-old Semen, thirteen-year-old Pavel, seven-year-old Petr; the daughters: nineteen-year-old Anna, twelve-year-old Alexandra), Mar'ia took over the family business. In 1832, she and her brother-in-law, Dmitrii Barkov, set up the trading house 'M. & D. Barkov' with a capital of 325,155 silver roubles. After Dmitrii's death in 1837, Anna decided to transact business together with her grown-up son Semen, then aged twenty-three. At that time, Mar'ia's capital in goods and promissory notes amounted to 223,415 silver roubles and 30 kopecks. At first, Mar'ia managed the business on her own, but then she decided that Semen was coping with his tasks well enough, and issued to him, on 13 April 1838, a power of attorney to transact all business in her name (the power of attorney was then prolonged in 1839 and 1840).[77] However, Semen turned out to be extremely inaccurate in handling transactions – he repeatedly failed to register in the books the data on payments made by purchasers, as well as his own debts for the goods delivered by the suppliers; moreover, he started to borrow money against promissory notes. Quite soon, on seeing that Barkov did not pay on time, the suppliers sounded the alarm. The scandal grew rapidly like a snowball rolled on snow. On 28 May 1840, the prominent Moscow textile manufacturer Semen Sopov initiated bankruptcy proceedings at the Commercial Court, against Mar'ia Barkova, his debtor.[78] On 29 May the Commercial Court heard the evidence of another twenty-five creditors of Barkova. It turned out that the debts against the bills personally signed by her amounted to nearly 30,000 silver roubles, and those against the liabilities signed by proxy by her son - to another 68,000 silver roubles; the total was 98,096 silver roubles and 53¾ kopecks. For meeting the claims, Barkova had 38,037 silver roubles and 70 kopecks in the form of real estate, movable property, cash and promissory notes of her debtors. On 30 May 1840, Barkova was declared bankrupt; her property was distrained and put to sale. In repayment of the debts, Barkova lost all her real estate and movable property, from the palatial house in Bol'shaia Ordynka street valued at more than 15,000 silver roubles (a three-storey building with six columns at the front, of the Empire style, it covered an area 126m long and 104m wide; the property included an immense garden with limes and apple-trees, two outbuildings, greenhouses and wells) to icons, furniture, tableware, clothes and even the family shop signboard. In her explanation to the Commercial Court, Barkova wrote that the cause of her undoing was the fact that

> wishing to strengthen the trade [she] entrusted the handling of all business matters to my eldest son, Semen Barkov, and issued to him an unlimited power of attorney, which he used, by the right conferred on him, and made debts not only against the documents registered in the book he was keeping, but also such debts that he had kept secret until the final days of the payment period.[79]

As a result, the Barkov family of nine (Mar'ia, her elderly sister, Praskov'ia, her son Semen with his wife and two children, her son Pavel with his wife, and her son Petr) were left without means of subsistence, and Barkova asked to monthly allot to her 63 roubles, or 7 roubles per capita, from the sums yielded by the auction. The 'infuriated' creditors were not unanimous in approving this request: there were nine in favour of the subsidy, and three votes against it. According to the law, Barkova should have been taken into custody in the presence of her 26 creditors. The Commercial Court prescribed that the creditors should arrive at Barkova's house by 8 o'clock in the morning on 2 July 1840, 'to consider the matter of confining the debtor Barkova under guard'. On their arrival, the creditors announced that they were against confining the fifty-four-year-old Barkova under guard, and considered unnecessary any restraining of her freedom 'because of her advanced age and ill health, as well as due to the fact that we absolutely do not suspect her of malicious bankruptcy'.[80]

The bankruptcy administration concerned with the affairs of the bankrupt Barkova existed at least until 1847. After the auctioning off of her property, the creditors received only 15 per cent of the sum they had demanded from Barkova. The last document from the Commercial Court's Barkova case is dated 7 May 1846 – Mar'ia 'is permitted to be absent' from Moscow for two months, and to go 'to worship the relics of the holy saints resting in peace in Kiev ... in order to keep her vow'. Barkova was planning to make the greater part of her pilgrimage on foot.[81] It is unknown whether Barkova indeed managed to go on pilgrimage after having drained the cup of woe, ruin and humiliation. According to the 1850 Census, at the end of her life the elderly Barkova lived with the family of her junior son, Petr, and his wife, Pelageia.

The collapse of a family business could have been prevented by the rigid regulation of relations between mother and children, consolidated in an official document. The way such relations within a merchant family could be shaped becomes clear from the archival document concerned with the foundation of the Shcheglovs' trading house. In July 1846, the honorary citizen and female merchant of the Second Guild Nastas'ia Shcheglova forwarded a petition to the Moscow City Duma, in which she asked to confirm the agreement she had concluded with her sons, Nikolai and Dmitrii, on the founding of the trading house 'N., N. & D. Shcheglov' for trading in silk. The period of the agreement was three and a half years. The office of the trade enterprise was in the 'patrimonial' house in Rogozhskaia district, trade was carried out in the three shops in the Gostinyi Dvor of Kitai-Gorod. It is apparent that the decision to found a trading house was taken because of its being the most convenient instrument for passing a business from mother to children without the former having relinquished control of the enterprise. One of the acts performed as early as 1846 in the course of setting up the firm was the brothers' purchasing from their mother of all the goods stored at the shops, for 33,857 silver roubles and 40 kopecks. In return, their mother consented to her sons' signature being sufficient for the execution of the firm's documents. In their announcement published in the newspapers, the brothers stated that 'by our mother's consent, we, Nikolai and Dmitrii, will be the sole managers of matters of trade thereat [at the trading house], and therefore, it will be solely we, the two brothers, who will be signing all documents as a joint firm 'N., N., & D. Shcheglov', while our mother, although taking part in this trading business, will not be signing'.[82] It was planned that after 3.5 years of transacting business the trading house would be closed, and all the goods and capital would be evenly divided between the partners. The City Duma gave its permission to set up the firm, and Nastas'ia Shcheglova continued her lucrative trade in silk fabrics until the early 1850s.

Conclusion

The 1830s and 1840s were the time when the economy of Russia, if we consider it as a regional case, was characterized by transition to the factory system, concurrent with a marked intensification of trade relations at the micro- and macro-levels. Although the concept of industrial revolution (and in particular the issue of the chronological framework) remains debatable in Russian historiography, there is a well-established point of view that the second quarter of the nineteenth century was the final stage of proto-industrialization. Apparently, both the influence of European technological achievements and the perception of an appropriate production organization pattern had a certain impact on the ongoing industrial restructuring and the slow decline of rural industry. As in Great Britain, the process of transition to industrial revolution in Russia was especially manifest in the small though dynamic textile industry (especially in the cotton and woollen branches), where 29 per cent of Russia's 5,500 enterprises were concentrated, and 11 per cent of owners were women.

A comparison between the industrial statistics of 1814 and 1832 has revealed a considerable growth in the number of enterprises owned by women – their absolute number increased by 2.9 times (from 165 to 484), while the proportion of women in the ranks of factory owners rose from 4.4 per cent to 9.1 per cent. Among the enterprises owned by women there were large establishments which employed between 150 and 900 workers.

In industry, the influence of noblewomen remained, as in the previous thirty years, an important factor of the development of female entrepreneurship. One half (49 per cent) of 'female-owned' industrial enterprises were on country estates. Women from the merchant estate possessed 35.6 per cent of enterprises, *meshchanki* – 9.9 per cent.

Women's participation in the management of industrial enterprises could be divided into two patterns, conventionally referred to as 'noble' and 'merchant'. They differed by the type of succession to an enterprise, by the style of management, by the importance of the factory or plant as a life-support resource for the family of the owner.

In 50 per cent of cases noblewomen either inherited enterprises or received them as gifts from their parents, and only in 19 per cent of cases from their husbands. Thanks to the possession of separate property which made them economically independent of their husbands, noblewomen enjoyed better investment possibilities for developing their own businesses. However, these possibilities were rarely used, because within the framework of a large landed estate, the enterprise was merely one of the elements of its infrastructure, and frequently represented an auxiliary rather than the main source of revenues. As far as management is concerned, a noble proprietress more often than not controlled her factory via the manager of the whole estate.

As regards women from the merchant estate, the pattern of acquiring an enterprise was very different: in 52 per cent of cases, women inherited factories after their husbands; in 21 per cent of cases, they inherited them after their parents; and in 12 per cent of cases created enterprises on their own. A merchant enterprise was the main source of income, guaranteeing the survival of the family; most frequently, the factory was situated within the owner's homestead, and was routinely controlled by the proprietress.

The 'merchant' pattern of business management (not only in industry, but in trade as well) was aimed at increasing the competitiveness of a family firm by optimizing the entanglement of personal relations within a corresponding family. In this case, only the existence of a strict hierarchy could enable the mechanism of a family business to work smoothly. There were frequent instances of relations between family members (for example, between mother and sons) being legally formalized with regard to disposal of capital, real estate, raw materials and finished goods. Each of those instances was an attempt to minimize the risk of bankruptcy; in this respect, formalization of family relations was a form of bankruptcy prevention. In this situation, the main reason for a widow to obtain, in accordance with her husband's will, full control of the family business and, simultaneously, full control of the family property was the desire to avoid a dispersal of property and to prevent conflicts within the family. In many instances women continued to head family businesses until the moment of death, even if they had adult (sometimes aged forty or fifty) sons who were mentioned in official documents as being 'attached to the mother'.

It is not unlikely that such a tandem of mother and her adult sons was the most efficient strategy of family business, which could also be denoted as 'active partnership'. Even when managerial functions were transferred to a son (by a notarially authenticated power of attorney valid for a specified period of time), it was the female owner who was the sole proprietor of the real estate and the major decision-maker, as well as the moral censor to be regularly accounted to by her son (sons) for the state of all business matters. For example, according to the 1838 data on commerce in Moscow, in 49 per cent of cases businesses were managed by sons in accordance with the letters of attorney issued to them by their mothers, who were officially deemed to be the firms' proprietresses; in 18 per cent of cases the proprietress acted 'herself' without being helped by her sons, husband or a hired clerks.

Apart from participating in industrial and commercial business (where 50 per cent of the 'female-owned' shops specialized in selling food and fabrics) and in the sphere of services (in the role of innkeepers, publicans and bath-house-keepers), businesswomen actively – and profitably – rented out business premises (inherited by them after their parents or specially acquired for this purpose). And they had the means to do this: for example, in Kitai-Gorod, the central commercial district of Moscow, 39.5 per cent of all business premises were owned by women.

In assessing those decades in the history of female entrepreneurship in Russia, it should be pointed out that the increased presence of women in the economy (practically unnoticed by the contemporaries, and therefore characterized in the title of this chapter as a 'hidden success') was just one aspect of the general picture which included the institutionalization of business, the establishment of a highly hieratic system of managing family businesses, and the development of a strict moral paradigm of personal thrift as a tool of consolidating family property. All this had one aim – to preserve and strengthen family business as the only resource of life-support for an economically independent urban family.

The extent of conformational change undergone by the patterns of female entrepreneurship in the following two decades – which were marked by a series of reforms causing radical alterations in the urban sphere and resulted in further development of Russia's market economy – will be considered in the next chapter.

3 FEMALE ENTREPRENEURSHIP IN THE 1850s–60s: AN UNSTABLE RISE: THE MOSCOW AND ST PETERSBURG CASES

As regards investigating the history of female entrepreneurship in the 1850s and 1860s, there exists a wider, although still not sufficiently exhaustive range of sources, which offers the researcher better opportunities of data collection and analysis.[1]

The onset of the industrial revolution had already revealed that Russia considerably lagged behind Europe in terms of the volume of industrial production and its by-branch diversity, as well as to the level of mechanization of enterprises.[2] This situation was fully appreciated by the governing circles and the educated society, and was being widely discussed on the pages of newspapers and magazines. The professor of statistics of the Academy of the General Staff A. Maksheev wrote:

> Factory industry is rather weakly developed in Russia, and therefore we export abroad a very negligible amount of articles (on average, about 6 percent of all exports), and even that amount goes predominantly to Asia, while receiving quite a lot of processed goods from abroad (about 20 percent of all imports). Meanwhile, the development of factory industry is one of the essential conditions of the wellbeing and, therefore, the power of any state.[3]

The 1850s and 1860s were marked by an upsurge in the business activity of women. The desire of female entrepreneurs to achieve economic independence was legally upheld on 10 June 1857 with the adoption of the Law 'On the Authorization to Issue to Merchants' Wives the Certificates for Carrying Out Trade Separately from the Husband'.[4] Isolated instances of married female merchants receiving individual guild certificates were observed as early as the beginning of the nineteenth century, but in each case the certificate was issued as an exception. The frequency of cases when each of the spouses had an individual business was gradually rising. It is known that the Finance Minister P. F. Brock addressed the State Council with a presentation of a similar case, that of the female merchant Belkina. Belkina had petitioned Emperor Alexander II with a request to permit her to trade independently of her husband. The case was then been submitted to the State Council, which passed a positive decision. The Law was supplemented with the following clarification: 'merchants' wives have the right to carry on trade in their own name' but, when paying duties, those women were obliged to submit to *uezd*[5] treasuries 'the written certificates verifying their husbands' consent thereto'.

This chapter will also focus on such issues as the economic characteristic of the epoch, and in particular the role played by proprietresses of industrial enterprises in the industrialization of Moscow (1853) and St Petersburg (1862). We are going to present the results of our analysis of female merchant groups (more than 1,000 persons in total), and offer a more detailed picture of the activities of those women, as well as the range of skills implicit to their managerial strategies.

1. The Epoch of the 1850s–60s: Demography, Urbanization, the Unevenness of the Regional Development of Entrepreneurship, the Concentration of Industry in Moscow and St Petersburg Provinces

According to the 1850 Census, the Russian Empire had a population of 65.1 million, with only 4.8 million persons (or 7.3 per cent) living in towns.[6] In 1858, its population increased to 67.9 million persons; 9.4 per cent of them resided in towns.[7] The highest level of urbanization was recorded in four of the forty-nine provinces: in the St. Petersburg (55.9 per cent) and Moscow (28.1 per cent) provinces centred on the capitals, and also in the two southern provinces (now Ukraine), Kherson (26.9 per cent) and Taurida (18.8 per cent). In 1863, the population size grew to 71.4 million persons (without Poland and Finland), 10.6 per cent of whom resided in towns.[8] In 1850, Russia accounted for 27 per cent of the whole population of Europe.[9]

The level of urbanization correlated with the development of industry and trade in towns and cities, and with the size of estate groups and their influence on city life. In 1856, the Empire had only three cities with a population of more than 100,000: St Petersburg (490,808), Moscow (368,765) and Odessa (191,320).[10] It should be noted that St Petersburg and Odessa were the largest points of maritime trade on the Baltic and Black Seas, while Moscow, situated in the centre of European Russia, was the terminus of trade routes from all the central provinces of Russia.

The two 'capital-city' provinces – Moscow and St Petersburg – were obvious leaders with regard to the number of industrial enterprises and the value of their output. In 1856, the aggregate value of industrial output in these two provinces amounted to 76.7 million roubles, or to 34.2 per cent of the value of the total industrial output of the country (224.3 million roubles).[11] Over the period of eight years, from 1856 to 1864, the share of the two provinces in the volume of production rose to 45.2 per cent.[12]

One of the outcomes of the uneven regional development of industry was that female entrepreneurship progressed most actively in the capital-city provinces. In 1863, of the fifteen biggest Russian female entrepreneurs who owned enterprises with the annual volume of production to the value of more than 100,000 silver roubles, six were transacting business in Moscow province, and two in St Petersburg Province. In Moscow and its province, the enterprises owned by women included the cloth mills of Kotova (284,000 roubles), Cherepakhina (122,112 roubles) and Tiuliaeva (108,815 roubles), and the cotton-weaving mill of Popova (105,420 roubles) in Moscow; the two cotton mills of Tret'iakova in Serpukhov (1,387,920 roubles); and Moshnina's stearine chandlery in Serpukhov *uezd* (122,500 roubles). In St Petersburg and its province, such businesses included the chemical plant of Rasteriaeva in St Petersburg (140,000 roubles) and the writing-paper factory of Kaidanova in St Petersburg *uezd* (110,000 roubles). The other provinces had seven major women-owned enterprises, including the cotton weaving mill of Protas'eva in Vladimir province (207,500 roubles), the wool-scouring mill of Ryzhova in Kharkov (188,200 roubles), the sugar refinery of Countess Pototskaia in Kiev province (140,000 roubles), the cloth mill of Verevkina in Simbirsk province (113,500 roubles), and three tanneries – Pribytkova's in Kazan' (115,500 roubles), Reshetnikova's in Tobol'sk province (103,250 roubles), and Savostina's in Orel province (100,000 roubles).[13]

Both provinces had a clear lead in the number of guild certificates.[14] In 1864, in St. Petersburg province, 484 first-guild certificates and 5,174 second-guild certificates were issued, while in the Moscow province – 569 and 7,218 respectively. This means that 36.2 per cent of all first-guild merchants (on the whole, 2,904 first-guild certificates were issued in the country) and 22 per cent of all second-guild merchants (on the whole, 56,123 second-guild certificates were issued) had their head offices in St Petersburg and Moscow.[15]

Information on the share of women in the merchantry could be found for the year 1869. In the St. Petersburg merchantry, the percentage of women was 13 per cent (501 persons), in the Moscow one – 11.6 per cent (583 persons). These groups will be dealt with in more detail below.

In the period under consideration women played an important part in the industrial sphere: thus, in Moscow they owned almost 12 per cent of industrial enterprises (1853). In the following section we will analyze the economic dimensions of this cohort of female entrepreneurs, paying due attention to the surviving biographic information so as to better understand the place occupied by female industrialists in the corresponding family hierarchies.

2. Female Entrepreneurs in Moscow Industry in 1853

Moscow, which was quite appropriately characterized by the American historian Daniel R. Brower as 'the epitome of the Russian mercantile city', had a number of advantages that promised the achievement of economic prosperity, such as

> its location in the major manufacturing region of the country, its access to most major rail lines, and its proximity to major markets – including its own booming population.[16]

An examination of the role of women in Moscow industry adds a new dimension to the understanding of the pattern of Russian women's direct involvement in the operation of Russian business. The 1853 statistics contains data on ninety-seven businesswomen who owned 99 industrial enterprises.[17] (See Table 3.1.) As before, the majority of those enterprises belonged to the textile industry – fifty-five out of ninety-nine (on the whole, Moscow had 839 such establishments). Of those fifty-five enterprises, twenty-seven were cotton mills, fifteen were woollen mills, eleven engaged in production of cotton fabrics, fifteen were silk mills, and two factories were auxiliary.[18]

Table 3.1. Number of Enterprises Owned by Women by Branch of Industrial Activity (Moscow, 1853)[19]

Industry	Number of female-owned enterprises (out of total number of 839)	Share of female-owned enterprises in total volume of production, in per cent / silver roubles	Share of female-owned enterprises, by number of workers, in per cent / persons
Textile industry	55 (out of 386)	10.0 per cent 1,904,253 out of 18,962,326	10.3 per cent 3,960 out of 38,327
Chemical industry	4 (out of 34)	3.1 per cent 49,060 out of 1,575,911	6.0 per cent 55 out of 917
Processing of fat and wax	7 (out of 41)	6.8 per cent 57,570 out of 849,476	10.2 per cent 31 out of 304
Tanning industry	4 (out of 32)	45.3 per cent 499,522 out of 1,103,247	47.7 per cent 394 out of 826
Metal-working industry	6 (out of 120)	6.1 per cent 217,005 out of 3,540,544	6.3 per cent 199 out of 3,170
Food production	3 (out of 37)	3.9 per cent 35,000 out of 901,990	8.1 per cent 39 out of 484
Paper production	2 (out of 9)	13.5 per cent 4,800 out of 35,433	18.5 per cent 24 out of 130
Tobacco	6 (out of 34)	2.5 per cent 39,183 out of 1,577,697	3.5 per cent 48 out of 1380
Carriage-making	4 (out of 44)	3.3 per cent 21,900 out of 666,545	6.8 per cent 57 out of 840
Furniture and pianos	2 (out of 37)	6.0 per cent 13,300 out of 220,270	3.4 per cent 20 out of 589

Industry	Number of female-owned enterprises (out of total number of 839)	Share of female-owned enterprises in total volume of production, in per cent / silver roubles	Share of female-owned enterprises, by number of workers, in per cent / persons
Clothes (hats and gloves)	1 (out of 16)	0.9 per cent 2,000 out of 210,653	2.6 per cent 5 out of 195
Earthenware and brick industry	2 (out of 19)	23.2 per cent 55,450 out of 239,310	10.1 per cent 260 out of 865
Other industries (clocks, matches)	4 (out of 30)	8.3 per cent 36,050 out of 434,261	9.4 per cent 56 out of 596
TOTAL	**99 (out of 839)**	**9,7 per cent 2,935,093 out of 30,317,663**	**10,6 per cent 5,148 out of 48,623**
Proprietresses	97		

Moscow industry was structurally dominated by the textile branch: in 1853 it accounted for 62.5 per cent of annual production and 79 per cent of labour force (more than 38 thousand persons); well behind it were the metalworking (11.7 per cent of annual production; 6.5 per cent of labour force), the tobacco (5.2 per cent and 2.8 per cent respectively), and the chemical (3.6 per cent and 1.9 per cent respectively) branches. The tanning industry was number five among the leaders (3.6 per cent and 1.7 per cent respectively). Among the enterprises owned by women, textile mills were also predominant: they accounted for 65 per cent of the annual output of the former and for 77 per cent of their labour force.

Businesswomen owned 11.8 per cent of Moscow-based industrial enterprises (99 out of the total of 839), which produced 9.7 per cent of the annual output of Moscow industry (to the value of almost 3 million silver roubles) and employed 10.6 per cent of the capital's labour force (more than 5,000 workers). The share of women-owned businesses was relatively high in the tanning industry (45.3 per cent of the annual output; 47.7 per cent of workers) and in the writing-paper industry, pottery manufacture and brick-making. As most of the proprietresses were widows, it can be suggested, when assessing the degree of influence exerted by women across a given branch of industry, that there was an element of chance in all of them, excepting the textile one. Nevertheless, 'also consistent with patterns found in Western Europe, widowhood created the greatest opportunity for merchant women to participate in family business'.[20]

Let us consider the issue of real-estate ownership, the parameters of ethnic and social status, and the data on a group of proprietresses of the largest industrial enterprises.

The issue of real-estate ownership was directly linked to attempts at minimizing the risks. Our estimates indicate that 73 per cent of enterprises were situated on the premises owned by their proprietresses, and only 27 per cent on rented premises. Rather frequently, real estate was divided among family members.

For example, the proprietress of a cloth mill Anna Vürgang, an ethnic German, owned the house in which her factory was situated. Her husband, Karl-Friedrich Vürgang, a merchant of the Third Guild, owned another house which had been made over to him. The houses stood close to each other, while being in separate ownership of the spouses. Anna was a Roman Catholic and a Russian subject, while her husband was a Lutheran and a Württemberg subject. The husband came to Moscow from St Petersburg after his marriage to Anna, who had inherited the mill after her father. Separate ownership of real estate was an effective way to prevent the loss of property in the event of bankruptcy of an enterprise, because under Russian laws a spouse was exempted from property liability for the other spouse's debts.

In the mid-nineteenth century, the ethnic composition of the cohort of proprietresses was becoming increasingly complex. Of the ninety-seven female factory owners, eighty-five were Russian, seven were German, four were French, and two were Italian. The most active businesswomen of foreign extraction were Germans. Most of the female factory owners of foreign parentage – eleven out of twelve – were Russian subjects.[21]

The group of seven German businesswomen included Julia Pigot (wool-scouring mills), Maria Junget (a wool dye house), Anna Vürgang (a cloth-finishing mill), Konstanzia Belhert (a factory for production of muslin and cotton curtains), Emilia Zindel (one of the largest cotton-weaving mills in Moscow), Elisabeth Getscher (a phosphoric-match factory) and Katharina Fürster (a piano factory). Three factories belonged to French businesswomen – Catherine Morelle (a dye and finishing works), Marguerite Meliard (a tobacco factory) and Hortensia Bouis (production of pomades and perfumes). The Italian Francesca Monigetti owned a silk-dye house, while her compatriot Maria Campioni – a workshop producing marble and granite monuments (mostly tombstones). We see that women of foreign extraction, as well as their Russian counterparts, operated, first of all, in the textile industry (seven out of twelve).

The social composition of the group reveals the predominance of factory proprietresses who were members of the merchant guilds (sixty-nine out of ninety-seven); the six women who were honorary citizens and represented the oldest merchant dynasties can also be classed with this category. Thus, 77 per cent of proprietresses of enterprises were female merchants. The rest of the businesswomen belonged to the nobility (two persons), to the *meshchanstvo* (seventeen persons) and to the *tsekhovye* (three persons).

The two noblewomen were Maria de Chario, wife of an official and also the proprietress of a distillery, and Anna Zenkovich, wife of an army officer and the proprietress of a bell foundry. Unlike the representatives of the high nobility whose histories are discussed in Chapter 2, de Chario and Zenkovich belonged to the landless middle strata of the nobility, not to its elite (composed of the titled nobles and of those whom their service had elevated into the first four classes of the Table of the Ranks). For both women, engagement in business augmented their family budgets with a subsidiary resource, which played a considerable role in the strategy for survival.

Let us turn to the history of Maria de Chario's business. Her example indicates that the 1850s were the period when the system of financial payments was still inadequately developed. Many an entrepreneur did not have enough spare capital, and therefore the system of issuance of goods on credit for six, eight, nine or twelve months with payment in instalments became wide-spread in Russia. This system involved a considerable risk for both the seller and the buyer.[22]

Maria de Chario owned a distillery founded in 1813 (in 1853, it employed 6 workers and produced goods to the value of 8,000 roubles), which was situated in the proprietress' own house. It can be assumed that the distillery was passed on to Maria from her parents. Maria's husband, Andre de Chario, descended from a Moscow family of the French origin; he was a minor official. In Moscow, the couple had two houses and resided in the one owned by the husband (it was valued at 22,000 roubles), while the house which belonged to the wife was used as premises for the enterprises. The products including pure alcohol, 'French vodka', brandy and rum were very popular among customers of modest means because of their low prices (a bottle of vodka cost 50 kopecks). In the catalogue of the 1863 exhibition of Moscow manufactured goods, the proprietress emphasized that 'the apparatuses for distilling alcohol were ordered from Paris' (such an advertisement could not fail with the Russian customer, who always preferred anything foreign to anything domestic). The family business was a success, and the couple decided to expand it. In the early 1860s, in addition to the Moscow enterprise, they leased a distillery on Prince Kochubei's estate in Nizhnii Novgorod province. As the second enterprise needed substantial investments, Maria de Chario took credits in cash from fourteen lenders to the total amount of 148,000 roubles. She expected to repay the loans by receiving the money from her numerous wholesale customers, who, in their turn, were purchasing consignments of her goods on credit for several months. The expectation that the customers, whose debts to Maria against promissory notes and invoices amounted to about 40,000 roubles, would be accurate in their payments and that the stock of products would be rapidly sold off (the shop in Kitai-Gorod had a stock of goods to the value of 20,000 roubles, and the storehouse in Moscow – to the value of 96,000 roubles) did not materialize. The creditors instituted a case against Maria before the Moscow Commercial Court and demanded that the money should be returned to them. She managed to repay only a fraction of her debts by re-pawning her securities – shares in the Moscow Insurance Company. In 1864, the firm was committed to outside management. As the inventory carried out in this connection showed that the value of the property exceeded the debts by 46,000 roubles, no bankruptcy proceedings were initiated. In order to save the business, Maria had to terminate the production of vodka in Nizhnii Novgorod province, and to retain only the Moscow enterprise. According to the 1868 data, the Moscow distillery employed fourteen workers, was equipped with a steam engine, and produced 8,000 *vedros*[23] of vodka to the value of 45,000 roubles. Its vodka was sold in Moscow and at the Nizhnii Novgorod Fair. The popularity of de Chario's vodka is attested to in literature. Thus, in his sketches expressively entitled 'Fragments of Moscow Life' (1884), the writer Anton Chekhov satirizes the primitive tastes of the Moscow commoner in a jocular description of an artisan who has bought 'chequered trousers, a cane in Tsvetnoi Boulevard, and a *sorokovushka from de Chario's distillery*, and subscribed to the fourth volume of 'The Brigand Churkin'.[24] The bottle of 40-per cent vodka distilled at de Chario's is included in the list of purchases which symbolized, in the eyes of a customer from the lower strata of urban population, a communion with 'the life of chic' achieved at a very moderate cost.

The case of de Chario clearly shows that, in the period under consideration, businesses (including those headed by women) were becoming visibly dependent on the institutionalization of the system of monetary payments. The slightest failure in the chain of payments for goods could immediately put at risk the very existence of a business.

In the group of women who were female honorary citizens (ranking next below noblewomen), all six proprietresses were widows who had inherited their businesses (three textile enterprises, one tannery, one tallow chandlery and one confectionery) after their husbands. In three cases (Alekseeva, Matveeva and Bakhrushina) the family factories were in the category of the biggest enterprises.

Judging by the number of workers employed, most of the ninety-nine enterprises could be characterized as medium-sized or small. (See Table 3.2.)

Table 3.2. Moscow enterprises owned by women, by number of workers employed (1853)

Number of workers	Number of enterprises
Less than 6	17
6–10	30
11–20	16
21–50	13
51–100	11
101–150	6
151–200	1
201–500	4
More than 500	1
Total	**99**

Let us focus on the group of the twelve enterprises with the maximum number of workers employed. That dozen of businesses (nine textile enterprises, two tanneries, one brickworks) had more than the lion's share of labour force – they employed 3,364 workers or 65 per cent of the total number of workers employed at 'women-owned' enterprises of Moscow, and produced goods to the value of 1,750,894 roubles, which amounted to 60 per cent of the total value of all those enterprises' output. (See Table 3.3.)

Five enterprises (three textile – Nosova's, Zündel's and Alekseeva's, and two tanneries – Bakhrushina's and Kudriavtseva's) were equipped with steam engines; not surprisingly, they were the most profitable among the businesses – by the value of their annual output they were the top five in the list of the ninety-nine female-owned Moscow enterprises. Among those leaders, the labour productivity per worker achieved by the textile mills amounted to 403 to 652 roubles, and that recorded at the tanneries – to 1,321 to 1,840 roubles (or, on average, to 942 roubles per worker). The businesses not equipped with steam engines achieved the productivity of labour per worker in the amount of 185 to 502 roubles at the textile enterprises, and 211 roubles at the brick works (on the average, 285 roubles per worker). A more relevant comparison between the textile enterprises alone reveals that the annual productivity of labour per worker achieved at the mills equipped with steam engines amounted to 516 roubles, and that achieved at the mills not equipped with such engines – to 297 roubles.

The enlargement of textile industrial enterprises and the increase in the volume of output were directly linked with the mechanization of the textile industry in the late 1840s and the 1850s, when, according to A. M. Solov'eva, the number of mechanical spindles increased by 2.5 times.[25]

The existing evidence indicates that in the initial period of the industrial revolution in Russia, the number of those who could afford the price of a steam engine was limited to the owners of large enterprises, and indeed only they had the opportunity to acknowledge the necessity of technological innovations. The sharp rise in the efficiency of production further increased the gap between the group of leaders and the rest of the enterprises, where manual machinery was still being used.

The history of the largest Moscow tannery – the Bakhrushin dynasty's plant – shows that at that time modernization of enterprises involved expenses so high that they were difficult to shoulder even by 'a well-off owner'. In the process of coping with the constantly emerging problems, the Bakhrushins developed a coherent strategy of managing their family business, which was based on partnership relations between the mother and her adult sons. The Bakhrushins' plant was founded in 1833 by Aleksey Bakhrushin (1792–1848); after his sudden death of cholera, it was headed in 1848–62 by his widow, Natal'ia (1793–1862).[26] According to a family legend, immediately after the funeral ceremony, the wid-

Table 3.3. Women-owned enterprises with more than 100 workers

Name	Status	Type of factory, presence of steam engine	Number of workers	Value of annual output, in roubles	Value of output per worker, in roubles
1. Natal'ia Nosova	Zvenigorod female merchant	wool-weaving, with steam engine	873	351,875	403
2. Emilia Zündel	female merchant of 2nd Guild	cotton-weaving, with steam engine	492	320,800	652
3. Anis'ia Alekseeva	female honorary citizen	cotton-weaving, with steam engine	485	236,160	492
4. Efimia Kudriavtseva	female merchant of 2nd Guild	tannery, with steam engine	117	215,260	1,840
5. Natal'ia Bakhrushina	female hon. citizen	tannery, with steam engine	160	211,300	1,321
6. Elizaveta Bogomazova	Voskresensk female merchant	cotton-weaving	390	174,110	190
7. Fedos'ia Shukhova	female merchant of 2nd Guild	wool-and cotton-weaving	130	55,052	423
8. Anna Matveeva	female honorary citizen	wool-and-cotton-weaving	103	51,729	502
9. Mar'ia Baidakova	female merchant of 2nd Guild	brick-works	240	50,650	211
10. Tat'iana Suchkova	female merchant of 3rd Guild	cotton-weaving	150	38,138	254
11. Olimpiada Popova	female merchant of 2nd Guild	cotton-weaving	105	23,860	227
12. Avdot'ia Koz'micheva	female merchant of 3rd Guild	cotton-weaving	119	21,960	185

owed Natal'ia (daughter of the merchant Potolovskii from Zaraisk, Moscow province, which was also the native town of her husband) and her three adult sons gathered together to audit the family business. It turned out that the coffers were empty and the enterprise was debt-ridden, because in 1844 the late owner had invested heavily (in the amount of 100 thousand roubles) in new mechanical equipment, which included an English steam engine (the first such engine ever installed in a Russian tannery). The three sons – the twenty-nine-year-old Petr, the twenty-five-year-old Alexander and the sixteen-year-old Vasilii – began to manage the business jointly with their mother, who became the official and actual head of the enterprise. Her great-grandson wrote in his memoirs that Natal'ia 'moved the whole mechanism as a hidden spring',[27] had a reputation as a resolute woman, and was literate, which made it possible for her to understand financial documentation. She managed to repay the debts and stabilize the firm. Her success was attested to by the fact that in 1851 the Bakhrushins were made hereditary honorary citizens.

According to statistics, during the fourteen years when the enterprise was headed by Natal'ia, its major parameters of production changed most positively: the number of workers increased from 160 to 290 (or by 1.8 times), and the value of output grew from 181,475 to 367,000 roubles per annum (or twofold).[28] In 1857, in addition to the already existing six brick factory buildings, a seventh two-storey brick building was built. The book entitled 'The Statistical Data on the Factories and Plants Whose Exhibits Received Prizes at the Manufacture Exhibition of the Year 1861' contains the following description of the equipment installed at the Bakhrushins' enterprise:

> The plant is set into motion by a 12-horsepower high-pressure steam engine. It has up to 200 vats for skin-tanning; also, there are 6 machines for wool-washing, 17 tables and 8 marble slabs for glossing and glazing morocco, 5 vats for boiling dyes and glue, 1 cylindrical press, 1 still and other apparatuses. Each year from 247 thousand sheep-skins, 10 thousand goat-skins and 11 thousand bull and calf skins, up to 257 thousand pieces of multicolour morocco, 8 thousand pieces of calf leather ..., up to 8 thousand *poods* of wool from sheep-hides, and 800 *poods* of glue boiled from parings of hides are produced. Sales are carried out in both capitals, Nizhnii Novgorod, Kyakhta and other places.[29]

In his review of the Exhibition, the professor of technology of Moscow University Modest Kittary noted that the leading position achieved by the Bakhrushins' enterprise was based on the use of state-of-the-art technologies:

> All the goods displayed at the Exhibition by this participant are of excellent quality; but the most important thing is ... that the plant of Mrs. Bakhrushina was one of the first to introduce improvements in Russian leather production, one of the first to adopt a steam engine, hoppers with rotating wings, etc, etc. And we can add that all these innovations were not kept secret: a special booklet with draughts and illus-

trations was published with regard to the new machinery, and besides, any person interested in the matter was invited to visit the plant.[30]

It should be mentioned that Bakhrushina managed to flexibly cooperate with the supervisory bodies, in particular with the sanitary inspectorate. In 1850, the architect Bykovskii from the Office of the Moscow Governor-General reprimanded the Bakhrushins for polluting the environment by openly dumping tannery waste into the Moscow river. This fact was confirmed in the Moscow Head Police-Master's report to Governor-General A. Zakrevskii. In order to prevent the closure of her enterprise for violation of sanitary regulations, Natal'ia Bakhrushina immediately made additional investments in equipment, although at that time, just two years after her husband's death, the enterprise was still not profitable enough. In particular, in less than a month, the two rafts for leather-washing which had been operating on the Moscow river were dismantled and replaced with scouring machines.[31]

It is apparent that the moral authority of the mother, the continuation of her late husband's policy of introducing technological innovations, and her creditworthiness in the eyes of both customers and creditors played an important role in stabilizing the firm. Entwined in her strategy were the emotional and the rational components of motivation. Firstly, when after the death of the owner it became clear that he had been financing the modernization of the enterprise by borrowing heavily, and that the debts on bills exceeded the value of the family's property, Natal'ia Bakhrushina chose to ignore the advice of her friends in the commercial world, who thought that it would be better for her to renounce succession as a heir and to declare the firm bankrupt in order to maximally compensate the creditors. She took the decision not to do this, 'lest the memory of the husband and father Aleksey Bakhrushin be compromised', and then managed to reach an agreement with the creditors concerning the postponement of the debt repayment. The established image of the company reflected its strategic approach to competition and its resolve to retain its leadership in the leather industry. Secondly, Natal'ia and her sons took the joint decision, which was later included in the firm's charter, to absolutely rule out any transactions on credit and to switchover to payments in cash.[32] The mother's authority and her dominance in business matters effectively prevented any conflicts among her children. After the death of Natal'ia, neither her three sons nor their descendants would divide the family business, and for fifty-five more years, until the 1917 Revolution, the enterprise would be operating under their joint management.

Natal'ia Bakhrushina was a widow who had inherited an already existing enterprise after her husband. Her breach with the traditional practice, when the lot of a woman was the domestic sphere was not very evident because a number of important managerial functions were taken over by the adult sons (it was noted in the documents that at the factory 'the owner himself is the foreman', which in this case meant the eldest son, Petr).

However, the successful female-owned enterprises of the 1850s included those whose proprietresses were always socially and culturally oriented to being independently engaged in business and had started their businesses from scratch. Take, for example, the case of Natal'ia Nosova. While the majority of enterprises were inherited by their proprietresses after their husbands, Nosova's wool-weaving mill was established by her on her own initiative, which is documentarily confirmed by her 1849 petition to Governor-General Zakrevskii, in which she applied for a certificate authorizing her to keep a factory. The application begins with the words: 'I have a factory in Moscow … in the houses of my sons … which was set up by me in the year 1829'.

In 1853 the mill, equipped with steam engines and mechanical machines, was the largest among enterprises headed by women. By the volume of production it ranked fifth from the top of the list of Moscow's 41 wool-weaving enterprises. The business employed 873 workers and annually produced finished goods to the value of 351,875 silver roubles. The raw materials for manufacturing shawls and woollen fabrics (flannel, costume cloth, etc.) were Russian and Spanish wool, and English and Russian cotton yarn.

Although we have not managed to reconstruct in detail all the circumstances in the history of the Nosov dynasty as yet (e.g., the social status of Natal'ia's parents, the source of her starting capital, the family's standard of living before the death of her husband), it is already clear that Natal'ia Nosova (1789–1853) played an important part in setting up and coordinating the business in which her sons were participants. In 1823, the widowed Natal'ia, then aged thirty-four, and her five children (four sons and one daughter), aged between four and thirteen, shifted from the *meshchanstvo* estate to the Third Guild. At first, she traded in flour from a rented shop in Yauza district. In 1829, after saving an amount of money, Natal'ia ventured to set up a factory manufacturing *dradedam* kerchiefs.[33] In 1838, she traded both in flour and in kerchiefs, for which purpose a second shop was rented in Kitai-Gorod. At that time, the shops were managed by Natal'ia's juniour sons (the twenty-six-year-old Ivan the Elder and the twenty-year-old Ivan the Younger), while she herself headed the factory where she was assisted by her two eldest sons, the twenty-eight-year-old Dmitrii and the twenty-seven-year-old Vasilii. Gradually, the focus of the business shifted to the factory, which became the main source of the family's income. By 1842, the factory was located in Moscow's industrial district of Lefortovo, where it occupied premises bought for this purpose for 6,000 roubles, and employed fifty workers. The building was registered by Natal'ia as a joint property of her sons. By 1849, a number of adjacent land-plots had been bought up, and another five brick buildings had been erected. In 1850, the mill's equipment included two steam engines (16 and 6 hp respectively) and more than 600 looms; by that time, the number of workers had risen to 1,000. Throughout the initial period of the mill's existence (1829–52), the enterprise was headed by Natal'ia Nosova. In 1852, she forwarded an appeal to the Office of the Governor-General, in which she expressed her decision to officially hand the mill over to her three sons on the grounds that she was no longer capable of managing the business 'because of the weakness of health'. The official certificate concerning the transfer of the mill into 'the complete ownership' of the sons Dmitrii, Vasilii and Ivan the Younger was issued on 9 December, 1853, twelve days before the death of Natal'ia Nosova.[34] The authoritarian character of Natal'ia, which fully manifested itself in the imposition of a very rigid subordination and discipline within the Nosov family, was reflected in her will which stipulated that one son, Ivan the Elder, should be excluded from the business 'in view of the intemperate life of his', and that a small subsidy from the interest on the sum of 2,857 silver roubles and 14 ⅔ kopecks deposited at one of the credit institutions should be allotted to him. The testator added that 'he, Ivan, should be content with this, and not demand more'. The daughter, Maria, was left a tiny sum of 571 silver roubles and 42 ⁶⁄₇ kopecks; for her it was recommended 'not to demand more ... and to prosecute no claims, because she [Maria] has been abundantly rewarded by me in my life-time and should be content forever'.[35] The fact that all her available capital as well as the sums earmarked for her children as heirs were meticulously calculated by Natal'ia Nosova, testifies to the unique thrift on the part of this businesswoman. The wellbeing of the family was achieved by her managing the business prudently to the extreme; even after she became a rich merchant, Natal'ia retained the habit of penny-pinching (which she never explained rationally), acquired at the time when she was a young widow with five small children on her hands. As she advanced in age, the peculiarity of her behaviour, which literally followed the proverb 'take the care of the pennies and the pounds will take care of themselves', became visible in a number of strange actions – thus, in order not to pay the guild levy in Moscow, where it was the highest (65 roubles), in 1851 she shifted to the Zvenigorod and then to the Eisk merchantry, because in those small towns the levy was lower (45 and 25 roubles respectively). This made the Moscow administration suspect that Nosova had avoided paying the tax in full, and so she had to wriggle out of trouble by making up a story that she had indeed planned to set up factories in those small towns, but could not do this quickly enough. Her strategy of business management was based on authoritarian control. Natal'ia wanted the 'iron' intra-family discipline to remain the core element of all the relations among her descendants, and expressed her last will in the following words:

on the termination of the life of mine, my body should be committed to the earth in accordance with the Christian rites, as it befits my rank; and I ask the children of mine to live in the fear of God and in brotherly love, and not to start any feuds or litigation between one another.[36]

The dying wish of the foundress of the family business was strictly observed, and in 1880 her sons established the joint-stock 'Partnership of the Brothers Nosov's Manufactories' with a capital of 3 million roubles, thus maintaining the family nature of the business.

The above cases clearly demonstrate that proprietresses of factories were experienced managers, exercising rigid day-to-day control over their enterprises and taking decisions either independently or in partnership with their adult sons.

The highest proportion of female industrialists in the Russian Empire were operating in Moscow. In order to analyse regional differences in female industrial entrepreneurship, we must now turn our attention to the situation in St Petersburg.

3. Businesswomen in St Petersburg's Industry in 1862

During the period under consideration, the role played by businesswomen in the industry of St Petersburg was smaller than that in Moscow. They accounted for 3.2 per cent of the annual value of production (about 1.25 million roubles), and employed 3 per cent of workers. By the general parameter of the number of workers per enterprise (58 persons), St Petersburg and Moscow were equal, but

Autograph signature of Natalia Nosova, head (in 1829–52) of a wool-weaving mill in Moscow. 1849. Courtesy of Mikhail Zolotarev, Moscow.

the average number of workers per enterprise in female ownership amounted to fifty-two in Moscow, and only to nineteen in St Petersburg. The absence of big enterprises owned by women can be explained by a higher social mobility of the St Petersburg population – by comparison with Moscow, the capital had much fewer merchant dynasties counting three or four generations. Therefore many small businesses were set up there by women (widows and married women) on their own initiative and without any expectations of getting outside help or capital.

In 1862, thirty-three St Petersburg businesswomen owned thirty-five enterprises out of 374 (see Table 3.4). Of the thirty-three female factory owners, there were twenty-seven Russians, five Germans, and one Englishwoman. The high percentage of foreigners (18 per cent) reflected the multi-ethnic composition of the St Petersburg population and the resulting strong influence of foreigners in St Petersburg entrepreneurship.[37]

Let us characterize in brief the structure of St Petersburg industry at that time. In 1862, the value of output of all the industrial enterprises in St. Petersburg amounted to 38.7 million roubles. By the annual volume of production, leadership was shared by the textile and food industries (31.5 per cent and 30.2 per cent respectively; at the same time, 75 per cent of the output of the food industry was accounted for by sugar refineries). They were followed by the metal-working (9.1 per cent), leather (7.0 per cent), tobacco (6.2 per cent), candle-making (4.2 per cent) and chemical (2.4 per cent) industries. Those seven branches of industry accounted for more than 90 per cent of the total output. Hired workers were divided into two categories – foremen (1,048 persons) and workers (20,782 persons, 78 per cent of whom were men, 14 per cent women, and 8 per cent children under fourteen).

In St Petersburg, businesswomen were especially active in fat and wax processing, and in the tobacco and leather industries. Four fat and wax processing enterprises accounted for 25.4 per cent of the value of the industry's output and employed 20.3 per cent of its labour force. We have managed to reconstruct the period of female ownership at three out of the four enterprises. The largest of those businesses, the tallow chandlery and soap boilery of Pelageia Davydova, which employed twenty-four workers and annually produced goods to the value of 306,625 silver roubles, was situated in a house in Ligovka Street, owned by its proprietress. The female merchant of the Second Guild Pelageia Davydova headed the enterprise for fifteen years, from the moment her husband, Timofei Davydov, died in 1852 until her own death in 1867; after which the business passed on to her son, Ivan Davydov.[39] Another large tallow chandlery belonged to the female merchant of the Second Guild Aleksandra Zhukova. She began to manage the chandlery and two candle shops in 1855, after the death of her husband. Aleksandra, then aged forty-five, had three sons – the eighteen-year-old Aleksandr, the twelve-year-old Vasilii and the ten-year-old Mikhail. When the sons grew older, they began to help their mother in business matters. For at least fourteen years (documents were found for the period of 1855–68), the chandlery (in 1862 it employed 6 workers and annually produced goods to the value of about 70,000 roubles) occupied rented premises. In the early 1860s, the son Aleksandr set up yet another tallow chandlery. The latest documents mentioning the chandlery or its proprietress date to 1870. The third widow, the female merchant of the Second Guild Ekaterina Kanbina, was rather successful for a long period of time (documents reflect the period of 1862–78). Ekaterina owned a house in Ligovka Street, which she had inherited in 1862 after her husband, a merchant, and was helped in business matters by her two sons – Makar and Petr. In 1862, Ekaterina was forty-five, and her sons were twenty-two and twenty years of age respectively. The junior son, Fedor, then aged eleven, did not take part in her business. He would become a participant at the age of eighteen. In 1862, the tallow chandlery employed eight workers and annually produced goods to the value of 31 thousand roubles. In 1869–77, it was recorded that apart from the tallow chandlery, Ekaterina owned a starch-making plant (no detailed information available). In 1878, each of the three sons participated in Ekaterina's business.[40]

As we see, the existing data on proprietresses of enterprises are not very informative. They clearly testify to only one thing – that in all the corresponding cases, widowed proprietresses performed the 'bridging function' by transacting business successfully enough to pass the enterprises on to their adult sons at the end of their lives.

In the tobacco industry (which held the first place in St Petersburg by the number of enterprises – thirty-nine), women owned seven tobacco-processing plants, six of which were small – with six to forty workers who annually produced goods to the value of 7,000–23,000 roubles. Although the tobacco industry of St Petersburg intensively employed female (31 per cent) and child (5 per cent) labour, the enterprises owned by women were characterized by much lower percentages (25 per cent and 3 per cent respectively).

The largest tobacco-processing plant which annually produced 14 million cigars, 15 million *papirosas* (Russian cigarettes with cardboard mouthpieces) and up to 280 million *poods* of smoking tobacco (to the value of 70,000 roubles), belonged to the noblewoman Anna Golenishcheva. The plant was situated in Nevskii Prospekt, the main street of St Petersburg. 22 per cent of its workers were women; child labour was not employed. The products were issued under the brand-name of 'Franz Heinrichs' and were extremely popular. The industrial expert Professor M. Kittary wrote in his review of the 1861 Exhibition: 'A. M. Golenishcheva's firm 'Franz Heinrichs' produces fairly much, and has up to 230 workers at her factory; the items of production are as follows: smoking tobacco, *papirosas* and cigars of very good quality'.[41]

Table 3.4. Number of Enterprises Owned by Women by Branch of Industrial Activity (St. Petersburg, 1862)[38]

Industry	Number of female-owned enterprises out of total number of enterprises (374)	Share of female-owned enterprises in total volume of production, in per cent/silver roubles	Share of female-owned enterprises by number of workers, in per cent/number of persons
Textile industry	4 (out of 75)	0.9 per cent 122,200 out of 12,203,204	1.1 per cent 85 out of 7,980
Chemical industry	3 (out of 23)	8.6 per cent 78,930 out of 912,860	19.3 per cent 47 out of 244
Processing of fat and wax	4 (out of 19)	25.4 per cent 409,162 out of 1,613,395	20.3 per cent 40 out of 197
Leather industry	5 (out of 18)	12.6 per cent 340,150 out of 2,698,820	11.4 per cent 110 out of 965
Metal-working industry	2 (out of 44)	0.7 per cent 24,125 out of 3,537,374	0.4 per cent 24 out of 5,655
Food production	2 (out of 26)	0.1 per cent 15,312 out of 11,681,841	0.7 per cent 13 out of 1,910
Tobacco industry	7 (out of 39)	6.0 per cent 144,697 out of 2,406,722	14.1 per cent 253 out of 1,795
Furniture and pianos	1 (out of 15)	9.9 per cent 25,000 out of 253,270	2.0 per cent 4 out of 202
Clothes (hats, gloves, uniforms)	2 (out of 9)	18.1 per cent 33,200 out of 183,747	19.4 per cent 34 out of 175
Earthenware and brick industry, construction materials	2 (out of 20)	17.8 per cent 48,370 out of 272,280	8.0 per cent 22 out of 276
Wood-working	1 (out of 14)	1.0 per cent 3,600 out of 368,598	2.4 per cent 10 out of 418

Industry	Number of female-owned enterprises out of total number of enterprises (374)	Share of female-owned enterprises in total volume of production, in per cent/silver roubles	Share of female-owned enterprises by number of workers, in per cent/ number of persons
Stone-working	2 (out of 12)	2.8 per cent 3,630 out of 128,160	8.7 per cent 11 out of 126
Other industries (machine-building, carriage-making, glass, writing-paper, rubber, etc. industries)	0 (out of 50)	0 out of 960,662	0 out of 621
TOTAL	35 female-owned enterprises	3.2 per cent 1,238,376 out of 38,695,505	3.0 per cent 653 out of 21,830
Proprietresses	33		

Among the female factory owners engaged in tobacco business, six of whom were Russians, there was one English proprietress, Sophie Lawrence (1810–85). Her rather modest enterprise employed ten workers and annually produced 636 thousand cigars and 293 thousand *papirosas* to the value of just 3,760 roubles. Sophie's husband, John Lawrence (1808–86), was a merchant of the Second Guild who traded in 'underwear and haberdashery'. At least since 1858, the husband and wife took out two certificates of the Second Guild, and followed separate paths in business. However, in the second half of the 1860s, only Sophie with her factory remained in the merchantry, while her husband shifted to the *meshchanstvo*. Apparently, at that time the tobacco-processing plant was the main source of income, or rather of the means of subsistence, for the whole family. The couple had four children – the sons Charles and Leopold, and the daughters Catherine and Elizabeth. The elder son, Charles, split off from the parents and took out a separate guild certificate; in 1867, he owned a commercial firm, 'Charles Lawrence & Co', which imported goods from Great Britain.[42]

The leather industry of St Petersburg had two Russian female factory owners – Praskov'ia Semenova and Agraphena Rasteriaeva, and one German Emilia Ginter. No biographical information has been found with respect to Semenova and Ginter. Prosopographic reconstruction is possible only in the case of Rasteriaeva.

There are no doubts that the female merchant of the First Guild Agraphena Rasteriaeva (1811–74) was the brightest and most prominent person among the female factory owners of St Petersburg. Agraphena took the helm of the family firm 'Sergei Rasteriaev' in 1861, after the death, in 1860, of her husband, the fifty-four-year-old merchant of the First Guild Sergei Rasteriaev.[43] Agraphena, then aged fifty, was helped in business matters by her three sons who were recorded to share 'one and the same capital' with their mother – the twenty-seven-year-old Ivan, the twenty-two-year-old Grigorii and the twenty-one-year-old Nikolai. Rasteriaeva owned two houses, including a brick one in the prestigious Troitskii Prospekt in the centre of the capital. Of the five enterprises inherited by Rasteriaeva after her husband, three were in St Petersburg – a tannery (in 1862, it employed one foreman and thirty-five workers, and produced goods to the value of 155,000 roubles); a chemical plant, founded in 1847 (it employed one foreman and forty workers, and produced 972 tons of sulphuric, nitric and hydrochloric acids and ammonia solution to the value of 64,280 roubles), and a small-shot foundry, set up in 1853 (it employed 1 foreman and 6 workers, and produced goods to the value of 22,450 roubles). In 1862, the three enterprises employed eighty-four workers and produced goods to the value of 280,015 roubles. Rasteriaeva also owned two brick-works (founded in 1855 and 1858) in the vicinity of St Petersburg. According to the 1865 data, they employed 200 workers, and produced 7 million 'red and scarlet' bricks to the value of 80 thousand roubles. One of the works was equipped with a steam engine.

Agraphena and her sons also inherited the commercial component of the family firm, that is, the trade in chemicals, metals, 'instruments' and hardware, carried on from three shops in St Petersburg (one was in Gostinyi Dvor and another two in Apraksin Dvor; both places were the capital's biggest shopping centres) and from an outlet in Moscow (in Gostinyi Dvor of Kitai-Gorod).[44] Trading in bricks was carried on in a special 'yard' in the centre of St Petersburg. The products of the tannery and the chemical plant were in high demand in Moscow, St Petersburg, Riga and other towns of the Russian Empire.[45] After the death of Agraphena, the business was partitioned by her three sons, two of whom then managed the St Petersburg enterprises (Ivan had got the small-shot foundry, and Grigorii – the rest of them), while the third, Nikolai, after having resettled in Moscow, headed the family trade in metals.

The case of Rasteriaeva demonstrates that the specific feature of the family business strategy was the creation and development of enterprises in two or more branches of industry. If a business on the whole was a success, the proprietress continued to run it without any intention of refocusing her activities on some single branch of industry. The ability to organize the production and the selling of various types of goods attested to the entrepreneurial talent of the proprietress.

After the death of Agraphena Rasteriaeva, her son Grigorii, who had inherited, in accordance with her will, most of the family business, successfully developed it as the firm 'Grigorii Rasteriaev'. He became one of the biggest traders in tools and metals. His position in the commercial elite was greatly enhanced by his marriage, *c.* 1865, to Tatiana Eliseeva, daughter of the biggest trader in wines and colonial goods, Chairman of the St. Petersburg Exchange Committee, Councillor of Commerce Grigorii Eliseev. Grigorii Rasteriaev's ascent in business was accompanied by a simultaneous rise in his social status – he became an elected member of the St Petersburg Exchange Committee, then was vested with the rank of Councillor of Commerce for taking part in philanthropy at the level of city community in the capacity of economic trustee, or treasurer, of the St Elizabeth's Almshouse established by the Eliseevs. Grigorii's highest achievement in gaining social status was his membership of the Emperor's Society of Trotting Races, an almost exclusively aristocratic and not very numerous (about 270 members) association of experts in horse-breeding, presided over by Grand Duke Dmitrii Konstantinovich, Director in Chief of the State Stud Farms and a representative of the reigning dynasty. Grigorii spent most of the income from his enterprises on purchasing real estate. In 1902, all the family real estate (excepting the family house on Troitskii Prospekt) was registered in the name of his wife Tatiana, who owned three multi-storey apartment houses in the centre of the capital, including one on Nevskii Prospekt. According to the municipality's estimates, their total value amounted to 815,555 roubles.[46]

The life stories of Davydova, Zhukova, Kanbina, Lawrence and especially Rasteriaeva illustrate the formation of a new type of independent women – proprietresses of enterprises. In the period when they headed family businesses, the enterprises technically modernized by them were all functioning smoothly. In the case of Rasteriaeva the fact of the female family head having been included in the public networks of business activity was attested to by the 'dynastic' marriage of her middle son. Always considering Grigorii to be the most promising of all her children, the mother bequeathed to him the lion's share of the family business and most of the real estate.

The remainder of this chapter explores the sociological aspects of the female merchants' groups in Moscow and St. Petersburg on the basis of evidence from the 'Reference Books'.

4. Female Entrepreneurs of Moscow and St Petersburg in 1869: Socio-Biographical Parameters and Economic Activity

From the second half of the 1860s onwards, information on persons taking out guild certificates of right to engage in business activities was published in the two capital cities, Moscow and St Petersburg, in the form of the so-called 'Reference Books'.[47] This source (we have used the 'Reference Books' for 1869) makes it possible to assess the role and influence of women in the industry and trade of the biggest commercial centres of Russia.

In St. Petersburg, women accounted for 13 per cent of the merchantry (501 persons out of the total of 3,864), in Moscow – for 11.6 per cent (583 persons out of 5,013).

Below we are going to consider the ethnic and age parameters of the group; its elite represented by female merchants of the First Guild; the distribution of businesswomen by trade specialization; and the marital status of the proprietresses of Moscow enterprises.

The Ethnic Parameters

In St Petersburg, the ranks of female merchants included 406 Russians (81 per cent), 43 Germans (8.6 per cent), 26 French (5.2 per cent), six English (1.2 per cent), five Italians (1 per cent), five Jewesses (1 per cent); the rest were represented by two Swedes, two Poles, one American, one Dutch, one Austrian, one Belgian, one Swiss and one Finn (2 per cent in total). The female merchantry of Moscow consisted of 531 Russians (91.9 per cent), thirty-three Germans (5.65 per cent), fifteen French (2.55 per cent), one Tatar, one Armenian, one Italian and one Belgian (0.7 per cent in total) (see Figure 3.1). These data correspond to the ethnic characteristic of the two capital cities.[48]

Figure 3.1. The ethnic composition of businesswomen in St Petersburg and Moscow (1869)

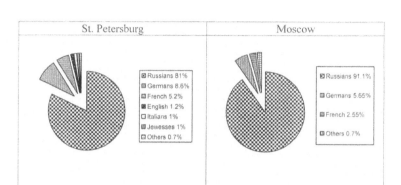

The Age Stratification

The most active group in St Petersburg was that of businesswomen aged 31 to 60, whose share amounted to 71.8 per cent, including aged 31 to 40 – 106 persons (21.2 per cent); aged 41 to 50 – 126 persons (25.1 per cent); and aged 51 to 60 – 128 persons (25.5 per cent). Five persons were under 20 (1 per cent); 42 persons (8.4 per cent) were aged 21 to 30; 94 persons were of senior age (18.8 per cent), including aged 61 to 70 – 72 persons (14.4 per cent); and aged over 70 – 22 persons (4.4 per cent).

The situation in Moscow was similar – the majority of businesswomen were aged 31 to 60, whose share amounted to 66.5 per cent, including aged 31 to 40 – 87 persons (14.9 per cent); aged 41 to 50 – 148 persons (25.4 per cent); 149 persons (25.6 per cent) were of senior age (including aged 61 to 70 – 116 persons, or 19.9 per cent); 33 persons (5.7 per cent) were over 70.

Despite the absence of any pronounced differences in age groups, the businesswomen of St Petersburg were, by and large, younger than those in Moscow (see Figure 3.2). The average age of a businesswoman in St. Petersburg was 47.7 years, while that of her Moscow counterpart was 54.4 years.

A comparison between the ethnic and age parameters reveals a greater openness and flexibility of the St Petersburg merchant corporation.[49] The differences in the business and social organization of St Petersburg and Moscow were also reflected in the composition of the group of female merchants of the First Guild.

Figure 3.2. The age of St Petersburg and Moscow businesswomen (1869, in %)

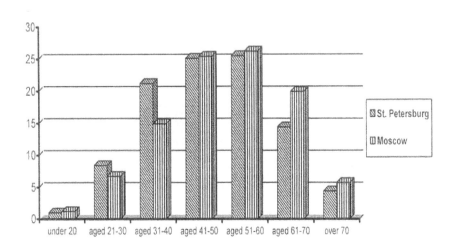

The Elite Group: Female Merchants of the First Guild

There was a significant difference between the two capitals in the numbers of the female merchantry of the First Guild. In 1869, there were fifteen women inscribed in the First Guild of the St Petersburg merchantry, which accounted for 3 per cent of its total membership of 501, while in Moscow the ranks of the First Guild included thirty-four women, which accounted for 6 per cent of its total membership of 583. This difference could be explained by a higher incidence in Moscow of longstanding family businesses. One can even speak in terms of a certain exclusiveness of the merchant elite of Moscow.

Of the fifteen St Petersburg female merchants of the First Guild, only four owned industrial enterprises. Two of them, Rasteriaeva and Kanbina, have already been mentioned above. The other two (Baird and Stenbok-Fermor) were noblewomen who regularly took out merchant certificates of right to engage in business activities.

The noble woman of English extraction Dorothea Baird, née Holliday (*c*.1810–*c*.1870), became a merchant in 1865, after the death of her husband Francis Baird (1802–64), and remained in the merchantry until 1869, when she transferred the management of the enterprise to her son George, then aged twenty-seven. The properties inherited by Dorothea included a number of big plants – 'a mechanical plant, an iron rolling mill, a foundry and a plant producing water-supply equipment' – and a shipping company. In 1828, Dorothea married Francis and had ten children by him. Francis in his turn had inherited the above enterprises after his father, the talented inventor and industrialist Charles Baird, an expatriate Scotsman who had built, in 1815, Russia's first steamship, the 'Elizaveta'.[50] In 1862, the Baird Works employed 862 workers, who produced goods to the value of 598 thousand roubles. After the death of Dorothea, her son George expanded production: in 1879, the steel foundry produced rails (the foundry equipped with four 1,334-horsepower steam engines, employing 950 workers, who annually produced goods to the value of one million roubles), the machine-building plant produced 'various mechanical items for shipbuilding and for factories' (it was equipped with fourteen 346-horsepower steam engines, and employed 1,514 workers, who annually produced goods to the value of 3.1 million roubles). In 1881, George Baird sold the enterprises to 'The Joint-Stock Society of the Franco-Russian Plants in St Petersburg' and returned to Great Britain, thus putting an end to the almost one-hundred-year-long epic of the Baird family's life in Russia.[51]

In 1849, Countess Nadezhda Stenbok-Fermor (1815–97) inherited eight metallurgical plants in Perm province in the Urals after her father, the Urals' biggest industrialist Aleksey Yakovlev (whose grandfather Savva Yakovlev had bought them from Demidov, Vorontsov and Yaguzhinskii; he was ennobled in 1762). From 1867 onward, Nadezhda took out certificates of the First Guild of the St Petersburg merchantry. In fact, she had been managing the family business since 1849, the year of her father's death. After becoming a widow at the age of thirty-seven, she devoted all her life to entrepreneurship: according to the memoirs of her relatives and acquaintances, she controlled the plants in the most meticulous way and overlooked no detail however insignificant it might be.[52] Nadezhda Stenbok-Fermor was Russia's second biggest producer of pig iron after the Demidovs (in 1867, her enterprises produced 12,333 tons of pig iron, which amounted to 4.9 per cent of Russia's total output), and iron (in 1867, they produced 14,109 tons of iron, which amounted to 7.1 per cent of Russia's total output). She also owned a number of gold fields (in 1866, they employed 1,577 workers and produced 560 kg of gold, which accounted for 31 per cent of the total amount of gold extracted at the privately-owned gold fields of the Urals, or for 7.1 per cent of Russia's total output) and copper smelting works (in 1867, they smelted out 512 tons of copper, which amounted to 11.5 per cent of Russia's total output).[53] In 1854, she bought from her brother-in-law (according to rumours, he was enmeshed by financial difficulties) the *Passazh* (arcade) on the Nevskii Prospekt – one of the most expensive commercial structure of St Petersburg (in 1874, the municipality valuated it at 528,855 roubles; in 1899 – at 612,899 roubles). It is noteworthy that after the death of the Countess, the Arcade, having been bequeathed to eleven persons selected from among her children and grandchildren, was once again recorded as being in 'purely female' ownership – now it belonged to the testatrix's daughter, Princess Nadezhda

Bariatinskaia, and three granddaughters – Anna and Irina Bariatinsky, and Nadezhda Bezobrazova (who had bought out the rest of the stakes from their relatives).[54] By the time of her death in 1897, Nadezhda Stenbok-Fermor had amassed one of the biggest personal fortunes in Russian history, evaluated at almost 41 million roubles.[55]

The remaining eleven St Petersburg female merchants of the First Guild engaged in trade. The specificity of entrepreneurship in a port city was reflected in the involvement of several businesswomen in maritime trade. (Their colleague, the above-mentioned Dorothea Baird, owned, among other things, a shipping company which operated on the sea-routes between St. Petersburg and Kronstadt, Revel, Riga and a number of ports of Great Britain.) Another shipping company operating on the 26km route between St Petersburg and Kronstadt belonged to the thirty-seven-year-old Aleksandra Beliaeva, the widow of a captain who had previously owned this business. One female merchant of the First Guild, Aleksandra Trikha, was engaged in 'wholesale trade at the port'.

In Moscow, of the thirty-four female merchants of the First Guild, seventeen were owners of industrial enterprises (eleven people owned textile enterprises; one owned a brick works; one person owned a copper and bronze works; one owned a tannery; one owned a distillery; one owned a wax chandlery; and one owned a stearine, chemical and soap works). Of the seventeen persons engaged solely in trade, seven traded in textiles (woollen fabrics, cottons, silks, brocade and thread), six traded in foodstuffs (of them, two traded in wine; two in tea and sugar; one in butter, and one in confectionery products), one kept a banking office (the French woman Anne Catoire), one traded in gold laces (Anna Bolotnova), one was engaged in money changing (Praskov'ia Bulochkina), and one traded in 'miscellaneous goods' (Anna Zernova).

By their marital status, of the thirty-four Moscow female merchants of the First Guild, thirty-one were widows, two were married, and one was a spinster. Of the thirty-one widows, only three were childless; they personally managed their businesses without any participation of their relatives. The remaining twenty-eight widows had one to six sons each. (For comparison: of the fifteen St. Petersburg female merchants of the First Guild, eleven were widows, two were married, and two were spinsters. Eleven persons had adult sons).

Let us consider the case of one businesswoman who was the mother of a large family. Elizaveta Bykovskaia (1791–1870), a descendant of the Alekseev family, owners of Russia's biggest gold-cloth factory, had six sons, born by her at the age of twenty, twenty-two, twenty-four, twenty-five, twenty-seven and twenty-eight. Elizaveta was widowed at the age of forty-two (her husband was sixteen years her senior; he died at the age of 58). The first years of her widowhood were difficult – in 1838 Elizaveta was a merchant of the lowest, Third, Guild. Together with her eldest son Semen, then aged twenty-seven, she traded in cotton yarn from her own shop in Kitai-Gorod. By the mid-1840s, when the sons were already advanced in age, she set up a firm, 'Elizaveta Bykovskaia & Sons', which traded in tea, sugar, cotton and cotton yarn – a clear indication that the family business had become stable and was expanding. In the late 1840s, Elizaveta returned to the First Guild. In 1852, after the death of her eldest son Semen, Elizaveta continued to transact business together with her five younger sons – Vladimir, Nikolai, Ivan, Petr and Aleksey. All the family members were recorded as 'being attached to their mother' (who would almost attain the age of eighty) and not having capital of their own. The firm had two major offices: one in Moscow (in the Gostinyi Dvor of Kitai-Gorod), and one in Orenburg (for trade operations in Siberia and Asia). Some additional income was generated by renting out the six shops owned by the family in Kitai-Gorod (in the Mirrors' Row, the main centre of the cotton trade in Moscow). After Elizaveta's death, the firm headed by her eldest surviving son, Vladimir, did not last for long. The Bykovskii brothers abandoned commerce and became rentiers, drawing income by renting-out their real estate (two houses and six shops in Kitai-Gorod).[56] During thirty-seven years at the helm of the family business, Elizaveta Bykovskaia managed to considerably diversify her trade. In addition to cotton yarn, she began to trade in tea, sugar and raw cottons, and invested the acquired income in purchasing real estate. As a result, she consolidated her position in the First Guild. The family relations during Elizaveta's reign epitomized the complete subordination of the sons to their mother for the sake of maximally coordinating the management of all business matters. Such a situation became possible, first of all, because the family's entire property belonged to the mother, and her children were, therefore, deprived of any freedom of action outside of the family firm. [57]

Women in Industry and Trade

The distribution of businesswomen by type of activities (industry, trade, other spheres – banking, renting-out of premises) has revealed a number of differences relative, first of all, to a more active participation of Moscow female entrepreneurs in industrial production. The summarized data are presented in Figure 3.3.

Let us consider the Moscow group of proprietresses of industrial enterprises (1869 – eighty-three persons). By their marital status, sixty-four businesswomen were widows, thirteen were married, and six were spinsters. The age-relating data are tabulated in Table 3.5, which demonstrates that the majority of proprietresses were in the age group 41–60 (63 per cent). For both guilds, the average age of female merchants was 51.5 years. As regards the number of children per businesswoman, the female merchants of the First Guild had, on average, 2.4 adult sons per family (N-14), and those of the Second Guild – 2.7 adult sons per

Figure 3.3. The distribution of St Petersburg and Moscow businesswomen by business specialization (1869)

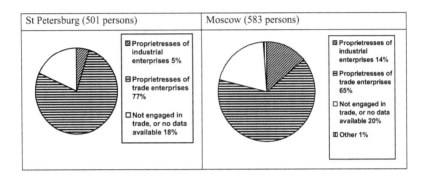

family (N-48). Three persons from the First Guild and eighteen persons from the Second Guild were sonless (26.5 per cent for both guilds).[58]

Table 3.5. The age of proprietresses of Moscow enterprises (1869)

	21–30	31–40	41–50	51–60	61–70	Over 70	Average age
1st Guild (N-17)	1	1	5	7	2	1	52.4
2nd Guild (N-66)	3	10	18	22	9	4	50.7
For 1st and 2nd Guilds	4	11	23	29	11	5	51.5
For both guilds, in per cent	5 per cent	13 per cent	28 per cent	35 per cent	13 per cent	6 per cent	100 per cent

The above data make it possible to depict a portrait of an average factory propri-etress – she was a widow aged forty-one to sixty, who lived in her own house (83 per cent were house owners), had adult sons (73.5 per cent) and combined the production of goods with trading in them from her own shop (in the First Guild – fourteen persons out of seventeen; for the Second Guild no data are available). This means that in the majority of cases the reason for the management of a fam-ily firm having been transferred to a woman was the death of her husband or his inability (due to old age) to manage the firm. As Russian legislation vested them with the full rights of disposal of property, businesswomen usually refrained from ceding the right of control and management to their sons, and preferred to remain at the top of the family hierarchy.

Although incomplete, the existing data on the share of women in the total industrial production of Moscow are representative enough. We have managed to find data for fourteen enterprises (out of seventeen) of the First Guild, and for seventeen enterprises (out of sixty-six) for the Second Guild. (The absence of data for the remaining forty-nine enterprises means that the value of their annual output was under 25,000 roubles; therefore the actual share of women must have been higher than the resulting figures presented by us.) The above thirty-one enterprises accounted for 11.8 per cent of total output (5.5 million roubles out of 46.7 million) and employed 36 foremen and 5,143 workers (8.7 per cent of the total labour force).[59]

Statistics indicate that labour productivity at female-owned enterprises was greater than the average. As is known, the achievements in this sphere directly depended on the level of mechanization in the context of the industrial revolution. Let us consider this crucial issue in more detail.

Steam engines were installed at 10 out of the 31 female-owned enterprises (for which data are available). All ten were textile mills – eight woollen, one cloth-finishing and one kerchief-and-cotton printing. The combined motive power of the steam engines installed at the female-owned enterprises amounted to 291 hp. Let us compare these data with those on the mechanization of Moscow enterprises as a whole. Steam engines were installed at 183 factories out of 516 (35.5 per cent); the average per-enterprise production of motive power amounted to 13 horsepower. Judging by statistics, mechanization was at its highest in the textile industry, where it was spearheaded by forty-eight wool mills whose steam engines produced 1,026 horsepower, or 22 horsepower per enterprise. On average, a female-owned textile mill possessed motive power amounting to 29 horsepower, and that in the wool industry – to 31 horsepower. The fact that the female-owned enterprises were better equipped with steam engines meant that the proprietresses of big and profitable businesses were more inclined to modernize their machinery than their male colleagues.

It was not infrequent that in the pursuit of modernization, businesswomen had to solve not only the problems of financing and reorganizing the production, but also had to overcome the resistance of their neighbours. Take, for example, the case of Afim'ia Belova.

The widowed female merchant of the First Guild Afim'ia Belova owned a wool-weaving mill, founded in 1814. In 1868, the family of Afim'ia, then aged seventy, was recorded to consist of her two sons, the forty-one-year-old Iakov and Vasilii, aged forty. The enterprise employed 371 workers (86 per cent of whom were male). The products were sold from her own shop in Kitai-Gorod and at the Niznii Novgorod Fair. In 1865, Belova took the decision to install a 15-horsepower steam engine and two steam boilers, as well as a whistle for signalling the beginning and the end of work. This led to a conflict with her neighbours, who lodged, in November 1865, a collective complaint, addressing it to the local police authorities and to the Office of the Moscow Governor-

General. They protested against the intended innovations mainly for the following three reasons: firstly, 'the whistle could frighten horses, thus resulting in accidents in front of our houses' (the houses of Belova and her neighbours were on the busy Semenovskaia Street, which was used as an access to a railway station); secondly, 'the loudness of the machines and the whistle could frighten young children in their sleep'; and thirdly, the steam engine could cause fires. In conclusion, the complaint, signed by the merchants Orlov, Zhdanov and Beliakov, the peasant Glazkov and the *meshchanka* Golysheva, reads: 'as to the installation of a machine with a whistle by the female merchant Belova, we have no intention of expressing our consent thereunto'. After receiving the complaint of the neighbours, the local police officer inspected the factory and reported to his superiors that the three-storeyed factory building was situated in the middle of Belova's estate (at a distance of 94 metres from Semenovskaia Street and 74 metres from the merchant Orlov's estate), that the closest neighbours, the Zabrodins and the Krasikovs, whose estates were distanced from the factory by 11 and 32 metres respectively, had not signed the petition, and that the steam engine would be installed in a brick annex which had been built for this purpose close to the factory building and, therefore, there would be no danger of fire. Moreover, the whistles and bells for signalling the beginning and the end of a workday, which had already been installed at many Moscow factories, did not frighten horses and certainly could not disturb the neighbours. After having been inspected by the police, the factory was visited and examined by engineer Drozzhin, one of the members of the City Architectural Inspectorate. He established that no regulations had been violated in the course of installing the steam engine and fifty mechanical looms at Belova's factory, and made an official statement to this effect. In December 1865, Afim'ia Belova received a certificate giving her the right to install the new equipment.[60]

This case testifies that the Moscow authorities introduced rigid regulations with regard to the mechanization of enterprises, fire safety, the increase and decrease in the number of workers, waste disposal (dumping of waste into rivers was prohibited, and it was prescribed that all waste should be treated), and the use of firewood (timber felling was declared illegal within the distance of 200 kilometres from Moscow, it was recommended that peat should be used as fuel).[61] The female merchant Belova had complied with all these requirements.

In the remaining pages of this chapter, I want to look at the sphere of commerce, where the majority of businesswomen were engaged, including 386 persons (or 77 per cent of all female entrepreneurs) in St Petersburg and 381 persons (or 65 per cent of their total number) in Moscow. The detailed data on specialization in commerce are presented in Table 3.6.

A comparison of figures for both capital cities reveals their close coincidence only in some segments of commerce, such as trading in foodstuffs and tobacco

Table 3.6. The specialization of the proprietresses of commercial enterprises in St Petersburg and Moscow, belonging to the First and the Second Guilds (1869)

Type of commerce	Specialization of commercial enterprises of St. Petersburg (number of persons)	As percentage of total number of commercial enterprises	Specialization of proprietresses of commercial enterprises of Moscow (number of persons)	As percentage of total number of commercial enterprises
Foodstuffs and tobacco	95	24.6	96	25.2
Service business (restaurants, inns, bathhouses, carriage of passengers)	66	17.1	58	15.2
Clothes, footwear, headgear	62	16.1	28	7.3
Tailor's, furrier's, leather-dresser's and shoe-maker's workshops	–	–	4	1.05
Textiles	20	5.2	58	15.2
Money-changing and money-lending	20	5.2	5	1.3
Transport (one shipping company – carriage of passengers and cargo)	–	–	1	0.3
Metals and metal items	14	3.6	17	4.5
Chemicals and cosmetics	13	3.4	8	2.1
Construction materials	12	3.1	22	5.8
Haberdashery	11	2.8	18	4.7
Tableware	8	2.1	4	1.05
Horse harnesses, equipages, wheels	5	1.3	6	1.6
Building contracts	6	1.6	5	1.3
Other	58	15.0	51	13.4
TOTAL NUMBER of proprietresses of commercial enterprises	**386**	**100 per cent**	**381**	**100 per cent**
No data, or trade is not made	90		113	
Renting-out of business and industrial premises			5	
Banking (one bank)			1	
Total	**476**		**500**	

(24–5 per cent) and the service business (15–17 per cent). In St Petersburg, women were amply represented among the owners of catering facilities – there were forty-two proprietresses of restaurants, coffee houses, confectionaries, eating-houses and other businesses of this kind. In Moscow, only thirty-two women specialized in the provision of such services. However, the women of Moscow were more active as innkeepers – nineteen persons as opposed to thirteen in St Petersburg.

One important question will inevitably arise: did there exist any feminized segments in commerce? The answer – not very precise but sufficiently representative – can be obtained by comparing the data on the structure of trade carried on in St Petersburg in 1869 with the 1863 generalized data on trade in St Petersburg. In 1863, St Petersburg had 7,041 commercial enterprises, most of which were selling food and tobacco (40.8 per cent) or services (restaurants, inns, bathhouses, carriage of passengers) (33.5 per cent). Despite the heavy presence of women in these segments of commerce, the percentage of male owners was still bigger. However, the following segments may be conditionally classed as feminized: trading in clothes and footwear (the percentage of female-owned shops selling these goods in the total number of shops – 6.2 per cent; their share in the total number of shops which belonged to women – 16.1 per cent); trading in textiles (1.6 per cent and 2.1 per cent); trading in metals (0.9 per cent and 3.6 per cent), trading in construction materials (1.5 per cent and 3.1 per cent); and money changing (0.3 per cent and 5.2 per cent).[62]

The differences in the structure of consumption in St Petersburg and Moscow are detectable in the clothes-and-footwear segment. In St Petersburg, trading in readymade clothes was well-developed (sixty-two enterprises), while only 20 shops sold textiles. In Moscow, the situation was just the opposite – readymade clothes and footwear were sold by twenty-eight enterprises, while fifty-eight enterprises traded in textiles; also, there were 4 workshops producing clothes and footwear (apart from tailors and shoemakers working privately). Although Moscow had twenty-two milliner's shops promoting the latest 'European fashion', most of the clothes and footwear worn by its residents continued to be home-made, and the transition to mass consumption in this city was much slower than in St. Petersburg with its Europeanized life-style. Typical of St Petersburg, the capital of the Empire, was a special kind of sartorial services – the tailoring of uniforms for government officials and military officers, the so-called 'manufacturing of officers' effects'; the city had 8 specialized female-owned shops for selling them.

When assessing the trade of St Petersburg and Moscow, one can come to the conclusion that European experience in trade was advanced among businesswomen, first of all, by the example of shops in the luxurious-goods segment of commerce, or by those gravitating towards it. In St. Petersburg, 75 per cent of the twenty-eight female retailers who kept fashion shops selling readymade clothes imported from Europe were foreigners (thirteen were French, five were Germans, one was Belgian, one was English and one was Italian), and only seven proprietresses were Russian. Foreign proprietresses were highly appreciated for their 'first-hand knowledge of the current trends in fashion'. In Moscow, of the twenty-two proprietresses of fashion shops, three were French, three were Germans and one was Belgian. Nearly all of the female foreigners trading in clothes and footwear retained the citizenship of their countries of birth, because the purpose of their coming to Russia was to quickly earn a capital which would enable the oldest of them to spend their retirement years in comfort and their younger counterparts – to set up businesses in their native countries.

For example, in the period between 1867 and 1876, one of the foreigners who traded in 'fashionable goods' in Moscow was Luise Becker, 'a citizen of Hamburg', whose shop was situated on Tverskaia Street, always crowded with potential buyers, all of them 'with money'.[63] Luise had come to Moscow together with her husband, Alexander-Friedrich, a merchant of the Third Guild, who adopted Russian citizenship.[64] After his death in 1868, the childless Luise, then aged fifty-four, continued to earn money in Moscow, planning to return to Germany and spend the rest of her life there without worries, comfortably well-off due to her savings. The life-story of Sophia-Ernestina Miller was different. In 1848, she came to Moscow from Mecklenburg-Schwerin at the age of twenty-nine, and traded in 'ladies' clothes' from a shop on Lubianka, in the central district of Moscow. As Sophie-Ernestina was single, her major aim was accumulation of capital.[65]

Unsurprisingly, St Petersburg businesswomen of Italian origin (who retained Italian citizenship) were especially active in the sphere of public catering. Thus, Elena Mardonini kept a confectionary, and Giakomina Canni – a 'café-restaurant'. The third Italian, Amalia Piazzo, owned a 'café-restaurant' in the 'Summer Garden' (*Letnii Sad*), the favourite promenade of the St. Petersburg aristocracy.

One of the strategies for survival in business adopted by Russian businesswomen was the creation of a chain of shops. If the first shop was a success, its proprietress, on having acquired experience in trade, would establish a second one, and so on. In St Petersburg, between 20 and 30 per cent of businesswomen operating in the commercial sphere had two or more shops. For example, seven years after setting up her business, Tatiana Ershova had three 'egg' shops (she managed the enterprise together with her son, Dmitrii). Liubov' Ershova owned three butcher's shops. Anna Glushkova had four greengroceries and wine shops. Anis'ia Danilova kept an eating-house and three 'wine cellars' (the eating house had been inherited by Anis'ia after her husband, while the cellars were set up on her own initiative in the course of her twenty-seven-year-long independent entrepreneurship; it is noteworthy that Anis'ia's income was sufficient for her to buy a brick house as a residence for herself and her two sons). Taisiia Zvezdina had three shops selling fur coats. But the absolute champion among them all was Matrena Il'ina who kept seven retail shops in the centre of the city, including one on the Nevskii Prospekt. The shops were inherited by her after her husband in 1865.[66] In 1869, forty-seven-year-old Matrena had two sons, aged twenty-four and twenty-two.

One further discrepancy between Moscow and St Petersburg was the social composition of the group. In Moscow, representatives of merchant dynasties were predominant, while in 'bureaucratic' St Petersburg, especially in the 1860s, 8 to 15 per cent businesswomen did not have merchant background. They were married women, as a rule, the wives of middle-ranking officers and officials, who set up businesses in order to obtain supplemental income to support their families and to serve their personal needs. For example, in 1869, the cohort of St Petersburg female merchants of the Second Guild included the wife of a second-captain Ksenia Agafonova, who kept a crockery shop; the wife of a sub-lieutenant Julia Leibrok, who kept a printing house, the wife of a Court Councillor Agrippina Andreanova and the wife of a Collegiate Secretary Sofia Gavrilenko, both of whom were moneylenders.

This group of St Petersburg businesswomen also included two representatives of the elite. Thirty-three-year-old Maria Korff, who had been taking out merchant certificates since the age of twenty-five, owned a spirit depot for wholesale trade. Forty-eight-year-old Pelageia Kovan'ko (1821–94), the wife of a major general, had been taking out merchant certificates since the age of forty-four. In partnership with the merchant Vargunin, Pelageia owned a chemical factory in the vicinity of St Petersburg; she was also the sole proprietor of a glassworks, established in the 1820s in Rozal'vino (the estate in St. Petersburg province inherited by Pelageia's husband after his parents). Pelageia was married to Aleksey Kovan'ko (1808–70), a prominent mining engineer and a member of the Mining Academic Council of the Ministry of Finance, who was eventually promoted to the rank of major general in the mining branch. Pelageia's male ancestors were all officers, including her father, Colonel Mikhail Basov.[67]

One of the cases is rather comical: the widow of a colonel, Sofia Okhotnikova, aged thirty-eight at the time of her husband's death, invested her money in establishing so-called 'family bathhouses' – one in her own house, and another on rented premises. The bathhouses were supervised by hired managers, while Sofia moved to Paris and lived there quite comfortably on income from her business (from 1866 until at least 1869).

In Moscow, the proportion of businesswomen of non-merchant descent was smaller, amounting to between 5 and 7 per cent. The most formidable representatives of this group were Anna Dislen, the wife of the censor of the Moscow Post Office, Anton Dislen, and the proprietress of a 'textiles-finishing enterprise' (in

1868, it employed fifty-two workers); Franziska Sviderskaia, the wife of a 'family teacher' and the owner of a shop selling tea and colonial goods; Maria Ermakova, the wife of an actor of the Emperor's St. Petersburg Theatres and the keeper of a readymade clothes shop.[68] By age, these four businesswomen belonged to the active, middle-age group; they were fifty, forty, thirty, and forty-two-years-old respectively.

The above cases testify to the existence of at least two trends. Firstly, entrepreneurs were recruited not only from the merchant and peasant strata, which happened during the whole first half of the nineteenth century, but also from the officialdom and, to a certain degree, from the service nobility (and not from the landed nobility as in the first half of the nineteenth century). Secondly, these changes bear witness to a gradual change in the prestigiousness of entrepreneurship in the eyes of society. In theatre plays and in the press the merchantry was subject to ridicule, but at the same time, more and more frequently, persons from 'educated society' were engaged in business in order to obtain supplemental (and sometimes their only) means of living. The formation, in the 1850s and 1860s, of a more complex social and occupational structure of the businesswomen group, bore witness to the development of market relations, which was accompanied by the diffusion of the entrepreneur class, including women.

Conclusion

The 1850s and 60s are characterized in historiography as the critical decades of Russian history. Economically, it was a period of structural change manifested, first of all, by the mass mechanization of big industrial enterprises and by the introduction of credit relations into the system mutual settlements between suppliers of raw materials, producers of finished goods, small retailers and consumers. Politically, those years was the time of rapid transformation, with the defeat in the Crimean War of 1853–6 giving strong impetus to the onset of the so-called Era of Great Reforms marked by the Emancipation of the Serfs in 1861, the introduction of the Self-Government such as the *Zemstvos* in rural areas in 1864, and of the Municipal urban administration in 1870.

The 1850s and 60s saw an upsurge in the business activity of women. At that time, the number of businesses owned by women entrepreneurs reached its historic high and was to remain at this level until the early 1890s (for example, ninety-nine out of the total number of 839 industrial enterprises existing in Moscow in 1853 were owned by women). However, many enterprises and firms were far from stable. In this period, businesses (including those headed by women) were becoming visibly dependent on the institutionalization of the system of monetary payments. Many an entrepreneur did not have enough capital when starting a business, and therefore the system of issuance of goods on six to twelve months' credit became widespread in Russia. This system involved a considerable risk, which is shown in this chapter on the example of the case of Natal'ia Bakhrushina, the proprietress of a tannery, and that of the vodka producer Maria de Chario.

When reconstructing family histories, we come across various models of family-business stabilization. As in the 1830s and 40s, the most widespread and stable construction of a family firm was the partnership between a mother and her adult sons which was held together by joint family capital and production, and by keeping a joint household. Some cases, presented in the chapter, clearly demonstrate that proprietresses of factories, contrary to the imagined gender stereotype, based on the 'separate spheres', were actually experienced managers, exercising rigid day-to-day control over their enterprises and efficient decision-making, either independently or in partnership with their adult sons.

Due to the lack of sources characterizing the all-Russian economic situation, female entrepreneurship in the period under study is illustrated by the data related to the two capital cities – St Petersburg and Moscow (with the attached provinces), whose role in industrial production was very important – by 1864, the share of those two provinces in the total volume of production had risen to 45.2 per cent. The participation of businesswomen in the industry of Moscow (1853) and St Petersburg (1862) had different patterns. In Moscow, female-owned enterprises accounted for 9.7 per cent of the volume of production and accumulated 10.6 per cent of the labour force; the biggest of such enterprises employed up to 1,000 workers. In St Petersburg, the role played by businesswomen in industry was more modest: their enterprises accounted for 3.2 per cent of the value of annual industrial output, and employed 3 per cent of the labour force. This difference was due to the existence in Moscow of a merchant core, which comprised several scores of merchant dynasties spanning three or four generations and successfully operating primarily in the textile and leather industries. In St Petersburg, women owned, as a rule, small and medium-sized businesses, often short-lived, this was indicative of the absence of protective mechanisms in the form of family capital and those women's involvement in the public networks. That the positions of Moscow factory proprietresses were strong is proved by the fact of their modernizing the equipment of the enterprises they owned: in this initial period of the industrial revolution in Russia, the number of those who could afford the price of a steam engine was limited to the owners of large enterprises, and indeed only they had the opportunity to acknowledge the necessity of technological innovations. The sharp rise in the efficiency of production further increased the gap between the group of leaders and the rest of the enterprises, where manual machinery was still being used.

The use of the merchant 'Reference Books' on Moscow and St Petersburg for the year 1869 as a source of historical data has enabled us to analyse the aggregate prosopographic data and economic parameters pertaining to 1,084 persons. The group of St Petersburg businesswomen (N – 501, or 13 per cent of all city merchants) was multiethnic (81 per cent were Russians, the rest were foreigners); the average age of its members was 47.7 years. The group was more active in trade (77-per cent involvement) than in industry (5-per cent involvement). 91 per cent of Moscow businesswomen (N – 583, or 11.6 per cent of all city merchants) were Russians; their average age was 54.4 years; 65 per cent of them were engaged in trade, and 14 per cent – in industry. As regards the specialization of trade, the situation in St. Petersburg and Moscow was similar in the major segments of retailing - a quarter of female shopkeepers were engaged in selling foodstuffs and tobacco, while 15 to 17 per cent operated in the service business (inns, restaurants, bathhouses, carriage of passengers). It is apparent that the organizational principles and the style of trade practiced in St. Petersburg were strongly influenced by the local foreign business community, which manifested itself in the St Petersburg customers' preference for buying readymade clothes rather than fabrics for subsequent custom tailoring (while the reverse was typical of Moscow).

In those decades, the creation of a favourable legal climate was conducive to the integration of women into the trading community. Business now attracted not only female merchants, who were entitled by the 1857 Law to carry on trade independently of their husbands, but also women outside the merchantry, including those related to the military and the officialdom strata.

The 1850s and 60s saw the rise of such prominent figures in female entrepreneurship as the factory proprietresses Princess Nadezhda Stenbok-Fermor, the noblewoman Dorothea Baird and the female merchant Agraphena Rasteriaeva in St. Petersburg, and the female merchants Natal'ia Bakhrushina and Natal'ia Nosova in Moscow. As a rule, the success of their businesses depended, first of all, on the authoritarian style of management practised by the proprietress, who occupied the top position in the family hierarchy, and also on her inclusion into public networks.

4 FEMALE ENTREPRENEURSHIP IN THE 1870s: FAMILY LEVERS IN BUSINESS REGULATION

The early 1870s signified a crucial change in the position of women in Russian society and on the labour market. Russia adopted a law on the admission of women to service at public and government institutions.[1] 'The Subjection of Women', a study written by British economist and philosopher John Stuart Mill, a strong advocate of women's rights, was translated into Russian and became immensely popular in society.[2]

Over that decade, the level of women's participation in entrepreneurship remained unchanged (in 1879, by comparison with 1869): women accounted for 10.5 per cent of guild merchants in Moscow (or 604 persons) and for 11.1 per cent in St Petersburg (or 545 persons).[3] In 1879, the number of women owing industrial enterprises amounted to more than 1,000, but their relative share was small (4 per cent).

This chapter will characterize industrial development in the 1870s, present relevant statistics on women's participation in industry and demonstrate how legal practice was becoming more versatile, with new precedents of commercial property (commercial and industrial enterprises) passing, within a family, into the hands of women. Frequently, conjugal ties served as an addition to business cooperation, as exemplified by the not so rare event of a husband taking wife's family name for the purpose of preserving the firm's brand and clients.

1. The Epoch of the 1870s: the Economic Situation as Illustrated by Demographic and Industrial Statistics

Economically, the 1870s were far from stable. In the mid-1870s Russia experienced a severe economic crisis, followed by a wave of bankruptcies among small and medium enterprises. Scores of firms went broke – in 1874–6, the bankruptcy cases of 237 firms were considered by the Moscow Commercial Court alone.[4] Economists agree that the major causes of the expansion and subsequent contraction of the internal market were the 1873 economic crisis, two years of bad harvest (1872 and 1875), and the rapid development of the railway network (according to P. Gatrell, 'the first major railway building boom in Russia lasted from 1868 to 1878; during that time the total track increased from 6,800 to 22,400km').[5]

The crisis was followed by the 1878–9 economic recovery. This revival was eloquently described by the well-known economist of that time, Vladimir Bezobrazov, as

> continually and rapidly growing, turning into febrile speculative agitation which caused an extraordinary intensification of production at all the old enterprises, as well as the opening of new ventures in almost every branch of the manufacturing industry ... In 1878, there was also an extraordinary rise in the import of all raw and semi-processed materials for our factories and plants (cotton, cotton yarn, silk, wool, dyed wool, pig metal, dyes, various chemical substances, etc.), despite a considerable rise in the customs tariff when it was converted into gold from 1 January 1877.[6]

Russia's population (less Poland and Finland) amounted to 77.1 million.[7] The dynamic of industrial development was characterized by the increase in the number of enterprises, between 1868 and 1879, from 18,840 to 26,067, and by the growth of the workforce from 575,000 to 711,097.[8] It should be noted that the number of workers had been growing before 1873, then the growth halted in 1874–6, resumed in 1877 and reached its peak in 1882.[9] In 1879, the volume of industrial production amounted to 1,103 million roubles (or £110.3 million).[10]

According to statistician Dmitrii Timiriazev, who worked at the Russian Ministry of Finance, the period between 1867 and 1879 saw a sharp rise in the volume of production, in the number of workers and in labour productivity in every branch of industry. For example, in the textile industry annual production grew twofold, the number of workers 1.3 times, and labour efficiency 1.35 times; in the paper industry 2, 1.4 and 1.6 times respectively; in the chemical industry 1.4, 1.2 and 1.4 times respectively; in the leather industry 2.6, 1.6 and 1.7 times respectively; and in machine-building industry 4.8, 3.1 and 1.6 times respectively.

Simultaneously, a number of industries were being restructured – in the context of mechanization, big enterprises were becoming ever bigger, while small enterprises were coming to ruin and were forced to drop out. Thus, although the general amount of enterprises in the textile industry rose 1.2 times (from 2,000 to 2,487), in the cotton-weaving sector this amount declined from 582 to 411, and in the linen sector – from 97 to 69. The number of chemical enterprises dropped from 339 to 182, and that of lard chandleries and soap works – from 855 to 816. [11]

By 1879, in the structure of Russian industry, the textile branch accounted for 31.6 per cent of annual production in money terms and for 47.9 per cent of the workforce. It was followed by the food industry (which accounted for no less than 20.1 per cent of annual production and for no less than 15.4 per cent of the workforce), the machine-building and metalworking industries (which accounted for 9.8 per cent of annual production and for 12.7 per cent of the workforce), and by the leather industry accounting for 4.7 per cent of annual production and for 7.8 per cent of the workforce. As in the previous decades, the clear leaders in terms of industrial production were Moscow Province (1879 – 17.7 per cent of the total volume of production, 23 per cent of the total workforce) and St Petersburg Province (15.2 per cent and 11.8 per cent respectively).[12]

The increase in the volume of production was caused, first of all, by technological modernization. In the period between 1866 and 1879, the share of cotton fabrics produced by power looms rose from 37 per cent to 58.4 per cent.[13] This could be explained by the fact that, starting from 1861 onwards (after the catastrophic defeat suffered by Russia in the Crimean War), the owners of machine-building plants were exempted from import duties on pig iron, iron and machinery (this exemption was later cancelled by the 1880 customs tariff). The favourable import regime had two important consequences. Firstly, the domestic machine-building industry started to actively develop (between 1856 and 1879, the number of enterprises rose from 24 to 247, and the volume of production – from 2.8 to 72.9 million roubles; in the second half of the 1870s, the value of locally produced goods became almost equal to that of imports).[14] British historian S. Thompstone characterizes the causes of the expansion of machinery imported from the UK as follows:

> The technological breakthrough in Britain's cotton textile sector in the late eighteenth century put that industry in a pre-eminent international position. Based for the most part in Lancashire, the textile machinery industry it spawned became from the 1830s the source of technological transfer to the textile industries of North America, Western Europe, the Far East, and from the 1840s to the cotton textile sector in Russia.[15]

In 1875, of 5,095 steam engines existing in Russian industry, 34 per cent (28 per cent of the total horsepower) was manufactured in Russia, 23 per cent (37 per cent of the total horsepower) – in the UK, and 15 per cent and 11 per cent (by 11 per cent of the total horsepower each) – in Germany and Belgium respectively. Of 1870 locomobiles, 85 per cent (84 per cent of the total horsepower) was manufactured in the UK.[16]

Russian experts of the last third of the nineteenth century considered the relatively low productivity of Russian factory workers (by comparison with Western Europe) to be a major obstacle to economic growth. Statistician Anton Radzig wrote:

In European Russia, in the year 1877, we had 2,850 thousand spindles and 50,149 mechanical looms. In that year, the number of workers engaged in spinning and weaving was 143,244; thus, there were 18 spindles and 0.35 loom per worker. ... As of the year 1878, in Great Britain, 482,903 were employed in the cotton industry on the whole, and there were ... 91.5 spindles and 1.0 mechanical loom per worker.[17]

Even in the leading 'textile' provinces of Russia – Moscow, St Petersburg, Vladimir and Tula (where 99 per cent of the mechanical equipment installed at Russian weaving and spinning mills was concentrated), modernization of equipment was carried out only at the biggest enterprises. Bearing in mind the gigantic size of the territory of Russia, this means that the intensive mechanization of enterprises began in the most economically advanced provinces, where key enterprises had already existed for decades.

An analysis of the above figures makes it possible to conclude that the considerable rise in the level of mechanization of big and medium enterprises in the 1870s bore witness to Russia's entry into the intensive phase of the industrial revolution.

This chapter will focus on the economic behaviour of female entrepreneurs under such conditions, and it will be investigated in which sectors of industry they were most confident of success, what the ethnic and estate characteristics of female industrialists were, and how these characteristics correlated with the regional distribution of female-owned enterprises.

2. Female Entrepreneurs in Russian Industry in the 1870s

In the 1870s, the situation regarding female industrial entrepreneurship was both complicated and dualistic. On the one hand, the beginning of the mass mechanization of industrial enterprises required considerable investments in equipment, unaffordable for businesswomen without spare capital. Those ladies had to depart from business. For example, in Moscow, the number of female-owned industrial enterprises dropped from 79 in 1871 to 56 in 1879. On the other hand, comprehensive sources indicate that, starting from the 1870s, the range of industrial activity of women entrepreneurs became very wide.

The following estimates concerning the participation of female entrepreneurs in industrial production are based on the data presented in '*Ukazatel' fabrik i zavodov*' (The Guide to Factories and Plants), which contains statistics for the year 1879. The estimates indicate that 1,045 female-owned enterprises with 45,901 workers produced goods to the value of 43.7 million roubles, which accounted for 4 per cent of Russia's total industrial output. The generalized results are tabulated in Table 4.1.[18]

Table 4.1. Number of Enterprises Owned by Women, by Branch of Industrial Activity (Russian Empire, 1879)

The branches are placed in the Table in descending order of the share of female-owned enterprises in total volume of production

Industry	Number of female-owned enterprises (out of total number of 26,067)	Share of female-owned enterprises in total volume of production, in per cent / silver roubles	Share of female-owned enterprises, by number of workers, in per cent / persons
Textile industry	114 (out of 2,516)	5.7 per cent 20,031,355 out of 349,203,740	8.2 per cent 27,737 out of 336,500
Food production	551 (out of 12,922)	7 per cent 15,375,985 out of 221,050,000*	7.1 per cent 8,017 out of 113,374*
Processing of fat and wax	45 (out of 1,582)	5.3 per cent 1,881,500 out of 35,447,000	3.2 per cent 314 out of 9,754
Leather industry	68 (out of 4,153)	3.6 per cent 1,852,750 out of 51,750,000	3.2 per cent 883 out of 27,227
Earthenware and brick industry*	87 (out of 3,562)	7.1 per cent 1,387,410 out of 19,569,000	7.1 per cent 3,824 out of 53,905
Machine-building and metal-working	46 (out of 872)	1.2 per cent 1,314,700 out of 108,034,000	2.8 per cent 2,509 out of 90,508
Chemical industry	22 (out of 417)	4.6 per cent 482,300 out of 10,754,000	5.4 per cent 406 out of 7,533
Paper production	15 (out of 126)	3.6 per cent 459,850 out of 12,924,000	5.1 per cent 676 out of 13,216
Wood-working	36 (out of 1479)	2.6 per cent 443,800 out of 16,831,000	6.6 per cent 1,017 out of 15,338
Tobacco	9 (out of 247)	305,900 out of 31,590,000	160 out of 17,570
Carriage-making	3 (out of 147)	54,100 out of 1,804,800	72 out of 2,840
Musical instruments	1 (out of 21)	2,000 out of 20,000	13 out of 773
Mining plants of Urals***	30 (out of 375)	No data	No data
Matches	9 (out of 229)	83,600 out of 1,770,000	273 out of 5,130
Rubber production	0 (out of 3)	0 out of 5,869,000	0 out of 2,337
TOTAL	1045 (out of 26,067)	4 per cent 43,675,295 out of 1,102,949,000	6.5 per cent 45,901 out of 711,097
Female Owners	991		

* *Less the value of the goods produced by female-owned distilleries and breweries (no data being available). The value of the annual output of flour mills is based on the author's estimations.*

** *Production of lime, bricks, earthenware, glass and construction materials.*

*** *Copper smelteries, cast-iron foundries, ironworks, steel works and rail-rolling mills.*

Let us consider the participation of women in the textile and food industries, the biggest by the volume of production and the number of enterprises. In each of these industries, the average annual volume of production per female-owned enterprise was higher than across that industry on the whole; in the textile industry it amounted to 175,713 roubles, and in the food industry – to 27,906 roubles (in the textile and food industries on the whole – to 138,793 roubles and 17,106 roubles respectively), which testified to the higher than average resource of stability in the proprietresses' management.

The development of the textile industry was determined by big mills situated in the central and Volga provinces of the Russian Empire. This was reflected in the female segment as well: goods to the value of more than 1 million roubles were annually manufactured by three enterprises, to the value of 0.5 to 1 million roubles – by 10 enterprises, and to the value of 0.1 to 0.5 million roubles – by 21 enterprises. The 34 enterprises belonging to thirty-three businesswomen annually produced goods to the value of 14.9 million roubles (which accounted for 4.3 per cent of the total output of Russia's textile industry). All these enterprises were mechanized. The data on the biggest enterprises (those annually producing goods to the value of 0.5 million roubles and more) are tabulated in Table 4.2.

In contrast to the textile industry, where seven out of 13 biggest enterprises were set up by the proprietresses' ancestors in the period between 1780 and 1841 (thus having already been in existence for 28 to 99 years), the food industry, to which belonged nearly half of all industrial enterprises and 53 per cent of female-owned ones, represented in the main a network of relatively new medium-sized and small enterprises, 60 per cent of these being situated on the noble estates of their proprietresses, predominantly in the southern (Ukrainian) and western provinces. Of 551 female-owned enterprises, 254 were distilleries, 113 were flour mills, 55 were vodka distilleries, 33 were breweries, 18 were beet-sugar mills, and 3 were sugar refineries. The rest were engaged in production of cereals, butter, cheese, malt, starch, macaroni and confectionery.

The distilling industry was characterized by a strict regional differentiation by size of enterprise. 197 enterprises had from four to thirty workers, and thirty-six enterprises – from thirty-one to fifty workers. More than half of the smallest enterprises (with four to ten workers) were situated in Minsk, Mogilev, Grodno and Vitebsk Provinces (presently Belarus); they belonged to proprietresses of Polish descent. Of thirty-six medium-sized enterprises (with thirty-one to fifty workers), twenty-five were situated in the central black-earth provinces (Orel, Kursk and Voronezh), where the grain crops were abundant enough for the enterprises to have sufficient reserves of raw materials necessary for their stable functioning. The category of 'big ones' comprised twenty-one enterprises (with fifty-one or more workers), including six enterprises with more than 100 workers. Most of the big enterprises were situated in the Volga and central provinces

Table 4.2. Female-owned textile enterprises with annual output in excess of 0.5 million roubles (Russian Empire, 1879)

Enterprise, location	Proprietress	Annual production, thousands roubles	Number of workers	Year of foundation	Presence of steam engine and mechanical equipment
1. Cloth mill 'The Babkin Brothers' (Moscow Province)	Female merchant of First Guild Maria Matveeva (née Babkina)	3,400	1,808	1800	127-horsepower steam engines, 1 turbine, 320 power looms
2-3. Two flax-spinning mills of 'Osip Sen'kov's Heiresses' (Vladimir and Kostroma provinces)	Female merchants Evdokiia Lenivova and Glafra Dediukhina (née Sen'kov)	Both – 1,404	Both – 1,490	1862	2 steam engines (25 and 30 horsepower)
4. Cotton-weaving mill (Kostroma Province)	Female merchant of First Guild Anna Krasil'shchikova	978	584	1820	2 36-horsepower steam engines, 500 power looms
5. Cloth mill (Moscow Province)	Female merchant of First Guild Glafra Remizova	858	915	1841	148 power looms
6. Cotton-printing mill (Ivanovo-Voznesensk, Vladimir Province)	Female merchant Ekaterina Kuvaeva	798	275	1818	2 35-horsepower steam engines, 4 printing machines, 2 calenders
7. Cloth mill (Simbirsk Province)	Baroness Sophie Stroemfeld	750	600	No data found	16-horsepower engine, 24 power looms
8. Cotton-printing mill (Ivanovo-Voznesensk)	Female merchant Praskov'ia Vitova	700	170	1780	2 24-horsepower steam engines/ 3 printing machines, 2 calenders
Cloth mill (Moscow Province)	Noblewoman Anna Tsurikova	648	1,007	1840	2 50-horsepower steam engines, 3 40-horsepower turbines, 3 40-horsepower turbines, 200 power looms
9-11. Three cloth mills (Tambov Province)	Noblewoman Vera Ragoza	In total – 628	In total -1,541	No data found	2 70-horsepower steam engines, 290 power looms
12. Flax-scutching mill (Tver' Province)	Female merchant Evdokiia Nemilova	500	1,000	1848	No data found
Total		**10,664**	**9,390**		

of European Russia; they belonged to noblewomen from the ranks of the Russian titled aristocracy, such as Countess Anna Tolstoy (fifty-five workers, Nizhnii Novgorod Province), Princess Sophia Kurakina (fifty-nine workers, Saratov Province), Countess Liubov' Musina-Pushkina (sixty-eight workers, Orel Province), and a member of the Russian Imperial Family, Grand Duchess Ekaterina Mikhailovna (127 workers, Poltava Province). Only two of the proprietresses of big enterprises belonged to the merchant estate: Anna Maslovskaia (132 workers, Kursk Province) and Maria Vinogradova (183 workers, Perm' Province).

113 flour mills were owned by 105 proprietresses. By estate composition, the category of proprietresses of flour mill was the most diverse: fifty-eight noblewomen, twenty-seven female merchants, eleven female peasants, seven *meshchanki,* one Cossack woman and one wife of a priest. For the most part, the mills scattered all over the territory of Russia were catering to the needs of the local customer. On average, a female-owned enterprise employed seven workers (the average per-enterprise number of workers in this industry being four), and the average volume of production was 31,500 roubles. Most of the enterprises were situated in Perm' [19] and Podolia provinces (sixteen in each). Only seven proprietresses owned big enterprises with the annual volume of production in excess of 100,000 roubles. Six of them were female merchants – Dina Gurvich (Vitebsk Province), Malka Kaufman (Grodno), Anna Maslovskaia (Kursk Province), Natal'ia Gladkova (Odessa), Anna Morskova (Olonets Province), F. Voitekhova (Perm' Province), and one was a noblewoman – the wife of Major-General Falkenhagen (Yekaterinoslav).

In the food industry, the category of big enterprises included, first of all, the beet-sugar mills (N-21) on the estates of the aristocratic elite in the 'Little Russian' provinces of Kiev (where 48 per cent of Russia's sugar was produced), Podolia, Volhynia and Kharkov (presently Ukraine), and in Tambov and Voronezh provinces in the southern part of Central Russia, and also sugar refineries in the towns and cities. The average number of workers per female-owned beet-sugar mill was 283 (the biggest number of workers employed at such enterprise being 433 – at Countess Maria Kleinmichel's mill in Kursk Province). The proprietresses included Princess Eugenia of Oldenburg, Princess Sophia Golitsyna, Princess Ol'ga Dolgorukaia, Countess Maria Apraksina, Countess Maria Potocka, Countess Leonia Vitztum and Countess Sophia Shuvalova. Most of these proprietresses inherited their estates and enterprises after their parents.

In 1878, Her Highness Princess Eugenia of Oldenburg (née Duchess Eugenia of Leuchtenberg), maternal granddaughter of Emperor Nicholas I, then aged thirty-three, bought the estate of Ramon' (4,000 *desiatinas* or 10,800 acres) in Voronezh Province. The estate with a beet-sugar mill and a distillery was purchased by her for 500,000 roubles. Ten years earlier, at the time of her marriage, Eugenia had received 100,000 silver roubles as a wedding gift from her uncle,

Emperor Alexander II, with the interest on this sum being at her disposal. Eugenia's personal capital (without taking into account the value of her jewellery and furniture) amounted to 726,214 silver roubles. In 1879, the value of the annual output of the Ramon' beet-sugar mill (where 319 workers were employed) amounted to 72,000 roubles. Princess Eugenia personally managed the estate: she reconstructed the sugar mill, set up a carpet factory and a confectionery (the latter was awarded a prize at the 1889 Paris Exhibition), built, at her own expense, a 20km branch line to Ramon', which was opened in 1901 and is still in operation, and established a school.[20] (Princess Eugenia was equally active in the social life of St Petersburg, where she chaired the Society for the Encouragement of the Arts and patronized a number of charitable institutions.) From 1886 onwards, Princess Eugenia took out merchant certificates of the Second Guild in St. Petersburg where she lived in winter.[21] By 1897, it became clear that the expanded business had to be managed more effectively, and so Princess Eugenia hired a manager, Koch. Koch bought yet another 4,000 *desiatinas* of land and reconstructed the sugar mill and the distillery. Although the proprietress had no spare capital, Koch embarked on a risky course of action by obtaining a loan from the Bank for the Nobility and then gambling with sugar prices. The business suffered enormous losses; in 1905 the deficit amounted to 4.2 million roubles. As a member of the Imperial Family, Eugenia was not left to sink – she received a 'relief' from the Treasury in the amount of 2.5 million roubles, and another 2 million roubles as a credit from the State Bank. Nevertheless, the Ramon' business remained on the brink of bankruptcy and the proprietress lost all her assets after the estate was included, in 1906, in the lands of the Crown Domain.[22] The case of Princess Eugenia shows that in a situation where the economic and social networks were becoming increasingly complex the proprietress was unable to fully control the affairs of her estate, the considerable flow of income from quite successful enterprises notwithstanding.

Of all the businesswomen engaged in the sugar industry, only Sophia Simirenko, the proprietress of the Sidorovsk mill in Kiev Province, did not belong to the elite of the nobility. Sophia and her husband Vasilii (1835–1915) were representatives of the third generation of a prominent Ukrainian merchant dynasty (which went bankrupt in the early 1870s), the Simirenkos. The Sidorovsk mill was not inherited – Vasilii bought it in an attempt to restore his business and secured the property to his wife so as to protect himself from any claims with regard to his former enterprises (because, according to legislation, 'in the event of insolvency of one of the spouses, it is only [that spouse's] property that is answerable for the debts').[23] The Simirenkos' mill employed 350 workers; the value of its output in 1879 was 160,000 roubles.

As far as the volume of production is concerned, sugar refineries, three of which belonged to women, were clearly among the leading enterprises of the food industry. Two of the three above-mentioned refineries were situated on big noble estates, where they operated alongside beet-sugar mills within the framework of a full-cycle enterprise. Countess Maria Potocka (1830–1910) and her father, Prince Roman Sangushko, co-owned a beet-sugar mill (founded in 1843) and a later-built sugar refinery in the small town of Shepetovka, Volhynia Province. In 1879, the mills employed 250 and 136 workers and generated output to the value of 154,000 roubles and 1,243,000 roubles respectively. Countess Maria Apraksina (1845–1922)[24] owned a beet-sugar mill (in 1879 she was renting it out) and a sugar refinery (in 1879, it employed 131 workers and generated output to the value of 660,000 roubles), which she managed herself. Both were situated on Countess Maria's estate of Velikii Bobrik, Kharkov Province, which she had inherited after her mother.

One of the biggest refineries was owned by a German woman and Prussian subject, Anna-Katharina Enners (1839 – after 1900). In 1861, it was established in Moscow by her first husband, Prussian subject Jakob-Wilhelm Gehner (1821–72), together with the native of Hamburg Alexander Reineke (who before long withdrew from the business). On Gehner's death, the property passed into the hands of his widow. In 1871, the refinery occupied a three-storeyed brick building, was equipped with 3 steam engines developing 30 horsepower, employed 100 workers, and generated output to the value of 148,240 roubles. Widowed at the age of thirty-three, Anna-Katharina was very energetic both in business matters and in managing her personal life. In 1874, after two years of widowhood, she remarried to Prussian subject Phillip Enners, and established a partnership of the First Guild, 'W. Gehner & Co'. Anna-Katharina invested a considerable amount of money – both her own and her second husband's – in expanding production and in purchasing land plots in the vicinity of the plant (where she immediately built warehouses, a boiler house and other outbuildings). As a result, in 1879 the number of workers employed at the refinery almost trebled (to 286), the volume of output increased thirteen times, and engine power rose to 60 hp. The value of sugar produced in 1879 amounted to 1,920,000 roubles, which placed Anna-Katharina's enterprise in the third position in the sugar industry of Moscow.[25]

An analysis of the estate and ethnic composition of enterprise proprietresses indicates that in the 1870s female merchants and noblewomen continued to be numerically predominant – 427 and 422 persons respectively (taken together, they accounted for 85.7 per cent of the total number of enterprise proprietresses). This social group included eighty-five *meshchanki* (8.6 per cent), forty-five peasant women (4.5 per cent), two Cossack women, one wife of a priest, and yet another nine persons whose estate status remains unclear.[26]

In accordance with the polyethnic and multi-confessional composition of the population of the Russian Empire, the country's entrepreneurial strata

Figure 4.1. The distribution of proprietresses of industrial enterprises by estate group (1879)

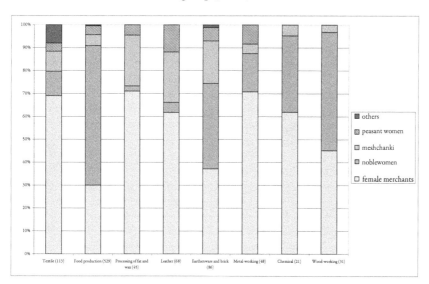

included representatives of various religious confessions and ethnic origins (see Figure 4.2). The substratum of female entrepreneurs included both foreigners and Russian subjects. Russians accounted for 75 per cent of businesswomen (750 persons). Numerically significant were the Polish, German, Jewish and Ukrainian groups of female entrepreneurs. Much less numerous were the English (N-5), French (N-5), Armenian (N-5), Tatar (N-4) and Lithuanian (N-3) groups of female entrepreneurs. Besides, the substrata included one Italian, one Serb, one Hungarian and one Crimean Tatar.

Let us consider the non-Russian ethnic groups of female entrepreneurs. The second most numerous group was Polish (N-95). Of ninety-five female entrepreneurs of Polish origin, seventy-six owned food industry enterprises, including fifty-four who owned a total of fifty-nine distilleries. Their enterprises were on noble estates, mainly in the western Provinces: there were twenty-three proprietresses in Volhynia Province, fifteen in Podolia Province, ten in Grodno Province, seven in Vitebsk Province, and six in Minsk Province. Some of them owned several enterprises each. For example, Princess Ludgarda Jablonowska, née Tyszkiewicz, owned two plants (for production of crockery-ware and glass bottles) in Volhynia Province. The most commercially active representatives of the 'Polish' group were five proprietresses from the dynasty of Counts Potocki. They owned eighteen enterprises.[27]

Figure 4.2. The ethnic composition of proprietresses of industrial enterprises (1879)

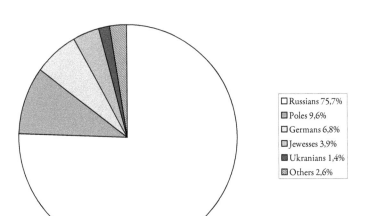

Russians 75,7%
Poles 9,6%
Germans 6,8%
Jewesses 3,9%
Ukranians 1,4%
Others 2,6%

German businesswomen ranked third (N-67). Ten of them were engaged in the textile industry, and another thirty-five – in the food industry. Most of the German proprietresses resided in big cities, primarily in St Petersburg (twelve persons) and Moscow (seven persons).

In the 1870s, Jewish businesswomen (N-39) were engaged in entrepreneurial activity within the limits of the Pale of Settlement (including twelve persons in Grodno Province, and five persons each in Volhynia and Podolia Provinces).[28] Only one female entrepreneur, Sophia Brodskaia, resided outside the Pale. She owned a tobacco factory in Voronezh (in 1879, it employed twenty workers and produced goods to the value of 20,000 roubles). Eleven Jewesses owned textile enterprises, and another four – vodka distilleries. The range of their industrial interests was broad – from production of lard candles and matches to leather and porcelain production.[29]

In the 1870s, the majority of non-Russian businesswomen still preserved their ethno-cultural identities in the domestic sphere, but in business matters they were all included in the all-Russian space of legal regulations and economic patterns. As in the past, the most important task of female entrepreneurs was to keep going their businesses, most of which were of a family nature.

3. The Various Forms of the Intra-Family Transfer of Rights in the Ownership of Business Objects to Women

In the decade under consideration, the methods by which a woman could obtain control over family enterprises were becoming more diverse. Alongside the traditional method of inheriting a property from parents or husband, which can be characterized as the 'vertical' transfer of property, there emerged a number of fresh solutions, brought to life by the introduction into commercial practice of credit relations and new organizational forms of business partnerships (e.g. joint-stock companies). One such method was to obtain a business as compensation for an outstanding debt. Since the relevant litigations and financial settlements frequently involved closest relatives belonging to the same generation, this method can be described as 'horizontal' transfer of property. Take, for example, the cases represented by the families of Babkins (Moscow) and Vyzhilovs (Uglich, Yaroslavl Province), where full control over enterprises was transferred to women.

Moscow female merchant of the First Guild Maria Matveeva (1821–after 1911) was for forty years (1842–83) the proprietress of the biggest cloth mill 'The Babkin Brothers' in the village of Kupavna, Moscow Province, including fourteen years when she was its single owner (1861–75). The biography of Matveeva is a history of her nineteen-year-long endeavours to become a complete owner of the enterprise, and of her achievements at the helm of it thereafter. On achieving her goal, Matveeva embarked on securing the legal immunity of her rights in the ownership of the enterprise. It was done so competently that in due course she became one of the first women to found a share partnership on the basis of private enterprise and to be appointed its director. The end of this story was not triumphal – in her old age Matveeva was deprived of any influence on the affairs of her own enterprise. The course and causes of her downfall will be analysed below.

It is not by chance that the history of Matveeva is told in the context of the chapter devoted to the 1870s. That decade saw a boom in the foundation of joint-stock companies, which had already picked up speed in the 1860s.[30] Characterizing this phenomenon, Thomas Owen notes:

> By 1870, the rapid increase in both new enterprises and reorganized partnerships created a unique, dual system of corporations, one that has scarcely been noted by historians despite its importance for an understanding of the economic and cultural peculiarities of Russian capitalism well into the twentieth century.[31]

When entering into a partnership with their own capital and enterprise, a female entrepreneur could now take a dominant position in a collective commercial firm.[32] This bore witness to the fact that, within Russia's business space, both the gender model of entrepreneurship and the role functions were undergoing significant changes, the Russian business community never before having articulated its acceptance of women in the role of equal partners. The 'Babkin Brothers' mill was one of those first enterprises reorganized into joint-stock companies where a woman was among the founders and later directors. The owner, Maria Matveeva, became one of the three founders of the Babkin Brothers Share Partnership; in due course she was included in its board of directors. The two other founders were her son Ivan Matveev and the Moscow merchant of the First Guild and big trader in wool Nikolai Baklanov. The charter of the partnership was approved by the Committee of Ministers on 21 February 1875.[33]

The role of females as proprietresses in the history of the Babkin Brothers Trading House was very prominent. One of Russia's oldest (and still existing) enterprises, it was established in 1800 by Prince Nikolai Yusupov, Minister and Member of the State Council. After his death in 1833, the business was bought by two brothers – Moscow merchants of the First Guild Petr (1784–1840) and Il'ia (1787–1842) Babkin.[34] In the late 1830s, they both were awarded the honorary title of Manufactory-Councillor for their achievements in industry. Il'ia had son Ivan, who was born in 1816 and died in his infancy, and daughter Maria, born in 1821; Petr had two daughters, Kapitolina and Avdot'ia, born in 1816 and 1818 respectively. Neither of the brothers had any direct male heirs.

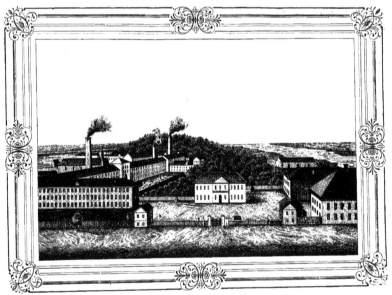

Купавинская суконная фабрика
БРАТЬЕВЪ БАБКИНЫХЪ.
въ Богородскомъ уюздю.

View of the biggest cloth mill 'The Babkin Brothers', which was owned for 40 years (1842–83) by the Moscow female merchant Maria Matveeva. 1840s. Source: L. Samoilov, Atlas promyshlennosti Moskovskoi gubernii (1845).

After the death of Petr Babkin, an agreement was signed between his daughters Kapitolina (married name Borodina) and Avdot'ia (married name Strakhova) and his brother Il'ia, confirmed by the Moscow City Duma, whereby on 7 September 1842 the Babkin Brothers Trading House was to be established to carry on trade in cloth and administration of the mill. The new company's stock was to consist of the movable and immovable property of the three co-owners to the total value of 716,000 silver roubles (with Il'ia owning half and his nieces a quarter each).[35] However, Kapitolina and Anna were only formal co-owners, having entrusted the conduct of affairs to their husbands. Later in 1842, Il'ia Babkin died, with his twenty-one-year-old daughter Maria (married name Matveeva) being the sole heir to her father's right to half of the family property. Thus, from 1842 onwards, the mill was co-owned by the two sisters and their female cousin. Maria's husband Mikhail Matveev (the eldest son of female merchant of the Second Guild and owner of a cotton-weaving mill Anna Matveeva) became its manager. In 1847, one of the sisters, Avdot'ia, died, leaving four young children between the ages of one and six in the care of their father, Nikolai Strakhov. In 1852, Maria Matveeva, then aged thirty-one, was left a widow with five children aged between three and eleven years, including two sons, Ivan and Mikhail. Apparently, the loss of her husband urged Maria to take drastic measures in order to establish her rights to the Babkins' factory (since she had nothing to expect from her late husband's family, her mother-in-law having made her junior son heir to the Matveevs' mill).

In 1853, Maria and her cousin Kapitolina reached an agreement as to the division of the joint property between themselves and Strakhov, aiming at preventing his children from making any claims to the mill. Accordingly, they brought a suit to the Moscow Chamber of the Civil Court, requesting an 'amicable division of property'. The joint property of the Babkins was valued at 222,000 silver roubles, including a) the mill – at 135,000 silver roubles, b) three houses and a vegetable plot in Moscow, two warehouses in Kitai-Gorod and a landed estate in Moscow Province – at 87,000 silver roubles. Because of Avdot'ia's having left no will, Strakhov as her heir and the children were entitled to 55,500 silver roubles worth of property. As Maria and Kapitolina most aspired to obtain the mill, the 'amicable division of property', carried out with the assistance of a conciliatory commission, resulted in the three houses, the land plots in Moscow and the provinces, as well as the warehouses in Kitai-Gorod, being passed to Strakhov. Since the value of this property exceeded Strakhov's share, he repaid Matveeva and Borodina 32,000 silver roubles. The latter invested this money in purchasing from Strakhov a consignment of wool manufactured at the Babkin's mill and worth 44,625 silver roubles.[36] At that time (1853), the mill employed 982 workers and annually produced goods to the value of 419,144 silver roubles.

After Borodina's death (around 1860), Maria Matveeva bought out her late cousin's share from her heirs and became the sole owner of the mill (1861), to remain in this position until 1875. It was under Matveeva that the mill became the leading enterprise of the cloth industry (number of workers: 1550 in 1865, 1402 in 1868, 1808 in 1879; value of annual output: 1.5 million silver roubles in 1865, 1.2 million in 1868, 3.4 million in 1879). The enterprise was equipped with British and Belgian steam engines (in 1872 their aggregate horsepower being 137hp), manufactured by 'John Musgrave & Sons', 'Hick, Hargreaves' and 'Perrot'.[37] Most of the cloth produced by the Babkin's mill (according to the prominent expert Skal'kovskii, this cloth was remarkable by its 'unique density and high quality')[38] was purchased by the Treasury for army needs, the rest being exported to China.

However, the severe economic crisis, whose effects were to be felt as early as 1873, frightened Matveeva, who witnessed the bankruptcies of many Moscow female entrepreneurs.[39] She was desperately looking for a solution and, believing that it would be provided by establishing a share partnership proposed by her business partner Nikolai Baklanov, she agreed. From February 1875, 'the mill with all the lands, forests, factory and residential buildings, engines and machines, warehouses, materials, offices, business premises and other property belonging to it' passed to the partnership (with a fixed capital of 2 million roubles in 2,000 shares).[40] Since Maria Matveeva had no spare capital left to buy out her shares, in September 1875 she was forced to pledge her two-storey brick detached house with a half-acre garden on the prestigious Prechistenka Street (bought in 1855 from nobleman Chashnikov) to the Moscow City Commercial Credit Society. Matveeva received a loan of bonds in the amount of 53,500 roubles, to be repaid in instalments within ten years.[41] Apparently, in addition to the purchase of the shares, part of the loan was invested in the gas works constructed in 1875–6 for the purpose of lighting the mill. Illuminating gas was supplied to all the factory blocks, fitted with almost 300 burners.[42] This made it possible for the mill to be switched over to working around the clock. (The practice was reluctantly abandoned only twenty-one years later, when the Law of 2 June 1897 limited the working day to 11.5 hours and introduced the mandatory Sunday off.) Owing to this sweating system, in 1879 output soared to its nineteenth century's historic high of 3.4 million silver roubles, subsequently (in 1884) dropping to 2.4 million.

In the early 1880s, age and poor health loosened Matveeva's grip on business, which was immediately taken advantage of by her partners. Baklanov, who now had practically everything under his thumb, reduced Matveeva's role to that of a mere shareholder. In 1885, she remortgaged her Prechistenka house for another twenty-five years, but got nothing for her pains. By the end of the 1880s she was completely out of business, her shares having been partly sold and partly passed to her son Ivan, who thus became the owner of twenty shares (or 1 per cent) in the partnership (1897). By that time, the Babkin Brothers Partnership had already lost its position as leader in the cloth industry. Moreover, by 1892 the partnership had been put on the brink of bankruptcy by the purchase of the 'K. Baklanov's Sons' Firm's assets by its executive director Nikolai Baklanov and his brother Ivan, another director of the partnership. In his position of Chairman of the Board of Directors of the Moscow Commercial Bank, N. Baklanov had no difficulty in convincing his colleague, Chairman of Management N. Naidenov, to grant the required credit of 2 million roubles (contrary to the rules, it was done without checking the solvency of the credit recipient). However, the partnership's situation was so shaky that the credit did not help. Only the decision of the Ministry of Finance to the effect that the State Bank should grant a 900,000 rouble loan to the 'Babkin Brothers' Firm saved both the firm and the Commercial Bank.[43]

In the early twentieth century the 'Babkin Brothers' Firm was, in effect, monopolized by the Baklanovs – their 'K. Baklanov's Sons' Trading House owning, in 1904, 568 shares in this enterprise, while another 215 shares belonged to eight other members of the Baklanov family. By 1911, the number of shares controlled by the clan had increased from 783 to 929, while the Babkins' descendants still owned the same twenty shares: Ivan Matveev owned seventeen, and his nephew Sergei owned three. At that time Maria Babkina, then aged ninety and out of business for nearly thirty years, was still alive – it is recorded that the Partnership's Board of Directors granted her an allowance of 3,000 roubles.[44]

In brief, Marveeva's business career can be summarized as follows. The newly created share partnership failed to become a reliable institutional and juridical basis for her business, the benefits of this strategy being short-lived and guaranteeing the 'Babkin Brothers' mill's stable existence only until the end of the 1870s. In the 1880s, when Matveeva was already an old woman, the complicated economic situation demanded new skills from managers in order to provide a sound legal backing for their businesses and become incorporated in the client networks of the commercial banks emerging in 1862–72. Matveeva failed to play by these rules (in particular, her only source of spare capital was the mortgage on her own house), which was used to their advantage by her partners, the Baklanovs, who totally excluded her from management and decision-making in the course of ten years.

When analysed on the basis of the newest interpretations of the theory of the industrial revolution, the Matveeva case brings us to the conclusion that the tragic finale of her entrepreneurial career was absolutely logical. In their book examining the 1700–1850 period of English history, British historians Steven King and Geoffrey Timmins single out the following three aspects of changes produced by the industrial revolution: technological change, development of the economic infrastructure, and work organization change. Such a radical transformation inevitably required the introduction of new financial mechanisms. In this connection the authors argue as follows:

> To cope with the long-term capital needs of businessmen the partnership form of organisation – often arising through kinship or religious connections – came to assume high significance, whilst to meet businessmen's working capital needs a massive expansion of credit networks took place, in which the emerging banking system came to play a key role. [45]

Now let us return to the second case of the 'horizontal' transfer of property.

The second case is represented by the change of ownership of the Vyzhilov's factory. This is yet another illustration of how necessary it was for a female entrepreneur to be legally competent and skilful in strategic matters. The family paper factory of the merchants Vyzhilovs, who resided in Uglich, Yaroslavl' Province, was initially owned by brothers Dmitrii and Aleksey. At some difficult point, apparently in view of the necessity of mechanizing their enterprise, Dmitrii and Aleksey borrowed a considerable sum of money from Aleksey's wife Anna. The receipt was made out on a bill of exchange form, but without a date.

After Aleksey's death in 1872, Dmitrii was appointed trustee of his late brother's estate. Dmitrii procrastinated debt repayment, and his major argument for not paying was that the bills had not been recorded in the business books of the Vyzhilovs. In the autumn of 1874, Anna decided that enough was enough, and so filed a debt claim with the district court of Rybinsk, a big commercial city in Yaroslavl' Province. She requested for recovery of debt in the amount of 13,000 roubles and the interest against two bills. As a proof, Anna submitted three documents: the originals of the two bills, a draft of the agreement between the brothers Vyzhilov concerning the method for using the joint property (including the factory), and Dmitrii's letter to Anna. On having examined the documents, the judges came to the following conclusions as to the proof of the debt's existence. Firstly, the debt receipts written on the bill of exchange forms contained the phrases 'we are due to pay' and 'which we received from her in cash'. By scrutinizing the bill of exchange forms, it was established that the ten-year period envisaged by legislation for presenting a bill for payment had not yet expired. Secondly, the draft agreement between the brothers Vyzhilov, written by Aleksey's hand and corrected by Dmitrii, stated that they owed Anna 13,000 roubles and that she was lending another 22,000 roubles, thus making a total of 35,000 roubles, 'against the amount of which the factory of theirs ... shall be passed to her, Anna, ... as a pledge'; moreover, the word 'owed' was changed to 'taken' by Dmitrii. Thirdly, in his letter to Anna, written after Aleksey's death on

5 December 1872, Dmitrii mentioned the money taken from Anna, which was expressed by the words 'from you'.

For all these reasons, the court passed a decision in favour of the plaintiff. Dmitrii Vyzhilov was obliged to repay his debt to Anna Vyzhilova. As the factory had already been pledged to Anna against the bills and Dmitrii had no money to repay the debt with, the property passed into Anna's full ownership. According to *Ukazatel' fabrik i zavodov*, in 1879 the registered owner of the factory was female merchant Anna Vyzhilova. That year, the factory employed sixty-six workers and produced 13,200 paper rims to the value of 30,200 roubles. It was equipped with a steam engine developing 30 horsepower. During the next five years, Anna installed one more steam engine with an output of 8 horsepower and managed to maintain her factory's performance level, with the same number of workers (sixty-six). In 1884, it produced goods to the value of 29,000 roubles.[46] The case of Vyzhilova, who belonged to the younger generation (approximately twenty-five to thirty years younger than Matveeva), indicates that even provincial female entrepreneurs could learn all the financial and legal intricacies of business, which made them capable of achieving success despite the increasing complexity of the market situation.

In order to protect their businesses, female entrepreneurs sometimes resorted to other methods – for example, continuing to use their family names as brands.

4. Husband's Family-Name Change as an Instrument of Brand Preservation

Not without interest, as a feature of inter-family business relations, are the cases when husbands took their wives' last names so as to keep both the brand and customers. These cases are a perfect illustration of the thesis that 'the marital partnership is the most fundamental economic relationship because, over time, it is one on which all other economic activities depend'.[47] The power of deciding as to whether or not a name change should be authorized belonged to the committee of deputies of each merchant corporation. For a case to be considered, it was necessary for a solicitor to file a petition and for three merchants to confirm in writing that 'there is no evil intention and harm to others on the part of the person who wishes to change his last name'. We have established that in the 1870s the Moscow Merchant Society considered four petitions for a husband to be permitted to take his wife's last name. Three were satisfied, and one denied. Let us analyse these cases in some detail.

In the first two cases, the remarried widows continuing the businesses of their late husbands decided to transfer the entrepreneurial functions to their second husbands, on condition that in the next generation control of each firm was to be vested in the children of their initial owners.

In 1871, merchant of the Second Guild Ivan Ivanov, then aged twenty-five, married Avdot'ia Tsyganova, the thirty-one-year-old widow of Moscow merchant of the Second Guild Ivan Tsyganov. Avdot'ia put her new spouse in charge of 'the hat trading business that had been established by her late husband and was in existence for more than 60 years'. In 1872, Ivanov filed a petition with the Moscow Merchant Society, whereby he requested for permission to change his last name to Tsyganov 'in order not to harm commercial affairs by changing the [name of the] firm'. The petition enclosed the solicitations of several Moscow merchants, including Avdot'ia's first husband's brother, honorary citizen Kondratii Tsyganov, all univocally attesting that Ivanov wanted to change his last name 'without any evil intention and with no harm to others, but solely in order to prevent any harm to the hat trading business taken over by him'. The name change was permitted. In addition to her three sons by her first marriage, Nikolai, Vasilii and Sergei, Avdot'ia had another son Aleksandr by her second marriage. Her second husband was head of the firm until his death in 1887, after which the hat trading business passed to his stepsons, Vasilii and Sergei.[48]

In 1875, the authorities considered a similar request made by thirty-three-year-old merchant of the Second Guild Aleksey Murashkintsev, also married to the widow of a Moscow merchant. As is stated in the petition, Aleksey had already 'taken over her comb trading business in accordance with the wishes of his wife, Ekaterina Nevezhina; now he decided to take her name as well. The main argument put forth by Murashkintsev was as follows: 'this trading business ... is known, especially among merchants from other towns, as Nevezhin's firm' (the first husband of Ekaterina, Gavriil Nevezhin, had traded in Kitai-Gorod since 1858; he died around 1871). The petition enclosed the written statements of Moscow merchants, certifying that the petitioner was acting 'without any evil intent and with no harm to others', and the ruling of the Orphan's Court that Ekaterina 'should be deemed to be the custodian of her children by her first marriage' (that is, of her sons Sergei, Mikhail and Nikolai). By her second marriage Ekaterina had another son, Gavriil, born in 1872. The name change was authorized.[49]

The third case was more complicated than the previous two. In 1875, a name-change petition was filed by Yegor and Nastas'ia Kulikov, married since 1863. At the moment of filing the petition, the husband and wife were aged fifty and forty-four respectively, and their son, Aleksandr, was nine years old. Yegor Kulikov had been Moscow merchant of the Second Guild since 1864 (prior to that – a *tsekhovoi),* and traded in 'timber materials and firewood'. His wife Nastas'ia, formerly a *meshchanka* and now a female merchant, was running a separate business and had taken out the merchant certificate of the Second Guild.

Like her husband, she traded in structural timber. Nastas'ia's maiden name was Pirogova. In the petition, the reason for the requested name change was stated as the wishes of Nastas'ia's father, *meshchanin* Aleksandr Pirogov. Most likely, the latter had promised to bequeath his capital and real estate to Yegor and Nastas'ia if they changed their last name to Pirogov. The request was satisfied. In the 1890s, Yegor and Nastas'ia Pirogov continued to trade separately, but instead of renting a flat, as they did in the 1870s, the couple was now living in a private house received from Nastas'ia's father. After Nastas'ia's death in the early 1900s, this house, according to the 1905 data, was recorded as belonging to Yegor, then aged seventy-six.[50] In the third case, the explicit motivation of pleasing an old man, whose business had already passed to his daughter, was augmented by some implicit agreements entailing economic benefits arising from the name-change applied for.

In the fourth case, Ivan Gel'tishchev, a former Tula *meshchanin* who inscribed in the Second Guild of Moscow merchants in 1879, one year before filing the petition had married Lidia, daughter of the late Moscow merchant Iakov Tikhonov, who by his first marriage had four daughters and by his second – another three (Lidia being the youngest) and a son (who died in infancy). Lidia's mother, female merchant of the Second Guild Anna Tikhonova, traded in chandler's goods (varnishes and sealing wax) produced at the Tikhonovs' varnish plant. She had inherited the business after her husband (a former *meshchanin,* who inscribed in the merchantry in 1858 and died in 1878). In 1879, the plant (established in 1845) employed sixteen workers and produced 14,150 *poods* (about 232 tonnes) of 'oil and spirit varnish' to the value of 163 thousand roubles.[51] As soon as Ivan Gel'tishchev, then aged twenty-five, married Lidia, his mother-in-law entrusted to him the post of a clerk at her enterprise. Apparently viewing him as a potential loyal business partner and her future successor, Anna also suggested that the young man should change his family name to Tikhonov. His petition to this effect was augmented by solicitations signed by Anna Tikhonova and five Moscow merchants. Since Gel'tishchev had been registered as merchant for only one year, it being prohibited for *meshchane* to change their names, the authorities denied his request. During the next twenty-seven years, Anna Tikhonova remained owner of both the plant and the chandler's goods shop in Kitai-Gorod. In 1888, she founded a trading house under the name of Anna Tikhonova & Co., whose only investor was Gel'tishchev. By that time Gel'tishchev had become a relatively prosperous businessman, as is testified by his acquisition of real estate in the form of three shops in the Honey Row of Kitai-Gorod. Anna Tikhonova died around 1906 at the age of seventy-eight. She left the business to her fifty-two-year-old son-in-law; in 1907 he renamed the family firm as 'Successor to the Trading House of Anna Tikhonova & Co, Ivan Gel'tishchev & Co'. Under this name, the business continued its existence until the 1917 Revolution.[52] As for the Tikhonova-Gel'tishchev case, it is absolutely clear that the widowed Anna Tikhonova was extremely cautious (and frequently suspicious) in matters of business management. She kept the reins until her dying day, never entrusting them to her son-in-law. Only after ten years of Gel'tishchev's clerkdom the widow relented and made him partner in the family business, while remaining in charge of the managerial and control functions. In this chain of actions and relations, the suggestion that Gel'tishchev should change his family name was the first test of the new relative's loyalty, the trial of his readiness to sacrifice his self-identity as independent person to the commercial ambitions of his mother-in-law, who represented herself as the keeper of the capital and the real estate of the Tikhonov family.

The cases of name-changing indicate that, for the sake of preserving his achieved social status and a merchant family's capital, the new member of that family was sometimes ready to relinquish his initial self-identity.

Conclusion

The economic conditions of the 1870s were difficult: Russian industry entered the intensive phase of the industrial revolution, while the market, heavily shaken by the 1873 world economic crisis, became extremely unstable. In these circumstances, it was highly important for every entrepreneur to increase his or her level of competitiveness and become a competent manager. The crucial step in this direction was to acquire sufficient knowledge of technological and legal matters. Those who played by these rules had better chances of survival. Thus, judging from our analysis of statistics, it was the strongest female-owned enterprises, those most capable of technological modernization (primarily in the textile and food industries), that managed to weather the storm of the crisis and stay afloat. During that decade, women preferred to increase their enterprises' reserves of survivability rather than to take risks, which are confirmed by the fact that the average annual production level of female-owned enterprises was higher than the annual average in nearly all industries. As for the estate and ethnic composition of the proprietresses (N-991), it remained more or less unchanged by comparison with the previous period – the groups of noblewomen and female merchants were equal in numbers (N-427 and N-422 respectively); taken together, they constituted 86 per cent of all proprietresses of industrial enterprises.

Some cases presented in the chapter serve as illustrations of the proprietresses' relations with their relatives and business partners. At the same time, they reveal the various aspects of the process of crystallizing property and ownership relations within the family. For example, there was a growing tendency to resolve business-related property disputes in courts of justice. Such suits, filed against the nearest relatives (as in the cases of Maria Matveeva and Anna Vyzhilova), testify to the stable institutionalization of Russian entrepreneurship, including its integral part – female entrepreneurship. In the course of court investigations, businesswomen demonstrated their substantial knowledge of the legal and financial intricacies of property ownership. In the cases under consideration, we can see those women not only as heads of households, with their activity being limited only to the family realm, but also as heads of robust businesses. Quite interesting, in terms of individual and family identity, are the cases of husbands adopting the family names of their wives in order to secure both the family brand and customers' loyalty. This is an indication that at the core of the daily practice of merchant families was the constant need to 'enhance' their economic immunity, motivated by the desire to increase the security of a family business and to stabilize its incomes.

5 FEMALE ENTREPRENEURSHIP IN THE 1880s: THE DICTATE OF MONEY INSIDE THE FAMILY CIRCLE

In the 1880s, the firms which had been on the market for no less than twenty years and had acquired a dynastic character started to play a key role in the business space. The new situation was accompanied by the establishment of firms (in the form of trading houses) where husband and wife were equal partners (the case of Maria Morozova).

One of the characteristics of that period was the 'dictate of money', when the actual leadership in a family was seized by the wife if she had considerable personal property (despite the principle that 'the wife is obligated to obey her husband as the had of the family, to live with him in love, respect, and unlimited obedience, and to render him all pleasure and affection as mistress of the household' having been endorsed in legislation).[1] To illustrate the 'dictate of money' pattern, we will devote a few pages to the history of the conflict in the Shchekin family of merchants.

Another feature of that decade was a rise in the number of female bankrupts. An analysis of bankruptcies considered by the Commercial Court (the cases of Kasheverova and Panina) will enable us to establish which of the risks could cause an irreversible decline of entrepreneurial activity.

In the 1880s, the numbers and influence of women engaged in entrepreneurship were approximately the same as in the previous decade: women accounted for 10.9 and 8.2 per cent (or 470 and 573 persons) of guild merchants (1889) in Moscow and St Petersburg respectively.[2] In 1884, the number of proprietresses of industrial enterprises rose by 25 per cent by comparison with 1879 (from 1,045 to 1,309); however, their relative share remained at the level of 4.8 per cent.

The chapter will present the major parameters of the Russian Empire's economic development in the 1880s; the statistics of women's participation in industry; and a number of life stories illustrating the tendencies of female entrepreneurship during that decade.

1. The Epoch of the 1880s: Parameters of Economic Development and Historiographical Debates

In their works of the 1960s, two American economists – Nobel Prize winner Simon Kuznets and the author of the backwardness model, Alexander Gerschenkron[3] – while using different research approaches, arrive at the same conclusion: that modern economic growth in Russia took off in the 1880s[4]. The issue of the rate of growth and the structure of Russia's economy was later considered in an historico-comparative perspective by Paul Gregory. One of his inferences was as follows:

> Russia began modern economic growth with a relatively high share of agriculture and a law share of industry, much like Japan. Unlike other countries beginning modern economic growth with high agricultural and low industrial shares, such as Japan, the United Kingdom, Denmark, Italy, the United States, and Canada, the decline in the *A* share (the rise in the *I* share) was more gradual in the Russian case. In this respect, Russia parallels the French experience a half century earlier.[5]

Gregory also made another remark, which is equally important for further analysis of the history of Russian entrepreneurship in general and female entrepreneurship in particular:

> Similar statistics could be cited for changes in the consumption, investment, and government shares of total product, but a casual examination of the available data suffices to indicate that the Russian 1885–1913 experience was generally similar to that of other countries during the early stages of modern economic growth.[6]

Unfortunately, historiography still lacks a strict academic interpretation of the socioeconomic characteristic of the 1880s. That decade continues to be the subject of debates which concentrate, among other things, on the issue of periodization of the industrial revolution in Russia.[7] The prominent Russian economic historian Valery Bovykin writes:

> So far as the economic history of Russia is concerned, the 1880s are in many respects a vague and puzzling period. Superficially, it might appear as near stagnation, because the dynamic of economic life is weakly manifested. But in the depth, some serious quantitative changes are taking place.[8]

As regards statistics, it is indicative of the following. On the one hand, when the figures for the beginning and ending dates of the period (1881 and 1890 respectively) are compared, a number of absolute indices demonstrate positive dynamics. The numbers of workers grew from 668,000 to 720,000; supply of foreign and Central Asian cotton increased from 9.1 to 11.5 million *poods*; and production of pig iron rose from 28.7 to 56.6 million *poods*. On the other hand, statistics indicate the presence of depression in the period of 1882–85. Over that period, supply of cotton dropped to 7.4–7.6 million *poods*; and the numbers of workers – to 616,000 (while only pig-iron production continued its steady growth).[9] According to the data prepared by Dmitry Mendeleev for the 1893 World's Columbian Exhibition in Chicago, Russian industrial output increased over the period 1881–90 from 1.287 to 1.656 billion roubles (the 1883–6 drop was insignificant: at its worst in 1883, output amounted to 1.304 billion roubles). Clearly indicative of the market's development was growth in the number of guild certificates taken out: in 1880, 3,300 first-guild and 70,700 second-guild certificates were taken out, while a decade later (1890) 4,900 and 113,800 were taken out respectively.[10]

Historians and economists offer different explanations as to causes of the rises and falls of the Russian economy during that period; however, they all admit the two following factors to be of paramount importance. The first factor is the influence exerted on the Russian economy by fluctuations of the world market (in Russia, as elsewhere in Europe and in the United States, the years 1882–5 were marked by industrial stagnation). The second factor is the government's attempts to start regulating economic processes. At the same time, the issue of the degree of state influence on the economy remains the subject of academic debate.[11] We believe to be relevant the opinion expressed by R. Munting: 'On the whole the state played a more indirect than direct role in industrial development in Tsarist Russia, but nonetheless a vital one'.[12]

The decade under study saw one important step forward, namely the development of factory legislation. The achieved progress attested to the implementation of the corresponding items of the economic programs engendered at the top levels of the bureaucracy. The adoption of the new laws was associated with the activity of N. Bunge (Minister of Finance in 1881–96 and Chairman of the Committee of Ministers in 1887–95). Bunge believed that the underdevelopment of Russian factory legislation by comparison with that of the West seriously impeded the industrial development of Russia. In his memorandum submitted to Emperor Alexander II in 1880, Bunge affirmed that 'in this respect, Russia lags behind Western Europe by half a century'.[13] Probably the most groundbreaking were two factory laws. The Law of 1 June 1882 forbade children younger than twelve to work in factories, and established an eight-hour working day for those between twelve and fifteen. The Law of 3 June 1886 introduced rules and regulations on recruitment, dismissal and payment of labour of industrial workers.[14] In 1882, a Factory Inspectorate was set up at the Ministry of Finance for the purpose of enforcing the new laws (on the lines of that introduced in the United Kingdom by the 1833 Factory Act).[15] The Juridical regulation of relations between the factory owner and the hired worker restricted the arbitrary treatment of the latter. Scores of cases were initiated in civil courts concerning workers' claims for untimely payment of wages and for disability compensation.

One of the examples coming up later in this chapter will give you a general idea of such conflicts.

2. Female Entrepreneurs in Russian Industry in the 1880s

In the 1880s, the positions of women engaged in industry became stronger despite the 1882–5 crisis. According to our estimates based on the official data for the year 1884 published in *Ukazatel' fabrik i zavodov* ('The Guide to Factories and Plants', 1887), the relatively short five-year period which had passed since the appearance of the '*Ukazatel*' containing the data for the year 1879 (published by the Department of Trade and Manufactories of the Ministry of Finance – see the previous chapter) was marked by a considerable growth in female entrepreneurship. The estimates indicate that 1,354 female-owned enterprises with 57,583 workers produced goods to the value of 63.6 million roubles, which accounted for 4.8 per cent of Russia's total industrial output. The generalized results are tabulated in Table 5.1.[16]

A comparison between the 1879 and 1884 data on result parameters shows that the value of output from female-owned enterprises increased by one and a half times – from 43.7 to 63.6 million roubles (while the aggregate output of Russian industry rose by 1.2 times); the number of workers increased by 1.25 times – from 45.9 to 57.6 thousand (the total number of industrial workers grew by 1.16 times). However, during the five-year period under consideration, there was little change in the trends of women's activity within individual branches of industry and in the regional perspective. In can be said that the trends described in the previous chapter remained essentially constant.

According to the 1884 data, 85 per cent of output from female-owned enterprises was accounted for by the food and textile industries. In these industries, the participation of women in entrepreneurship was the highest – their businesses accounted for 9.2 per cent and 7.7 per cent of the annual output of the food and textile industries respectively.

The period from 1879 to 1884 saw no major changes in the estate and ethnic composition of proprietresses of industrial enterprises. Taken together, noblewomen (N-572) and female merchants (N-553) comprised 85.9 per cent of the group. Despite their growth in numbers, the percentage of *meshchanki* and peasant women remained the same – 8.9 per cent (N-116) and 4.7 per cent (N-61) respectively. Also, the group included two Cossack women and two wives of priests.[17]

An ethnicity analysis has indicated that the number of businesswomen of Russian origin grew in absolute terms – from 750 to 863, but their percentage dropped from 75.7 per cent to 65.9 per cent. In the early 1880s, female entrepreneurs from ethnic minorities were becoming increasingly active.

There was a growth in the numbers (from 95 to 167 persons) and in the share (from 9.6 per cent to 12.5 per cent) of the Polish group, mainly accounted for by establishment of small-scale agricultural enterprises (distilleries, wind- and water mills, etc.) on landed estates in the southern and western provinces. 137 of 167 Polish businesswomen operated in the food industry, including 114 in the distilling and flour-grinding sectors. For the same reasons, the Ukrainian group also increased – from fourteen to forty-two persons (or from 1.3 per cent to 4.2 per cent), 36 of whom owned agricultural processing enterprises. Women belonging to the Polish titled aristocracy (a virtual 'caste' apart) played a crucial role in beet-sugar production: the enterprises of Countess Maria Potocka (three mills), Maria Branicka (three mills), Julia Branicka (two mills), Alexandra Potocka and Helena Tyzskiewicz (located in the Kiev, Podolia and Volhynia Provinces) accounted for 7 per cent of Russia's annual sugar output.

The group of German female entrepreneurs increased from 67 to 126 persons (or from 6.8 to 9.6 per cent). The picture of the activity of German female entrepreneurs reveals a rather wide spectrum of their industrial interests, which included textile production, dyeing, mechanical and metalwork, soap-boiling, confectionary, etc. The personal cases of those women also demonstrate their preference for installing state-of-the-art technical equipment at their plants and factories, as well as a remarkable stability of their businesses: by the turn of the twentieth century, the age of most female-owned factories was between twenty and forty years. Of 126 businesswomen, eighty-eight were engaged in the food industry, where they owned forty distilleries and twenty-two breweries. German female entrepreneurs were very successful in the textile and machine-building industry (eleven and ten enterprises respectively). Most of their textile enterprises were located in Moscow (five enterprises) and St Petersburg (four enterprises).

One of the biggest textile enterprises of Moscow belonged to Alexandrina-Helena Knörzer, née Fischer. Alexandrina, the wife of Paul Knörzer (broker at Moscow Stock Market in 1863–74), became a widow at the age of forty and, in 1874, applied for 'her being registered as a Moscow Second Guild Merchant beginning with the year of 1875'. Having become a businesswoman, Alexandrina established in her house on Danilovskaia Street a cloth mill with a dyery. She remained registered as the mill's owner for the subsequent thirty years, although her family included two adults – her son Nikolaus Karl Heinrich and her daughter Emilia Margarita. In 1881, the mill employed seventeen workers; by 1886, the number of workers had increased to about 100. That year it produced goods to the value of 301,000 roubles. The enterprise was equipped with a steam-engine manufactured by the Swiss company 'Sulzer', three steam-boilers, eight shearing devices, two dryers and six washing machines – forty-seven machines all told.[18]

Table 5.1. Number of Enterprises Owned by Women, by Branch of Industrial Activity (Russian Empire, 1884)

The branches are placed in the Table in descending order of the share of female-owned enterprises in the total volume of production

Industry	Number of female-owned enterprises (out of total number of 26,067)	Share of female-owned enterprises in total volume of production, in per cent / thousand roubles	Share of female-owned enterprises, by number of workers, in per cent / persons	Number of female-owned enterprises equipped with steam engines
Food production	769 (out of 12,397) 734 owners	9.2 per cent 30,882 out of 335,338*	11.9 per cent 21,652 out of 181,641*	207
Textile industry	136 out of 2,916 139 owners	6.7 per cent 23,096 out of 345,046	6.5 per cent 24,227 out of 370,610	51
Earthenware and brick industry**	128 (out of 3,582) 121 owners	7.3 per cent 1,758 out of 24,034	7.9 per cent 4,836 out of 61,220	6
Leather industry	86 (out of 3,820) 84 owners	3.6 per cent 1,675 out of 45,946	2.9 per cent 780 out of 27,261	2
Tobacco	14 (out of 419) 15 owners	3.4 per cent 1,536 out of 45,670	4.6 per cent 1,333 out of 28,783	2
Machine-building and metalworking	57 (out of 1030) 56 owners	1.8 per cent 1,528 out of 84,211	2.3 per cent 1,864 out of 79,400	20
Chemical industry	26 (out of 370) 25 owners	5.5 per cent 1,031 out of 18,880	6.6 per cent 532 out of 8,085	4
Processing of fat and wax	55 (out of 1,388) 56 owners	2.4 per cent 798 out of 33,158	3.6 per cent 357 out of 9,817	None
Wood-working	47 (out of 1634) 43 owners	2.4 per cent 497 out of 20,557	4.9 per cent 1,289 out of 26,392	16
Paper production	17 (out of 211) 17 owners	2.0 per cent 372 out of 18,515	3.4 per cent 560 out of 16,330	6

Industry	Number of female-owned enterprises (out of total number of 26,067)	Share of female-owned enterprises in total volume of production, in per cent / thousand roubles	Share of female-owned enterprises, by number of workers, in per cent / persons	Number of female-owned enterprises equipped with steam engines
Matches	11 (out of 240) 11 owners	12.5 per cent 311 out of 2,486	6.7 per cent 560 out of 8,149	1
Carriage-making	5 (out of 124)	54 out of 1,814	90 out of 2,408	1
Salt production	1 (out of 24)	47 out of 413	37 out of 203	No data
Production of mineral and lubricating oils	1 (out of 46)	8 out of 4,552	7 out of 1,522	1
Musical instruments	1 (out of 30)	3 out of 1,203	19 out of 978	No data
Other: gun powder production, rubber production	0 (out of 2) 0 (out of 3)	0 out of 6,885 0 out of 5,869,000	0 out of 1,727 0 out of 2,337	
Mining plants of Urals	No data	No data	No data	
TOTAL	1354 (out of 27,235)	4.8 per cent 63,596 out of 1,329,602	7 per cent 57,583 out of 826,794	317
Female Owners	1309			

* Less the value of the goods produced by female-owned distilleries (no data being available). The value of the annual output of flour mills is based on the author's estimation.

** Production of lime, bricks, earthenware, glass and construction materials.

The number of Jewish proprietresses increased from thirty-nine to sixty-four (or from 3.9 per cent to 4.9 per cent). As before, they operated within the Pale of Settlement.

Among the female entrepreneurs who were Russian subjects there were seven Tatars, six Armenians, four Lithuanians, one Karaim, one Moldavian and one Greek (Maria Sinadino, the daughter of Kishinev's mayor, resided in Odessa where she had a tobacco factory employing thirty-three workers and annually producing goods to the value of 38,000 roubles). The most noteworthy among the Tatar businesswomen were two representatives of the Akchurin merchant dynasty, who headed two of the seven cloth mills which the Akchurins owned in Simbirsk Province. For example, in 1880, Fahri-Banu Akchurina's mill in the village of Liakhovka employed 100 workers and produced goods to the value of 400,000 roubles; it was equipped with one English and one Belgian steam engines.[19]

Anna Gabai, a Karaim[20] woman, owned a tobacco factory in Moscow (presently, the *Java* tobacco factory) which was founded in 1863 (in 1884 it employed 175 workers and produced goods, including 10,000 poods of tobacco and 33 million of *papirosy*, to the value of 259,000 roubles; in 1890, the number of workers increased to 300, production of *papirosy* climbed to 60 million, output included 10,000 *poods* of tobacco, and the value of goods produced over that year was 750,000 roubles). Anna took over the factory in 1880, at the age of thirty-eight, after the death of her husband, merchant Samuel Gabai. Although the factory was big (in the late 1880s it ranked second among Moscow tobacco enterprises after the Bostandzhoglo factory), Anna invariably took out certificates of the Second Guild. Anna's motivation for not ascending to the First Guild (although the gigantic scale of her business clearly corresponded to the criteria for membership in the First Guild) illustrates the behaviour of a businesswoman from an ethnic minority. It has two possible explanations: it was difficult for Anna Gabai to achieve stability because of her not belonging to the ethnic Russian merchantry and because her Judaism may have made the police suspicious of her. Thus, Anna's 'artificial' (or 'non-adequate') belonging to the Second Guild reflected the behaviour of newcomers, who preferred to keep a low profile in the formal merchant hierarchy of Moscow and not to compete with the old Muscovites of Greek origin - tobacco merchants Bostandzhoglo (who had dominated the tobacco industry for decades), and who besides were close relatives of N. Alekseev, Mayor of Moscow from 1885 to 1893.[21]

Apart from the above-mentioned group of German businesswomen, the ranks of enterprise proprietresses of European origin included seventeen French women (for example, Anna Craft and Julie Simon owned two chocolate factories in St Petersburg); five English women; one Finnish citizen (Laura-Maria Forsbom, owner of a pig-iron foundry in St Petersburg – in 1884, it employed fifteen workers and produced goods to the value of 16,000 roubles); one Danish subject, Klifus (the first name is not indicated), owner of a small brickworks near St Petersburg, one Austrian subject, Theresa Stolz, who owned a brewery in Pskov (in 1885, it employed seven workers and produced goods to the value of 6,000 roubles); and one Luxemburg subject, Elizabeth Nussbaum, owner of a brewery (established in 1882) in Kamyshin, a small town in the Saratov Province (in 1884, it employed thirteen workers and produced goods to the value of 14,000 roubles).

Our reconstruction of the life story of Janet Smith, who was a Moscow businesswoman and a subject of the United Kingdom, indicates that she spent almost fifty years in Russia. Her husband, Richard Smith, came to Moscow in 1848 in order to set up his own business. On 20 December 1856, he submitted a petition to the Office of the Minister of Finance whereby he asked for a permission to set up an enterprise for producing 'steam engines and all the instruments necessary for their functioning, iron furnaces with boilers, reservoirs, iron bridges, rafters and beams for buildings, grates, copper boilers, etc.' The note from the police, attached to the petition, verified that 'Richard Smith ... of good behaviour and way of life, has enough wealth and can be entrusted with the running of the undertaking appealed for.'[22]

The recommendation from the Moscow Department of the Manufactory Council reads:

> the proliferation, in Moscow, of mechanical industry is all the more desirable because the serious shortage thereof creates an obstacle to the adequate development of our manufactories.[23]

In 1857, the authorities gave the permission for a plant with twenty-five workers to be set up. In 1865, the plant employed fifty workers; in 1871, their numbers rose to 146.[24] In 1871, it produced goods to the value of 90,000 roubles. By 1871, steam engines (developing between 5 and 20 horsepower) manufactured at the Smith plant had been installed at thirteen Moscow facilities, including eleven textile mills, one perfume factory (owned by Dutfois, a big French firm), and the famous Chelyshev bathhouse.[25]

In 1872, Richard Smith died. In 1873, his forty-nine-year-old widow Janet inscribed in the Second Guild and took over the management of the plant. In 1874, the Office of the Governor General permitted her to install an additional steam engine in order to get rid of manual labour at the enterprise. Janet was an efficient manager, which made it possible for her to escape the negative effects of the economic crisis (in 1884, her plant employed 154 workers and produced goods to the value of 101,000 roubles). As Smith's products were in high demand, and so there was an urgent need to optimize their supply, in the early 1890s the firm opened an office on Miasnitskaia Street, one of the major commercial arteries of Moscow. In 1895, Janet continued to manage the business herself, apparently having decided for the time being not to pass it on to her sons, John and Richard. John was his mother's assistant for many years. It was not until 1895 that she gave her consent to his taking out a personal guild certificate. John was already forty-eight at that time. In 1895, Richard, then aged thirty-five, left his ancestral home, rented a flat in another district of Moscow, and set up his own mechanical plant.[26]

Janet Smith was one of the first Moscow businesswomen summoned to court after the introduction of the 1886 Factory Law. The plaintiff was her worker Petrov. When he was working on a drilling machine, three of the fingers on his right hand were caught in the cog-wheels and crushed, after which Petrov spent two months in St Catherine's Hospital in Moscow. He became permanently disabled. The first court that considered his case passed a ruling that Petrov should be paid a monthly disability allowance of 8 roubles (or 96 roubles per annum). Petrov then filed an appeal with a court of higher instance whereby he demanded that Janet Smith pay him 200 roubles per annum starting from the date of the accident, 30 September 1888, until his death. Petrov's arguments in favour of his demand were limited to proving that the factory owner, Janet Smith, was guilty of violating job safety rules: firstly, the drilling machine had not been fitted with guards to prevent contact with the cog-wheels; secondly, 'the countershaft is placed too far from the machine … and in the event of an accident, the worker cannot stop the machine himself'. After having reconsidered the case, the court passed the following ruling: 'it is proved that the plaintiff's disability was caused by negligence on her [Janet Smith's] part', and so she had to pay the required compensation to the plaintiff.[27]

Turning back to the characteristic of female entrepreneurs engaged in industry, it should be said that several of the enterprises owned by them annually produced goods to the value of more than a million roubles. They included the 'Georg Landrin' Confectionery Factory owned by female merchant Evdokia Maksimovich (in 1884, the factory named after Evdokia's first husband was employing 287 workers and produced goods to the value of 1,014,000 roubles), and the cotton-weaving mill of Anna Krasil'shchikova, female merchant from the Kostroma Province. In 1884 her mill employed 1,120 workers and produced goods to the value of 1,347,000 roubles. The proprietresses of these facilities managed their businesses themselves and knew all the details of both the production process and the relations with their workers, suppliers and wholesale buyers.

Coming next is a biographic portrait of one of the representatives of this cohort of millionairesses – Maria Morozova, who made millions by manufacturing cotton textiles.

3. Female Manufacturer Maria Morozova – the Genius of Profit and Propriety

Both in terms of personal wealth and the degree of influence, the undisputed leader among Russian female merchants-entrepreneurs was Maria Morozova (1830–1911).[28] After the death, in 1889, of her husband, Timofei, Maria became the head of Russia's largest textile enterprise – the Partnership of the Nikolskaia Manufactory of 'Savva Morozov's Son & Co'. Morozova was one of the richest women of Russia: the capital she inherited after her husband amounted to 'just' 6 million roubles; twenty-two years later, the property left by Maria to her heirs was valued at 30 million roubles[29]. Contrary to the stereotypes created by the playwright A. Ostrovskii (who, in the words of 19th-century literary criticist N. Dobroliubov, sarcastically depicted the life of merchants as a 'kingdom of darkness'), Morozova was an educated woman, knowledgeable of literature and foreign languages, while at the same time – a brilliant captain of industry, who succeeded in developing a flawless business strategy for her family firm.

Maria descended from an old merchant clan founded by her great-grandfather, Andrei Simonov, who was a member of the Third Guild of the Moscow merchantry in the year 1795.[30] Her grandfather, Ivan Simonov, a merchant of the Second Guild, owned a silk and cotton mill in Moscow. Maria's father, Fedor, expanded the business by buying two textile mills in Moscow Province; as a result, by the 1840s he possessed three enterprises where 1,300 workers were employed.[31] In 1829, Fedor married Maria Soldatenkova, from a well-known family of textile manufacturers belonging to the community of Old Believers. The Moscow factories of the Simonovs and the Soldatenkovs were situated close to each other. Thus, the marriage clearly had some business motives, as it helped to develop a coordinated strategy of production and to gain competitive advantages in the marketing sphere. From childhood, Maria (Masha) was very resolute, persistent and eager to learn. She was taught privately by the best Moscow teachers and was most successful at mathematics, German and French. When Masha was sixteen, her father suddenly died. The future husband was handpicked for the girl by her maternal uncle – the wealthy factory owner, banker and philanthropist Koz'ma Soldatenkov (childless, he helped his sister to bring up and educate her children). The potential husband had to answer two major requirements: to be both a rich textile manufacturer and an Old Believer. As a result, a perfect match was found in the person of Timofei Morozov, the twenty-five-year-old heir to the fortune of a famous Russian textile dynasty. In 1848, Masha was married to him. Thus, from the very beginning, the purpose of this marriage was clearly the creation and stabilization of a valuable family and business network.

Maria's father-in-law, Savva Morozov, was Russia's biggest manufacturer of cotton yarn. In 1860, which was the last year of his life, he founded the trading house 'Savva Morozov and Sons' with a capital of more than 4.5 million roubles. The firm was co-owned by Savva, his two sons – Timofei and Ivan (their stake amounted to 75 per cent), and Savva's two nephews, Abram and David.

Just one year later, with the role of his relatives having been reduced to that of stake-holders, Timofei, in fact, became the sole manager of the firm. In 1869, in the course of the business being re-registered, its fixed assets were increased to

Portrait of Maria Morozova, head (in 1889–1911) of Russia's largest textile enterprise – the Partnership of the Nikolskaia Manufactory of 'Savva Morozov's Son and Co'. Courtesy of Mikhail Zolotarev, Moscow.

5 million roubles, with Timofei's stake amounting to 3 million. In 1871, Timofei split from his cousin partners, got the Nikolskaia manufactory in Moscow Province, and became head of a new firm, 'Savva Morozov's Son & Co'. T. S. Morozov's high business reputation reflected on his social status: he was elected chairman of the Moscow Stock Exchange Committee (1868-76) and headed the board of one of the biggest banks, 'The Moscow Merchant Mutual Credit Society' (1869–74).[32]

So far as their human qualities were concerned, both Timofei and Maria were independently-minded and strong-willed. However, their family life became one of the rare examples of spouses complementing one another, not competing with one another. The happy marriage of Timofei and Maria Morozov produced nine children, three of whom (two boys and a girl) died in their infancy. With four daughters surviving, Maria gave birth to her last children, the long-awaited sons, Savva and Sergei.[33] The property status of Maria was strengthened in 1872, when she inherited three shops in Kitai-Gorod after the death of her bachelor brother, merchant of the Second Guild Aleksey Simonov.[34] Previously, she had received a substantial inheritance after the demise of her parents and her sister Nadezhda, and so all the wealth accumulated by four generations of the Simonov family was now concentrated in her hands. She invested this money in the family business and in the bringing-up of her children. When the Charter of the Morozovs' firm was being authorized in 1873, Maria was included by her husband in the number of the founders.[35] In the course of corporatization, the firm's fixed capital of 5 million roubles was divided into 5,000 shares of 1,000 roubles each. According

View of the Nikolskaia manufactory. 1890s. Courtesy of Mikhail Zolotarev, Moscow.

to the Charter, the ownership of shares was restricted to family members. In the early 1880s, Timofei and Maria owned 3,462 and 1095 shares respectively.[36] Thus, 91 per cent of shares in the firm belonged to the husband and wife, 1.6 per cent – to their children, and another 7.4 per cent – to their business partner, provider of British-made weaving equipment (via the Manchester firm of 'De Jersey & Co') Ludwig Knoop and to certain senior employees of the Morozovs' firm - its chief accountant and engineers.[37]

After Timofei's death on 10 October 1889, Maria, who had been married to him for forty years, immediately made up her mind and so on 10 October succeeded her late husband in the position of Executive Director of the Nikol-skaia manufactory.[38] Timofei had prepared Maria for the job well in advance. In 1883, he had furnished her with a full power of attorney to manage the estates, purchase land and to receive money.[39] In his will drawn up in 1888, Timofei had stated the following:

> I hereby give and bequeath to my wife, Maria Fedorovna Morozova, in full, excep-
> tional and independent ownership and unlimited possession and disposal, all the
> movable and immovable property having been acquired by me which may remain
> after my death, whatever and wherever it might be.[40]

The total value of the inheritance was estimated at 6.1 million roubles, includ-ing 2.4 million roubles worth of shares in Nikolskaia manufactory and 12,000 desiatinas (32,400 acres) of land.[41] By Timofei's will, 90 per cent of property passed to Maria. Thus, the family business was prevented from being divided.[42] A distinctive system of inheritance based on the right of primogeniture was clearly in the making in the merchant community, when all the property was passed to one heir picked up from among a large family. The two sons and three daughters had to put up with getting only five inheritance shares of 100,000 roubles each.

From that moment onwards, Maria Morozova was in charge of both the fam-ily and the business. According to one of her contemporaries, 'she was a very strong-willed woman, with bright mind, much tact and independent views. A true head of a family'.[43]

One of her relatives wrote that Morozova managed her family 'with indis-putable authority and energy'.[44]

The Nikolskaia manufactory included six main factories (a cotton-spinning, a cotton-weaving, a cotton-printing and a cotton-bleaching mills, a dyery, and a textile-finishing plant) and nine auxiliary works (including a pig-iron foundry, a gas works, a chemical plant, a fitting shop, a turner's shop, an electric power station, and a peat works), located on 409 desiatinas (1,104 acres) of land. Seven offices in Moscow and at the mills were responsible for communicating with suppliers and clients.[45] According to the Ministry of Finance, in 1890 the Nikol-skaia manufactory was Russia's second largest industrial producer in terms of annual output: that year it manufactured goods to the value of 13.3 million roubles (and employed 17, 252 workers).[46]

It is noted in Irina Potkina's book that, when Maria took over the enterprise, she transformed the system of its management: the principle of individual decision-making was replaced by that based on group leadership, with the responsibilities being strictly divided among the four company directors[47] – Maria's two sons, her son-in-law and the accountant Kolesnikov. Twenty-seven-year-old Savva Morozov (educated in England as a chemical engineer) was in charge of production, including the issues of equipment and product quality. Maria's twenty-nine-year-old eldest son, Sergei Morozov (educated as a lawyer), though nominally a director, devoted most of his time to charity, not business. The third director, Maria's son-in-law Nazarov, was in charge of raw-material supply, financial settlements with foreign partners (cotton was purchased on the Liverpool Exchange), and the running of the head office in Moscow. The fourth director, Kolesnikov, was responsible for trade and for the circulation of documents.

So far as the distribution of shares is concerned, in 1893 Maria owned almost one-half of the whole block (48.2 per cent or 2,413 shares); her sons, Savva and Sergei, owned 13 per cent each; and her daughters and sons-in-law had 3–5 per cent each.[48]

In the days of Maria Morozova, the firm's strategy of development consisted of three major components: technological modernization, optimized crediting and innovations in selling.

Technological modernization had been planned by Timofei Morozov; it was carried out in 1889–90 by his successor, Maria, who, among other things, replaced gas lighting by electricity and installed new spinning machines. In the late 1890s, the old English steam engines were replaced by the more economical steam engines manufactured by the Görlitz machine-building plant (Germany), 'Sulzer-Brüder' (Switzerland) and by the Morozovs' own mechanical plant.[49]

Maria Morozova put an end to the practice of obtaining bank credits from the Moscow Commercial Bank and the Moscow Office of the State Bank (at a 5–7 percent annual rate), and instead started to get credits from the personal capital of the owners, at a 3-percent annual rate. Thus, in the 1882–3 operational year, Morozova used her own funds for providing a 3.4-million-rouble credit to the Nikolskaia manufactory; in the 1903–4 operational year – for providing another credit in the amount of 2.25 million roubles.[50] It is not inconceivable that this scheme was devised in order to eliminate the possibility of external creditors initiating bankruptcy proceedings against the firm, by Morozova herself.

As regards the sales policy of the enterprise, it should be noted that the emphasis shifted from wholesale seasonal sales at the Nizhnii Novgorod and other fairs to all-year-round wholesale trading through the permanent representations of the firm established in St Petersburg, Nizhnii Novgorod, Kharkov, Rostov-on-Don and Irbit. The Moscow office in Kitai-Gorod remained the headquarters. It handled up to 60 per cent of sales. The fabrics produced by the Nikolskaia manufactory were known for their high quality, elegant design and fast colours. Extremely popular in Russia, they were also exported to China and Persia. The volume of production of fabrics, cotton wool, thread and yarn was increasing year on year. Owing to the company's great success on the market, its fixed capital increased from 5 million roubles in 1873 to 15 million roubles in 1907. All this was achieved due to the far-sighted strategy of the firm's proprietress.

Maria Morozova did not quit the company even after the demise, in 1905, of her beloved son Savva, who died under suspicious circumstances at a hotel in Cannes (France), where he had come for medical treatment. Maria kept her grief to herself, and it was made evident only by the mourning dresses she never ceased wearing after the day of her son's death, and by her long prayers. The content of Morozova's testament demonstrates her meticulously developed strategy for strengthening the family's financial position. All the executors appointed by Morozova were her closest male relatives: her son Sergei; Sergei's brother-in-law Aleksandr Krivoshein (Minister of Agriculture under Stolypin); her son-in-law Grigorii Krestovnikov (who was a banker, a member of the State Council and Chairman of the Moscow Exchange Committee); and her grandson Sergei Nazarov.[51] All those persons were professional lawyers, which also pay tribute to Maria's thorough approach to managing her business.

The total value of the inheritance amounted to 30.2 million roubles. The shares in the Nikolskaia manufactory were worth almost 7 million roubles. More than half of Maria's wealth (approximately 16 million roubles) was in the form of securities: among her favourites were state annuity certificates with a fixed interest rate of 4 per cent per annum (6.6 million roubles); bonds of the Russian 4.5 per cent Loan of 1906 (1 million roubles); 4.5 per cent bonds of the Moscow-Kiev-Voronezh Railway; and 4 per cent bonds of the Riazan' – Urals Railway (1.1 and 1.55 million roubles respectively).[52] As regards foreign paper, the Moscow millionairess clearly trusted German securities, because some of her money was invested in bonds of the Baden, Hessen and Prussian Loans (280,000 roubles).[53] Her trust in the reliability of the German banking system is reflected by the fact that her only foreign bank account was with the Berlin branch of Deutsche Bank. The inheritance was divided into five shares received by Maria's son Sergei, her daughters Anna and Julia, and the children of the late Savva and Aleksandra. 'In order that [they] remember the grandmother', Morozova bequeathed 10 thousand roubles to each of her twenty-seven grandchildren.

The funeral of Maria Morozova became a memorable event for every Muscovite. Moscow Governor Vladimir Dzhunkovskii wrote that the death of

Morozova 'has deprived the merchant Moscow of one of the prominent and colourful representatives of its womanhood'.[54] In accordance with her wishes and in compliance with Orthodox rites, food and money were distributed to the poor, and on the day of the funeral two Moscow charitable canteens served free dinners to one thousand persons. More than 26,000 workers of the Morozov mills received money (approximately in the amount of their daily wages) and 'victuals for the funeral repast'.[55]

In her private life, Morozova was wilful, and contemptuous of certain generally accepted rules. According to one memoirist, Maria's son, Savva Morozov, once described his mother as follows:

> She dressed and acted like a gentlewoman, loved to read novels, was acquainted with many Slavophiles, and yet would not permit electricity in her home because she considered it a supernatural force. She busied herself with philanthropy and ... loved no one, could not even find a tear to shed at the death of her husband, and ruled over her sons with an iron fist.[56]

In our opinion, this seemingly very tough characteristic can be explained by the apparent underlying similarities in the characters of Maria and her son. The nature of their strong personalities was essentially egocentric.

As in the case of other Moscow female entrepreneurs, the main reason for Morozova's assuming entrepreneurial functions was the death of her husband. The difference between her case and the earlier ones consists in the fact that Timofei Morozov began initiating his wife in the management of the family business almost twenty years before his death – as soon as their children had come of age. Maria Morozova accomplished her mission successfully due to her becoming a businesswoman capable of turning her capital, knowledge and information into a lucrative business potential.

If a family was not united in its approach to business or was not ambitious enough to aspire after high social and financial status, this inevitably led to conflicts and could result in the destruction of that family, as it happened in the Shchekins case.

4. The Dictate of Money: the Shchekins Case

When a woman had a considerable personal wealth, it could create a dictate-of-money situation. When this woman descended from a family whose social status was much higher than that of her husband's family, it could further complicate matters. But when the woman in question owned a business, the situation could become really explosive, as it happened in the case of Moscow female merchant Nadezhda Shchekina, née Khludova. The details of the Shchekin family's conflict were considered at the highest level – by Prince Vladimir Dolgorukov,

Governor General of Moscow, and by the Assembly of Deputies of the Moscow Merchant Society.

In June 1882, the Office of the Governor General instructed the Merchant Society to consider the petition of honorary citizen Sergei Shchekin, filed to the effect that a trusteeship be imposed on the property of his wife Nadezhda 'for the reason of her wastefulness and inappropriate behaviour'. In accordance with the existing procedure, a police investigation was carried out, and a number of witnesses from among the Shchekins' neighbours and acquaintances were questioned.[57]

The following circumstances were thus revealed. In 1860, Nadezhda Shchekina, daughter of Nazar Khludov who belonged to a prominent dynasty of textile manufacturers, married Sergei Shchekin. The bride was sixteen years old, and the groom was twenty-six. Sergei's father, Il'ia Shchekin (1792–1864), was a well-known cloth manufacturer, merchant of the First Guild, and former Mayor of Moscow (in 1849–51). The peasant ancestors of both Sergei and Nadezhda hailed from the neighbouring villages of the Riazan Province; they were distant relatives. In 1871 Nadezhda bore a son, Mikhail.

In 1864, Sergei Shchekin and his four brothers jointly inherited their father's cloth mill (in 1854 it employed 500 workers), which quite soon went out of business. Sergei began to trade in yarn, but turned out to be rather inept: in a few years' time he was deep in debt. In 1867, Shchekin's creditors initiated legal proceedings against him with the Commercial Court. Shchekin's debts amounted to 468,330 roubles, while the property he owned was valued at 278,485 roubles – clearly not enough to cover the indebtedness. The list of creditors included approximately forty persons and firms.[58] On 13 March 1868, after a six-month-long investigation, Sergei was declared to be an insolvent debtor. However, Sergei was rescued by his wife. Nadezhda reached an amicable arrangement with the creditors (with the debt to be paid off for as little as 14 kopecks on the rouble), and repaid some of her husband's debts out of her own pocket. Sergei was faced with the inevitability of arrest and detention in a debtors' prison, but was saved from this ordeal by his wife's vouching for him. On 22 March 1868 Nadezhda picked Sergei up from the police station, after having signed the following document:

> I, the undersigned, hereby certify ... that, in accordance with Resolution of 19 March, No 78, of the Administration established to supervise the case of my husband, honorary citizen Sergei Il'ich Shchekin, I have bailed the above-named husband of mine on condition of his not leaving Moscow, and have undertaken to produce him [before the authorities] at the request of the Administration.
>
> Signed: Honorary citizen Nadezhda Nazarovna Shchekina.[59]

In June 1869 the case was closed. In 1870, Sergei completely abandoned commerce. To keep him occupied, Nadezhda appointed him manager of her two rental houses (responsible for collecting rent, paying taxes, purchasing victuals and paying the servants). The houses located in prestigious districts (the Arbat and Pokrovka Street) were a source of considerable profit – Nadezhda's annual income from the thirteen flats she was renting out was expected to be 8,210 roubles. However, according to Nadezhda, her husband, 'while residing with her and not having any property of his own, wasted her money, collected the incomes and did not hand over the money'. Meanwhile, Nadezhda set up her own business by opening a children's clothes shop in the fashionable 'Solodovnikov's Arcade'. From 1879 onwards, she was recorded as member of the Second Guild of the Moscow merchantry. The relations between the spouses increasingly deteriorated with the passage of time. In due course, the confrontation reached its climax: on orders from Nadezhda, her servants 'threw away' (as a female neighbour described their action to the police) Sergei's bed and mattress from the family bedroom into the closet. The hostilities were not limited to domestic level, also spreading to the legal sphere – with Sergei submitting the aforementioned petition to the Governor General of Moscow.

In the course of further investigation it was revealed that earlier, in April 1882, Sergei had given his wife a separate-residence permit.[60] In May Nadezhda and her son Mikhail left for one of the southern European health resorts to 'bathe in the sea'. It was exactly at that time that Sergei initiated legal proceedings for the imposition of a trusteeship on Nadezhda's property on the pretext of her wastefulness. On having been informed about this, Nadezhda wrote a letter to the Governor General whereby she asked that consideration of her case be suspended until her return to Moscow. At the same time, she pointed out that the witnesses 'of her reputedly luxurious life' put forward by Sergei were her former servants sacked for laziness. Also, Nadezhda refuted Sergei's affirmations of her having had several affairs with their son's tutors. Nadezhda asked the authorities that some additional witnesses, apart from those recommended by her husband, be also heard, and in particular her cousins – Varvara Morozova (owner of the Tverskaia manufactory), Ol'ga Lanina (wife of the owner of the biggest Moscow mineral water and fruit processing plant and editor of the liberal newspaper *'Moskovskii Courrier'* (the Moscow Messenger), Vasilii Khludov (director of the Egor'evskaia manufactory, a well-known intellectual and a virtuoso pianist), her mother (in her second marriage Princess Tenisheva), and a number of others.

In the course of the questioning of these witnesses, it turned out that 'at first [that is, after his marriage] Shchekin behaved depravedly ... permitted himself to consume alcoholic beverages and indulged his other indecent inclinations' and thus had squandered all his property. In business matters he was a complete failure. After having been recommended by the Khludovs to a number of private commercial firms, 'he nowhere demonstrated any success' and was sacked.

In August 1882, Nadezhda Shchekina sent another letter to the Merchant Board, whereby she interpreted the motives of her husband as follows:

> bearing in mind the specific circumstances of her marital position and that her husband, who does not have any occupation or any property, has given her a separate-residence permit and therefore cannot use her fortune in a legal way, the aim of his pursuits consists in achieving by all means, including libel, the imposition of a trusteeship on her … property and in making … all her estate subject to his control.

Then Nadezhda pointed out that

> attention should also be paid to the fact that the person who accuses me of wastefulness has absolutely no means, that he squandered everything he got from his parents and became insolvent; while I, whom he calls wastrel, was and is doing trade, and by now not only have not diminished my means, but significantly increased them. Hence, I am asking the Merchant Board to critically assess the personalities [of the witnesses] and the essence of the testimonies referred to by my husband.[61]

In the end, witnesses were divided into two camps. Those who supported the husband were accusing the wife of having an anxious and fidgety character (while at the same time admitting that she was a kind woman and by no means a miser), of being prone to luxury (Matveev, who rented a flat from Shchekina, considered it a sign of luxury that she kept a rented carriage) and to receiving guests; and they noted the calm disposition of Sergei Shchekin (Braun, a student of Moscow University who had been giving lessons to the Shchekins' son, said that 'Shchekin always behaved modestly, and humoured his wife in everything, while she treated him with disdain'). Those who supported the wife stated that they had never noticed Nadezhda being prone to luxury, wastefulness and insobriety (Maria Flei, saleswoman from Shchekina's shop: 'Shchekina does not live grandly, but in accordance with her means'), and that Nadezhda visited her shop daily and stays there from 12 am to 3 am, personally controlling the trade. Nevertheless, after having considered the arguments put forth by the parties, the Assembly of Deputies of the Merchant Society found no grounds for continuing the investigation and passed a ruling that Sergei Shchekin's request concerning the imposition of a trusteeship on his wife's property should be satisfied. A report to this effect was immediately sent to Governor General Prince Dolgorukov.

However, Prince Dolgorukov refused to confirm this ruling, because he believed that Shchekina's wastefulness and negative influence on her son had not been proven. The Shchekins case was forwarded to the Head Police-Master of Moscow for further investigation. The ruling of the Assembly of Deputies was declared to be unfounded. A special opinion was expressed by Chairman of Moscow Exchange Committee Nikolai Naidenov (it is noteworthy that in

1859–67 his predecessor in this position had been Nadezhda's uncle, Aleksei Khludov, in whose family she was brought up after her father had fallen gravely ill and then died in 1858). Naidenov did not agree with the arguments put forth by the Governor General and stated that the Assembly had based its ruling on the information that seemed to be reliable, and had acted 'according to their conscience'. He also said that the Governor General had the right to take a decision differing from that of the Assembly of Deputies. As a result, the Assembly decided not to hurry with passing its verdict and to re-examine the full amount of evidence.

A short time later, Shchekin withdrew his petition. He moved into his mother's house, which was in a walking distance from his conjugal nest. In order to vex his wife and to prevent her from travelling abroad, Shchekin hampered her being issued a separate-residence permit (which had to be renewed periodically). In 1887, to achieve her ends, Nadezhda wrote a petition to the Emperor, requesting that such permit be granted to her.[62]

The Shchekins case is curious in several of its aspects. We see that the evolution of conjugal relations took place in the context of a crucial stage in the process of female emancipation.[63] Sergei Shchekin was a representative of a patriarchal merchant family which had been dominated, over the course of two generations, by the pattern of absolute subjection of the wife to the authority of her husband (reflected in legislation by the formula: 'The wife must live with her husband in love, respect and total obedience'). The first ten years of the Shchekins' marriage had passed in accordance with this rule. Having got married at the age of sixteen, Nadezhda was still immature and therefore could not soberly analyze the economic and behavioural situations within which her family lived. For Nadezhda, the strong impetus for re-assessing her self-identification came from her realization that Sergei was incapable of transacting his own business (trading in yarn). To make matters worse, her husband became depressed and made no attempts at resolving his business problems. Nadezhda, then aged twenty-seven, took the situation under her control, examined the legal aspects of the problem and repaid the debts out of her own pocket. After having been saved from bankruptcy, her husband continued to play truant. Nadezhda saw that the cultural and psychological dissonance between her and Sergei was ever increasing.

Apparently, her main motivation was the desire to prevent any dishonour descending on the family, and to remain in the ranks of the Moscow merchant elite where she belonged from the day she was born. The Khludov family was known for its high spiritual and aesthetic demands, charity activities and patronage of the arts. Nadezhda's grandfather had a peasant background, whereas his five sons, including Nadezhda's father Nazar, were europeanized Russian merchants who, according to memoirists, as early as 1860s had established an office in Britain (in Liverpool; it was run by Nadezhda Shchekina's first cousin, Ivan

Khludov). In order to characterize the Khludov family, we are going to cite here two memoirs. Thus, N. Varentsov wrote: 'The Khludovs, undoubtedly clever, energetic, enterprising, with decisive character, stood apart from other representatives of their estate'.

Margarita Morozova was less flattering in her judgement:

> The Khludovs were known in Moscow as very gifted, clever but extravagant people, one had to be always wary of them as of those who were unable to fully control their passions.[64]

The well-known Moscow Anglophile and art collector, Nadezhda's uncle Gerasim Khludov, wrote this in his journal (which he kept from 1835 to 1877) about his younger brother – Nadezhda's father: 'Nazar ... He can be called, if only this is possible, a philosopher of the 19th century. A writer.'[65]

This was the environment in which Nadezhda had grown up.

At the age of thirty-five, in the nineteenth year of her marriage, Nadezhda chose her own way of emancipation by starting a business. Before that, she had never experienced any material troubles: having been provided with a substantial dowry by her parents (Nadezhda's father, who died in 1858, bequeathed 986,908 roubles to his wife and three children),[66] she also was receiving income from renting out her apartments, which enabled her to keep several servants, a tutor for her son, and to invite students of Moscow University as crammers. Besides, every year she went on vacation to Europe. In this case, Nadezhda was motivated in starting her business not by a need for profit, but by a desire to act in contradiction the contemporary gender stereotypes, which were fully complied with by her husband, whose proneness to passivity was further widening the gap between the spouses.

As additional arguments in favour of interpreting in this light the case of Nadezhda Khludova-Shchekina, we can point to the reaction of the Assembly of Deputies of the Moscow Merchant Society to this conflict between husband and wife. Although during the collapse of her husband's enterprise Nadezhda had displayed a sensible conduct and keen business intuition (by acting in a more energetic fashion that Sergei), the majority of merchants-deputies spoke against Nadezhda, who had demonstrated the free spirit of an emancipated female merchant. They viewed this freedom as a threat to the rigid genderized pattern, when only widows, in view of their exceptional position consolidated in legislation,[67] were allowed to engage in business activity on their own, but without getting into any disputes with the senior members of the self-governed merchant corporation, where males were indisputable rulers. As for Nadezhda, by her behaviour she had disrupted the gender-segregated socialization.

So, what course did Nadezhda's life take in later years? She succeeded in freeing herself psychologically from her former life (by obtaining a separate-residence permit). She sold her house, where she had lived for nineteen years with her husband, to her neighbours, the famous Moscow confectioners Abrikosovs, and then moved to the Arbat district, where she bought two houses. In one of these houses she lived herself, and the other was rented out. Her strong character and analytical mind, backed by her capital, enabled her to lead an independent life.

She was never faced with the problem of her own bankruptcy, to which many female entrepreneurs fell victim in the 1880s.

5. Bankruptcies: Businesswomen Faced with Financial Distress

In a discourse in economics, bankruptcy represents one of the serious conflicts arising in the course of the development of Russia's modern market economy and business culture.[68]

Below we are going to consider two bankruptcy cases. In the first one (the Kosheverova case) the female entrepreneur abstained from any business activity, having completely entrusted it to her son-in-law, who then brought the family firm to its collapse. In the second one (the Panina case) the businesswoman was acting on her own, but the insufficiency of her starting capital and the situation characterized by the onset of an economic crisis in 1882 (when merchants in their mutual settlements switched over to transactions in cash, and discontinued selling goods on credit for the time being) forced her to close down her business, which had existed for six years.

The Kosheverova Case

In the previous chapter we discussed the case of Anna Tikhonova, who based her relationship with her son-in-law, the latter being her only partner in the family business, on strict discipline and regular reports. This pragmatic strategy consistently implemented by Tikhonova, was entirely reasonable, because it allowed her firm to successfully survive until the 1917 Revolution. Quite the opposite happened in the family of the female merchant Glafira Kosheverova: she entrusted her firm to her son-in-law, and in the next twenty years his efforts resulted in the complete ruin of the Kosheverovs' family business.

In October 1885, the newspaper *'Senatskie vedomosti'* placed the information concerning the Moscow female merchant Glafira Kosheverova being declared to be insolvent. Kosheverova, who had been widowed in 1861 at the age of thirty-nine years, was the owner of a wholesale trade in cotton fabrics in Kitai-Gorod. In 1872, Glafira belonged to the First Guild, owned two houses on Bolshaia Ordynka (a street where many rich merchants were also residents), a shop in Kitai-Gorod, and two shops at the Nizhnii-Novgorod Fair. Twelve years later her business was subject to bankruptcy administration. On 15 October 1885, Glafira (accompanied by her lawyer) had to appear in person before a general meeting of creditors, where she was presented with claims amounting to the enormous sum of 420,739 roubles (approximately £42,000).[69] The majority of Glafira's creditors were suppliers for her wholesale business – either owners of textile mills (as the cotton manufacturers, Moscow Germans Emil Zündel and Albert Hübner, her debt to each of them being approximately 24 thousand roubles), or the biggest wholesale traders in textiles (as the silk merchants - Vladimir Shchenkov, the debt to whom amounted to more than 170 thousand roubles, and the Grachev brothers with 60,000 roubles to claim). This means that the debts had resulted from her failure to pay for goods taken on credit.

At the creditors' meeting, Glafira Kosheverova submitted a written appeal, in which she explained that 'her trade business, with the right to buy on credit, has been managed since 1861, on the basis of a power of attorney, by her son-in-law Vladimir Serikov, who in the course of that trade made debts involving substantial amounts of money, and that she, Kosheverova, at the present time is unable to satisfy the creditors from the property owned by her for the reason of the total decline in trade'.[70] It turned out that one of her houses was mortgaged to the merchant Golofteev for 70,000 roubles, the other was mortgaged to the Moscow City Credit Society for 12,000 roubles, 'all the flats in these houses are leased out, and the money thereof has been received in advance'.

In the period from 15 October 1885 to 15 February 1886, Kosheverova's finances were audited, and then the issue of auctioning off her Moscow houses and the shops in Moscow and Nizhnii-Novgorod was raised. An inspection of Kosheverova's office in Kitai-Gorod revealed that the main commercial books were missing, while the entries in those that were available were inaccurate. On 17 February 1886, Kosheverova submitted a new written explanation, where she recollected certain facts that had not been reflected in the first document. Thus, she stated that she had learned about the decline in her affairs from her son-in-law Serikov only in September 1885, after which she had had to mortgage her houses. From the money received by Kosheverova, her son-in-law asked her to give him 42,000 roubles, saying that he needed to urgently make payments against the promissory notes issued to him by the Mikhail Serikov & Sons Trading House (owned by his brothers). Kosheverova gave him the money, but later, reconstructing in her memory the events of recent years, she realized that her son-in-law had simply wheedled that sum from her by taking advantage of her moment of weakness. She insisted that 'for several years already neither she nor her attorney Vladimir Serikov, as far as she knows, have bought any goods from the Serikovs' trading house, and besides the turnovers of her trade were by no means so extensive that a big debt could have arisen'. Then Glafira wrote that from her son-in-law she 'did not demand any accounts of the trade, fully trusting him as the husband of her daughter',[71] and in this connection her son-in-law was not paid any salary. She annually spent 3,000–4,000 roubles on her own personal needs.

On 19 December 1886, the Bankruptcy Administration (its decision being coordinated with the Trade Statute) ruled that Kosheverova's insolvency had resulted 'not from any deliberate intention and fraud on her part, but from carelessness and risk in respect of [her] unlimited trust in [her] clerk son-in-law', and therefore she should be recognized as 'an unfortunate debtor', 'victim of deception on the part of … the clerk son-in-law, on whose unfair acts she could rely to a lesser extent than on those committed by any unrelated persons'.[72] After the sale of Kosheverova's property, the sum of 54,181 roubles was received for the redemption of her debts, and so her creditors were able to receive only 12.5 kopecks on the rouble. Instead of her former status as a merchant of the First Guild, Kosheverova now found herself to be a poor *meshchanka*, dependent on the charity of her relatives.

The investigation now became focused on her son-in-law Serikov. It was found that he had taken advantage of Glafira Kosheverova's trust in him and used it for his own enrichment. From 1871 onwards Serikov, behind Kosheverova's back, had been mortgaging to banks the promissory notes issued by her to various persons, and from 1879 onwards he had also been registering, with various persons and banks, promissory notes allegedly issued by Kosheverova to the Mikhail Serikov & Sons Trading House. He made no entries in the commercial books with regard to these promissory notes, gave nothing to the Serikov brothers, but used the money he had been receiving to purchase the country estate 'Butovo' near Moscow and to start there the construction of a *dacha* settlement, on which he had spent 50,000 roubles. Serikov's case was forwarded to a court of justice.[73]

It should be added that by no means all Kosheverova's creditors agreed with the ruling of the Commercial Court. Some of them declared that 'if Kosheverova had demanded annual accounts from her son-in-law she would not have been ruined',[74] and so they demanded that she be punished more severely. However, they remained in minority, and thus the main punishment for Kosheverova became the loss of all her property and her formerly high social status, as well as the shame that befell her at the end of her life because of her own naivety, gullibility and indisposition to personally manage and rigidly control her own business.

The Panina Case

In 1884, the Moscow Commercial Court considered the case of Maria Panina. In 1878, Moscow *meshchanka* Maria Panina, then aged twenty-two, inscribed in the Second Guild of merchants, and had remained its member ever since. By that time, she was married and had three children. With her husband, *meshchanin* Aleksandr Panin, and their children she lived in her own two-storey house, bought in 1878 from *meshchanin* Medvednikov (on an instalment arrangement: 3,200 roubles was paid by Panina lumpsum, while she took upon herself the obligation to pay the rest of the sum, amounting to 4,000 roubles, over the next year, in respect of which she gave him a bill of exchange).

At first (in 1878–81), Panina traded in textiles in Kitai-Gorod. In 1878 she established a factory for manufacturing rubber bands in one of the wings of her house. As she had no starting capital, she spent her own savings (generated from her trading profits and the rent payments for the flats in her rental house) on purchasing the necessary equipment. On 15 May 1881, apparently in the hope that new technologies would guarantee a market success of her goods, she took a loan of 8,000 roubles from a rich Ukrainian merchant, Mikhail Bocharov, in order to further equip her factory.[75] The loan was to be repaid in three years at an interest rate of 10 per cent. For two years, her business was developing rather successfully. Panina paid her debts accurately, in particular in 1884 she repaid 5,000 roubles plus interest to Bocharov, and then further extended the loan agreement against the remaining sum of 3,000 roubles. Between 1879 and 1883, she gave birth to three more children, with yet another pregnancy ending up in a miscarriage. In spring 1883 Panina, who had hitherto been making on her own all the decisions concerning her factory, gave her husband, Aleksandr Panin, the power of attorney 'to fully administer and manage' the house and the factory.

Previously Panina had loaned, against promissory notes, 8,000 roubles from St Petersburg merchant Meinhardt who, because of her failure to repay the dept, filed a suit against her with the Moscow Commercial Court. At that time, as a result of the onset of the economic slump, the demand for the products of the rubber-band factory plummeted. Panina loaned 1,000 roubles 'to enhance the volume of trade turnover' (and later another 1,200 roubles) from her factory's foreman, *meshchanin* Itsyk Shapiro; but she was unable to repay even this debt. In summer 1883, the situation became very bad, Panina frantically taking money from new creditors in order to repay her previous debts. In the autumn she once more turned to Bocharov who, having been intending for a long time to settle in Moscow, suggested that she sell to him the entire property of her factory (the steam boiler, the Roley steam engine, 20 rubber-weaving machines, all the bench tools and finished products), of which, on 30 December 1883, a contract worth 25,100 roubles was signed.

In May 1884, on Meinhardt's petition, a case was opened at the Moscow Commercial Court. Meinhardt demanded that Panina be declared an insolvent debtor and so be placed in the debtors prison ('placed in custody'). Panina objected, putting it forth as her main argument that she owned a property consisting of a two-storeyed residential building with 16 rooms, a three-storeyed factory building, and a two-storeyed dormitory building for her workers. The value of all these buildings was estimated to be 40,000 roubles. The residential building was insured for 13,700 roubles.

When the case against Panina was investigated, it turned out that the amount of her debts was higher than the value of her property. Panina had to mortgage her house to the Credit Society. Meinhardt, through his attorney, continued to demand that she repay the money or be imprisoned. However, during July and August 1884 a police officer failed to find Panina at home, while her husband explained that she had gone first to Kiev and then to Piatigorsk (in the Caucasus). The search for Panina conducted by the police in Kiev and Piatigorsk yielded no results. In early September, Panina returned to Moscow, where a summons to appear in court on 5 September had been awaiting her. One day before the beginning of the court proceeding she submitted a certificate from her physician, dated as of 3 September, confirming the fact of her pregnancy 'complicated by a disorder of the nervous system'. With due regard for Panina's affliction, the members of the Commercial Court on 6 September came in person to her house in order to inspect her property. It turned out that the factory buildings and the house where she lived had been leased to Bocharov.[76]

On 8 October 1884, by a court decision, Panina was declared to be 'an insolvent trade debtor'. On 15 October, a detention order for Panina was issued. On 19 October, before being taken to prison, Panina was examined in her house by the staff gynecologist of the Moscow City Police, Bazhenov, and by municipal physician Glazkov. In the medical-inspection report, it was certified that the twenty-eight-year-old Panina was in the fifth month of her eighth pregnancy, 'of medium built, and suffering from attacks of hysteria'. On the basis of the physician's conclusion, since Panina had once already had a miscarriage in the third month of her pregnancy, this was recognized as a predilection to premature birth, which could happen again if Panina was placed in prison. The physician recommended that Panina should not be imprisoned.

On 20 November, a group of creditors came to Panina's house and made an inventory of her property. The only remnants of her former wealth in the sixteen rooms of the house were the furniture and curtains, including a walnut sofa with a green woollen reps upholstery and four similar armchairs, an oak dining table, a walnut card-table, twelve birch chairs, and woollen and gauze draperies on the windows and doors, together worth 42 roubles. On the same day, depositions concerning her debts and property were taken from Panina, her husband, and 'Shapiro and Prokhorov, employed as her servants'.

Panina admitted that for several months in 1884 she had failed to settle her debts, and so conveyed all her property to Bocharov in payment on her mortgage, while he at the same time took upon himself her debts to her other creditors. She was aware of the cause of her collapse, and stated it clearly in her deposition to the Commercial Court:

> Concerning the decline in my trading, I can point it out that it resulted from the very limited means with which [I] had started my business and from the non-issuance of goods on credit in recent time... Trading matters were managed at first [1878-spring 1883] by myself, and then my husband Aleksandr Panin on a power of attorney...[77]

The picture became more complete with the deposition of Aleksandr Panin. First, Panin confirmed that during the first five years his wife had managed the factory on her own (because she was the owner of all the immovable and movable property), and he had taken over the management only during the last year on the basis of the power of attorney given to him by his wife. He stated that the causes of his wife's bankruptcy were as follows:

> a) 'the high interest rates on the capital borrowed by her in order to establish her factory business', b) the decline in demand for rubber goods, c) 'the high costs of the upkeep of a family consisting of the children, relatives and servants, numbering 18 persons', and lastly d) 'all the operations in the factory business were started with borrowed capital, while my wife's own capital had been less than three thousand'.[78]

After the sale of her factory equipment to Bocharov, Panina managed to repay some of her debts. When all her immovable property had been transferred to Bocharov in compensation for the credit granted by him, he made a commitment to satisfy the claims of Panina's creditors. In their turn, the creditors recalled their suits filed with the Commercial Court, and on 21 January 1885 Panina's bankruptcy case was closed. Maria Panina's life in later years could not be traced. It is only known that she never again undertook any business.

The case of Panina is interesting, first of all, in that it provides answers to the questions raised in the discussions on 'separate spheres'. Modern researchers base their judgments on the experience of present-day life, which rather contradicts the notion that a woman who gave birth nearly every year could indeed combine her maternal and conjugal functions with an independent management of her own business. Panina's example can explain many things, if not all. It was the following factors that enabled a mother of many children to carry on with her business: her factory was one of the segments of her household; the system of long-term credits existing prior to the crisis helped to cover the deficit of financing; the availability of servants (even to persons with modest means, like Panina) made it possible to cope with the upbringing of children.

However, even a minor flaw in this fragile structure could lead to fatal consequences, which is testified to by the collapse of Panina's business.

Conclusion

A comparison of the aggregate data from *Ukazatel' fabrik i zavodov* for the years 1879 and 1884 has demonstrated that, during that five-year period, the number of proprietresses of enterprises increased 1.32 times (from 991 to 1309 persons), while that of female-owned enterprises – 1.29 times (from 1045 to 1354). These rates were higher that the overall rate of industrial development: in the same five-year period the number of all enterprises increased 1.04 times (from 26,067 to 27,235). The share of females in the total rouble volume of production grew from 4 per cent to 4.8 per cent, while in absolute values it rose by 1.5 times, to 63.6 million roubles in 1884. The number of workers at female-owned enterprises increased to 57.6 thousand. A quarter of all female-owned enterprises were equipped with steam engines, the highest levels being demonstrated by the textile industry (37.5 per cent of enterprises), machine-building (35 per cent), and the woodworking industry (34 per cent), which corresponded to the average mechanization level in those sectors.

The cases studied here demonstrate that the behaviour of these women could either be compatible with, or go contrary to the gender patterns that had emerged earlier. Inside the social group of the entrepreneurial elite, to which Morozova and Shchekina belonged, the boundaries of gender roles were by no means stable and unchangeable. Those women who owned substantial capital and real estate of their own could enjoy a higher degree of economic independence, including possibilities for making their own decisions concerning their participation in family businesses, or for the establishment of their own enterprises.

In the 1880s, there emerged amongst the owners of industrial enterprises several female magnates of merchant origin. This chapter features a biographical portrait of Maria Morozova, who in 1889, after her husband's death, became the Executive director of the Nikolskaia manufactory – Russia's second biggest industrial enterprise with more than 17,000 workers. The apogee of Morozova's successful career in business was the fivefold increase of her private wealth (from 6 million to 30 million roubles) during the twenty-two years of her being at the helm of her family business, and as a result she became one of the country's wealthiest individuals. This was the upshot of the cumulative effect of several factors: her substantial dowry and thus the opportunity to own a big personal estate early in her married life; good education; mutual understanding between the spouses and their orientation to the success of their family business; Morozova's participation in developing their firm's strategy until her husband's death, and then as his widow; and her belonging to the social network of the Moscow business elite. It was her enormous capital and strong character that made it possible for Morozova to avoid gender discrimination in her entrepreneurial activity.

As opposed to Morozova's case, that of Shchekina, who came from the elite merchant family of the Khludovs, shows that the differently vectored interests of husband and wife could have a deteriorative effect on both their family life and their family's business potential. Although Shchekina possessed a substantial estate of her own, which made it possible for her to be independent of her husband and to rely on her income from the lease of real estate, her marriage to a man without any entrepreneurial ambitions prevented Shchekina from realizing her potential as a successful business woman, and did nothing to elevate her social status. Moreover, when considering Shchekina's case, the deputies of the Moscow Merchant Society (only males being eligible to these posts) acted as staunch supporters of domestic ideology, and it was only the Governor General's interference which prevented the adoption of an unfair decision that Shcheki-na's personal property should be subject to the imposition of a trusteeship.

The chapter contains the life stories of two females whose businesses failed in the years of the 1882–5 crisis. The causes of their bankruptcy were as follows: the lack of a distinctly defined distribution of responsibility and control between the partners in a family business (the Kosheverova case); the insufficiency of the initial capital needed for establishing a factory and for its further development; the sharp decline in consumer demand for its products; and the crisis-imposed suspension of operations in the crediting system acting as an additional risk factor (Panina case).

However, among the four life stories described in this chapter there are by no means only those that can produce a rather depressing vision of the familial relationships between husband and wife in the merchant milieu. Morozova's case (and probably that of Panina, who had the benefit of her husband's psychological support both before and after her bankruptcy) can be estimated as stories of companionship and affection.

6 FEMALE ENTREPRENEURSHIP IN THE 1890s: A BREAKTHROUGH TOWARDS INDEPENDENCE

By the end of the nineteenth century, female entrepreneurship had started to play an important role in the Russian economy. As a result, there emerged a stratum of women with considerable personal wealth. By presenting figures and stories, we are going to demonstrate how the substantial personal fortunes of women from the merchant elite made it possible for their owners to be integrated in the process of investing in industry and trade. In the 1890s, as biggest family firms were being reorganized into joint-stock companies, women demonstrated their considerable degree of influence in business by acting as board directors and stakeholders.

The First All-Russian Population Census that took place on 28 January 1897 (with the Empire's population numbering 125.7 million, 13.4 per cent of whom resided in towns) revealed that, among persons owning independent trade businesses, women constituted 13.3 per cent (35,694 out of 267,989); among these, 166 women were heads of the biggest firms (2.9 per cent of a total of 5,695).[1]

Women's positions in industry and their control over enterprises are analysed on the basis of data taken from *Perechen' fabrik i zavodov* (The Guide to Factories and Plants, 1897) and similar analytical documents issued by the Ministry of Finance. The number of female owners of enterprises rose 29 per cent by comparison with 1884 (from 1,309 to 1,684), their relative share amounting to 6 per cent.

A special section addresses the socio-biographical parameters and economic activity of the female entrepreneurs of Moscow and St Petersburg in 1895 (set against similar parameters discussed in the chapter on the 1860s), thus making it possible to compare the female entrepreneurship structures existing in the two capitals in 1869 and 1895. In the 1890s, women accounted for 10.7 per cent of the guild merchantry in Moscow and for 8.7 per cent in St Petersburg; however, the range of their commercial interests was now much broader than during previous decades.[2]

The chapter ends with the story of Vera Firsanova, one of Moscow's richest female entrepreneurs. Firsanova attempted to repossess her personal commercial property which she had, at the time of her marriage, formally handed over to her husband 'in a fit of love passion'. However later, once being convinced of her husband's infidelity, Firsanova resorted to legal means in order to once again become owner of her property.

1. The 1890s: a Decade of Economic Growth

The 1890s were the time of rapid progress in Russian industry. During that period, while the volume of industrial production nearly doubled between 1890 and 1900 (from 1,582 million to 3,086 million roubles), production became mainly concentrated at big and medium-sized enterprises (the total number of enterprises decreasing by 26.5 per cent (from 31,979 to 23,488).[3] The highest production growth rate was noted in the extractive industries sector – in the oil (by 6.6 times, with its share in total production increasing from 1.9 per cent to 6.4 per cent) and coal (by 1.7 times, with its share in total production increasing from 1.5 per cent to 2.7 per cent) industries. However, the most significant phenomenon in the restructuring of Russian industry was the increased share in the total production volume of the metal-processing and machine-building sectors. While in 1890 the textile sector was an absolute leader (31.4 per cent), followed by the food sector (31.3 per cent), with metal-processing and machine-building occupying only the third place (16.5 per cent), by 1900 the role of metal-processing and machine-building had become more prominent (22.1 per cent), the shares of the textile and food sectors in the total production volume now accounting for 26.1 per cent and 24.9 per cent respectively.[4]

As summarized by L. Kafengauz, 'the overall dynamics of the whole industry in 1887–1900 ... characterizes the evolution of all the main groups of industry'. Annual growth of gross output in 1891–1900 was between 7.3 per cent (1894) and 13.9 per cent (1899); thus, on the basis of his resulting analysis of all the indices, Kafengauz noted 'a slump in 1890–1891 and a lengthy boom, uninterrupted from 1892 to 1900'.[5]

As before, the weak component of economic growth, despite the increase in absolute values, was the low number of steam engines being applied in Russia, as compared to that in developed countries of the West. In the early 1890s, the total horsepower capacity of steam engines applied in Russia's industry was 325,000 horsepower, whereas in Germany this index was higher by 5.7 times, in the United Kingdom - by 10.8 times, and in the USA – by 21.8 times. This lagging behind was less noticeable in railway transport, where the total horsepower capacity of steam engines in Russia was two million, thus being near the level of Germany (2.3 million horsepower), while amounting to one-half of that in the United Kingdom and to one-eighth of that in the USA.[6]

2. Female Entrepreneurs in Russian Industry in the 1890s

In the 1890s, the degree of women's participation in industrial production increased still further, reaching the century's historic high. Our estimations are based on the official data published by the Ministry of Finance in *Perechen' fabrik i zavodov*, encompassing 39 thousand enterprises, and the 1897 issue of *Materialy dlia torgovo-promyshlennoi statistiki* (Materials for Commercial and Industrial Statistics).[7] After excluding the more than 4,000 of enterprises in Poland, we analysed the data on the remaining 34,723 enterprises.

According to the *1897 Perechen'*, there existed 1,684 female-owned enterprises, belonging to 1,711 individuals.[8] In thirteen years (since 1884) the number of such businesses had risen by 1.29 times. The estimates indicate that these 1,684 enterprises with 105,799 workers produced goods to the value of 150.4 million roubles, which accounted for 6.0 per cent of Russia's total industrial output. The generalized results are tabulated in Table 6.1.

When we compare the data for 1884 and 1897, it becomes obvious that production volume (in money terms) at female-owned enterprises increased 2.4 times – from 63.6 million roubles to 150.4 million roubles (while the aggregate output of Russian industry rose by 1.9 times); the number of workers increased by 1.8 times – from 57.6 thousand to 105.8 thousand (the total number of industrial workers grew by 2.2 times).[9]

As before, the sphere of female industrial entrepreneurship was dominated by the textile and food industries, their aggregate share amounting to 84 per cent.

In the textile industry female-owned enterprises accounted for 10.6 per cent of Russia's total production volume. Among 201 enterprises, the lion's share was produced by family companies, which had been reorganized (in the late 1870s–early 1890s) into share partnerships. It was these companies – as a rule, based on family relationships – that flourished most during the 1890s, their production volume reaching its peak. A typical phenomenon of the 1890s became the participation of women in the management of enterprises in the capacity of directors of boards and stakeholders, their influence on decision-making – including financial decisions – being quite considerable (this fact is testified to by the minutes of board meetings, where the presence of women is recorded, with their personal signatures under the boards' decisions). Full-fledged members of a board consisting of three (or sometimes four or five) directors were often the widows, wives, sisters and daughters of male owners. In the previous chapter we described, by way of example, the case of Maria Morozova, who headed the Partnership of the Nikol'skaia Manufactory of 'Savva Morozov's Son & Co'. According to the *1897 Perechen'*, in the textile industry there existed twenty-five

Table 6.1. Number of Enterprises Owned by Women, by Branch of Industrial Activity (Russian Empire, 1897)

The branches are placed in the Table in descending order of the share of female-owned enterprises in the total volume of production

Industry	Number of female-owned enterprises (out of total number of 34,723)	Share of female-owned enterprises in total volume of production, in per cent / thousand roubles	Share of female-owned enterprises, by number of workers, in per cent / persons
Textile industry	201 out of 3,706 / 209 owners	10.6 per cent 85,738 out of 807,551	9.9 per cent 52,452 out of 527,306
Food production	927 (out of 14,852) / 930 owners	6.9 per cent 40,982 out of 591,462*	11.6 per cent 26,377 out of 226,758*
Machine-building and metalworking	97 (out of 2,055) / 100 owners	1.6 per cent 4,232 out of 265,490	2.9 per cent 5,537 out of 193,535
Tobacco	15 (out of 260) / 15 owners	10.6 per cent 3,205 out of 30,136	12.8 per cent 4,558 out of 35,705
Earthenware and brick industry*	119 (out of 2,935) / 124 owners	4.1 per cent 2,816 out of 68,851	4.9 per cent 6,277 out of 127,121
Leather industry	77 (out of 3,145) / 84 owners	3.2 per cent 2,300 out of 71,995	3.5 per cent 1,634 out of 46,108
Wood-working	66 (out of 2005) / 68 owners	2.5 per cent 2,300 out of 90,281	2.9 per cent 2,251 out of 77,260
Processing of fat and wax	33 (out of 1,051) / 33 owners	4.9 per cent 2,222 out of 45,175	4.1 per cent 521 out of 12,596
Paper production	35 (out of 452) / 35 owners	5.5 per cent 2,155 out of 39,043	5.6 per cent 2,323 out of 41,637
Chemical industry	43 (out of 533) / 43 owners	3.9 per cent 1,857 out of 47,115	5.6 per cent 998 out of 17,807
Matches	21 (out of 159) / 20 owners	13 per cent 1,753 out of 14,222	12.3 per cent 1753 out of 14,222
Carriage-making	5 (out of 204)	24 out of 7,430	61 out of 3,941
Musical instruments	2 (out of 50)	94 out of 2,076	71 out of 1,521
Printing shops	43 (out of 352)	766 out of 2,895	1,086 out of 4,545
Other: oil processing, rubber production, etc.	0 (out of 160)	0 out of 45,735	0 out of 1,727
	0 (out of 27)	0 out of 21,468	0 out of 2,337
	0 (out of 186)	0 out of 7,171	0 out of 7,189
Mining plants of Urals	No data	No data	No data
TOTAL	1,684 (out of 34,723)	6.0 per cent 150,444 out of 2,506,252	5.9 per cent 105,799 out of 1,797,698
Female Owners	1,711		

* Production of lime, bricks, earthenware, glass and construction materials.

partnerships with women as members of their boards of directors.[10] Now let us discuss a few examples of this phenomenon.

The post of Executive Director of the Tverskaia Manufactory Partnership (founded in 1859) was occupied in 1883–92, after the death of Abram Morozov, by his widow, Varvara Morozova, née Khludova (1848–1917). The Partnership's three directors during that period were her two eldest sons (Abram and Varvara had three sons) – Ivan and Mikhail, and their relative, an eminent businessman Alekseev. In 1893, Varvara handed over the reins to Ivan, but remained a director until 1916. The Tverskaia Manufactory was one of Russia's biggest enterprises (in 1897 its annual production was to the value of 6.7 million roubles, and it employed 5,772 workers). On Varvara Morozova's initiative, the Tverskaia Manufactory Partnership's factories had a hospital, a maternity 'shelter', a nursery, an orphanage, a retirement home, a 'shelter for the chronically ill', a library, a school, a theatre, and night classes for the workers. Varvara was the most prominent female philanthropist in Moscow, where she was born and lived all her life. She donated over one million roubles to health care and education, including 500,000 roubles to the psychiatric clinic of the Medical Department of Moscow University, the dormitory of the Imperial Higher Technical School, and the city's largest public library (the Turgenev Library). Morozova was chairperson of the Moscow Female Club, and her mansion near the Arbat hosted fashionable musical and literary society. After being widowed, she became a common-law wife of Professor of Moscow University Sobolevskii, editor-in-chief of the influential liberal newspaper '*Russkie vedomosti*'. In defiance of public opinion, she bore him two children.[11]

One more case: Marina, the widow of an owner of a textile factory, Griaznov, and his daughter Serafima (married name – Sadovnikova) were two (out of three) directors of 'The Pokrov Cotton and Shawl Printing Manufactory of P. N. Griaznov' partnership (founded in 1878) in Ivanovo-Voznesensk. In 1897, the Griaznovs' manufactory employed 609 workers and produced goods to the value of 3.2 million roubles.[12]

After three generations of male managers, women came to occupy the dominating positions in the family business of the Kuvaevs, owners of a cotton mill (founded in 1817) in Ivanovo-Voznesensk. In 1897, after the death of the mill's head, Kharlampii, who represented the family's third generation, it was headed in 1865–72 by his widow Ekaterina, and then by their only daughter, Nadezhda, who was married to a scion of a prominent 'textile dynasty', the Burylins. In 1887, the Burylin couple set up 'The Kuvaevs' Cotton-Printing Manufactory Share Partnership', where Nadezhda became one of its three directors (the other two being her husband and their relative, a businessman).[13] In 1897, the partnership employed 1,601 workers and produced goods to the value of 5.5 million roubles.

The overwhelming majority of big textile enterprises in dominating positions in management belonged to women were cotton-processing ones; these were situated in central Russia, mainly in Moscow and Vladimir Provinces (75 out of 201 enterprises).

The reason why big enterprises were predominant in the Russian textile industry was explained by the eminent German economist Gerhart von Schulze-Gävernitz, who visited Russia in the 1890s:

> In the West, big industrial enterprises evolved gradually out of the medium-sized and small businesses. In Russia large-scale production emerged at once, by the will of big capitalists. Thus, the development of Russian industry began with the already existing substantial capital concentration... It has turned out that the number of spindles per factory in Moscow and Vladimir is higher than in England and Germany.[14]

Schulze-Gävernitz wrote that 'the cotton industry in Russia emerged and developed while relying on local mass-scale consumption',[15] and he cited some examples of the rapid reorientation of society's lowest strata from homespun products to cotton fabrics:

> In 1895 I visited a small shop at one large village in Voronezh Province, in order to get some idea of the contemporary demand for goods on the part of peasants. Various cotton goods were predominant; women preferred for their festive outfits the brightly coloured calicos, which had totally ousted the bleak homespun products. Cotton machine-made yarns served as material for the rich and elaborate embroideries. The only item of non-Russian origin was the red yarn known under the name 'Müllhouse' – a distortion of the real name of the place where it is produced ... (Muhlhausen) in Thuringia. Men have also switched over to cotton clothes ... As usually there are very high temperatures in peasants' log houses, men and women alike wear cotton clothes at home, even in winter. When going out into the yard, they put on a coat and top boots.[16]

Thus, the development of the textile industry and the growing wealth of the proprietresses of textile enterprises were directly linked to changes in a model of consumption. The cheaper, durably dyed mass produced textiles were inevitably ousting the products of home weavers.

As for the food industries sector, its pattern changed little in comparison to the 1880s. A multitude of small and medium-sized flour mills and distilleries (situated mainly in western and southern provinces) were neighbours of sugar-processing giant plants belonging to female representatives of the Polish aristocracy and the Ukrainian bourgeoisie. The leaders by the numbers of enterprises were Kiev (sixty-four enterprises) and Volhynia (fifty-seven enterprises) Provinces. Among the provinces populated by ethnic Russians, the greatest number of food enterprises (forty-nine) were in Voronezh Province, with its well-developed agriculture.

The big landowner Countess Maria Branicka owned eleven enterprises in Kiev Province: four mills (all leased out), two distilleries, one brewery and four beet-sugar plants. Their aggregate annual production in 1897 (less the revenues from the lease of the mills) amounted to approximately 2.2 million roubles, and they employed a total of 2,010 workers. The 1890s saw the emergence, among the leaders of beet-sugar production, of Ukrainian female entrepreneurs who descended from two families of sugar magnates. The plant of Nadezhda Tereshchenko in Kiev Province employed 464 workers and annually produced goods to the value of 415,000 roubles. Natal'ia Kharitonenko owned a plant in Kharkov Province (in 1897, the output value was 1,142,846 roubles; the number of workers was 891).

The 1890s saw an increase in the activity of female entrepreneurs in the Baltic provinces – Estlandia (thirty-three enterprises) and Liflandia (eighteen enterprises). The specific feature of this region was the development of food enterprises (supplying their products to the markets) on country estates, the majority of whose owners belonged to the elite of the local nobility of German, Swedish and Danish origins (the so-called Baltic barons). Among the female owners of small and medium-sized enterprises with annual output to the value of between 3,000 and 25,000 roubles, which produced potato alcohol, cheeses, butter, and flour, there were Baroness Natalia von Ikskul (five enterprises, including three distilleries, one flour mill and one cheese dairy), Baroness Alexandra von Tiesenhausen (two enterprises), Anna von Buksgevden [von Buxhöwden] (two enterprises), and also Baronesses Justina von Wrangel, Elena von Ramm, Paulina and Molly von Dehn, Luise von Rennenkampf, Karoline von Lilienstadt, Josephine von Baggovuth [von Baggehufwudt], Maria von Wrede, and some others.

To illustrate the highly polyethnic character of female entrepreneurship (despite being represented by numerous examples, it cannot be precisely estimated), we can note the appearance in the 1890s of Greeks and Armenians among the owners of food enterprises in the southern provinces with the ethnic Russian population (e.g., in the territory of the Don Host). One Greek female entrepreneur (Kolimira Nomikos) in Taganrog owned two macaroni factories (with aggregate annual production to the value of 43,350 roubles, with thirty-seven workers); another Greek, Polyxenia Apodiako, owned one macaroni factory (annual production to the value of 6,970 roubles, ten workers). The Armenian Persane Nalbandova established her own trading house for the sale of macaroni produced by her factory (annual production 35,000 roubles, twenty-two workers). The initial capital for 'The Trading House of Nalbandova & Co', alongside Persane's own investments, was provided by two male stakeholders.

The regional dimension also became more complex. According to the *1897 Perechen'*, a number of large-scale female entrepreneurs operated in the food sector in Siberia. For example, the female merchant Guseva in the village of Shushenskoe near Minusinsk, Yenisei District, established, in 1874, a mill (in 1897, it employed nineteen workers and produced goods to the value of 63,610 roubles), and later, in 1889, a sugar refinery (in 1897 it employed 161 workers, and the value of its output was 153,127 roubles).

During that decade there occurred a new phenomenon – a successful development of enterprises with entirely female collective management, including in those branches of industry which had previously never belonged to feminized segments of entrepreneurship, e.g., in the manufacture of metal products. Some interesting material has been provided by our reconstruction of the history of the sisters Zav'ialov's firm, one of the best-known in Russia manufacturers of table knives and other types of cutlery, including scissors and razors. The Zav'ialovs had originally come from the village of Vorsma (Nizhnii-Novgorod Province), which had been famous since the eighteenth century for its production of knives; in the mid-nineteenth century it was home to 100 smitheries. Vorsma (just as Ivanovo, Russia's textile centre) belonged to Count Sheremetev, and so Ivan Zav'ialov, who in 1825 founded his first family enterprise, was Sheremetev's serf who ransomed himself in the late 1850s. After Ivan's death, the plant was inherited by his eldest son Alexei and then (*c.* mid-1870s) passed on to Alexei's widow Anna and his unmarried sisters Anfisa and Liubov'. They jointly owned the enterprise which manufactured:

> table knives with various mother-of-pearl, bone, stone, metal and wooden handles; pen knives with mother-of-pearl, tortoise-shell, ivory, mammoth and walrus ivory, reindeer, buffalo and simple horn, and wooden handles; travel knives...; daggers...; garden knives ...; razors, scissors - office, garden, tailor's, and ladies' of different kinds; tools - surgical, bench, joiner's and carpenter's, turner'...[17]

The products of the Zav'ialovs' plant were famous for their fine finish, which was confirmed by their being awarded the 'Honoris Causa' medal for the samples of their steel knives presented at the 1862 International Exhibition in London. This fact is mentioned in Dostoyevsky's novel *Teenager*, where one of the characters says:

> Patriotic feeling is gratified as well: for example, there is another story that the English promised Zav'ialov a million on condition that he shouldn't put his stamp on his hardware.[18]

While being managed by women in the second half of the period 1870s–90s, the firm was becoming increasingly stronger: thus, between 1879 and 1897 its annual output value rose from 100,000 roubles to 214,819 roubles, and the number of workers – from 300 to 1,055. In addition to the one in Vorsma, there was also another plant (manufacturing only tableware) in Vladimir Province.[19] In the late 1870s (after Anna's death) the Zav'ialovs' enterprise was transformed into a partnership with headquarters in Moscow, owned by the two sisters - Anfisa and Liubov'. From 1878 onwards, the elder sister, Anfisa Zav'ialova, then aged 34, inscribed in the Second Guild of Moscow merchants.[20] Both sisters remained single, and their business became their life. In Moscow, in Kitai-Gorod (on Nikol'skaia Street), they leased, in Anfisa's name, the premises for their office and head store from one of the Counts Sheremetev. The products were supplied to Moscow, St Petersburg, Ukraine, Siberia, Poland, the Caucasus and Persia.

The case of the Zav'ialovs demonstrates that the proprietresses focused their efforts not only on developing production. Their strategy also incorporated some other elements: the transfer of their head office to Moscow and the entry into the Moscow merchant community, through which they joined the all-Russian entrepreneurial network; the development of a second plant in Vladimir Province, in close proximity to Moscow; and expansion of their sales network, which thus encompassed all the regions of the Empire.

By way of summarizing our analysis of the role of female entrepreneurs in industrial development, we should point to two more circumstances that were not reflected in industrial statistics until the 1890s. Firstly, there was a marked progress in the production of printed matter: the *1897 Perechen'* contains information on forty-three female-owned printing shops (out of a total of 352): in 1897 they employed 1,086 workers, and their aggregate output value was 766,000 roubles. Secondly, there emerged a new branch – the manufacture of readymade clothes. The *1897 Perechen' 1897* offers details concerning thirteen enterprises, including eight in Moscow, one in Kazan', one in Yekaterinburg, one in St Petersburg, and two in Kharkov and Kharkov Province. Most of these factories were established in the 1890s. One example is the firm operating under the name of its female owner – 'Maria Nadezhina-Cherkasova'. Under this brand, various fur items were manufactured: winter coats, round cloaks, muffs and hats. The factory's output in 1897 was to the value of 10,000 roubles; it employed twenty-two workers. Another factory, owned by Klavdia Murav'iova and situated in Moscow Province, manufactured men's and ladies' overcoats which were then sold in Moscow shops. Murav'iova employed only men (twenty-five persons). The factory's output value in 1897 amounted to 10,000 roubles.

The end of the nineteenth century brought about certain qualitative changes in the structure of consumption. This became a determining factor in the development of female-owned industrial enterprises. Below we are going to discuss the extent to which it influenced the structure of 'female' commerce.

3. Female Entrepreneurs of Moscow and St Petersburg in 1895: Socio-Biographical Parameters and Economic Activity

As before (see Chapter 3), our analysis of the socio-biographical parameters and the structure of economic activity is based on the data taken from the 1895 'Reference Books' for St. Petersburg and Moscow.[21] The choice of Moscow and St

Petersburg, as was noted earlier, is motivated by the exclusive roles played by the two 'capitals' in the Empire's trade and industrial life. According to the 1897 Census, the shares of merchants and honorary citizens[22] were as follows: for the whole Empire – 0.49 per cent, for the provinces of European Russia – 0.59 per cent, the highest figures being demonstrated by St. Petersburg and Moscow – 3.98 per cent and 3.95 per cent respectively.[23]

In 1895, female merchants accounted for 8.7 per cent of St. Petersburg merchants (530 out of 6,064 persons), and for 10.7 per cent of Moscow merchants (564 out of 5,274 persons). By comparison with the 1869 indices, the number of female entrepreneurs increased in St. Petersburg (1869 N-501), while in Moscow it became lower (1869 N-583).

Below we are going to discuss parameters of ethnicity and age, relating to the elite group – the female merchants of the First Guild; and the distribution of female entrepreneurs by their occupation and marital status.

Ethnic Parameters

The female merchant community of St Petersburg comprised 410 Russians (77.4 per cent), fifty-four Germans (10.2 per cent), twenty-three Jewesses (4.3 per cent), nineteen French (3.6 per cent) and six English (1.1 per cent); the other ethnic groups (3.4 per cent) were represented by four Finns, three Swedes, two Swiss and two Belgian women, and by one person of Ukrainian, Polish, Austrian, Armenian, Greek, Karaim, and Bulgarian origin each. In Moscow, the female merchant group included 429 Russians (76.1 per cent), forty-one Germans (7.9 per cent), twelve French (2.3 per cent), and ten Jewesses (1.8 per cent); besides, there were six Austrians, three English and three Karaims and two persons of Swedish, Swiss, Belgian and Ukrainian origin each; besides, there were one person of Armenian, Greek and Finnish origin each. In fact, the parameters pertaining to the ethnic composition of the St Petersburg and Moscow communities of female entrepreneurs in the 1890s differed very little. The more prominent 'foreign' component (which increased from 8.9 per cent in 1869 to 23.9 per cent in 1895) among female entrepreneurs in Moscow is indicative of that group's overall internationalization – the process that also involved Moscow's commercial life at large.

Age Stratification

The most active group in St Petersburg was that of businesswomen aged thirty-one to sixty, whose share amounted to 72 per cent, including aged 31 to 40 - 108 persons (20.4 per cent); aged forty-one to fifty – 135 persons (25.5 per cent); and aged fifty-one to sixty – 140 persons (26.4 per cent). Five persons were under twenty years of age (0.9 per cent); forty-four persons (8.3 per cent) were aged twenty-one to thirty; ninety-eight persons were of senior age (18.5 per cent), including aged sixty-one to seventy – seventy-six persons (14.3 per cent); and aged over seventy – twenty-two persons (4.2 per cent). The oldest in the St Petersburg group was the eighty-two-year-old female merchant of the Second Guild Taisia Zvezdina, who came from the city of Rybinsk, Yaroslavl' Province. She had been a St Petersburg merchant since 1859 (or for thirty-six years), and traded in winter coats.[24]

The situation in Moscow was similar – the majority of businesswomen were aged thirty-one to sixty, whose share amounted to 75 per cent, including aged 31 to 40 - 130 persons (23.1 per cent); aged forty-one to fifty – 162 persons (28.7 per cent); aged fifty-one to sixty – 133 persons (23.6 per cent). Three persons were under twenty years of age (0.5 per cent); fifty persons (8.9 per cent) were aged twenty-one to thirty. Eighty-three persons (15.2 per cent) were of senior age (including aged sixty-one to seventy – seventy-three persons, or 12.9 per cent); and thirteen persons (2.3 per cent) were over seventy. Moscow's oldest female merchant was the eighty-year-old Pelageia Serebrennikova from Tula Province, who inscribed in Moscow merchantry at the age of sixty-six years (prior to that she had been inscribed in local merchantry). Pelageia traded in bread at the largest of Moscow's six railway terminals – Kursk Station.[25]

Statistics demonstrate that, by comparison with 1869, the age stratification of St Petersburg and Moscow entrepreneurs changed only slightly, while at the same time there was a closer similarity between the average age indices in the two cities – as a result of their having gone down in Moscow (in 1869 – 54.4 years, in 1895 – 51.1 years) and having become a little higher in St. Petersburg (in 1869 – 47.7 years, in 1895 – 48.6 years). This happened due to the increased share of married women belonging to the active age groups among female merchants.

An analysis of ethnic and age parameters has led us to the conclusion that the Moscow merchant corporation had equalled the St Petersburg one by the degree of its openness and flexibility – as recorded by the 1869 data for St Petersburg.

Below we are going to consider the similarities and differences then existing between female merchants of the First Guild in St Petersburg and Moscow.

The Elite Group: Female Merchants of the First Guild

By 1895 the number of female merchants of the First Guild had risen on the year 1869 by 1.9 times in St Petersburg, and by 1.3 times in Moscow. In 1895, there were 28 women inscribed in the First Guild of the St Petersburg merchantry (1869 N-15), which accounted for 5.3 per cent of its total membership of 530 (1869 N-501), while in Moscow the ranks of the First Guild included forty-four women (1869 N-34), which accounted for 7.8 per cent of its total membership of 564 (1869 N-583).

So far as their ethnicity is concerned, among the twenty-eight St Petersburg female merchants there were sixteen Russians, five Germans, five Jewesses, one

French and one Swede. Non-Russian female entrepreneurs accounted for 43 per cent of women inscribed in the First Guild of St Petersburg merchants (the average for both guilds being 19.4 per cent). In Moscow, of the forty-four female merchants, thirty-three were Russians, seven Jewesses, three English and one French (the share of non-Russian entrepreneurs being 25 per cent).

In our opinion, such a situation had to do, first of all, with the 'Jewish Question'. Among the Jewish female entrepreneurs of the First Guild, five were in St Petersburg and seven in Moscow. Under then existing legislation the permission to reside permanently outside of the Pale of Settlement[26] was granted (1859) only to merchants of the First Guild, who thus could live in either of the two capitals with their families (however, only with those of their children who were still minors), on condition of their having a previous five-year experience of successful economic activity within the Pale. After ten years of residence in a capital they could acquire the right of permanent residence there. Their children, on coming of age, usually also stayed on in the capitals by right of being students of the higher educational establishments there. This interpretation can be confirmed by the fact that some of the Jewesses who were paying the Guild tax at St Petersburg still lived within the Pale of Settlement, while having the opportunity at any time (for example, in an event of pogroms) to leave for the capital.

In 1895, of the twenty-eight St Petersburg female entrepreneurs of the First Guild, six owned industrial enterprises. Of these, three were merchants (Volkova, Gausch, Maksimovich), and three were noblewomen (Stenbok-Fermor,[27] Polovtsova, Karageorgievich). The female owners of industrial enterprises can be characterized as follows. The forty-five-year-old Alexandra Volkova, who had been inscribed in merchantry since 1874, was married (her husband also being a merchant) and operated her own independent business – a vodka plant, producing alcoholic beverages under the brand name 'Gothard Martini'. Another factory owner, the German Amalia-Luise-Leontina-Matilda Gausch (age unknown), had a leather factory 'Gausch & Co' (founded in 1868). In 1897 her factory employed thirty-three workers and manufactured sole leather and driving belts for machinery to the value of 130,000 roubles. In order to manage the factory, Matilda (this was the name by which she was known in St Petersburg) had established a partnership where the two shareholders beside herself were Theodor Gausch (evidently, Matilda's husband) and Georg Hans.[28] The third factory owner was Evdokia Maksimovich, owner of the huge 'Georg Landrin' Confectionery Factory.[29]

All the three noblewomen were representatives of the aristocracy, the core of all their businesses being mining plants in the Urals.

Countess Nadezhda Stenbok-Fermor (1815–97), as before, was one of the biggest producers of iron and rolled steel in Russia.[30]

The twenty-one-year-old Aurora Karageorgievich, née Demidova, Countess San-Donato (1873–1904), began to take out merchant certificates from 1895 onwards as a participant in the Demidovs' trading business – that family being owners of several dozens of plants in the Urals (which by their production volume were ahead of those owned by Stenbok-Fermor). Aurora represented both her own interests and those of her minor brother Pavel. Aurora was married to Prince Arsen Karageorgievich.[31]

The third noblewoman, Nadezhda Polovtsova (1843–1908), was the adopted daughter[32] and only heir of the manager of the State Bank of Russia (in 1860–6), Baron Alexander Stieglitz, whose enormous estate shortly before his death was estimated at 38 million roubles. At eighteen, Nadezhda married the twenty-nine-year-old Alexandr Polovtsov, who was member of the Senate and had ahead of him a promising career of a courtier (his father being Minister of State Domains, and his mother belonging to the eminent Tatishchev family). In 1885 Polovtsov achieved the highest rank of the 'Table of the Ranks' that of actual privy councillor and in 1883–92 he occupied the post of State Secretary to Emperor Alexander III, while at the same time being a member of the State Council and the Committee of Finance. From 1885 Nadezhda Polovtsova had been taking out guild certificates for the right to manage the mining plants in Perm Province in the Urals, which had been purchased in her name. In 1894 the metallurgical plant was built, which was named after her ('Nadezhdinskii') and became the biggest in the Urals. Together with her husband, Nadezhda was shareholder in a number of leading joint-stock companies, including the Krenholm Cotton Manufactory at Narva (presently in Estonia), the Neva Cotton Spinning Manufactory, and the Neva Thread Manufactory. In addition to the mining and metallurgical enterprises, Nadezhda Polovtsova also owned, according to the *1897 Perechen'*, four enterprises in the food sector: two in Voronezh Province – a flour mill (with annual output to the value of 206,775 roubles, and 138 workers) and a distillery (no data); and two in Tambov Province – another distillery (with annual output to the value of 59,150 roubles, and 64 workers) and a small starch works (with annual output to the value of 9,281 roubles, and nine workers).[33] Count Witte (Minister of Finance in 1892–8), irritated by Polovtsov – who was more successful in his career as a state official, in addition to his being a rich man and the owner of one of the most resplendent mansions in St. Petersburg – gave in his memoir a vitriolic characteristic of Polovtsov's entrepreneurial activity, the latter being the manager of his wife's affairs. Witte wrote that Polovtsov

> was all the time ... busy with various shady transactions: he would sell, buy, speculate – and speculated to such an extent that he speculated away nearly all of his wife's estate.[34]

Evidently, in this opinion Witte was guided by his dislike of Polovtsov, although the latter's entrepreneurial style in managing his wife's business is described very accurately.

Now let us look at the occupations of the other twenty-two female merchants of the First Guild. Of these, seven traded in textiles (three were Russian: Anna Dernova, Anna Kirikova, Anna Chiuvaldina; two – Jewish: Tsyva Monoszon and Vera Striziver; one German – Katharina Berg; and one French – Claude-Marie Giraud). They were all widows aged forty-two to sixty-three, who inherited their businesses after their husbands.

Another two female entrepreneurs, also widowed, owned steamship companies.[35] Elena Grigor'eva had, for forty years (1853–93), 'been attached to the capital of her husband', whose company kept steamers and coasting vessels at St Petersburg, on the rivers Volga and Kama, and on the Caspian Sea. From 1893 onwards, she managed the business on her own. Beside the ships, Elena also inherited a wharf and three houses at St Petersburg and one house at Sebastopol.[36] Elena was assisted in her business by her twenty-four-year-old son Vladimir. (Regretfully, we could find no materials concerning the turnovers of the Grigor'evs' company.) The other steamship company was inherited by Iroida Konetskaia (age unknown) after the death of her husband, who had been developing it for eighteen years. Iroida was the mother of eight children aged between twelve and twenty-five (five sons and three daughters). The third female entrepreneur associated with sea trade was a German, the 64-year-old Augusta-Elisabete Kron, who owned wholesale trade in wines 'at port' which she had inherited in 1889 after her husband Karl Kron, who had been managing this business for the previous twenty-five years (since 1864).

Two entrepreneuring widows had businesses in the financial sphere: the German Luzia-Nathalia Braun took on 'commissions', and the Jewess Anna Weisbrem had a banking office in Grodno (which was her permanent place of residence).

The other ten persons traded in a variety of goods, including sugar, eggs, firewood and clocks. The sixty-year-old Alexandra Petrovskaia (who never married) traded 'wholesale at the exchange'.

In Moscow, the share of female industrialists (seven persons out of forty-four) was smaller than in St Petersburg, having significantly decreased since 1869 (when seventeen female factory owners had been inscribed in the First Guild). Among the seven female-owned industrial enterprises, two manufactured textiles, while the other five produced sugar, pig iron, factory equipment, bricks, and leather.

The previously mentioned Anna-Katharina Gehner's sugar plant continued to operate successfully.[37] According to the *1897 Perechen'*, its annual production rouble volume and the number of workers had both increased (1879 – 1.9 million roubles, 286 workers; 1897 – 2.4 million roubles, 397 workers).

The British subject Elizabeth Hopper (b. 1834) was the owner of a big cast-iron foundry, founded in 1843 by her husband William Hopper (and which is still in operation today). The foundry had passed to her after her husband's death in 1885. In 1886, together with her two sons, Elizabeth founded the trading house 'W. Hopper & Co'. According to the *1897 Perechen'*, it employed 134 workers and annually produced goods to the value of 161,725 roubles.

Zinaida Fedotova (1829–97) was the owner of a big wool weaving mill founded in 1857. In 1862, after her husband's death, the thirty-three-year-old Fedotova inscribed in the Second Guild. During the thirty-five years of her being the factory's manager, Zinaida expanded her business by establishing, in 1874 in the village of Durykino, Moscow District, a second enterprise, which manufactured yarn for the Moscow-based factory. Fedotova had three sons, Pavel, Konstantin and Nikolai, with whom in 1883 she founded a trading house under the name 'Z. A. Fedotova & Co' for managing the two factories and the sale of finished products. This institutional transformation was the evidence of her desire to make the management process more efficient. The success of her business was testified to by the growing economic indices of her 'old' Moscow factory (1871 – annual production to the value of 140,000 roubles, 150 workers; 1890 – 184,000 roubles and 220 workers; 1897 – 242,500 roubles, 329 workers respectively). In 1897, her second factory's employed eighty-two workers and produced goods to the value of 87,000 roubles. Both factories were mechanized: the Moscow-based one was equipped with a 12-horsepower kerosene engine, the one in Durykino – with two locomobiles with an aggregate capacity of 22 horsepower (1897).[38]

Among the thirty-seven persons whose only occupation was commerce, thirteen traded in textiles, nine in foodstuffs (including seven in tea and sugar; one in butter and one in meat), and one in tobacco; two owned banking offices (the Russian Evdokia Chizhova in Moscow, and the Jewess Sheina Braude in Minsk, where she resided permanently), and one was a moneychanger. The others traded in footwear, writing-paper, needles, copper, furs, jewellery and sewing machines. One female entrepreneur kept furnished rooms. Another two were paying the First Guild tax, but did not actually engage in trade.

Female Entrepreneurs in Industry and Trade

In the 1890s, as is seen by the distribution of female entrepreneurs by their occupation (industry, trade, banking, etc.), the differences between the groups of female entrepreneurs in Moscow and St Petersburg became minimal. A more prominent trend was that of intergenerational changes. If a comparison is to be drawn with the year 1869, one can see that in 1895 the share of non-trading female merchants became much smaller (these were merchants' widows who, while not engaged in entrepreneurial activity, were willing to pay the Guild fee in order to maintain their high social status). This was indicative of the fact that the young and medium-aged generations of female entrepreneurs were much more interested in participating in economic activities alongside men and in displaying their independence as a mark of self-identification, in their attempts to go contrary to the patriarchal gender model and beyond their habitual domesticity pattern – rather than in simply maintaining a formal status.

In this chapter, instead of discussing in detail the owners of industrial establishments in St Petersburg and Moscow (thirty-five and forty-two factories for both Guilds), we are going to focus on the issue of married women as heads of enterprises. An analysis of the 'Reference Books' leads to the conclusion that the proportion of married women among female owners of enterprises was constantly on the rise (for the year 1869 we estimated this index as being 5–7 per cent, for 1895 – as no less than 20 per cent). For example, in St Petersburg the forty-nine-year-old wife of a Swedish subject Elizaveta Johansson, who had been inscribed in the merchantry since 1867, kept the 'Bruno Hofmark' mechanical plant; and Anna Korotkaia, the forty-year-old wife of a staff captain of the Life-Guards Grenadier Regiment (her second husband), owned the tobacco factory 'The K. & P. Petrov Brothers'.

The case of the owner of one of Moscow's confectionary factories, Ekaterina Lenova, demonstrates that women could indeed play the leading part in a family business. The Lenovs' confectionery company entered the period of fast expansion only in 1890s, despite being one of the oldest enterprises in Moscow. In 1826, a craftsman, Sergei Lenov, had opened a small confectionery workshop in a quiet Moscow street. The workshop manufactured only hard-boiled candy and fondant, and initially processed only 80 kg of sugar per day. The manufacturing process was quite primitive: drops of boiled sugar syrup were cooled on a slab of marble over a thin coating of olive or almond oil. The workshop had a limited output because it served only the local neighbourhood. The family income was insignificant, and so they could not afford the fee required for joining a merchant guild. The Lenovs' social status remained low. Over several decades of hard work they gradually expanded their production capacity, while the range of their loyal customers kept growing; eventually they opened a warehouse in central Moscow, from where their products were being transported to other towns. Ekaterina Lenova (1853–1912), the wife of Sergei's grandson Georgii Lenov (1850–1916), was very active in the development of the family business. Apparently, she (née Baryshev) was a daughter of a rich Moscow merchant, and it was her dowry that had helped to expand the business. She had received a good education and became the company's bookkeeper. It was she who insisted on officially incorporating the company as her property. After the Lenovs' wedding, in the 1880s the company started growing at a very fast rate. The Lenovs' work-shop was granted the status of a factory. Ekaterina purchased the neighbouring land plots and expanded the production facilities. In the 1890s the company acquired new machinery and the most advanced electrical equipment. Now, in addition to popular brands of candy, the company was manufacturing fruit marmalade and fruit-flavoured marshmallows, jelly and paste. In 1890 the company employed sixty-eight workers, and its earnings amounted to nearly 38,000 roubles.[39] In the early twentieth century the workforce grew to 170, and then to 215 employees, and the earnings increased considerably. In 1914, the Lenovs company had 400 employees and annual earnings of one million roubles. By 1916, the Lenov company had become the fourth largest confectionery manu-facturer in Moscow after the companies of von Einem, Abrikosov and Sioux. The company had more than a thousand employees and was equipped with the most advanced electric-powered production machinery. Ekaterina Lenova, with her commercial acumen, decided that the demand for cheap products of a suf-ficiently high quality on the part the low-income consumer would continue to grow steadily, and so she adjusted accordingly her company's business strategy. Until her death in 1912, Ekaterina Lenova had remained the managing director of the company, while her husband Georgii was chairman of its board of direc-tors, and their son Nikolai (1885–1952) and his wife Nadezhda (1883–1963) were the board's members. Until the 1917 Revolution the Lenov company pre-served the appearance of a family business.[40]

Now let us look at the sphere of trade – the occupation of the majority of female entrepreneurs, including 462 persons in St. Petersburg and 489 persons in Moscow (87 per cent and 87 per cent of all female entrepreneurs respectively). The detailed data as to the specialization of their trade are tabulated in Table 6.2.

As in 1869, the majority of female entrepreneurs were engaged in four trade segments: foodstuffs; textiles; readymade clothes and footwear; and provision of services.[41] In 1895, the aggregate share of these four segments changed against that recorded in 1869: in St. Petersburg it rose from 63 per cent to 64.9 per cent, while in Moscow it declined from 62.9 per cent to 60.2 per cent. However, in absolute terms the number of entrepreneurs engaged in these types of business activity increased in St. Petersburg from 243 to 300, and in Moscow – from 240 to 314, thus being indicative of the feminization of these segments of trade.

In St Petersburg, the leading activity of female entrepreneurs in the 1890s became the services sphere, followed by the former leader – trade in foodstuffs and tobacco. In Moscow, it was the similar situation, while trade in textiles remained in the third place. The number of female entrepreneurs trading in tex-tile products increased 1.3 times (from fifty-eight to seventy-eight persons), that

Table 6.2: The specialization of the proprietresses of commercial enterprises in St Petersburg and Moscow, belonging to the First and Second Guilds (1895)

Type of commerce	Specialization of proprietresses of commercial enterprises of St Petersburg (number of persons)	As percentage of total number of commercial enterprises	Specialization of proprietresses of commercial enterprises of Moscow (number of persons)	As percentage of total number of commercial enterprises
Foodstuffs and tobacco	87	18.8	91	18.6
Service business (restaurants, inns, bathhouses)	90	19.5	97	19.8
Clothes, footwear, headgear	56	12.1	48	9.8
Tailor's, furrier's, leather-dresser's and shoe-maker's workshops	5	1.1	2	0.4
Textiles	67	14.5	78	16.0
Money-changing and money-lending	3	0.7	6	1.2
Transport (one shipping company – carriage of passengers and cargo)	14	3.0	6	1.2
Metals and metal items	22	4.8	26	5.3
Chemicals and cosmetics	20	4.3	23	4.7
Construction materials	24	5.2	19	3.9
Haberdashery	11	2.4	21	4.3
Tableware	8	1.7	2	0.4
Horse harnesses, equipages, wheels	2	0.4	7	1.5
Building contracts	2	0.4	2	0.4
Other	51	11.1	61	12.5
TOTAL NUMBER of proprietresses of commercial enterprises	**462**	**100 per cent**	**489**	**100 per cent**
Trade is not made	28		31	
Renting-out of business and industrial premises	3		–	
Banking	2		2	
Total	**495**		**522**	

of those trading in chemicals and cosmetics – threefold, while the number of those trading in metals and metal products – 1.5 times.

The most important features of the transformations going on in the sphere of female-owned trade businesses in Moscow and St. Petersburg that became evident in the 1890s were as follows: the emergence of new types of female-owned businesses, and a significant inflow of female entrepreneurs from non-merchant strata.

As is noted by the American historian Alfred Rieber:

> The structure of the merchant *soslovie* underwent a transformation. Its hereditary character virtually disappeared, and the link between economic function and social status was broken.[42]

Here are the facts of the matter. In St. Petersburg, from 1890 onwards, the forty-five-year-old widow of a senator, Alexandra Kalmykova, ran a bookshop at her own house. From 1890 onwards, the thirty-nine-year-old widow of 'an engineer from the town of Helsingfors', Maria Bade, from 1890 owned a warehouse of lighting equipment. A physician's wife, the thirty-two-year-old Anna-Maria Gorinevskaia, owned a shop of hygienic appliances.[43]

In Moscow, Elena Tubenthal, the fifty-one-year-old wife of a government official, who had been inscribed in the merchantry since 1878, owned a sewerage business (the creation of such an enterprise had been necessitated by the provision of high-grade Moscow dwellings with sewerage and running water). Another female entrepreneur, Natal'ia Pechkovskaia, a forty-four-year-old spinster and a major general's daughter, who had been inscribed in the Second Guild since 1880 and rented an apartment in one of Moscow's most expensive blocks of flats, established an agency offering subscriptions to newspapers and magazines. A third, the thirty-six-year-old spinster daughter of a priest, Sofia Pogozheva, since 1893 had owned a music shop selling sheet music and instruments near the Moscow Conservatoire. A fourth, the twenty-nine-year-old Alevtina Murina, the wife of a graduate of the Law Faculty of Moscow University, ran a bookshop attached to her house in the prestigious Arbat District of Moscow. A fifth, the forty-eight-year-old widow of a major general, Maria Savicheva, owned the hotel 'Arcadia'.[44]

All the aforesaid cases testify to the fact that business was the domain of well-off women, who by their income level belonged to the middle class, which is also confirmed by their ownership of real estate or tenancy of apartments in prestigious blocks of flats. In this case they had other motivation, in addition to the purely economic ones. The female entrepreneurs of these younger generations, who started their businesses in the 1880s and 90s, viewed their own independent source of income and acquisition of professional skills as a means for self-realization.

One of the signs indicative of these intergenerational changes became the transformation of the marital status parameter of female entrepreneurs. For the period of the 1890s, this issue can be investigated on the basis of the demographic data obtained during the First All-Russian Population Census (1897). But let us begin with taking a look at the estimations based on data from the 'Reference Books' (1895).

Of the twenty-eight St Petersburg female merchants of the First Guild, nineteen were widows (sixty-six per cent), six were married (including Maksimovich, who was in her third marriage), one was single, and two were of unknown marital status. Of the forty-four Moscow female merchants of the First Guild, thirty-seven were widows (84 per cent), three were married (7 per cent), and four were spinsters (9 per cent). In St Petersburg, among the female merchants of the Second Guild, there were 241 widows (48 per cent); 166 married women (33 per cent), twenty of whom were married for the second time; 94 spinsters (19 per cent) and one divorced woman. Our calculations relating to the data on the Moscow female merchants of the Second Guild demonstrate that 265 female entrepreneurs were widows (51 per cent); 193 were married (37 per cent), ten of whom were married for the second time; and sixty-two were single (12 per cent).

The resulting data for the two guilds in St Petersburg have yielded the following picture: 260 widows (49 per cent), 172 married (33 per cent), 95 single (16 per cent) and one divorced woman; in Moscow, there were 302 widows (53 per cent), 196 married (35 per cent) and sixty-six single women (12 per cent).

Now let up compare these data with those of the Census. The Empire's averages are: widows – 13.4 per cent, married – 64 per cent, and single women (aged fifteen years and older) – 22.3 per cent (the marital status of 0.3 per cent being undetermined). However, the indices recorded in the two capitals, both of them megapolises, considerably differed from the national average: the number of unmarried women was higher, and that of the married ones was lower. Thus, in St Petersburg, widows constituted 18.4 per cent, married women – 41.3 per cent, and single women – 39.7 per cent; in Moscow the percentages were 21.7 per cent, 43.7 per cent, and 34.1 per cent respectively.[45] This demographic situation influenced both the 'business behaviour' of female entrepreneurs and the motives that determined their involvement in this activity. The access of women to education, including secondary and sometimes even higher education(by the late 1870s, higher women's education courses had been opened in Moscow, St. Petersburg, Kiev and Kazan),[46] equipped them with the skills necessary for efficient management of their businesses, for example, the knowledge of accounting and of the ways of dealing with customers.

The issue of unmarried female entrepreneurs deserves some special attention.[47] A very large proportion of single women in the two capitals were forced to create their own sources of income – thus, according to the 'Reference Books' (1895), the total number of single businesswomen in St Petersburg and Moscow was 162.

The quintessence of entrepreneurial activity within this subgroup of female entrepreneurs was the event of a business being passed from female to female – usually from a mother to her unmarried daughter. Thus, for example, the thirty-five-year-old St Petersburg female merchant of the Second Guild Paraskeva Kornilova had inherited, at the age of twenty-six years, an eating house after her mother (the latter having been its owner for twelve years). Another St Petersburg female merchant of the Second Guild, the fifty-one-year-old Paraskeva Zherebtsova, had inherited her dry-saltery at the age of thirty-six years upon the death of her mother who had run it for forty years (1839–80).

These cases, as well as the statistical data, bear witness to the existence of some other phenomena besides the economic, demographical and legal shifts. By the end of the nineteenth century the self-identity of female entrepreneurs had also undergone a certain change, thus promoting their self-sufficiency and independent conduct in society. One such emancipated entrepreneur was Vera Firsanova.

4. The Firsanova Case: a Victim of Love

In the last third of the nineteenth century, the growing complexity of market relations and the development of the legal base designed to regulate property relationships quite often gave rise to intricate situations where female entrepreneurs found themselves entangled by difficulties. Such situations could be characterized by a conflict produced by the incompatibility of several gender roles that a female entrepreneur was forced to play. The role of an independent female entrepreneur protecting her own economic interests thus went contrary to that of a wife, the latter being obliged, in accordance with the traditional 'patriarchal' scenario, to display in the context of private life her weakness and dependence on her male partner. The marriage of a rich female entrepreneur in such a situation could thus produce one of the most frequently encountered collisions in judicial practice – a conflict of the spouses' property interests.

As stated earlier, the following two postulates of Russian legislation were important in regulating the property rights of spouses: a) marriage did not result in the emergence of a joint estate of spouses, each of whom could still own and acquire his or her separate property; b) a wife's dowry, as well as the property acquired by her or in her name during her married life (by means of purchase, gift, or inheritance), was recognized as her separate property.[48]

From the last two decades of the nineteenth century onwards, so-called 'sham transactions' became more frequent. These were not considered to be contrary to the law if there were no mercenary motives. In the event of a sham transaction, a husband could gain access to the management of his wife's property in the following three ways: 1) by a power of attorney, issued by his wife, to manage her affairs; 2) by receiving property from her for management on the basis of a deed of gift; 3) by concluding a false transaction of purchase and sale not involving any actual cash payment. All these methods were conducive to the consolidation of family wealth when one or another agreement between spouses was based on mutual trust. A conflict of interests was usually the result of a deteriorating personal relationship. M. Vinaver, an eminent specialist in civil law, wrote as follows with regard to such legal phenomena:

> Given the absolute separateness of spouses' property which is prevalent [in this country], in the presence of an aspiration (characteristic of good family relationships) for undivided use of earthly goods and a woman's natural search for a stronger [partner] to serve as a foundation for her life and business, – the chain of relationships becomes so entangled that, formally, the wife's separate property becomes not only the joint property of both spouses – it becomes the other spouse's separate property.[49]

One vivid example of how a wife, who had transferred to her husband property under a feigned transaction, very nearly lost a considerable part of her estate is provided by the story of Vera Firsanova. Firsanova (1862–*c*.1928) was the most prominent owner of urban real estate in Moscow in the late nineteenth and early twentieth centuries. She had eighteen expensive estates in downtown Moscow, including blocks of flats, the '*Petrovskie Linii*' arcade, the Sandunov Bath House, the 'Prague' restaurant, and a mansion on Nikitskii Boulevard. She had inherited all this property at the age of eighteen, after the death of her father.

Her father, Ivan Firsanov (1817–81), had been contracted by the Treasury to supply firewood to army barracks and timber construction materials to the Army. Prior to becoming the Treasury's supplier, he had worked as a merchant's clerk at Shchegleev's jewellery shop in Kitai-Gorod. The shop owner would dispatch Firsanov to the houses of the nobility, entrusting him with purchasing their family jewellery. Firsanov, while buying French and Italian antique jewellery for his master, would pocket some of the items. This was the origin of his initial savings which he used, even before the 1861 Reform, for purchasing from the impoverished nobility their country estates with good forests. In 1859 alone, he bought 2,119 desiatinas (5,721 acres) of land in Moscow Province.[50] By supplying wood to private customers he earned enough money to buy a house in the centre of Moscow. After the death of his childless elder brother Semen, Ivan, as the only heir, received another ten houses in downtown Moscow. In 1869 Firsanov bought the Sandunov Bath House – the capital's largest public facility of this kind.

Busy with his pursuit of profit, Ivan Firsanov remained single for a long time. At the age of forty-four he married Aleksandra Nikolaeva, an orphan from a noble family and graduate of the Institute for Noble Maidens, who was twenty-five years his junior. At the age of forty-five Firsanov became a father; he doted on his only daughter Vera and spoiled her.[51] Vera grew up to be a beautiful woman. Her first marriage was at seventeen, to the banker Vladimir Voronin – the popular belief was that she had simply wanted to get rid of her father's oppression.

Firsanov died a year later, and it was a terrible death. He kept his banking documents and jewellery at home, in a safe deposit box, the key to which was hidden under his pillow. Gradually everybody began to notice that the thoughts of this key were becoming the cause of a mental distress. According to one memoirist,

> before the onset of his agony, he would jump up, give a glance, with mad glassy eyes, at all those present in the room, and then with pain and fear pick up the key and try to push it into his nose.[52]

Having inherited from her father a millionaire's estate, Vera decided to leave her husband, their relationship being a failure. However, in accordance with the law, a divorce was possible only in an event of infidelity on the part of one of the spouses. Article 44 of the Civic Laws went as follows: 'A marriage can be dissolved ... at the request on one of the spouses in the event of a proven adultery of the other spouse'.[53]

Vera offered to her husband indemnity in the amount one million roubles, so that he would take the blame upon himself. The divorce was duly granted, but Vera was by no means in a hurry to remarry (there were rumours of her love affairs with representatives of the bohemian world). By the age of thirty Vera, at last, had found the man of her dreams. This was Aleksey Gonetskii, a handsome cornet from St Petersburg, whose father was the Master General of the Peter and Paul Fortress in St Petersburg. The noble Gonetskii family was known since the sixteenth century, and so, evidently, the prospects of marrying into the aristocracy became the decisive factor for a descendant of merchants from Serpukhov. In 1892, Vera married Gonetskii. Trusting her husband completely, she, as it was later recorded in the files of the Secret Department of the Moscow Governor General's Office,

> conferred on him full power of attorney to manage her affairs, with the right to mortgage and sell estates, and transferred in his name, under a deed of gift, her acquired house, and under a deed of purchase, without receiving its price, her inherited estate, the Sandunov Bath House in Moscow.[54]

The romantic idyll thus continued for six years before, in 1898, Vera was shocked to learn that her husband had a mistress with whom he had left for Europe, and was squandering his wife's money.

It had always seemed to Vera that her husband was wholeheartedly protecting her commercial interests. It had been Gonetskii who initiated the construction of a new building for her Sandunov Bath House. It had been his idea that the new bathhouse should be unrivalled in its splendour and profitability. Vera was impressed. Together with her husband, she travelled several times to Europe in order to learn how this business was practiced in different countries.

The inner yard of the Sandunov Bath House in Moscow, owned by Vera Firsanova. Late 1890s.
Courtesy of Mikhail Zolotarev, Moscow.

The new bathhouse (actually, it was a business centre with the baths attached to it) was built in two years' time to the design of the fashionable architect B. Freidenberg. It was opened in May 1896. The complex consisted of eight buildings (the ninth, a garage for the clients' cars, was added in 1910). The property was insured for 1.2 million roubles by the First Russian Insurance Society.[55] The exquisite decoration materials included Italian and Norwegian marble; the tiles were from England, Germany and Switzerland. Income from the new bathhouse was growing from year to year. Between 1901 and 1913 it increased from 109,250 roubles to 112,385 roubles. Approximately 60 per cent of this sum was received from the bathhouse business, and the other 40 per cent – from the lease of commercial premises and apartments in a three-storey residential building (where Vera occupied the best eight-room apartment).

The cheated Vera realized that it was necessary to urgently rescue her property. She enlisted the services of the famous lawyer F. Plevako, on whose advice she then wrote a petition to Emperor Nicholas II, asking the sovereign to protect her property interests. Vera presented a claim to Gonetskii in the amount of 2.7 million roubles and petitioned that a decision be made at the highest level as to the nullity of her deed of purchase without money and of her deeds of gift, thus creating legal grounds for the property being returned to her.

As the grounds for the appeal, Vera's lawyers under Plevako's leadership offered the formula of 'insult to her conjugal rights'.[56] This formula could entail the application of the civil law norm envisaging 'the return of a gift in an event of an evident lack of respect on the part of the person who has received the gift'. Article 974 of the Civic Laws reads as follows:

> A gift received by the person for whom it has been intended shall not return to the giver; but if the person who has received the gift makes an attempt on the life of the giver, or inflicts on him a beating or threats, or in general demonstrates an evident lack of respect for him, the giver shall have the right to demand that the gift be returned to him.[57]

A husband's infidelity could be estimated as 'an evident lack of respect', which served as legal grounds for the return of the gift.

The case was submitted for an expert examination at the Ministry of Justice, but Minister Murav'ev did not support the appeal by the insulted wife, noting that he

> does not see any grounds for the consideration of the case in an extraordinary procedure, because Gonetskaia's appeal should be subject to comprehensive consideration by a court of law if the applicant's husband should indeed be declared to be an insolvent debtor and if the creditors should claims their rights to the property transferred by the husband to the wife under the deeds of gift, – which, however, has not happened so far.[58]

The process of salvaging her property was thus further complicated, but Vera did not despair. She managed to get an audience with the Moscow Governor General, Grand Duke Sergei (Emperor Nicholas II's uncle). The Grand Duke, in his own name, wrote a letter concerning Firsanova-Gonetskaia's case to Minister of Internal Affairs Sipiagin. The case was revived.

Soon, a scandalously publicized divorce followed, after which Vera got back her bathhouse, the *'Petrovskie Linii'* arcade (the annual income from which in 1906–13 was between 107 and 152,000 roubles),[59] and reverted to her maiden name. From the formal point of view, Gonetskii returned this property to her on his own free will. However, it was rumoured that Vera had to pay to him one million roubles (just as had been the case with her first husband) for signing all the necessary documents. After the divorce Gonetskii left for South Africa, to fight in the Anglo–Boer War.

The wizened Vera Firsanova never married again. Due to her incomes from real estate, she was becoming increasingly wealthy. She became a renowned patron of the arts. After her divorce, she began to rearrange her two country estates worth over 195,000 roubles. In particular, she built the railway station Firsanovskaia.[60] In 1914, at the country estate Serednikovo, which she had bought from the noble Stolypin family, Vera erected a monument to poet Lermontov (who had stayed there with his relatives in 1829–32).

Only legends have survived as to Vera Firsanova's life after the 1917 Revolution, when she lost all her property. One story goes that in the mid-1920s, making use of her connections in artistic circles she managed to leave for Paris as a costumier for a Soviet theatre troupe on a tour abroad. After that, her trail went cold.

The case of Firsanova testifies to the changes that occurred in the late nineteenth century in the social and material status of big female entrepreneurs, as well as in their legal skills. Firsanova possessed enormous wealth, undreamed of by any female merchant just a few decades previously. Vera was well-educated; she was knowledgeable of accounting procedures, which enabled her to progressively develop her business. She managed on her own the leases of her considerable commercial properties. After her father's death she successfully invested her capital in a complete reconstruction, by applying newest construction technologies, of her bathhouse and arcade, thus making these premises the best in Moscow and very attractive for prospective leasers. The few years during which she attempted to retire and reduce her role only to that of a wife proved to be the least successful – in terms of both her entrepreneurial and feminine functions. Her strategic mind helped her to find a way out of a difficult situation; however, she never again tried to place her female interests above those of her business.

Conclusion

Under conditions of modern economic growth which, as economists believe, began from 1885, the development of female entrepreneurship became part of the overall context of the Russian economy's vigorous growth. In the last decade of the nineteenth century the volume of industrial production doubled (in money terms), and one important factor of the economic evolution became the concentration of production at big enterprises.

A comparison of the data on female-owned industrial enterprises in 1884 and 1897 demonstrates that their production rouble volume increased 2.4 times – from 63.6 million roubles to 150.4 million roubles, and the number of workers increased by 1.8 times – from 57.6 thousand to 105.8 thousand. The share of female-owned enterprises' production volume in industry rose from 4.8 per cent to 6 per cent. The highest indices of production were achieved by female entrepreneurship in the textile industry (10.6 per cent of the overall output volume of that industry), where women were heads of some largest enterprises with the annual production rouble volume of one million to six million roubles. The transformation of family firms into share partnerships in Russia, similarly to Europe, was followed by 'the introduction of managerial hierarchies into family-controlled enterprises',[61] where women could occupy prominent and sometimes even leading positions.

An analysis of the *Reference Books* (1895) has shown that in the sphere of trade the number of female entrepreneurs was the highest, in particular in St Petersburg with its 462 women traders (87 per cent of all female entrepreneurs in 1895; 77 per cent in 1869) and in Moscow which had 489 women traders (87 per cent of all female entrepreneurs; 65 per cent in 1869). The growth of the share of 'active' female entrepreneurs, whose formal status corresponded to their actual participation in business, by comparison with 1865, could happen due to a dramatic reduction in the number of 'non-trading' persons – those who would take out guild certificates in order to maintain their high status (once achieved by their deceased husbands or fathers) within the estate stratification.

An important sigh of the changed self-identity of female entrepreneurs became the numerous facts of family firms being given female names (in 1895 in Moscow, eighteen out of the 168 trading houses of the First Guild were named after their female owners, for example 'Anna Belousova & Sons', 'Popova & Co.', 'Frada Weil & Son', 'Anna Sergeeva & Co.', 'Zinaida Fedotova & Co', and so on). This is the evidence of the market having been actively penetrated by 'feminized' brands, which served as an impulse for creating new 'clichés' in the mechanism of customer preferences.

In industry and trade alike the share of the multiethnic group of female entrepreneurs became higher, which reflected the overall process of integration of representatives of ethnic minorities in market relations. The megapolises, first of all St Petersburg and Moscow, joined the process of modernization and thus were involving hundreds or even thousands of ethnic Russians and representatives of other ethnic groups (both Russian and foreign subjects) in the development of new forms of production and exchange, based on model legal regulation and rigidly institutionalized management forms. In the group of female entrepreneurs the ratio between ethnic Russians and other ethnic groups in the late nineteenth century was approximately 4:1. The source materials analysed in our study point to the increased commercial activity of Jewish entrepreneurs (including women) and their settling down outside of the Pale of Settlement, which indicates that from the late 1880s the Russian economy had enough windows of opportunity to attract Jewish capital and promote integration of Jews into the bourgeois class of the Russian Empire.

Our comparison of the empirical data from the 'Reference Books' (1895) with the demographic data for the whole of the Russian Empire obtained during the First All-Russian Population Census (1897) made it possible to reveal a trend towards a decrease of the share of widows in the overall number of female entrepreneurs, coupled with a simultaneous growth in the number and importance of married women and spinsters. This is the evidence of a gradual deterioration of the patriarchal gender roles model. The pursuit of business activity was conducive to financial and legal independence, and so it became one of the channels whereby women were entering the economic and social arena.

CONCLUSION

Female entrepreneurship in the Russian Empire had indeed come to play an important role by the beginning of the twentieth century. However, a closer look at the picture of female entrepreneurship in Russia reveals the fact of it being rather diverse. The female owners of enterprises and commercial facilities were representatives of various social strata – first of all those of the landowning aristocrats and merchants.

The patterns of ownership and the social composition of the female entrepreneur strata were changing over the course of the century. In the first half of the nineteenth century the core of female entrepreneurs' wealth was, for most part, inherited property, while later on the balance began to steadily shift in favour of newly acquired property and capital actively used in commercial transactions.

When examining the history of women's participation in the Russian economy of the nineteenth century, one should never ignore the issue of the influence of gender ideology on female entrepreneurship. For the past fifteen years the European historiography has been reflecting the most heated debates regarding this problem, because an analysis of some regional models confirms the 'separate spheres' paradigm, while certain new facts revealed in the course of examining other countries and regions add weight to the arguments for the existence of a 'segmented sphere'. Some scholars are keen to prove that 'the pre-industrial concept of a 'joint sphere' was resilient and adaptable to new circumstances'.[1]

The history of female entrepreneurship in nineteenth-century Russia makes it possible to suggest the existence of a symbiotic model. On the one hand, the Russian situation was unique, because over the whole course of the nineteenth century women possessed and realized equal rights with men, be it property rights or the right to engage in business. (The only restriction consisted in the prohibition for a merchant's wife 'to sign a promissory note in her own name without her husband's consent', but this prohibition did not extend to the cases when a woman transacted trade 'in her own name').[2] This made Russia different from European countries, the majority of which were steadily toughening restrictions on women's property rights until the last quarter of the nineteenth century, which had negative effects on the development of the independent entrepreneurship of married women.

But at the same time we find some manifestations of the 'separate spheres' paradigm in the persistence of the masculine character of entrepreneurial public organizations and institutions. Women could take part in partnerships' board meetings as directors and stakeholders, but they were not admitted to meetings of local Exchange and Merchant Societies. At least since the 1860s, several hundred of Moscow female entrepreneurs had the right to vote in elections of deputies to the local bodies of merchant self-government, but they were not permitted within the voting room. In accordance with the charter of the Moscow Merchants' Association, a woman was obliged to put her signature on the courier list to verify the reception of the invitation to take part in the voting, and then to entrust her proxy vote to any male family member of the full legal age.[3] The pressure of gender ideology also manifested itself in the prohibition for women from the merchant estate to attend the Emperor's court (in accordance with a 1807 decree[4]), which remained in force throughout the nineteenth century.[5] Despite all the restrictions on the self-representation of businesswomen in public networks, the economic characteristics of Russian female entrepreneurship revealed by our study are sufficiently impressive.

Aggregate data on the participation of female entrepreneurs in industrial development demonstrate that, whilst in 1814 there were only 165 female-owned enterprises (out of a total of 3,731), by 1832 their number had increased to 484 (out of 5,349), by 1879 – to 1,045 (out of 26,067), by 1884 – to 1354 (out of 27,235), and by 1897 – to 1,684 (out of 34,723). (See Figure 7.1.) At the same time, the share of female-owned enterprises by their production volume (in money terms) was 4 per cent in 1879, 4.8 per cent in 1884, and 6 per cent in 1897. The achieved historic high of industrial female entrepreneurship (1897) is expressed in the following figures: 105,799 workers produced goods to the value of 150.4 million roubles.

An analysis of statistical data has revealed that, in the 1880s–90s, 85 per cent of output from female-owned enterprises was accounted for by the textile and food industries. In these industries, the participation of women in entrepreneurship was the highest: their businesses produced 9.2 per cent and 6.7 per cent (1884) and 10.6 per cent and 6.9 per cent (1897) respectively of the annual output of the textile and food industries. In 1897, sufficiently high indices were achieved in some other sectors as well: in the tobacco industry – 10.6 per cent, and in the production of matches – 13 per cent.

Throughout the nineteenth century, the one sector where the role of women (mainly those of merchant origin) remained unchangingly prominent was the textile industry. In 1832, 11 per cent of all enterprise owners in the Russian textile industry were women, and in 1897 their number was nearly the same – 12.2

Figure 7.1. The share of female-owned enterprises (1814–97)

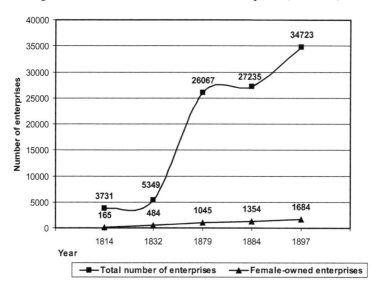

per cent. A direct consequence of the industrial revolution was the enlargement of textile industrial enterprises and the increase in the volume of their output, noted since the late 1840s. In the last quarter of the nineteenth century the development of the textile industry was determined by the performance of the big mills situated in the central and Volga provinces of the Russian Empire. Women were the owners of several dozens of these enterprises – which, for example, in 1879 produced goods to the value of 14.9 million roubles (thus accounting for 4.3 per cent of the total output of Russia's textile industry).

The second most important segment of female entrepreneurship – the food industry – represented in the main a network of relatively new medium-sized and small enterprises, 60 per cent of them situated on the estates of their noble proprietresses, predominantly in the southern (Ukrainian) and western (Belarusian and Baltic) provinces. The dynamic development of this sector was a clear sign of the formation, in the second half of the nineteenth century, of an all-Russian agrarian market.

So far as the sphere of trade and services is concerned, the number of businesswomen there was eight to ten times higher than that of female factory owners. More than half of female-owned shops specialized in selling food and fabrics. In the sphere of services, female entrepreneurs were innkeepers, publicans and bathhouse-keepers. One of the strategies for survival in business adopted by Russian female entrepreneurs was to create a chain of shops. In St Petersburg and

Moscow, between 20 and 30 per cent of businesswomen operating in the commercial sphere owned two or more shops.

The female-owned industrial enterprises of the nineteenth-century Russian Empire were characterized by the mixed social backgrounds of their proprietresses. The statistical analysis did not confirm our initial hypothesis that noble businesswomen were gradually being ousted in this role by female merchants. Despite the progressive decline in noble landownership after the 1861 Emancipation of the Serfs (by 1.5 times between 1862 and 1897[6]), the role of noblewomen in industrial development became no less prominent, and they preserved their parity with female merchants, with the additional small but constant presence of *meshchanki* and peasant women. In 1814, noblewomen comprised 46 per cent, and female merchants – 38 per cent of all female factory owners; in 1832 these figures were 50 per cent and 36 per cent (with 49 per cent of female-owned industrial enterprises being situated on country estates); in 1879 – 42 per cent and 43 per cent; and in 1884 – 44 per cent and 42 per cent respectively (no exact data being available for the year 1897).

The post-Great Reforms period brought a new phenomenon – that of women entering business ownership (more often in trade than industry) not only from the merchant and peasant strata, which had happened during the whole first half of the nineteenth century, but also from the officialdom and, to a certain degree, from the service nobility. In the 1890s, in Moscow and St Petersburg, among the persons taking out merchant certificates for the right to transact business, there were one senator's widow; major generals' widow, wife and daughter; and even the wife of a State Secretary to Emperor Alexander III (Nadezhda Polovtsova). These changes bear witness to a gradual change in the way entrepreneurship was perceived by public opinion in terms of its prestigeousness. These women were engaged in business in order to obtain a supplemental (and sometimes their only) income. For the younger generations of female entrepreneurs coming from the educated strata, their engagement in business was becoming not only a way to go beyond the patriarchal gender model and thus to achieve economic independence, but also a vehicle of social ascent.

Another factor responsible for the emergence of pluralism was the multi-ethnic and multi-confessional character of female entrepreneurship: apart from women of local extraction (Russian, Tatar, German, Ukrainian, Jewish) the sisterhood actively engaged in organizing businesses in Russia also included some of their foreign counterparts (mostly German, but also English, French, Italian, Belgian, Dutch, Austrian, Swedish, etc). The main trend in the changing ethnic composition of this group of entrepreneurs was the diminishing share of ethnic Russians. Thus, between 1869 and 1895 the share of female entrepreneurs of Russian origin in St. Petersburg decreased from 81 per cent to 77.4 per cent, and in Moscow – from 91.9 per cent to 76.1 per cent. According to the 1879 data on the situation in industry, Russians accounted for 75 per cent of businesswomen, while the Polish, German, Jewish and Ukrainian groups of female entrepreneurs were also numerically significant. For 1884, an ethnic analysis has indicated that the number of businesswomen of Russian origin grew in absolute terms from 750 to 863, while their percentage dropped from 75.7 per cent to 65.9 per cent. In the 1880s-90s, female entrepreneurs from ethnic minorities were becoming increasingly active.

During the nineteenth century, the dimension of marital status underwent some noticeable changes as well. Beginning from the 1860s, the main reasons for a woman to become an independent manager of a business were no more her widowhood or spinsterhood, as it always used to be in the past. We have some examples of remarried merchant's widows managing their business independently of their second husbands, while the latter could be merchants, state officials or army officers. In the 1890s, the share of widows among the women taking out merchant certificates in St. Petersburg and Moscow amounted to 49–53 per cent, that of married women – to 33–5 per cent, and that of spinsters – to 12–16 per cent. The growth in the number and importance of married women and spinsters serves as the evidence of a gradual deterioration of the patriarchal gender roles model. It means that the self-identity of female entrepreneurs had also undergone a certain change, thus promoting their self-sufficiency and independent conduct in society.

In this connection, one cannot overlook the issue of the business strategies of female entrepreneurs. Under Russian legislation, women enjoyed absolute freedom in disposing of their own property, but there was also the other side to it: they also bore sole personal responsibility for business losses.

In the nineteenth century any business was conducted, as a rule, within a family framework.[7] The ever-present goal of a female entrepreneur was to minimize the risk of bankruptcy. In order to achieve this, they applied different means. Thus, for example, they could resort to formalization of family relations, expressed in the passing on to a widow, in accordance with her husband's will, of full control over the family business – and, simultaneously, full control of their family property. The reason for using such a pattern was the desire to avoid a dispersal of property and to prevent conflicts within the family. In many instances women continued to head their family businesses until the moment of death – even if they had adult sons who were mentioned in official documents as being 'attached to the mother'.

This pattern invites us to delve deeper into the mechanisms of partnership between mother and her sons within the framework of a family business. The research has made it possible for us to obtain a definite answer to the question as to whether the women who figured in the documents as the owners were only formal possessors or actually managed the businesses. According to the 1838 data pertaining to Moscow, in 18 per cent of cases the female owner managed her business 'herself'; in 49.3 per cent it was managed by her adult son (or sons), in 19.1 per cent, if there were more than one enterprise to handle, the female owner assigned her son/sons, her husband, or her clerks to manage the less important undertakings. Some cases presented in the book demonstrate that, contrary to the gender stereotype based on the 'separate spheres', proprietresses of industrial and trade enterprises were actually experienced managers.

However, the subsequent institualization of business and the establishment of a managerial hierarchy within family firms conduced to the rise of the tendency to resolve business-related property disputes in courts of justice, which was clearly manifested from the 1870s onwards.

Within the framework of the issue of business strategies, the monograph considers two more aspects of the development of female entrepreneurship in the last third of the nineteenth century. First, the numerous facts of female names being given to family firms provide the evidence of the market being actively penetrated by 'feminized' brands which became an important sigh of the changed self-identity of female entrepreneurs. Second, there are the cases of husbands adopting the family names of their wives in order to secure both the family brand and customers' loyalty.

The bankruptcy cases, examined on the basis of documents of the Commercial Court, indicate that they were caused by the lack of a distinctly defined distribution of responsibility and control between the partners in a family business; the insufficiency of the initial capital needed for establishing a factory and for its further development; the sharp decline in consumer demand for its products; and the suspension of operations in the crediting system at the time of crisis acted as an additional risk factor. Starting from the 1870s, bankruptcies were becoming increasingly frequent in conditions of world economic crises, thus reflecting on the dynamics of the economic development of Russia, which by that time had become involved into global market relations.

We should like to quote here the characteristic of the development of the Russian Empire in 1881–1905, laconically and precisely formulated by Catherine Evtuhov:

> Russia's transformation into a modern industrial state involved not only growth in military power but the evolution of an infrastructure of urban life, from the penetration and consolidation of powerful industrial firms, to newspaper publishing and advertising, to restaurants, cafés, and concert halls.[8]

In the last quarter of the nineteenth century, the reorganization of family companies into share partnerships became the dominant trend. The 1890s brought with them the participation of women in the management of enterprises in the capacity of board directors and stakeholders, their influence on decision-making

being quite considerable. Another innovation of that decade was the successful functioning of enterprises with entirely female collective management (the
Zav'ialovs' case).

By the end of the nineteenth century, female entrepreneurship had started to
play an important role in the Russian economy. As a result, there emerged a stratum of women with a significant personal wealth. The ownership of considerable
capital had its impact on the transformation of the gender roles of female entrepreneurs both on the family and social planes. Sometimes, a female entrepreneur
could even experience a certain psychological dissonance, when her business
interests came into conflict with her aspiration for formal well-being in the role
of wife and mother (the cases of Firsanova and Shchekina). But such cases were
the exception rather than the rule.

In 1882, the reading public was gobbling up the novel 'Kitai-Gorod' by Petr
Boborykin. The plot of the novel was a convoluted love story, whose protagonist
was twenty-seven-year-old Anna Stanitsyna, a colourful representative of the
female entrepreneur breed. Anna's parents descended from a prominent family
of the Volga Old Believers; she received a good education ('graduated second
in her class from a boarding school'). Having received her parents' factory as
her dowry, Anna married a merchant's son, heir to a dynasty of Moscow textile
magnates. Anna gave birth to two children, but the marriage was not a success:
her husband turned out to be a rake who preferred to squander money in Paris
and at fashionable European resorts. The young man appeared in Moscow only
occasionally – to get money for settling his current debts. During one of his rare
stays at home Anna, realizing that his factories (which were to be passed on to
her children) were under threat of bankruptcy, resorted to some tough measures. During a meeting with her husband at her office in Kitai-Gorod, where
she went every day to attend to business matters, she declared that, as his own
business was on the brink of ruin, from now on he would be allotted only 30,000
roubles a year as an 'allowance'. At first, the indignant husband made an attempt
to increase the amount of this 'allowance', but then, fearing that his wife might
refuse to redeem his promissory notes, and so his firm would go bankrupt, he
conferred on Anna the power of attorney to manage his inherited 'factories'.

The character of Anna has certain features that are remarkable from the
point of view of a historian. Thus, while the Stanitsyns' firm is facing bankruptcy, Anna's own factory is very successful. Anna is a keen businesswoman,
her acumen being highly acclaimed by the most experienced of her clerks: she
personally controls the daily flow of her financial documentation and knows the
minutest details of all her products and pricelists. Besides, Anna has established
and provides the funding for the school at her factory. She is a close friend of
journalist and philosopher Yermil Bezrukavkin[9], with whom she discusses articles published in 'thick' journals and whose advice she seeks when conducting

her financial affairs. To crown it all, Anna is a typical Russian beauty, with a well-shaped body, and her outfits are tasteful and expensive: thus, taking leave of one of her admirers, nobleman Paltusov, she allowed him to kiss her arm 'a little above her wrist where, over her glove, there coiled – up to her elbow – a finely shaped platinum snake bracelet'. During her encounter with Paltusov, Anna at first is very distressed that he found her in her office, busy with accounting records, but then she managed to overcome her uneasiness in front of a representative of the nobility:

> She is a merchant woman, the owner of a factory worth a million, she does her business, and she does it well. There is nothing to be ashamed of. It would be good for everybody to follow her example.[10]

The facts found in various historical sources provide an ample and convincing proof that the character of Stanitsyna is by no means the product of the author's fantasy. The Russian entrepreneurial milieu, especially in the last third of the nineteenth century, was represented by a large cohort of women who were heads of firms and managed them quite successfully.

As noted by Paul Gregory,

> Russia on the eve of World War I was one of the worlds' major economic powers. General works typically rank Russia as the world's fourth or fifth largest industrial power behind the United States, the United Kingdom, France, Germany and perhaps Austria-Hungary.[11]

The industrial revolution came to Russia fifty to sixty years later than to the United Kingdom, and twenty-five to thirty years later than to Germany. However, Russia managed to take advantage of her 'backwardness' by borrowing 'readymade' technologies from the West, which insured a high rate of industrialization, especially in the late 1880s – early 1890s, and thus at the turn of the century became one of the world's leaders in economic development.

In this process of Russia's evolution towards modernization, the role of female entrepreneurs was notable, indispensable and invariably creative. But it was undoubtedly beyond their power to change the course of events inexorably leading the country to its doom in the twentieth century.

NOTES

Abbreviations

ch.   chast' [part]
d., dd.   delo, dela [file, files]
f.   fond [collection]
l., ll.   list, listy [folio, folios]
op.   opis' [inventory]

PSZ   Polnoe sobranie zakonov Rossiiskoi imperii [Complete Collection of Laws of the
          Russian Empire]
RGADA   Rossiiskii gosudarstvennyi arkhiv drevnikh actov [Russian State Archive of Ancient
          Acts]
SZ   Svod Zakonov Rossiiskoi imperii [Digest of Current Russian Law]
TsIAM   Tsentral'nyi istoricheskii arkhiv Moskvy [Central Historical Archive of the City of
          Moscow]

Spisok 1830   Spisok kuptsov goroda Moskvy, ob'iavivshikh kapitaly na 1830 god,
                     spokazaniem imeiushchegosia pri nikh semeistva, chem torgovliu
                     proizvodiat i gde zhitel'stvo imeiut [The List of Merchants of the City
                     of Moscow for the Year 1830] [Moscow, 1830]

Spisok 1832   Spisok fabrikantam i zavodchikam Rossiiskoi imperii 1832 goda (St
                     Petersburg: tipografiia Departamenta vnesh. torg., 1833) [The List of Fac-
                     tory-Owners and Manufacturers of the Russian Empire for the Year 1832]

MDIMK Skazki   Materialy dlia istorii moskovskogo kupechestva. Revizskie skazki
                     (Moscow: Tipolitografiia I. N. Kushnereva i Ko., 9 vols, 1883–9). [The
                     Materials for the Moscow Merchantry History. Census Files]

MDIMK Prigovory   Materialy dlia istorii moskovskogo kupechestva. Obshchestvennye
                     prigovory (Moscow: Tipolitografiia I. N. Kushnereva i Ko., 11 vols,
                     1892–1909) [The Materials for the Moscow Merchantry History. Mer-
                     chant Corporation Decisions]

SK Moscow   Spravochnaia kniga o litsakh, poluchivshikh kupecheskie svidetel'stva
                     po 1 i 2 gil'diiam v Moskve na [1869–8] god (Moscow. 1869–98) [The
                     Reference Book of Moscow Merchants for a year ... 1869–98]

SK St. Petersburg   Spravochnaia kniga o litsakh, poluchivshikh na [1867–98] god kupecheskie svidetelstva po 1 i 2 gil'diiam, (St. Petersburg, 1867–98) [The Reference Book of St. Petersburg Merchants for a year ... 1869–98].

Introduction

1. A. Orlov, *Anna, kupecheskaia doch', ili barkhatnyi ridicul' iz Galantereinogo Riadu* (Moscow: Universitetskaia Tipografia, 1832), pp. 9–10.
2. M. L. Marrese, *A Woman's Kingdom: Noblewomen and the Control of Property in Russia, 1700–1861* (Ithaca , NY and London: Cornell University Press, 2002), p. 117.
3. Let us address the case of the United Kingdom. As is noted by Maxine Berg, 'research on property-holding for England, from the early modern period to the nineteenth century, indicates a decline in women's rights and status regarding property over the course of the eighteenth century to the constrained mid-Victorian times'. See M. Berg, 'Women's Property and the Industrial Revolution', *Journal of Interdisciplinary History*, 24:2 (1993), p. 234. Married women's rights to maintain separate property were introduced by the Married Women's Property Acts of 1870 and 1882. According to Mary Shanley, The Married Women's Property Act of 1882 'not only gave to married women the legal capacity to act as autonomous economic agents, but struck a blow at the whole notion of coverture and the necessary subordination of a woman's will to that of her husband'. See: M. L. Shanley, *Feminism, Marriage, and the Law in Victorian England* (Princeton, NJ: Princeton University Press, 1993), p. 103. On the contrary, in Russia women's property rights were being extended in the course of the eighteenth and first half of the nineteenth centuries.
4. *Polnoe sobranie zakonov Rossiiskoi Imperii (Complete Collection of Laws of the Russian Empire)*. Sobranie I, 45 vols (St Petersburg: Tipografiia II Otd. Sobstvennoi E. I. V. Kantseliarii, 1830-43, hereafter *PSZ* I), vol. XIII, No 10111.
5. Ibid., vol. XL, No 30472.
6. See: *Svod Zakonov Rossiiskoi imperii (Digest of Current Russian Law)*, 15 vols, (St Petersburg: Tipografiia II Otd. Sobstvennoi E. I. V. Kantseliarii, 1833, hereafter *SZ*), vol. X, part 1, arts 80-81; N. Reinke, 'Dvizhenie zakonodatel'stva ob imushchestvennykh pravakh zamuzhnei zhenshchiny', *Zhurnal grazhdanskogo i ugolovnogo prava*, 3 (1884), pp. 69–70.
7. A. Lindenmeyr, 'Review on Marrese, A Woman's Kingdom', *Journal of Social History*, 38:2 (2004), p. 553.
8. B. A. Engel, *Women in Russia, 1700–2000* (Cambridge: Cambridge University Press, 2004), p. 35.
9. W. G. Wagner, *Marriage, Property, and Law in Late Imperial Russia* (Oxford: Clarendon Press, 1994, 2nd edn 2001).
10. N. Basch, *In the Eyes of the Law: Women, Marriage and Property in Nineteenth-Century New York* (Ithaca, NY: Cornell University Press, 1982); L. Holcombe, *Wives and Property: Reform of the Married Women's Property Law in Nineteenth-Century England* (Toronto, ON: University of Toronto Press, 1983); S. Staves, *Married Women Separate Property in England, 1660–1833* (Cambridge, MA: Harvard University Press, 1990); M. Salmon, *Women and the Law of Property in early America* (Chapel Hill, NC: University of North Carolina Press, 1986), etc.
11. Wagner, *Marriage, Property, and Law*, p. 66.

12. Marrese, *A Woman's Kingdom*, pp. 4–9, 44–70.

13. L. A. Farrow, *Between Clan and Crown: The Struggle to Define Noble Property Rights in Imperial Russia* (Newark, DE: University of Delaware Press, 2004).

14. L. Davidoff and C. Hall, *Family Fortunes: Men and Women of the English Middle Class, 1780–1850*, 2nd edn (Chicago, IL: University of Chicago Press, 1991), p. 277.

15. A. S. Nevzorov, *Russkaia zhenshchina v deistvuiushchem zakonodatel'stve i v deistvitel'noi zhizni* (Revel, 1892), p. 39.

16. A. V. Koval'chuk, *Manufakturnaia promyshlennost' Moskvy vo vtoroi polovine XVIII veka* (Moscow: Editorial URSS, 1999), pp. 95–6, 100.

17. For more details concerning the history of women in Imperial Russia (the eighteenth –early twentieth centuries), see D. Atkinson, A. Dallin and G. Lapidus (eds), *Women in Russia* (Stanford, CA: Stanford University Press, 1977); R. Stites, *The Women's Liberation Movement in Russia. Feminism, Nihilism, and Bolshevism, 1860–1930* (Princeton, NJ: Princeton University Press, 1978); L. H. Edmondson, *Feminism in Russia, 1900–1917* (London: University of London Press, 1981); G. A. Tishkin, *Zhenskii vopros v Rossii v 50–60 gg. XIX v.* (Leningrad: izdatel'stvo LGU, 1984); D. L Ransel, *Mothers of Misery: Child Abandonment in Russia* (Princeton, NJ: Princeton University Press, 1988); D. B. Clements, B. A. Engel and C. Worobec (eds), *Russia's Women. Accommodation, Resistance, Transformation* (Berkeley, CA: University of California Press, 1991); B. A. Engel, *Between the Fields and the City: Women. Work and Family in Russia, 1861–1914* (Cambridge: Cambridge University Press, 1994); O. A. Khasbulatova, *Opyt i traditsii zhenskogo dvizheniia v Rossii, 1860-1917* (Ivanovo: Izdatel'stvo IvGU, 1994); L. Bernstein, *Sonia's Daughters: Prostitutes and their Regulations in Imperial Russia* (Berkeley, CA: University of California Press, 1995); A. Lindenmeyr, *Poverty is not a Vice: Charity, Society, and the State in Imperial Russia* (Princeton, NJ: Princeton University Press, 1996); R. Marsh (ed.), *Women in Russia and Ukraine* (Cambridge: Cambridge University Press, 1996); B. Clements, *Bolshevik Women* (Cambridge: Cambridge University Press, 1997); N. Pushkareva, *Women in Russian History From the Tenth to the Twentieth Century* (Armonk, NY: M.E. Sharpe, 1997); B. Pietrow-Ennker *Russlands 'neue Menschen': Die Entwicklung der Frauenbewegung von den Anfängen bis zur Oktoberrevolution* (Frankfurt-New York: Campus Verlag, 1999); D. L Ransel, *Village Mothers: Three Generations of Change in Russian and Tataria* (Bloomington, IN: Indiana University Press, 2000); B. A. Engel, *Mothers and Daughters. Women of the Intelligentsia in Nineteenth Century Russia* (Ewanston, IL: Northwester University Press, 2000); *Russian Women, 1698-1917: Experience and Expression, An Anthology of Sources*, compiled by W. G. Wagner and others (Bloomington, IN: Indiana University Press, 2002); D. Raleigh (ed.), *The Emperors and Empresses of Russia: Rediscovering the Romanovs* (Armonk, NY: M. E. Sharpe, 1996); C. Ruane, *Gender, Class, and the Professionalization of Russian City Teachers: 1860–1914* (Pittsburgh, PA: University of Pittsburgh Press, 1994); W. Rosslyn, *Deeds, Not Words. The Origins of Women's Philanthropy in the Russian Empire* (Birmingham: University of Birmingham Press, 2007); I. Yukina, *Russkii feminism kak vyzov sovremennosti* (St Petersburg: Aleteia, 2007); N. Pushkareva, *Gendernaia teoriia i istoricheskoe znanie* (St Petersburg: Aleteia, 2007).

18. C. Kelly, 'Teacups and coffins: the culture of Russian merchant women, 1850-1917', in Marsh (ed.), *Women in Russia and Ukraine*, p. 55.

19. M. Joffe and A. Lindenmeyr, 'Daughter, Wives, and Partners: Women of the Moscow Merchant Elite', in J. L. West, Iu. Petrov (eds), *Merchant Moscow: Images of Russia's Vanished Bourgeoisie* (Princeton, NJ: Princeton University Press, 1997), p. 103.

20. Marrese, *A Woman's Kingdom*, pp. 128–33.

21. N. Kozlova, 'Khoziaistvennaia aktivnost' i predprinimatel'stvo kupecheskikh zhen i vdov Moskvy v XVIII v.', in *Torgovlia, kupechestvo i tamozhennoe delo v Rossii XVI-XVIII vekov* (St Petersburg, 2001), pp. 139–44; idem, 'Imushchestvennoe pravo i polozhenie zhenshchiny v kupecheskoi sem'e Moskvy XVIII v.', in *Stolichnye i periferiinye goroda Rusi i Rossii v srednie veka i rannee novoe vremia* (Moscow, 2003), pp. 259–75.

22. O. V. Fomina, *Imushchestvenno-demograficheskaia kharacteristika moskovskoi kupecheskoi sem'i v poslednei treti XVIII v.* [Avtoreferat ... kand. ist. Nauk] (Moscow, 2003).

23. M. N. Tikhomirova, 'Uchastie zhenshchin v promyshlennom proizvodstve Rossii v kontse 60-kh-nachale 70-kh godov XIX veka (na materialakh Tverskoi Gubernii)', in *Zhenshchiny. Istoriia. Obshchestvo.* (Tver', 1999), pp. 34-46; I. V. Potkina, *Na Olimpe delovogo uspekha: Nikol'skaia manufaktura Morozovykh. 1797–1917* (Moscow: Mosgorarchive, 2004); G. Ulianova, 'Predprinimatel': tip lichnosti, dukhovnyi oblik, obraz zhizni', in *Istoriia predprinimatel'stva v Rossii*, 2 vols (Moscow: Rosspen, 1999), vol.2, pp. 441–66; idem, 'Tuche, Schnaps und Farben; Unternehmerinnen aus Deutschen Familien in Russland im 19. Und zu Beginn des 20. Jahrhunderts', in D. Dahlmann, K. Heller, T. Igumnowa, J. Petrow, K. Reschke (eds), *«Eine Grosse Zukunft». Deutsche in Russlands Wirtschaft* (Berlin-Moskau, 2000), pp. 90–7; idem, 'Die Unternehmerinnen als Wohltäerinnen in Moskau. 1850–1914', in G. Hausmann (ed.), *Gesellschaft als lokale Veranstaltung. Selbstwervaltung, Assoziierung und Geselligkeit in den Städten des ausgehenden Zarenreiches* (Goettingen: Vanderhoeck & Ruprecht, 2002), s. 405-432; idem, 'Merchant Women in Business in the Late Eighteenth and Early Nineteenth Centuries', in W. Rosslyn and A. Tosi (eds), *Women in Eighteenth-Century Russian Culture and Society* (London: Palgrave, 2007), pp. 144–67.

24. A. Rieber, *Merchants and Entrepreneurs in Imperial Russia* (Chapel Hill, NC: University of North Carolina Press, 1982); J. A. Ruckman, *The Moscow Business Elite, A Social and Cultural Portrait of Two Generations, 1840–1905* (DeKalb, IL: Northern Illinois University Press, 1984); M. Hildermeier, *Bürgertum und Stadt in Russland 1760–1870: Rechtliche Lage und Soziale Struktur* (Köln: Böhlau Verlag, 1986); A. Aksenov, *Genealogiia Moskovskogo kupechestva XVIII veka* (Moscow: Nauka, 1988); B. V. Anan'ich, *Bankirskie doma v Rossii, 1860–1914 gg. Ocherki istorii chastnogo predprinimatel'stva* (Leningrad: Nauka, 1991); T. C. Owen, *The Corporation under Russian Law, 1800–1917* (Cambridge: Cambridge University Press: 1992); A. N. Bokhanov, *Krupnaia burzhuaziia Rossii, konets XIX v. – 1914 g.* (Moscow: Nauka, 1992); J. L. West, I. Petrov (eds), *Merchant Moscow: Images of Russia's Vanished Bourgeoisie* (Princeton, NJ: Princeton University Press, 1997); Y. A. Petrov, *Moskovskaia burzhuaziia v nachale XX veka: predprinimatel'stvo i politika* (Moscow: Mosgorarchive, 2002).

25. E. W. Brownlee and M. M. Brownlee, *Women in the American Economy: a Documentary History, 1675 to 1929* (New Haven, CT: Yale University Press, 1976); W. Gamber, *The Female Economy: the Millinery and Dressmaking Trades, 1860–1930* (Urbana, IL: University of Illinois Press, 1997); A. Kwolek-Folland, *Incorporating women : a history of women and business in the United States* (New York: Twayne Publishers, 1998); J. M. Oppedisano, *Historical Encyclopedia of American Women entrepreneurs: 1776 to the Present* (Westport, CT: Greenwood Press, 2000); R. Beachy, B. Craig and A. Owens (eds), *Women, Business, and Finance in Nineteenth-century Europe: Rethinking Separate Spheres* (Oxford and New York: Berg, 2005); H. Barker, *The Business of Women. Female Enterprise and Urban Development in Northern England, 1760–1830 (New York: Oxford University Press, 2006); N. Phillips, Women in Business, 1700-1850* (Woodbridge, Suffolk-Rochester, NY: Boydell Press, 2006); E. Sparks, *Capital Intensions: Female*

Proprietors in San Francisco, 1850–1920 (Chapel Hill, NC: University of North Carolina Press, 2006). The most important articles are as follows: W. Gamber, 'Gendered Concerns: Thoughts on the History of Business and the History of Women', *Business and Economic History*, 23:1 (1994), pp. 129–40; M. Finn, 'Women, Consumption and Coverture in England, c.1760–1860', *Historical Journal*, 39:3 (1996), pp. 703–22; A. Owens, 'Property, Gender and the Life Course: Inheritance and Family Welfare Provision in Early Nineteenth-Century England', *Social History*, 26 (2001), pp. 297–315; D. R. Green, A. Owens, 'Gentlewomanly Capitalism? Spinsters, Widows and Wealth Holding in England and Wales, c. 1800–1860', *Economic History Review*, 56 (2003), pp. 510–36; A. C. Kay, 'Small Business, Self-Employment and Women's Work-Life Choices in Nineteeth-Century London', in D. Mitch, J. Brown, M.H.D. van Leeuwen, *Origins of the Modern Career* (Aldershot: Ashgate, 2004), pp. 191–206; idem, 'Retailing, Respectability and the Independent Woman in Nineteenth-century London', in Beachy, Craig and Owens (eds), *Women, Business, and Finance*, pp. 152–66.

26. Davidoff and Hall, *Family Fortunes* (see p. 277).
27. A. Vickery, 'Golden Age to separate spheres? A review of the categories and chronology of English Women history', *Historical Journal*, 36:2 (1993), pp. 383–414.
28. Berg, 'Women's Property and the Industrial Revolution', p. 241.
29. Ibid., pp. 242–3.
30. W. Gamber, 'A Gendered Enterprise: Placing Nineteenth-Century Businesswomen in History', *Business History Review*, 72 (Summer 1998), p. 217.
31. A. Kwolek-Folland, Gender and Business History, *Enterprise & Society*, 2:1 (2001), p. 1.
32. Beachy, Craig and Owens (eds), *Women, Business, and Finance in Nineteenth-century Europe*, p. 9.

1 Female Entrepreneurship in the 1800s–20s: Business and the Issue of Property

1. C. Evtuhov and R. Stites, *A History of Russia: Peoples, Legends, Events, Forces Since 1800* (Boston, MA and New York: Houghton Mifflin Company, 2004), p. 1.
2. V. O. Kliuchevsky, 'Kurs russkoi istorii', in V. O. Kliuchevsky, *Sochineniia*, 9 vols, (Moscow: Mysl', 1987–90), vol. 5 (1989), p. 190.
3. *PSZ* I, vol. XX, No 14327, art. 3; vol. XXX, No 23503, arts 3, 6; vol. XXXIX, §43, 45; *PSZ* II, vol. XL, No 41779. For a thorough analysis of Russia's property rights legislation (from 1649 to the early nineteenth century), see Marrese, *A Woman's Kingdom*, pp. 17–100.
4. *PSZ* I, vol. XX, No 14327.
5. Ibid., vol. XXII, No 16188 ['Charter on the Rights and Benefits for the Towns of the Russian Empire', bi-lingual text in *Catherine II's Charters of 1785 to the Nobility and the Towns*, ed. D. Griffiths and G. E. Munro, *The Laws of Russia Series II: vol. 289* (Bakersfield, CA: Schlacks Publishers, 1991), pp. 22–60.
6. Ibid., vol. XXII, No. 16188, arts 104, 110, 116. The criteria and capital levels governing division between guilds could vary. Thus in 1794, because of inflation, the government raised the financial threshold for the merchant guilds: required capital now became 16,000–50,000 roubles for the first guild, 8,000–16,000 for the second, 2,000–8,000 for the third. See Koval'chuk, *Manufakturnaia promyshlennost'*, p. 33.

7. 'In the eighteenth century the term *meshchane* in Russia was used in two senses: either it meant the entire commercial-artisan class in the towns and cities ... or, in a limited sense, it designated only the lower groups of the city population, the petty tradesmen, crafts-men and the like. In the nineteenth century it had only the latter meaning', *Dictionary of Russian Historical Terms from the Eleventh Century to 1917*, comp. S. Pushkarev, ed. G. Vernadsky and R. T. Fisher Jr (New Haven, CT and London: Yale University Press, 1970), p. 60. See also, Hilderneirer, *Bürgerten und Stadt in Russland*, pp. 437–56.

8. *PSZ* I, vol. XXII, No 16188, art. 90.

9. See *Proekt torgovogo ulozheniia Rossiiskoi imperii* (St Petersburg: Tipografiia Komissii Sostavleniia Zakonov, 1814), pp. 9–11.

10. On estate stratification in Russia see: G. L. Freeze, 'The *Soslovie* (Estate) Paradigm and Russian Social History', *American Historical Review*, 91 (1986), pp. 1–36; A. J. Rieber, 'The Sedimentary Society', in E. W. Clowes, S. D. Kassow, J. L. West (eds), *Between Tsar and People: Educated Society and the Quest for Public Identity in Late Imperial Russia* (Princeton, NJ: Princeton University Press, 1991), pp. 343-66.

11. *PSZ* I, vol. XXXVIII, No 21484 (decree of 24 October 1804 'Concerning the rules for registration of peasants in the merchantry').

12. Ibid., and *PSZ* I, vol. XXXVIII, No 21811.

13. *PSZ* I, vol. XXXVIII, No 21811.

14. 'Treasury' peasants belonged to the state and paid a quit-rent to the Treasury. In 1765 their ranks were enlarged by merger between them and the 'economic' peasants, previ-ously the property of monasteries, who had been placed under the control of the state College of Economy in 1764 after the dissolution of the monasteries. Appanage peasants belonged to members of the Imperial family (decree of 5 April 1797, 'Statute concerning the Imperial family'). See *Otechestvennaia istoriia. Istoriia Rossii s drevneishikh vremen do 1917 goda. Entsiklopediia*, 3 vols to date, (Moscow: Bol'shaia Rossiiskaia entsiklopediia, 1994 onwards), vol. 3, pp. 135, 138, 140; *Dictionary of Russian Historical Terms*, pp. 46–8.

15. *PSZ* I, vol. XXXVIII, No 21484.

16. Ibid., vol. XXV, No 18714 (decree of 22 October 1798 'Concerning the release of set-tlers under the jurisdiction of the Appanage Department into the *meshchanstvo* and merchantry').

17. Ibid., vol. XXX, No 23020, para. 2, art. 7.

18. Ibid., vol. XXXVI, No 19576 ('Concerning the duty of Fiscal Chambers to exact from peasants and persons of other estates who register in the merchantry and the *meshchanstvo* all lawful taxes due from them, until a new tax census, according to the requirements of both estates').

19. Ibid., vol. XXXVII, No 28855 (decree of 31 December 1821 'Concerning the registra-tion of Appanage peasants in the merchantry and *meshchanstvo* on the same basis as that on which manumitted landlords' peasants enter these callings').

20. Tsentral'nyi istoricheskii arkhiv Moskvy (Central Historical Archive of the City of Mos-cow, hereafter TsIAM), f. 2, op. 1, d. 123, l. 2.

21. TsIAM, f. 2, op. 1, d. 114, l. 1. 4.

22. Ibid., d. 87, ll. 1–4.

23. Ibid., f. 2, op. 1, d. 137, ll. 1–4; d.140, ll. 1–2; d.148, ll. 1–2; d.170, ll. 1–2; d.176, ll.1–4; d. 204, l. 1.

24. Aksenov, *Genealogiia Moskovskogo kupechestva XVIII veka*.

25. Ibid., p. 64.

26. Koval'chuk, *Manufakturnaia promyshlennost'*, pp. 91–4.

27. *Vedomost' o manufakturakh v Rossii za 1813 i 1814 gody* (St Petersburg: Tipografia Pravitel'stvuiushchego Senata, 1816), p. 226.

28. *Materialy dlia istorii moskovskogo kupechestva. Revizskie skazki*, 9 vols (Moscow: Tipolitografiia I. N. Kushnereva i Ko., 1883–9, hereafter *MDIMK Skazki*), VI (1887), p. 196.

29. TsIAM, f. 2, op.1, d. 204, l. 1.

30. See *Vedomost' o manufakturakh*.

31. The wives of army conscripts (commonly called *soldatki*) were usually left behind when their husbands were taken into military service, which lasted many years. Their social position thereafter was often precarious, and they might have to find means of livelihood outside of ordinary peasant roles. See P. P. Shcherbinin, *Voennyi faktor v povsednevnoi zhizni russkoi zhenshchiny v XVIII-nachale XIX vv.* (Tambov: Iulis, 2004), p. 26.

32. *PSZ* I, vol. VI, No 3711 (decree of 18 January 1721 'Concerning the purchase of villages for factories'); vol. XXII, No. 9004 (decree of 27 July 1744 'Concerning permission for manufacturers to buy villages for factories').

33. See V. I. Semevskii, *Krest'iane v tsarstvovanie Imperatritsy Ekateriny II*, 2 vols (St Petersburg: Tipografia M. M. Stasiulevicha, 1901–3), vol. 1, pp. 540–7. *PSZ* I, vol. XVIII, No 13374 (decree of 13 October 1769 'Concerning permission to all who so wish to set up weaving looms').

34. *Vedomost' o manufakturakh*, p. 6.

35. *Starosta* and *shliakhtich, shliakhta* (below) were Polish designations of (male) noble social status.

36. *Vedomost' o manufakturakh*, pp. 11–13.

37. Ibid., pp.100, 106, 136.

38. Ibid., pp. 66, 93, 95.

39. Ibid., pp. 65–80.

40. *Pood* is equal to about 36.11 pounds (16.38 kilograms).

41. *Vedomost' o manufakturakh*, pp. 114, 119.

42. Ibid., p. 87.

43. *MDIMK Skazki*, V (1887), p. 350; VI, p. 243.

44. Ibid., IV (1886), returns for 1794, p. 400.

45. Some of the most interesting examples of the recent scholarship include A. Vickery, *The Gentleman's Daughter: Women's Lives in Georgian England* (New Haven & London: Yale University Press, 1998); Yu. A. Tikhonov, *Mir veshchei v moskovckikh i peterburgskikh domakh sanovnogo dvorianstva (po novym istochnikam pervoi poloviny XVIII veka)* (Moscow: Kuchkovo pole, 2008).

46. R.G. Eimontova, 'Dvenadtsatyi god. Nashestvie' in *Istoriia Moskvy s drevneishikh vremen do nashikh dnei*, 3 vols (Moscow: Mosgorarchive, 1997–2000), vol. 2, p. 34.

47. TsIAM, f. 50, op. 14, d. 423, l. 1.

48. Ibid., l. 2.

49. Ibid., l. 4.

50. Ibid., l. 8.

51. In conversion to metric measure the plot was 6.5 m long and wide and had an area of 42.25 square metres.

52. TsIAM, f. 50, op. 14, d. 423, l. 25.

53. Ibid., l. 29.

54. Ibid., f. 51, op. 22, dd. 23, 33, 46, 85, 196, 231, 284; *MDIMK Skazki*, IV, pp. 595, 290, 74; V, pp. 327, 139, 21.

55. *MDIMK Skazki*, IV, p. 595.
56. TsIAM, f. 51, op. 22, d. 23, l. 1.
57. Ibid., d. 196, ll. 1-5.
58. *MDIMK Skazki*, V, p. 139.
59. TsIAM, f. 51, op. 22, d. 85, ll. 1–34.
60. *MDIMK Skazki*, IV, p. 74; V, p. 21.
61. TsIAM, f. 51, op. 22, d. 46, ll. 1–5.
62. *Vedomost' o manufakturakh*, p. 230.

2 Female Entrepreneurship in the 1830s–40s: a Hidden Success

1. *Spisok fabrikantam i zavodchikam Rossiiskoi imperii 1832 goda* (St Petersburg: tipografiia Departamenta vneshnei torgovli, 1833, hereafter *Spisok 1832*); L. Samoilov, *Atlas promyshlennosti Moskovskoi gubernii* (Moscow: Moskovskoe otd. Manufacturnogo soveta, 1845).
2. TsIAM, f. 14, op. 9, d. 6675.
3. On *meshchanstvo* estate (*meshchane*) see Chapter 1, note 75.
4. B. N. Mironov, *Sotsial'naia istoriia Rossii perioda Imperii (XVIII-nachalo XX v.). Genezis lichnosti, demokraticheskoi sem'i, grazhdanskogo obshchestva i pravovogo gosudarstva*, 2 vols (St Petersburg: Dmitry Bulanin, 1999), vol. 1, p. 315.
5. The data are for 1858; no earlier data are available. See Ya. E. Vodarsky, *Dvorianskoe zemlevladenie v Rossii v XVII – pervoi polovine XIX v.* (Moscow: Nauka, 1988), p. 238.
6. A. M. Solov'eva, *Promyshlennaia revoliutsia v Rossii v XIX v* (Moscow: Nauka, 1990), p. 32. Between 1820 and 1852 the annual output of cotton fabrics increased from 35 million *arshins* to 257.1 million *arshins*. *Arshin*, the old Russian measure of length, was established by Emperor Peter I at 28 inches; thus, the output rose from 81.7 million feet to 599 million feet (or, in metric terms, from 24,850,000 m to 182,541,000 m). Ibid., p. 33.
7. TsIAM, f. 14, op. 9, d. 3516, l.220; d. 6675, l. 9; d. 6746, l. 219; f. 46, op. 2, d. 560, ll. 3, 6, 16; *Spisok kuptsov goroda Moskvy, ob'iavivshikh kapitaly na 1830 god, s pokazaniem imeiushchegosia pri nikh semeistva, chem torgovliu proizvodiat i gde zhitel'stvo imeiut* (Moscow, 1830, hereafter *Spisok 1830*), 3rd Guild, No 687; VIII (1889), p. 155; IX (1889), p. 141; *Spravochnaia kniga o litsakh, poluchivshikh kupecheskie svidetelstva po 1 i 2 gil'diiam v Moskve na [1869–1898] god* (Moscow, 1869–98, hereafter *SK Moscow*), (1869), p. 91; K. Niström, *Moskovskii adres-kalendar' dlia zhitelei Moskvy*, 4 vols (Moscow: Tipografia S. Selivanovskogo, 1842), vol. 4, p. 241.
8. *Spisok 1832*, pp. 52, 73, 75, 191–2, 280, 574.
9. Because of the absence of data for the 1830s and 1840s, we use the data for 1848, presented in *Sbornik statisticheskikh svedenii o Rossii, izdavaemyi statisticheskim otdeleniem Imperatorskogo Russkogo Geograficheskogo obshchestva* (St Petersburg, 1851), vol. 1, p. 8–10.
10. According to the Table of Ranks, which was in effect from 1722 to 1917, all men of service were divided into 14 categories; the ranks of privy councillor and actual state councillor corresponded to the third and fourth categories respectively, while the rank of colonel corresponded to the fourth category.
11. *PSZ* I, vol. V, No 2829.
12. The *desiatina*, an old Russian unit of measure, amounted to 2.7 acres.

13. *Prilozheniia k trudam Redaktsionnykh komissii dlia sostavleniia Polozhenii o krest'ianakh, vykhodiashchikh iz krepostnoi zavisimosti. Svedeniia o pomeshchich'ikh imeniiakh*, 6 vols. (St Petersburg, 1860), vol.2, *Orel guberniia*, p. 72.

14. *Spisok 1832*, pp. 198, 703, 705.

15. *Ukazatel' Vystavki rossiiskikh manufakturnykh izdelii, byvshei v St. Peterburge v 1839 godu* (St Petersburg, 1839), p. 93.

16. This is known from the memoirs mentioning her son Ivan Miatlev (1796–1844), a high ranking official of the Ministry of Finance, remembered in the history of Russian literature as a poet and a friend of Aleksandr Pushkin.

17. RGADA, f. 1271 (Miatlevy), op. 1, d. 104, ll. 20–1.

18. F. F. Vigel', 'Zapiski', in *Russkie Memuary. Izbrannye Stranitsy: 1800–1825* (Moscow: Pravda, 1989), p. 446.

19. Ibid.

20. *Spisok 1832*, pp. 296–7.

21. *Zhivopisnaia Rossiia*, 19 vols (St Petersburg: tov. M. O. Wolf, 1879–1901), vol. Litovskoe i Belorusskoe Poles'e, (1882), p. 366.

22. The estimates are based on data from *Prilozheniia k trudam Redaktsionnykh komissii*, vol. 6 Minsk guberniia, p. 2, 16, 218, 24, 28, 30-56; *Vitebsk guberniia*, p. 12; *Vil'na guberniia*, p. 2, 10.

23. A. O. Smirnova-Rosset, *Vospominaniia, pis'ma* (Moscow: Pravda, 1990), p. 85.

24. See: A. K. Golubovich, *Arkhiv Radziwillov-Wittgensteinov v Bundesarchive, Germania*, www.niab.belhost.by/stat/arh_radz/, accessed 15 April 2008.

25. *Spisok 1832*, p. 595.

26. On Count Kirill Razumovsky, see K. G. Fedorchenko, *Rossiiskaia imperiia v litsakh. Entsiklopediia biografii*, 2 vols (Krasnoiarsk-Moscow: OLMA-Press, 2001), vol. 2, p. 291.

27. The estimates are based on the data from *Prilozheniia k trudam Redaktsionnykh komissii*, vol.6 Poltava guberniia, p. 18.

28. A. M. Anfimov, 'Karlovskoe imenie Mecklenburg-Strelitskikh v kontse XIX-nachale XX v.', *Materialy po istorii sel'skogo khoziaistva i krest'ianstva SSSR* (Moscow: izdatel'stvo Akademii nauk SSSR, 1962), p. 353.

29. P. A. Viazemsky, *Staraia zapisnaia knizhka* (Leningrad: Izdatel'stvo pisatelei, 1929), pp.228–32.

30. According to the memoirists M. Dmitriev and A. de Custine, la Valle was created a count after the Restoration of the Bourbons for having provided the exiled Louis XVIII with a large amount of money during the latter's stay in Mittau, Kurland (presently Elgava, Latvia) in 1798–1800.

31. Marrese, *A Woman's Kingdom*, p. 199.

32. Ibid, p.191.

33. Estimates: The total number of enterprises – 805, including 529, or 65 per cent, textile (79 woollen mills, 117 silk mills, 238 cotton mills, 15 linen mills, 79 dye works and cotton-dyeing and printing mills, and 1 spinning mill); 18 factories manufacturing gold and silver braid, lace and other trimmings, 10 writing-paper mills, 102 tanneries, 11 soap-boileries, 22 chandleries, 10 tallow-boileries, 11 wax refineries, three snuff-box factories, three pomade factories, three tobacco processing plants, one sugar refinery, five vinegar distilleries, 11 dyestuff factories, 4 sealing-wax factories, 19 chemical plants, one needle factory, one glass factory, 18 porcelain and pottery factories, and 19 copper mills.

34. The analysis of this parameter is based on a correlation of the 1832 data with the existing lists of real estate for 1818 and 1842.
35. V. Androssov, *Statisticheskaia zapiska o Moskve* (Moscow: Tip. S. Selivanovskogo, 1832), p. 23.
36. M. M. Bogoslovsky, 'Moskva v 1870–1890-kh godakh', in M. M. Bogoslovsky, *Istoriographia, memuaristika, epistoliaria* (Moscow: Nauka, 1987), p. 108.
37. The Chetverikovs – N. A. Dobrynina Family Archive, Sergey Chetverikov, *The Memories (manuscript)*, part 3, l. 20.
38. Androssov, *Statisticheskaia zapiska*, pp. 31, 52.
39. Ibid., p. 50.
40. TsIAM, f. 14, op. 9, d. 3515, l. 116; d. 6746, l. 182.
41. Ibid., dd. 1389, 3516, 6746, 6675; Samoilov, *Atlas promyshlennosti*, p. 2, 25, 35.
42. TsIAM, f. 14, op. 9, d. 6675, ll. 18-19; *Spisok 1830*, 3rd Guild, No 371; Samoilov, *Atlas promyshlennosti*, p. 2; *MDIMK Skazki*, VII, p. 40; VIII, p. 43-4; Niström, *Moskovskii adres-kalendar'*, vol. 4, p. 54.
43. TsIAM, f. 14, op. 9, d. 6746, ll. 220-1; *Moskovskii Nekropol'*, 3 vols (St Petersburg: tipografiia M. M. Stasiulevicha, 1907–8), vol. I (1907), p. 116; Samoilov, *Atlas promyshlennosti*, p. 28; *MDIMK Skazki*, V, p.302; VI, p. 70; VII, p. 69; VIII, p. 87; Niström, *Moskovskii adres-kalendar'*, vol. 4, p. 32; S. Tarasov, *Statisticheskoe obozrenie promyshlennosti Moskovskoi gubernii*, (Moscow: tipografiia Velomostei Mos. gor. politsii, 1856), p. 62.
44. TsIAM, f. 14, op. 9, d. 6746, ll. 219-20; *Spisok 1830*, 3rd Guild, No 6; Samoilov, *Atlas promyshlennosti*, p. 26; *MDIMK Skazki*, VII, p. 13; VIII, p. 9.
45. Koval'chuk, *Manufakturnaia promyshlennost' Moskvy*, p. 263.
46. *Spisok 1830*, 3rd Guild, No 23; *MDIMK Skazki*, IV, p. 810; V, p. 388; VI, p. 27; VII, p. 23; VIII, p. 24; Niström, *Moskovskii adres-kalendar'*, vol. 4, p. 24.
47. *Spisok 1830*, 2nd Guild, No 9; Samoilov, *Atlas promyshlennosti*, p. 4; *MDIMK Skazki*, V (1887), p.195; VI, p. 127; VII, p. 137; VIII, p. 300; IX, p. 275; Niström, *Moskovskii adres-kalendar'*, vol. 4, pp. 110, 237; M. Rudolf, *Ukazatel' mestnosti v Kremle i Kitaegorode stolichnogo goroda Moskvy*, vol. 1, Kreml i Kitai-gorod (Moscow: Tipografia A. Semena, 1846), pp. 93-5; Tarasov, *Statisticheskoe obozrenie*, p. 22; *SK Moscow*, 1869, p. 81; P. A. Orlov, *Ukazatel' fabric i zavodov Evropeiskoi Rossii i Tsarstva Polskogo* (St Petersburg: tipografia R. Golicke, 1887), p. 65.
48. *PSZ* I, vol. XXVI, No 19692; vol. XXIX, No 22522.
49. Ibid.,vol. XXV, No 18663, 'The Statute of the Capital City of Saint Petersburg'. Ch. V. § 6; No 18822, 'The Statute of the Capital City of Moscow', Ch. V. § 6. In accordance with the Statutes of the capital cities adopted on 12 September 1798 and 17 January 1799 respectively, peasants had the right to establish shops of three types: for the first type they were to pay 100 roubles to the city treasury, whereupon they were authorized to trade in 'foreign' (imported) and native vegetables, tea, coffee, and sugar; for the second type they were to pay 50 roubles, whereupon they could trade in all the aforesaid goods excepting tea, coffee, and sugar; the payment for the third type was 25 roubles, and the foodstuffs to be traded in were exclusively Russian.
50. Androssov, *Statisticheskaia zapiska, p.* 39.
51. The estimates are based on the data from Rudolf, *Ukazatel' mestnosti v Kremle i Kitaegorode*.
52. The estimates are based on the data from Rudolf, *Ukazatel' mestnosti v Kremle i Kitaegorode*, pp. 47, 51-2, 55, 63, 65, 68-9, 71-4, 76, 79, 83, 104.

53. TsIAM, f. 50, op. 14, d. 1164, ll. 23-4, 86.
54. Ibid., l. 52.
55. Ibid., f.14, op. 9, d. 6675, l. 27.
56. Ibid., l. 294; d. 6746, l. 173.
57. Ibid., ll. 201-15.
58. Ibid., ll. 186-7.
59. See G. N. Ulianova, *Blagotvoritel'nost' moskovskikh predprinimatelei, 1860–1914* (Moscow: Mosgorarchive, 1999), pp. 461–2.
60. S. I. Chetverikov, *Nevozvratnoe proshloe* (Moscow: izdatel'stvo Territoria, 2001), p. 12.
61. Ruckman, *The Moscow Business Elite*, p. 53.
62. TsIAM, f.14, op. 9, d. 6675, ll. 201-2.
63. Ibid., ll. 232-3.
64. See Samoilov, *Atlas promyshlennosti*.
65. TsIAM, f.14, op. 9, d. 6675, ll. 93-4; Spisok 1830, 2nd Guild, No 218; *MDIMK Skazki*, VI, p. 171; VII, p. 175; VIII, p. 301; V.D. Metelercamp, K. Niström, *Kniga adressov stolitsy Moskvy* (Moscow: Tipografia S. Selivanovskogo, 1839), p. 184; Niström, *Moskovskii adres-kalendar'*, vol. 4, p. 161; Rudolf, *Ukazatel' mestnosti v Kremle i Kitae-gorode*, p. 86; *Materialy k istorii Prokhorovskoi Trekhgornoi manufactury i torgovo-promyshlennoi deiatel'nosti sem'i Prokhorovykh. Gody 1799-1915* (Moscow, 1915), pp. 5-6, 72, 137.
66. Ya. P. Garelin, *Gorod Ivanovo-Voznesensk ili byvshee selo Ivanovo i Voznesenskii Posad (Vladimirskoi gubernii)*, 2 vols (Shuya: lito-tipografia Ya. I. Borisoglebskogo, 1884–5), vol. 1 (1884), p. 210.
67. *Spisok 1830*, 2nd Guild, No 84; *Spisok 1832*, p.409; *MDIMK Skazki*, VI, p. 221; VII, p. 115; VIII, p. 130; Metelercamp, Niström, *Kniga adressov*, p. 259; Niström, *Moskovskii adres-kalendar'*,, vol. 4, pp. 202, 209–10; Samoilov, *Atlas promyshlennosti*, p. 51; Rudolf, *Ukazatel' mestnosti v Kremle i Kitae-gorode*, p. 78; N. Matissen, *Atlas manufacturnoi promyshlennosti Moskovskoi gubernii* (Moscow: tipografia A. Ris, 1872), p. 136.
68. TsIAM, f.14, op. 9, d. 6746, ll. 225–39.
69. Ibid., d. 3515, l. 115.
70. Ibid., d. 6746, l. 232; d. 6675, l. 245; *Moskovskii Nekropol'*, vol. III (1908), p. 221; Spisok 1830, 3rd Guild, No 1380; Samoilov, *Atlas promyshlennosti*, p. 51; *MDIMK Skazki*, IV, p. 218; V, p. 94; VII, p. 206; VIII, p. 230.
71. TsIAM, f.14, op. 9, d. 6675, l. 11–12; *Spisok 1830*, 3rd Guild, No 219; *MDIMK Skazki*, IV, p. 131; V, p. 60; VI, p. 45; VII, p. 41; VIII, p. 35; IX, p. 30; *SK Moscow*, 1869, p. 604.
72. TsIAM, f.14, op. 9, d. 6675, l. 232; *Spisok 1830*, 3rd Guild, No 974; *MDIMK Skazki*, III (1884), p. 651; IV, p. 762; V, p. 379; VII, p. 171; VIII, p. 189; Metelercamp, Niström, *Kniga adressov*, p. 246; Niström, *Moskovskii adres-kalendar'*, vol. 4, p. 198; *SK Moscow*, 1872, p. 292.
73. *PSZ* II, vol. VIII, No 6108.
74. TsIAM, f.14, op. 9, d. 6675, l. 198; *MDIMK Skazki*, V, p. 245; VI, p. 238; VII, p. 236; VIII, p. 262; Niström, *Moskovskii adres-kalendar'*, vol. 4, p. 121.
75. TsIAM, f.14, op. 9, d. 6675, l. 189; f. 78, op. 1, d. 325, ll. 40–1; f. 78, op. 1, d. 326, l. 1–81; *Spisok 1830*, 1st Guild, No 69; *Moskovskii Nekropol'*, vol. I (1907), p. 78; *MDIMK Skazki*, VII, p. 262; VIII, p. 306; Niström, *Moskovskii adres-kalendar'*, vol. 4, p. 17.
76. TsIAM, f. 78, op. 1, d. 328, ll. 19–20.
77. Ibid., l. 34.
78. Ibid., d. 330, ll. 11–16.

79. Ibid., d. 325, ll. 40–1, 120–4.
80. Ibid., l. 14.
81. Ibid., d. 330, l. 49.
82. Ibid., f. 14, op. 10, d. 3904, l. 2.

3 Female Entrepreneurship in the 1850s and 1860s: an Unstable Rise – the Moscow and St Petersburg Cases

1. This increase in the number of source materials is due to the activity of the Central Statistical Committee, founded in 1852 to collect and publish data on the Empire as a whole and on its provinces, as well as to publish regional collections of data on the state of industry. Unfortunately, there is no all-Russian collection of statistical data on industrial enterprises with concrete names of their owners. Thus, it is impossible to estimate the participation of women in industrial production in general, and in its branches in particular. However, we can get some idea of the various aspects and parameters of the process of development of female entrepreneurship by addressing a number sources, first of all the lists of industrial enterprises of Moscow (1853, 1868) and St Petersburg (1862), as well as the list of merchants of Moscow and St Petersburg (both for the year 1869).

2. The chronology of the industrial revolution in Russia was the subject of numerous discussions in the 1920s and then in the 1960s–80s. So far as the industrial revolution is concerned, Russia lagged behind Western Europe by several decades. In generalizing works the accepted dates are the 1850s–90s. See P. G. Ryndziunsky, *Utverzhdenie kapitalizma v Rossii, 1850-1880 gg* (Moscow: Nauka, 1978), p. 21–48; Solov'eva, *Promyshlennaia revoliutsia*.

3. A. Maksheev, *Voenno-statisticheskoe obozrenie Rossiiskoi Imperii* (St Petersburg: Tipografiia F.Sushchinskogo, 1867), p. 189.

4. *PSZ* II, vol. XXXII, No 31974.

5. *Uezd* (district) was a subdivision of the province.

6. N. V. Varadinov, *Istoriia Ministerstva vnutrennikh del*, 3 vols (St Petersburg: Tipografiia Ministerstva vnutrennikh del, 1862), vol. 3, p. 607.

7. *Statisticheskie tablitsy Rossiiskoi imperii, izdavaemye po rasporiazheniiu ministra vnutrennikh del Tsentral'nym statisticheskim komitetom* (St Petersburg: Tipografiia II Otdeleniia Sobstvennoi E. I. V. kantseliarii, 1863), vol. 2, *Nalichnoe naselenie imperii za 1858 god*, pp. 182–3, 187. (The tables are concerned with forty-nine provinces of European Russia, which accounted for 90 per cent of Russia's total population).

8. *Voenno-statisticheskii sbornik*, vol. 4 Rossiia (St Petersburg: v Voennoi Tipografii, 1871), pp. 46, 134.

9. Mironov, *Sotsial'naia istoriia Rissii*, vol. 1, p. 20.

10. *Statisticheskie tablitsy Rossiiskoi imperi za 1856 godi,sostavlennye i izdannye po rasporiazheniiu ministra vnutrennikh del statisticheskim otdelom Tsentral'nogo statisticheskogo komiteta* (St Petersburg: Tipografiia II Otdeleniia Sobstvennoi E. I. V. kantseliarii, 1858), p. 222.

11. Ibid., p. 275.

12. In 1864, Moscow province had 1,036 enterprises with 73,480 workers, which produced goods to the value of 65.3 million roubles; the St Petersburg province had 536 enterprises with 39,355 workers, which produced goods to the value of 60.6 million roubles. The estimates are based on the data of the Ministry of Finance in *Svedeniia o fabrikakh*

i zavodakh, deistvovavshikh v 1864 godu (St Petersburg: Tip. Maikova, 1866), pp. 20, 25–6, 29–30.

13. *Statisticheskii vremennik Rossiiskoi Imperii* (St Petersburg: Tsentral'nyi statisticheskii komitet, 1866), pp. 64-71.

14. When obtaining those certificates, the entrepreneurs were guided by the new 'Regulation on the Duties to be Paid for the Right to Carry Out Trade and Crafts', adopted on 1 January 1863. According to this Regulation, the division into three guilds was replaced by the division into two guilds. Merchants of the First Guild who paid levies in the amount of 265 roubles per year were entitled to the following rights: a) to carry out wholesale and retail trade in Russian and foreign goods throughout the territory of the Empire, and therefore to keep an unlimited number of warehouses and shops (for each shop, the so-called ticket charge in the amount of 30 roubles was to be paid); b) to gain contracts; c) to keep factories and other industrial enterprises. Merchants of the Second Guild who paid levies in the amount of 25 to 65 roubles per year (depending on the size of the town where they transacted business) were entitled to the same rights as merchants of the First Guild, although in their case the place of trading was limited (to the town or *uezd* where the certificate was issued); the sum of contracts was limited to 15,000 roubles. For each shop, second-guild merchants had to additionally pay 5–20 roubles. See: *PSZ* II, vol. XVIII, No 39118.

15. *Statisticheskii vremennik Rossiiskoi Imperii (1866)*, pp. 182–3; the first time a comprehensive survey on merchantry structure was presented is in Hildermeier, *Bürgertum und Stadt in Russland*, pp. 470–504.

16. D. R. Brower, *The Russian City between Tradition and Modernity, 1850–1900*, (Berkeley, CA: University of California Press, 1990), p. 59.

17. The estimates are based on the data in Tarasov, *Statisticheskoe obozrenie*.

18. According to the 1863 official data, within the structure of Russian industry, the textile branch accounted for 28.2 per cent, the food branch – for 13.2 per cent, the metal-working branch – for 11.2 per cent, the fat and wax processing branch (candles and soap) – for 8.9 per cent, and the tanning branch – for 6.9 per cent of products. Well behind them were the writing-paper branch with 2.4 per cent, the chemical branch with 2.2 per cent, the wood-working branch with 2.1 per cent, the glass branch with 2.0 per cent, the mining branch with 1.5 per cent, and the other branches with 21.4 per cent of products. Within the food industry, the sugar branch accounted for 9.1 per cent, the milling and malting branch – for 3.3 per cent, and the butter and dairy produce branch – for 0.8 per cent of products. The estimates are based on the data in *Statisticheskii vremennik Rossiiskoi Imperii (1866)*, pp. 56–60.

19. The estimates are based on the data in Tarasov, *Statisticheskoe obozrenie*.

20. Joffe and Lindenmeyr, 'Daughter, Wives, and Partners', in West and Petrov (eds), *Merchant Moscow*, p. 103.

21. According to the law, Russian citizenship could be acquired after five years of residence in Russia. See: *PSZ* II, vol. III, No 1737.

22. The various credit regimes as element of business strategies are analysed in: J. Smail, 'The Culture of Credit in Eighteenth-Century Commerce: The English Textile Industry', *Enterprise & Society*, 4:2 (2003), p. 299–325; P. Hudson, 'Capital and Credit in the West Riding Wool Textile Industry *c*.1750–1850', in P. Hudson (ed.), *Regions and Industries. A Perspective on the Industrial Revolution in Britain* (Cambridge: Cambridge University Press, 1989), pp. 69–99.

23. *Vedro* (pail) is equal to 12.3 litres (3.25 gallons). The mentioned *sorokovushka* is equal to 0.3 litre.

24. Tarasov, *Statisticheskoe obozrenie*, p. 83; *Moskovskii Nekropol'*, vol. III (1908), p. 329; *Ukazatel' V moskovskoi vystavki russkikh manufakturnykh proizvedenii. 1865* (Moscow, 1865), p. 120; TsIAM, f.78, op. 3, d. 687, ll. 3, 7; *Statisticheskii vremennik Rossiiskoi Imperii*, II, No 6 (St Petersburg: Tsentral'nyi statisticheskii komitet, 1872), pp. 192-3; A. Chekhov, 'Fragments of Moscow Life', in A. Chekhov, *Polnoe sobranie sochinenii i pisem*, 30 vols (Moscow: Nauka, 1974-83), vol. 16 (1979), p. 105.

25. Solov'eva, *Promyshlennaia revolutsia*, pp. 66–7.

26. Y. Bakhrushin, *Vospominaniia* (Moscow: Khudozhestvennaia literatura, 1994), p. 301.

27. Ibid., p. 327.

28. TsIAM, f.16, op. 24, d. 3970, l. 3; *Statisticheskie svedeniia o fabrikakh i zavodakh exponentov, poluchivshikh nagrady na manufakturnoi vystavke 1861 g.* (St Petersburg, 1862), p. 97.

29. *Statisticheskie svedeniia o fabrikakh i zavodakh exponentov*, p. 97.

30. M. Ya. Kittary, *Obozrenie Sankt-Peterburgskoi vystavki russkoi manufakturnoi promyshlennosti 1861 goda* (St Petersburg: Tipografia Lermantova i Ko, 1861), p. 215.

31. TsIAM, f.16, op. 24, d. 3970, ll. 7–9.

32. See: Bakhrushin, *Vospominaniia*, pp. 325–6.

33. Dradedam – *drap des dames*, ladies' light woolen cloth with a stripe woven ornament.

34. TsIAM, f. 14, op. 9, d. 6675, l. 9; f. 16, op. 24, d. 3693, ll. 1, 5, 7-8, 14-18, 23, 27, 33; f. 46, op. 2, d. 654, ll. 3, 5, 13–20; *MDIMK Skazki*, VII, p. 160; Niström, *Moskovskii adreskalendar'*, vol. 4, p. 241.

35. TsIAM, f. 16, op. 24, d. 3693, l. 33.

36. Ibid.

37. Among the owners of big enterprises, the proportion of foreigners amounted to 12.1 per cent (11.1 per cent in the metal-working industry, 15.6 per cent in the textile industry, and 11.1 per cent in the tobacco industry). See N. V. Yukhneva, *Etnicheskii sostav i etnosotsial'naia struktura naseleniia Peterburga, vtoraia polovina XIX - nachalo XX v.: Statisticheskii analiz* (Leningrad: Nauka, 1984), p. 69. See also M. Busch, *Deutsche in St Petersburg, 1865–1914: Identität und Integration* (Essen: Klartext, 1995), pp. 42–3.

38. The estimates are based on the data in *Statisticheskie svedeniia o fabrikakh i zavodakh v Sankt-Peterburge za 1862 god* (St Petersburg: izd. St Peterburgskogo statisticheskogo komiteta, 1863).

39. *Spravochnaia kniga o litsakh, poluchivshikh na [1867-1898] god kupecheskie svidetelstva po 1 i 2 gil'diiam* (St Petersburg, 1867-1898, hereafter *SK St Petersburg*), (1867), p. 20, (1878), p. 339; *Vseobshchaia adresnaia kniga Sankt-Peterburga* (St Petersburg: Goppe i Kornfeld, 1867-8), p. 214; *Peterburgskii Nekropol*, 4 vols (St Petersburg: Tip. M.M. Stasiulevicha, 1912–13), vol. 2 (1912), p. 318.

40. *SK St Petersburg* (1867), p. 139; *Vseobshchaia adresnaia kniga*, p. 184.

41. Kittary, *Obozrenie*, p. 230.

42. *SK St Petersburg*, (1869), p. 235; *Vseobshchaia adresnaia kniga*, p. 286; *Peterburgskii Nekropol'*, vol. II, p. 693

43. *SK Moscow* (1869), p. 529; *Vseobshchaia adresnaia kniga*, p. 397; *Peterburgskii Nekropol'*, vol. 3 (1912), p. 548.

44. Rasteriaeva's specialization in metal items was due to the fact that her late husband had been one of the founders and the biggest shareholders of the joint-stock company 'The

Company of the St Petersburg Metal Works', although we have found no information concerning his shares having been passed on to his widow.

45. *SK St Petersburg* (1869), p. 45; *SK Moscow* (1869), p. 529; *Vseobshchaia adresnaia kniga*, p. 397; *Statisticheskie svedeniia o fabrikakh i zavodakh v Sankt-Peterburge*, pp. 10, 15, 19; *Ukazatel' V moskovskoi vystavki (1865)*, p. 158–9.

46. See: *Ves' Peterburg na 1902 g.* (St Petersburg, 1902), pp. 977, 45, 72, 250; A. V. Krasko, *Eliseevy* (St Petersburg: VIRD, 1998), p. 20; *Tabel'naia kniga nedvizhimykh imushchestv g. Sankt-Peterburga* (St Petersburg: tipo-lit. Schrödera, [1900]), Liteinaia chast', p. 25, Spasskaia chast', pp. 176, 141.

47. The 'Books of Reference' [*Spravochnye knigi*] (published in St Petersburg and Moscow from 1865 and 1867 onwards respectively; the early issues are not available) contained information on every person, including name, age, date of entering the merchantry, type of business, place of residence (sometimes, the ownership of real estate), names and age of the sons, and ethnicity (in case of foreigners).

48. By comparison with other cities, St Petersburg had a much higher proportion of foreigners among its population: they accounted for up to 20 per cent thereof. In 1869, of the 667.2 thousand of its residents, 45.6 thousand (or 6.8 per cent) were Germans, 3.1 thousand (or 0.5 per cent) were French, and 2.1 thousand (or 0.3 per cent) were English. See Yukhneva, *Etnicheskii sostav, pp.* 28-32. As regards Moscow, in 1871 its population included no less than 95 per cent Russians, while about 4 per cent were Germans, Englishmen and Poles, and 0.9 per cent were Jews. See I. N. Gavrilova, *Demograficheskaia istoriia Moskvy* (Moscow: Fast-Print, 1997), p. 277.

49. For an interesting analysis of a comparable situation in Birmingham and Sheffield, see Berg, 'Women's Property and the Industrial Revolution'.

50. Dorothea's father-in-law was the prominent Scottish engineer Charles Baird (1766–1843), who, at the age of nineteen, was invited to Russia to establish a small arms factory at Petrozavodsk. From there Baird moved to St Petersburg where he set up his own business (Baird Works). At first, Charles Baird specialized in steam-driven machinery, but later turned his attention to steamship routes from St Petersburg to Kronstadt and to iron bridge-building in St Petersburg. See: R. W. Rennison, T. Cox, *Biographical Dictionary of Civil Engineers in Great Britain and Ireland* (London 2002); *Memoir of the late Charles Baird, esq., of St Petersburg, and of his son, the late Francis Baird, esq., of St Petersburg and 4, Queens Gate, London* (London, 1867).

51. *Statisticheskie svedeniia o fabrikakh i zavodakh v Sankt-Peterburge*, p. 7; P. A. Orlov, *Ukazatel' fabrik i zavodov Evropeiskoi Rossii* (St Petersburg: Tip. Br. Panteleevykh, 1881), pp. 357, 367.

52. Nadezhda's parents had nine children, five of whom died in infancy, while two died young; only two of them survived their father – Chamberlain and State Councillor Ivan (1804–82, who moved to Paris at the age of twenty-five and rarely visited Russia), and Nadezhda (1815–97) who inherited the whole property after her father's death in 1849. In 1835, Nadezhda married Lieutenant of the Life-Guards Horse Regiment Alexander Stenbok-Fermor, a descendant of the Swedish General Count Stenbok, who died in 1852. In 1825, because of the extinction of the Fermor family, her father-in-law Johann Magnus Stenbok was permitted by the Tsar to take the family name of his mother, the only daughter of the Russian General-in-Chief Count William W. Fermor. See A. B. Lobanov-Rostovskii, *Russkaia rodoslovnaia kniga*, 2 vols (St Petersburg: izd. A. S. Suvorina, 1895), vol. 1, pp. 453–8; L. A. Chereiskii, *Pushkin i ego okruzhenie* (Leningrad: Nauka, 1988), p. 522.

53. *Voenno-statisticheskii sbornik*, pp. 290, 298, 304, 306
54. *Tabel'naia kniga*, Spasskaia chast', p. 3.
55. See N. V. Mikhailov, *Lakhta: piat' vekov istorii. 1500-2000* (Moscow: Ves' mir, 2001), p. 47.
56. *Moskovskii Nekropol'*, vol. I, p. 161; *SK Moscow* (1869), p. 23; *SK Moscow* (1872), p. 14; TsIAM, f. 14, op. 9, d. 6675, l. 97.
57. For a well-founded interpretation of the issue, see Barker, *The Business of Women, pp. 134-66* (Chapter 'Family, Property and Power').
58. Hereinafter, the estimates are based on the data in *SK Moscow* (1869); *Statisticheskii vremennik Rossiiskoi Imperii* (1872); *Moskovskii Nekropol'*.
59. In 1868, Moscow had 516 plants (equipped with 183 steam engines producing 2,404 horsepower), which manufactured goods to the value of 46.7 million roubles, employed 817 foremen (802 men and 15 women) and 59,291 workers (47,012 men and 12,279 women). See *Statisticheskii vremennik Rossiiskoi Imperii* (1872), pp. 392-3.
60. TsIAM, f. 16, op. 24, d. 488, ll. 86-91.
61. *PSZ* II, vol. XXVI, No 25090.
62. The estimates are based on the data in *Pamiatnaia knizhka Sankt-Peterburgskoi gubernii na 1864 god* (St Petersburg: izd. St.-Peterburgskogo statisticheskogo komiteta, 1864), pp. 292-9.
63. TsIAM, f. 3, op. 2, d. 261, l. 17.
64. *MDIMK Skazki*, IX, p. 156.
65. *SK Moscow* (1869), p. 438.
66. *SK St Petersburg* (1869), pp. 143, 159, 180.
67. *Adres-calendar'. Obshchaia rospis' nachal'stvuiushchikh i prochikh dolzhnostnykh lits po vsem upravleniiam v Rossiiskoi imperii na 1870 g.*, 2 vols (St Petersburg: Dep-t gerol'dii pravit. Senata, 1870), vol.1, p. 536; *Peterburgskii Nekropol'*, vol. 2, pp. 413–14; *Prilozhe-niia k trudam Redaktsionnykh komissii*, vol.3. *St Petersburg guberniia*, pp. 2–3.
68. *SK Moscow* (1869), pp. 284, 545, 557.

4 Female Entrepreneurship in the 1870s: Family Levers in Business Regulation

1. *PSZ* II, XLVI, No 49137.
2. The book was widely discussed in Russia. See: Stites, *The Women's Liberation Movement in Russia*, pp. 73–5.
3. These estimates are based on the data in *SK Moscow* (1879), *SK St. Petersburg* (1879).
4. M. Tugan-Baranovskii, *Russkaia fabrika v proshlom i nastoiashchem. Istoriko-ekonom-icheskoe issledovanie* (St Petersburg: Izdatel'stvo O.N. Popovoi, 1900), p. 328.
5. P. Gatrell, *The Tsarist Economy, 1850–1917* (London: B.T. Batsford Ltd, 1986), p. 150.
6. V. P. Bezobrazov, *Narodnoe khoziaistvo Rossii*, 3 vols (St Petersburg: Dep-t torgovli i manufaktur), vol.1 (1882), p. 287.
7. The estimates are based on the data in Yu. E. Yanson, *Sravnitel'naia statistika Rossii i zapadnoevropeiskikh gosudarstv* (St Petersburg: Tip. M. Stasiulevicha, 1878), vol. 1, p. 20; V. de Livron, *Statisticheskoe obozrenie Rossiiskoi Imperii* (St Petersburg: Tip. T-va 'Obshchestvennaia pol'za': 1874), Tables, pp. 25-6. No data for the end of the decade are available. In western European countries, the size of the population was as follows:

Germany – 42.8 million (1875), France – 36.1 million (1872), the United Kingdom – 32 million (1871). See: Yanson, p. 20.

8.   Yanson, *Sravnitel'naia statistika*, p. 109; de Livron, *Statisticheskoe obozrenie*, Tables, p. 37; Orlov, *Ukazatel' fabrik i zavodov* (1881), p. 695. Included are the enterprises paying the excise (the distilling, beet-sugar, tobacco and match industries).

9.   Tugan-Baranovskii, *Russkaia fabrika*, p. 317. Tugan-Baranovskii noted the coincidence between the fluctuations in the numbers of Russian workers and the fluctuations in English imports (first of all, raw cotton, yarn, steam engines and power looms for the textile industry) into Russia: 'The parallelism of fluctuations in English exports and in the numbers of factory workers in Russia is astonishing. One could think that in this case we are dealing with the curves related to one and the same country.' He arrived at the conclusion that 'reflected in the development of out industry ... is the periodicity typical of capitalist production all over the world', and disagreed with those economists who explained the dynamics of Russian industrial production by the dependence on harvests inside Russia (ibid., pp. 321–4)

10. Orlov, *Ukazatel' fabrik i zavodov* (1881), p. 695. For the ratio between the British pound and the rouble as it was in the 1870s (£1 = 10 roubles), see: S. Chapman, *Merchant Enterprise in Britain from the Industrial Revolution to World War I* (Cambridge: Cambridge University Press: 1992), p. 316.

11. The estimates are based on the data in D. A. Timiriazev, *Razvitie glavneishikh otraslei fabrichno-zavodskoi promyshlennosti v Rossii s 1850 po 1879 god* (St Petersburg: Tip. Kirshbauma, 1881), pp. 5–13.

12. The estimates are based on the data in Orlov, *Ukazatel' fabrik i zavodov* (1881). No complete data with regard to the food industry are available.

13. Solov'eva, *Promyshlennaia revoliutsia*, p. 157.

14. N. Labzin, *Istoriko-statisticheskii obzor promyshlennosti Rossii. Gruppa IX. Mashiny, apparaty i ekipazhi* (St Petersburg: Tip. A. S. Suvorina, 1882), pp. 95, 98.

15. S. Thompstone, Russkoe Tekhnicheskoe obshchestvo i import britanskogo tekstil'nogo oborudovaniia, in S. Thompstone (ed.), *Rossiiskaia tekstil'naia promyshlennost'; tekhnologicheskii transfer, syr'e, finansy* (St Petersburg: Olearius Press, 2006), p. 15.

16. The estimates are based on the data in *Materialy dlia statistiki parovykh dvigatelei v Rossiiskoi imperii* (St Petersburg: Tsentral'nyi statisticheskii komitet, 1866), pp. 163, 166-7.

17. A. Radzig, *Khlopchatobumazhnaia promyshlennost' Rossii* (St Petersburg: Tip. Severnogo telegrafnogo agentstva, 1891), p. 36–7. In France (1873), there were 50 spindles and 0.7 looms per worker, in Germany (1881) – 78.8 spindles (Ibid., pp. 38–9). There is no precise information for other countries.

18. The estimates are based on the data in Orlov, *Ukazatel' fabrik i zavodov* (1881); sometimes they do not agree with the figures contained in other sources, for example, in the work by Timiriazev. The eventual figures concerning the number of factories, the volume of production and the number of workers in the Russian Empire (less Poland and Finland) are taken from '*Ukazatel'*' (p. 695).

19. In the territory of the Urals Mining District.

20. This case is a good illustration of Marrese's point that 'women's legal status as owner of property in their own right all conspired to guarantee that noblewomen acted as administrators of their own or their family estates'. See Marrese, *A Woman's Kingdom*, p. 175.

21. *SK St. Petersburg* (1889), p. 742.

22. A.M. Anfimov, *Krupnoe pomeshchich'e khoziaistvo Evropeiskoi Rossii, konets XIX-nachalo XX veka* (Moscow: Nauka, 1969), pp. 269–70; E. Annenkova and Y. Golikov, *Printsy Ol'denburgskie v Peterburge* (St Petersburg: Rostok, 2004), pp. 317, 338–9, 345–9.

23. Svod Zakonov, vol. X, part 2, art. 2268–76.

24. She was a daughter of Elizaveta Rakhmanova, mentioned in Chapter 2, and the wife of Major-General Anton Apraksin.

25. TsIAM, f. 16, op. 25, d.437, ll. 1-6; f. 142, op. 5, d.655, ll. 2. 101, 131; *SK Moscow* (1869), p. 225; *SK Moscow* (1875), p. 302; N. Matissen, *Atlas manufacturnoi promyshlennosti Moskovskoi gubernii* (Moscow: Tip. T.Ris, 1872), p. 146; Orlov, *Ukazatel' fabrik i zavodov* (1881), p. 557.

26. The Cossack woman Zinaida Avdeeva owned a flour mill in Orenburg Province, the Cossack woman Anna Shakina – a brick works in Don Oblast', and the wife of a priest, Anna Deriabina – a flour mill in Perm' Province. For information on Cossack women, see S. O'Rourke, 'Women in a Warrior Society: Don Cossack women, 1860–1914', in R. Marsh (ed.), *Women in Russia and Ukraine* (Cambridge: Cambridge University Press, 1996), pp. 45–54.

27. Maria Romanovna, Maria Ksaver'evna, Anna, Aleksandra, Wanda.

28. 'The Statute Concerning the Organization of the Jews', of 9 December 1804, specified the limits of the Pale of Settlement, which was to include the following 15 provinces: Bessarabia, Vil'no, Vitebsk, Volhynia, Grodno, Ekaterinoslav, Kovno, Minsk, Mogilev, Podolia, Poltava, Tauria, Kherson and Chernigov. The Jews of Kiev Province had a special status: they were allowed to reside in the whole territory of the province, excepting Kiev. See *PSZ* II, vol. XXXIV, No 34247. In accordance with the Law of 16 March 1859, the right of residence and trade outside the Pale were granted only to merchants of the First Guild. See *PSZ* II, vol. XXXIV, No 34248. See also: B. Nathans, *Beyond the Pale: The Jewish Encounter with Late Imperial Russia* (Berkeley, CA and London: University of California Press, 2004), pp. 48, 215.

29. On the establishment of civil equality for all religious faiths in the 1867 Constitution and subsequent big proportion of Jewish businesswomen in Vienna during 1870s–90s see: I. Bandhauer-Schöffmann, 'Businesswomen in Austria', in Beachy, Craig and Owens (eds), *Women, Business and Finance*, pp. 119–20.

30. According to our estimates, in 1865–9 the Committee of Ministers approved the charters of thirty-two industrial partnerships, in 1870–4 – of 104 partnerships, and in 1875–89 – of 89 partnerships (see *PSZ* II). Women were among the founders of approximately 25 per cent of the partnerships.

31. Owen, *The Corporation under Russian law, 1800–1917*, p. 51. Owen writes that this dualistic system consisted in the following: 'The typical joint-stock company (*aktsioner-naia kompaniia*...), newly formed for a large undertaking like a railroad, steamship line or bank, raised its basic capital in the sale of a large number of shares, called *aktsii*, commonly priced at 100, 200, or 250 rubles. In contrast, a moderately sized share partnership (*tovarishchestvo na paiakh*), typically established to provide limited liability for an existing enterprise such as a cotton-textile factory, raised less capital ... and did so by selling to a small circle of the partners' relatives and friends a relatively small number of shares (*pai*), often priced at between 500 and 25,000 rubles each. ... *Pai* almost always displayed the name of owner'.

32. In the 1870s, during an intensive industrial transformation, the similar process of women entering into joint-stock companies took place in Sweden. See T. Petersson, 'The Silent Partners; Women, Capital and the Development of the Financial System in Nineteenth-

century Sweden', in Beachy, Craig and Owens (eds), *Women, Business and Finance*, pp. 46–7.

33. *PSZ* II, vol. L, No 54405.

34. They were sons of Moscow *meshchanin* Vasilii Iakovlev. After the death of their mother, seven-year-old Petr and five-year-old Il'ia were adopted by their godfather, the childless merchant Semen Ivanov, and his wife. Prior to his inscribing in the merchantry and setting up a cloth mill of his own, Semen worked as a foreman at Semen Babkin's cloth mill. In accordance with the testimony of Semen Ivanov, who died in 1810, Petr and Il'ia inherited his Moscow mill. In 1811, they adopted the family name Babkin in honour of the former employer of their godfather. In order to buy the Kupavna mill, the brothers sold their Moscow enterprise. The success of the Babkins' business was attested to by their purchasing in the centre of Moscow, in the 1830s, of three detached houses valuated at 88,570 silver roubles. See *MDIMK Skazki*, IV, pp. 389, 406; V, p. 195; VI, p. 127; VII, p. 160; Niström, *Moskovskii adres-kalendar'*, vol. 4, p. 15.

35. Apart from 'the property representing articles of home life..., namely Holy icons, clothes, furniture, diamonds, silver and other precious things, horses, carriages, tableware, etc.' (TsIAM, f. 50, op. 5, d. 12336, l. 14)

36. TsIAM, f. 50, op. 5, d. 12336, ll. 1-6.

37. *SK Moscow* (1875), p. 35; Tarasov, *Statisticheskoe obozrenie,* p. 171; Matissen, *Atlas*, pp. 8–9; *Statisticheskii vremennik Rossiiskoi Imperii* (1872), p. 212; Orlov, *Ukazatel' fabrik i zavodov* (1881), p. 24; Orlov, *Ukazatel' fabrik i zavodov* (1887), p. 16.

38. K. Skal'kovskii, *Vserossiiskaia manufakturnaia vystavka v promyshlennom otnoshenii* (St Petersburg: Tip. Imp. Akademii Nauk, 1870), p. 50.

39. Thus, in the files of the Moscow Commercial Court, we have found the 1872-4 documents concerning the bankruptcy of the following female merchants: the proprietress of a mechanical plant Agnia Vetchinkina (TsIAM, f. 78, op. 19, d. 1971), the trader in silk Liubov' Nemirovskaia (op.19, d.2681), the trader in mirrors Maria Kalashnikova (op. 4, d. 2449–50), etc.

40. *PSZ* II, vol. L, No 54405, art. 2.

41. TsIAM, f. 117, op. 9, d. 290, ll. 1–5.

42. Ibid., f. 16, op. 25, d. 983, ll. 2–3; f. 715, op. 1, d. 26, l. 11.

43. Y. Petrov, *Kommercheskie banki Moskvy. Konets XIX v.– 1914* (Moscow: Rosspen, 1998), p. 37; N. Varentsov, *Slyshannoe. Vidennoe. Peredumannoe. Perezhitoe. [Memoirs]* (Moscow: Novoe literaturnoe obozrenie, 1999), pp. 326-7.

44. TsIAM, f. 715, op. 1, d. 178, l. 10, 24.

45. S. King and G. Timmins, *Making Sense of the Industrial Revolution: English Economy and Society, 1700–1850* (Manchester: Manchester University Press, 2001), pp. 102–3.

46. Ibid., f. 131, op. 58, d. 1539, ll. 3, 22-3; Orlov, *Ukazatel' fabrik i zavodov* (1881), p. 136; Orlov, *Ukazatel' fabrik i zavodov* (1887), p. 99.

47. A. L. Erickson, 'The marital economy in comparative perspective' in M. Ågren, A. L. Erickson (eds), *The Marital Economy in Scandinavia and Britain 1400-1900* (Aldershot: Ashgate, 2005), p. 3.

48. *MDIMK Prigovory,* IX (1909), p. 61; *MDIMK Skazki*, IX, p. 146; *SK Moscow* (1869), p. 659; *SK Moscow* (1875), p. 283; *SK Moscow* (1895), p. 246; *Vsia Moskva* (1899), pp. 1925, 1028, 1431.

49. *MDIMK Prigovory,* IX, p. 165; *SK Moscow* (1869), p. 465; *SK Moscow* (1875), p. 202.

50. *MDIMK Prigovory,* IX, p. 205; *SK Moscow* (1869), p. 385; *SK Moscow* (1875), p. 217, *SK Moscow* (1905), p. 101.

51. On *pood* see note 40, Chapter 1.
52. *MDIMK Prigovory*, IX, p. 43; *SK Moscow* (1869), p. 618; *SK Moscow* (1875), p. 264; *SK Moscow* (1884), p. 250; *SK Moscow* (1895), pp. 32, 230; *SK Moscow* (1905), p. 60; *SK Moscow* (1910), p. 45; *SK Moscow* (1916), p. 159; AKM-88,, 757; *Vsia Moskva* (1899), p. 1086; Orlov, *Ukazatel' fabrik i zavodov* (1881), p. 188; Orlov, *Ukazatel' fabrik i zavodov* (1887), p. 159.

5 Female Entrepreneurship in the 1880s: the Dictate of Money Inside the Family Circle

1. *SZ* (1857), vol. X, part 1, art. 107.
2. The estimates are based on the data in *SK Moscow* (1889), *SK St. Petersburg* (1889).
3. Both of them were born in the Russian Empire in the early twentieth century.
4. See: S. Kuznets, *Modern Economic Growth* (New Haven, CT: Yale University Press, 1966); A. Gershenkron, *Economic Backwardness in Historical Perspective* (Cambridge, MA: Harvard University Press, 1962), essay 1.
5. P. Gregory, *Russian National Income 1885–1913* (London: Cambridge University Press, 1982), p. 167. Using the data from Kuznets, *Modern Economic Growth*, as the base, Gregory analyzed the structural change at the beginning of modern economic growth and over the next thirty years, by three sectors (agriculture, industry, services) for thirteen countries, including Russia. In all those countries the change consisted in an increase of the percentage share of the industrial sector and in a decrease of the percentage share of the agrarian sector in national product (in the services sector, no common trend was detected). The earliest starting point of modern economic growth was in the United Kingdom (1786), the latest being in Italy (1895). Russia's starting point was the year 1883 (see Gregory, *Russian National Income*, p.166, Table 7.3).
6. Ibid., p. 167.
7. W. O. Henderson, *The Industrial Revolution on the Continent: Germany, France, Russia, 1800–1914* (London: Frank Cass & Co., 1967), pp. 202–5, 211–21; L. E. Shepelev, *Tsarism i burzhuaziia vo vtoroi polovine XIX veka* (Leningrad: Nauka, 1981), pp. 134–90; Solov'eva, *Promyshlennaia revoliutsia*, pp. 208–48.
8. V. Bovykin, 'Ekonomicheskaia politika tsarskogo pravitel'stva i industrial'noe razvitie Rossii, 1816–1900', *Ekonomicheskaia Istoriia. Ezhegodnik 2002* (Moscow: Rosspen, 2003), p. 24.
9. The data have been collected from Tugan-Baranovskii, *Russkaia fabrika*, p. 313.
10. D. Mendeleev, 'Vvedenie. Obzor fabrichno-zavodskoi promyshlennosti i torgovli Rossii', in *Fabrichno-zavodskaia promyshlennost' i torgovlia Rossii* (St Petersburg: Tip. V. Balasheva i Co i V. Demakova, 1893), pp. 8, 44–5.
11. See, for example, Bovykin, 'Ekonomicheskaia politika' and J. P. McKay, *Pioneers for Profit. Foreign Entrepreneurship and Russian Industrialization 1885–1913* (Chicago, IL: University of Chicago Press, 1970). Arcadius Kahan, Professor of Economic History at the University of Chicago, characterizes the economic situation as follows: 'The process of accepting the goal of industrial development as a component of policy decision-making on the part of the Russian government is not tantamount to policy-making that is a priori conducive to industrial growth. Thus, one of the two major controversies among economic historian studying the modern period of Russian development concerns the role of the government in the Russian economy, while the other (not unrelated

to the first) concerns the role of foreign versus domestic capital invested in the Russian economy during this period'. See A. Kahan, *Russian Economic History: the Nineteenth Century*, ed. R. Weiss (Chicago, IL and London: University of Chicago Press, 1989), p. 67.

12. R. Munting, 'Industrial Revolution in Russia', in M. Teich and R. Porter (eds) *The Industrial Revolution in National Context: Europe and the USA* (Cambridge: Cambridge University Press, 1996), p. 336.

13. Cited in A. P. Pogrebinskii, 'Finansovaia politika tsarizma v 70-80-kh godakh XIX v.', *Istoricheskii arkhiv*, 2 (1960), pp. 135–6. For Bunge's role in political and economic life of the 1880s, see V. Stepanov, *N. Kh. Bunge: Sud'ba reformatora* (Moscow: Rosspen, 1998), pp. 110–227.

14. *PSZ* III, vol. I, No 49.

15. For labour legislation of the 1880s, see Tugan-Baranovskii, *Russkaia fabrika*, pp. 385–430; B. Anan'ich, 'Novyi kurs. 'Narodnoe samoderzhavie' Aleksandra III i Nikolaia II', in B. Anan'ich (ed.), *Vlast' i reformy. Ot samoderzhavnoi k sovetskoi Rossii* (St Petersburg: Dmitry Bulanin, 1996), pp. 383–4.

16. The estimates are based on the data in Orlov, *Ukazatel' fabrik i zavodov* (1887); sometimes they do not agree with the figures contained in other sources. The eventual figures concerning the number of factories, the volume of production and the number of workers in the Russian Empire (less Poland, Finland and the Tauria Province which had not submitted the data) are taken from '*Ukazatel*' (p. 755).

17. A. Korelin explained the entrepreneurial activities of nobles by their desire to compensate themselves for the decline in receipts from land after the emancipation of the serfs. See A. P. Korelin, *Dvorianstvo v poreformennoi Rossii 1861–1900* (Moscow: Nauka, 1979), pp. 106–22.

18. *MDIMK Skazki*, VIII, p. 136; IX, p. 119; *SK Moscow* (1872), p. 157; TsIAM, f. 3, op. 1, d. 958, l. 1; f. 1629, op. 2, d. 116, ll. 56–7, 134–5.

19. Orlov, *Ukazatel' fabrik i zavodov* (1881), p. 188; N. Tairov, *Akchuriny* (Kazan': Tatarskoe knizhnoe izd-vo, 2002), p. 26.

20. The Karaims are a Turkic ethnic group converted to Judaism, originating from the Crimea.

21. On Alekseev's policy in Moscow merchant and municipal life see B. A. Ruble, *Second Metropolis. Pragmatic Pluralism in Gilded Age Chicago, Silver Age Moscow, and Meiji Osaka* (Cambridge: Woodrow Wilson Center press & Cambridge University press, 2001), pp. 333–49.

22. TsIAM, f. 16, op. 24, d. 4573, l. 4,

23. Ibid., l. 6.

24. Ibid., ll. 1–11; d.1480, l. 5.

25. Matissen, *Atlas*, pp. 11, 110.

26. *SK Moscow* (1879), p. 248; *SK Moscow* (1895), p. 219; Orlov, *Ukazatel' fabrik i zavodov* (1887), p. 342; TsIAM, f. 3, op. 1, d. 958, l. 1; f. 1629, op. 2, d. 116, ll. 56–7, 134–5.

27. TsIAM, f. 131, op. 59, d. 3231, ll. 1, 17–19.

28. The latest historiography reflects a growing interest in biographies of female magnates. Robert Beachy has examined the model of effective management on the example of a female representative of the family of Germany's largest locomotive manufacturer – widow Sophie Henschel. See: R. Beachy, 'Profit and Propriety: Sophie Henschel and Gender Management in the German Locomotive Industry', in Beachy, Craig, Owens (eds), *Women, Business, and Finance*, pp. 67–80. Life stories of two German female entre-

preneurs from Krupp family is presented in S. van de Kerkhof, 'How Women Became Principals – Business Networks and Regional Variations in Rhineland-Westfalia and Upper-Silesia, in A. Owens, M. Schulte-Beerbühl (eds), *Women and Business Networks in the Early Industrialization* (Oxford: Oxford University Press, 2009, forthcoming).

29. Y. A. Petrov, *Moskovskaia burzhuaziia v nachale XX v.*, pp. 380–1.
30. *MDIMK Skazki*, V, pp. 256–7.
31. Samoilov, *Atlas promyshlennosti*, pp. 11, 28, 114.
32. See *Ocherk deiatel'nosti Moskovskogo kupecheskogo obshchestva vzaimnogo kredita za dvadtsatipiatiletie (1869–1894)* (Moscow, 1895).
33. See *Morozovy. Dinastiia fabrikantov i mezenatov. Opyt rodosloviia* (Bogorodsk: Bogorodskii pechatnik, 1995), pp. 6-7, 12-15.
34. TsIAM, f. 357, op. 1, d. 11, l. 3.
35. *PSZ* II, vol. XLVIII, No 52490.
36. M. Lebedev, 'K istoriko-economicheskoi kharakteristike byvshei Nikol'skoi manufaktury', in *Istoriko-kraevedcheskii sbornik*, 2 (1959), p. 15.
37. Potkina, *Na Olimpe*, p. 117.
38. Ibid., p. 129.
39. TsIAM, f. 357, op. 1, d. 31, ll. 1–3.
40. Ibid., d. 47, l. 9.
41. Ibid., ll. 9-13.
42. See Y. A. Petrov, 'Lichnye sostoianiia Morozovykh-'Timofeevichei', in *Trudy Pervykh Morozovskikh chtenii* (Bogorodsk: Bogorodskii pechatnik, 1995), p. 35.
43. P. A. Buryshkin, *Moskva kupecheskaia* (Moscow: Vysshaia shkola, 1991), p. 126.
44. K. A. Krivoshein, *Aleksandr Vasil'evich Krivoshein: sud'ba rossiiskogo reformatora* (Moscow: Moskovskii rabochii, 1993), p. 43.
45. *Orekhovo-Zuevskii kalendar' i zapisnaia knizhka na 1903 g.* (Orekhovo, 1903), pp. 29-32, 39.
46. P.A. Orlov and S.G. Budagov, *Ukazatel' fabrik i zavodov Evropeiskoi Rossii* (St Petersburg: Tip. V. Kirshbauma, 1894), p. 41.
47. See Potkina, *Na Olimpe*, p. 129.
48. Ibid., p.138.
49. Ibid., pp. 71–2.
50. Ibid., p. 65.
51. *Otchiot dusheprikazchikov po dukhovnomu zaveshchaniiu Marii Fedorovny Morozovoi* (Moscow, 1913) p. 81.
52. The issue of women's investment in government securities is analysed in Green and Owens, 'Gentlewomanly capitalism', pp. 510–36. The authors come to the important conclusion that 'the relationship between gender ideology and economic activity was more complex than this in the sense that public and private spheres were interdepended rather than separated' (p. 531).
53. *Otchiot dusheprikazchikov*, pp. 1–5.
54. V. F. Dzunkovskii, *Vospominaniia*, 2 vols (Moscow: izd. Sabashnikovykh, 1997), vol. 1, p. 588.
55. TsIAM, f. 357, op. 1, d. 167, l. 15-103.
56. Cited in Ruckman, *The Moscow Business Elite*, pp. 86–7.
57. TsIAM, f. 3, op. 1, d. 1550, ll. 2-3.
58. Ibid., f. 78, op. 18, d. 1341, ll. 3, 5; d.1343, l. 331.
59. Ibid., d. 1341, l. 174.

60. As it was extremely difficult for spouses to obtain official divorce (see: Wagner, *Marriage, Property, and Law*, pp. 70–1, 95–6), they sometimes resorted to its palliative in the form of a separate-residence permit. In 1882 alone, the office of the Moscow Governor General permitted 221 women to reside separately from their husbands. Estimated from the data in TsIAM, f. 16, op. 72.

61. TsIAM, f. 3, op. 1, d. l. 9.

62. She submitted it to His Imperial Majesty's Chancery for the Reception of Petitions Addressed in His Most Exalted Name.

63. Nadezhda Shchekina-Khludova grew up in the period of the Great Reform, the time of liberalization of social life, when, for the first time in Russian history, girls were permitted to attend St Petersburg University as occasional students. See B. Pietrow-Ennker, *Russlands «neue Menschen»: Die Entwicklung der Frauenbewegung*, pp. 74–5.

64. Varentsov, *Slyshannoe*, p. 202; M. Morozova, 'Moi vospominaniia', in *Moskovskii al'bom* (Moscow: Nashe nasledie, 1997), p.199. Varentsov notes that some representatives of the Khludov family became prototypes of the characters in a number of works of literature : for example, in A. Ostrovskii's play *'The Hot Heart'* (where Khludov figures as Khlynov), N. Leskov's *'Hellriser'* and N. Karazin's *'In the Distant Borderlands'*.

65. *Kupecheskie dnevniki i memuary kontsa XVIII-pervoi poloviny XIX veka* (Moscow: Rosspen, 2007), p. 48.

66. TsIAM, f. 78, op. 18, d. 1343, l. 202.

67. *SZ*, (1899), vol. IX, art. 541.

68. On bankruptcy in international discourse see P. Di Martino, Approaching Disaster: A Comparison between Personal Bankruptcy Legislation in Italy and England (*c.* 1880–1939), *Business History,* 47:1. (January 2005), pp. 23–43; P.-C. Hautcoeur and N. Levratto, 'Bankruptcy law and practice in 19th century France', *PSE (Paris School of Economics) Working Papers*, 2007–29.

69. See note 10 to Chapter 4.

70. TsIAM, f. 78, op. 8, d. 140, l. 49.

71. Ibid., l. 51.

72. Ibid., l. 71.

73. No archival data on the outcome of the Serikov case have been found.

74. TsIAM, f. 78, op. 8, d. 140, l. 73.

75. Bocharov was the owner of a big beet-sugar plant in Kharkov Province (in 1884, the value of its output amounted to 540,000 roubles).

76. In 1884, the factory which had passed from Panina to Bocharov produced goods to the value of 60,000 roubles. See *Ukazatel' fabrik i zavodov* (1884), p. 49; on Bocharov, p. 607.

77. TsIAM, f. 78, op. 9, d. 62, l. 128.

78. Ibid., l. 130.

6 Female Entrepreneurship in the 1890s: a Breakthrough Towards Independence

1. *Obshchii svod po Imperii rezul'tatov razrabotki dannykh Pervoi vseobshchei perepisi naseleniia Rossiiskoi Imperii, proizvedennoi 28 ianvaria 1897 g.*, 2 vols, (St Petersburg, 1905), vol. 2, p. 288.

2. The estimates are based on the data in *SK Moscow* (1895), *SK St. Petersburg* (1895).

3. V. Bovykin, *Formirovanie finansovofgo kapitala v Rossii, konets XIX v.-1908 g.* (Moscow: Nauka, 1987), p. 72.

4. Our calculations are based on data from V. Bovykin, 'Ekonomicheskaia politika', p.27.

5. L. B. Kafengauz, *Evolutsia promyshlennogo proizvodstva Rossii (posledniaia tret' XIX v. - 30-e gg. XX v.)* (Moscow: Epifania, 1994), p. 60.

6. See Solov'eva, *Promyshlennaia revoliutsia*, p. 243.

7. *Perechen' fabrik i zavodov* (St Petersburg: Tip. I. A. Efrona, 1897), pp. 1-1047; *Materialy dlia torgovo-promyshlennoi statistiki. Svod dannykh o fabrichno-zavodskoi promyshlennosti v Rossii za 1897 g.* (St Petersburg: Tip. V. Kirshbauma, 1900), pp. i–xxiii. The 1897 source has been selected because *Spisok fabrik i zavodov* (St Petersburg, 1903) containing industrial statistics for 1900 cannot provide complete data. Regretfully, the 1897 *Perechen's* structure does not correspond to that of the Guides to Factories and Plants (with statistical data for the years 1879 and 1884), which makes it impossible, in particular, to fully reconstruct the estate and ethnic parameters of the female entrepreneur group.

8. The difference in the numbers of enterprises and their owners can be explained by the fact that some of the owners had several enterprises; and, vice versa, one enterprise could be owned by several female representatives of one family (see examples in the text).

9. The decline both in the overall number of enterprises and in the number of those owned by women is noted only in the fat-melting industry, which probably was associated with the gradual switchover from candles to electric light by enterprises, public premises and households.

10. The indices for these firms are included in our calculations presented in Table 6.1.

11. Ch. M. Ioksimovich, *Manufakturnaia promyshlennost' v proshlom i nastoiashchem* (Moscow: Knizhnyi magazin manufakturnoi prom-sti, 1917), p. 35–8; Ulianova, *Blagotvoritel'nost'*, pp. 406–8.

12. In the last third of the nineteenth century, the Griaznovs, similarly to other factory owners of the Central Region of European Russia, were permanently residing in Moscow, although their enterprises were situated 300km from the capital. In memory of her late husband, Marina Griaznova, in 1894, donated to the Moscow Merchant Society a house with a plot of land (to the value of 20,000 roubles) and a capital of 60,000 roubles for the establishment of a charitable institution for the elderly. See Ulianova, *Blagotvoritel'nost'*, p. 332.

13. Ioksimovich, *Manufakturnaia promyshlennost'*, pp. 260–1.

14. G. von Schulze-Gävernitz, *Krupnoe proizvodstvo v Rossii (Moskovsko-Vladimirskaia khlopchatobumazhnaia promyshlennost')* (Moscow: Izd. Magazin Knizhnoe delo, 1899), p. 49.

15. Ibid., p.14.

16. Ibid., p.11.

17. A. Smirnov, *Pavlovo i Vorsma, izvestnye stal'no-slesarnym proizvodstvom sela Nizhegorodskoi gubernii* (Moscow: Tip. I. Chuksina, 1864), pp. 12–13. The Zav'ialovs' plant still exists and manufactures surgical instruments.

18. F. Dostoevsky, *'Podrostok'* ('Teenager'), in F. Dostoevsky, *Sobranie sochinenii*, 15 vols (Leningrad: Nauka, 1988–96), vol. 8 (1990), pp. 337–8.

19. Orlov, *Ukazatel' fabrik i zavodov* (1881), p. 378; *Perechen'* (1897), pp. 320, 358.

20. *SK Moscow* (1879), p. 131.

21. *SK Moscow* (1895), *SK St Petersburg* (1895). As a source we selected the reference books for the year 1895, which contain data comparable with the data presented in the previ-

ous chapters. After the adoption of the Law on Business Taxation (1898) the principle of gaining access to entrepreneurial activity was changed.

22. For the hereditary honorary citizens, see Chapter 2, p. 53.
23. *Obshchii svod ... perepisi naseleniia*, vol. 1, p. 64.
24. *SK St Petersburg* (1895); for Zvezdina, see Chapter 3.
25. *SK Moscow* (1895), p. 212.
26. See Chapter 4, note 8.
27. See Chapter 3, pp. 97–8.
28. *Perechen'* (1897), p. 546.
29. See Chapter 5, p. 144.
30. See Chapter 3, pp. 97–8.
31. His elder brother Peter I was King of Serbia (1903–18), King of Serbs, Croats, and Slovenes (1918–21).
32. There were rumors at the court that Nadezhda was an illegitimate daughter of Grand Duke Mikhail (brother of Emperor Nicolas I) and one of the maids of honour.
33. *Perechen'* (1897), pp. 636–9, 910–13.
34. S. Y. Witte, *Vospominaniia*, 3 vols (Moscow: Izdatel'stvo sotsial'no-ekonomicheskoi literatury, 1960), vol. 1 p. 181.
35. As was already noted in Chapter 3, p. 98, the involvement of female entrepreneurs in maritime trade was one of the specific features of St Petersburg as a sea port.
36. A port on the Black Sea.
37. See Chapter 4, p. 120.
38. *Moskovskii Nekropol'*, vol. III (1908), p. 329; Orlov and Budagov, *Ukazatel' fabrik i zavodov* (1894), p. 26; *SK Moscow* (1895), p. 47.
39. Orlov and Budagov, *Ukazatel' fabrik i zavodov* (1894), p. 558.
40. See: G. Ulianova et al., *Two Centuries of Confectionery Industry in Russia* (Moscow: Gosinkor, 2003), pp. 20–6.
41. According to the 1897 Census, 123,561 independent owners of service industry businesses were male, and 30,909 (or 20 per cent) were female. Of this latter group, 8,001 women owned hotels and furnished rooms for rent; and 6,422 women owned restaurants, cafes and canteens. See *Obshchii svod ... perepisi naseleniia*, vol. 2, p. 292.
42. Rieber, *Merchants and Entrepreneurs in Imperial Russia*, p. 82.
43. *SK St Petersburg* (1895), pp. 150, 324, 360.
44. *SK Moscow* (1895), pp. 59, 192–3, 210, 233.
45. *Obshchii svod ... perepisi naseleniia*, vol. 1, *Prilozhenie*, pp. 48, 52–6.
46. A. E. Ivanov, *Vysshaia shkola Rossii v kontse XIX – nachale XX veka* (Moscow: Institut rossiiskoi istorii, 1991), p. 102–3.
47. The intensification of the business activity of single women was a general trend both in Russian and western European big cities. A. Owens and D. Green note that 'in comparison with the other major cities, London was distinctive by virtue of its relatively large component of single women, particularly spinsters' (according to the 1851 Census, 32.3 per cent women were widows, 14.4 per cent – spinsters). See Green, Owens, *Gentlewomanly Capitalism*, p. 513. Béatrice Craig presents detailed statistics on female merchants, traders and manufacturers in Lille, France, according to which the share of single women engaged in business was steadily growing from 14.7–23.8 per cent in the first half of the nineteenth century to 19.7–26.8 per cent in the second (simultaneously, the share of widows dropped from 60.3–76.5 per cent to 42.3–52.5 per cent, and that of married women increased from 4.8–7.9 per cent to 13.8-29.5 per cent). See B. Craig, 'Where

have All the Businesswomen Gone? Images and Reality in the Life of Nineteenth-century Middle-class Women in Northern France', in Beachy, Craig, Owens (eds), *Women, Business, and Finance*, p. 58.

48. *SZ* (1833), vol. X, part 1, art. 80–1.
49. Vinaver M.M. Grazhdanskaia khronika, *Vestnik grazhdanskogo prava*, 2 (1913), p. 90.
50. TsIAM, f. 142, op. 5, d. 42, ll. 1, 6–8.
51. Varentsov, *Slyshannoe*, p. 535.
52. Ibid., p. 536.
53. I. M. Tiutriumov, *Zakony grazhdanskie (Svod zakonov, t. X, ch. 1, izd. 1900 g.) s raz"iasneniami Pravitel'stvuiushchego Senata i s kommentariiami russkikh iuristov, izvlechennymi iz nauchnykh trudov po grazhdanskomu pravu* (St Petersburg: tip. 'Trud', 1905), p. 7.
54. TsIAM, f. 16, op. 89, d. 67, l. 2.
55. Hereinafter: TsIAM, f. 179, op. 62, d. 16146, ll. 1–22.
56. TsIAM, f. 16, op. 89, d. 67, l. 2.
57. Tiutriumov, *Zakony grazhdanskie*, p. 433.
58. TsIAM, f. 16, op. 89, d. 67, l. 3.
59. Ibid., f. 179, op. 62, d. 16233, ll. 2-4.
60. *Pamiatnaia knizhka Moskovskoi Gubernii na 1899 god* (Moscow: Mosk. Statisticheskii komitet, 1899), p. 493, 497.
61. The problem was examined in A. Colli, *The History of Family Business, 1850-2000* (Cambridge: Cambridge University Press, 2003), pp. 49–65.

Conclusion

1. Beachy, Craig, Owens, 'Introduction', in Beachy, Craig, Owens (eds), *Women, Business, and Finance*, p. 11.
2. *PSZ II*, vol. VII, No 5462.
3. TsIAM, f. 3, op. 1, d. 255, ll. 10–127.
4. *PSZ I*, vol. XXIX, No 22418, art. 17.
5. It should be noted that estate discrimination affected male merchants as well. At the Kremlin ceremonies marking the Emperor's visits to Moscow in the 1880s–90s, merchants were topographically separated from nobles. The Monarch met with the leading members of the Moscow merchant and artisan communities in St Vladimir's Hall of the Great Kremlin Palace, while his meeting with families belonging to the first four classes of the nobility took place in St George's Hall. See: TsIAM, f. 143, op. 1, d. 5, ll. 46–8, 98–100.
6. From 87.2 to 58.4 million *desiatinas* (or from 235.4 to 157.7 million acres). See S. Becker, *Nobility and Privilege in Late Imperial Russia* (DeKalb, IL: Northern Illinois University Press, 1985), p. 32.
7. For the efficiency of the family firm as a form of organization and management, see Colli, *The History of Family Business, 1850-2000*; D. Arnoldus, *Family, Family Firm and Strategy: Six Dutch Family Firms in the Food Industry,1880–1970* (Amsterdam: Aksant, 2002); D. S. Landes, *Dynasties: Fortunes and Misfortunes of the World's Great Family Business* (New York: Viking, 2006).
8. Evtuhov and Stites, *A History of Russia*, p. 158.
9. The model for this character was Vasilii Botkin.
10. P. Boborykin, *Kitai-Gorod* (Moscow: Moskovskii rabochii, 1985), pp. 77, 75.
11. Gregory, *Russian National Income*, p. 154.

WORKS CITED

Archival Sources

TsIAM (Tsentral'nuy istoricheskii arkhiv Moskvy -Central Historical Archive of the City of Moscow), fonds (collection) 2, 3, 14, 16, 50, 51, 78, 117, 131, 142, 179. 357, 715.

RGADA (Rossiiskii gosudarstvennyi arkhiv drevnikh actov – Russian State Archive of Ancient Acts), fond (collection) 1271 (Miatlevy).

The Chetverikovs - N.A. Dobrynina Family Archive, Sergey Chetverikov, *The Memories (manuscript)*, pictures.

Primary Sources

Adres-calendar'. Obshchaia rospis' nachal'stvuiushchikh i prochikh dolzhnostnykh lits po vsem upravleniiam v Rossiiskoi imperii na 1870 g., 2 vols (St Petersburg, 1870).

Androssov V., *Statisticheskaia zapiska o Moskve* (Moscow, 1832).

Bakhrushin, Y., *Vospominaniia* (Moscow, 1994).

Bezobrazov, V. P. *Narodnoe khoziaistvo Rossii*, 3 vols (St Petersburg, 1882).

Garelin, Y. P. *Gorod Ivanovo-Voznesensk ili byvshee selo Ivanovo i Voznesenskii Posad (Vladimir-skoi gubernii)*, 2 vols (Shuya, 1884–5).

V. F. Dzunkovskii, *Vospominaniia*, 2 vols (Moscow, 1997).

Golubovich, A. K., *Arkhiv Radziwillov-Wittgensteinov v Bundesarchive, Germania*, www.niab.belhost.by/stat/arh_radz/, accessed 15 April 2008.

Ioksimovich, C. M., *Manufakturnaia promyshlennost' v proshlom i nastoiashchem* (Moscow, 1917).

Kittary, M. Y., *Obozrenie Sankt-Peterburgskoi vystavki russkoi manufakturnoi promyshlennosti 1861 goda* (St Petersburg, 1861).

Labzin, N., *Istoriko-statisticheskii obzor promyshlennosti Rossii. Gruppa IX. Mashiny, apparaty i ekipazhi* (St Petersburg, 1882).

Livron V. de *Statisticheskoe obozrenie Rossiiskoi Imperii* (St Petersburg, 1874).

Lobanov-Rostovskii, A. B., *Russkaia rodoslovnaia kniga*, 2 vols (St Petersburg, 1895).

Maksheev, A., *Voenno-statisticheskoe obozrenie Rossiiskoi Imperii* (St Petersburg, 1867).

Materialy dlia istorii moskovskogo kupechestva. Obshchestvennye Prigovory, 11 vols (Moscow, 1892–1909).

Materialy dlia istorii moskovskogo kupechestva. Revizskie skazki, 9 vols (Moscow, 1883–9).

Materialy dlia statistiki parovykh dvigatelei v Rossiiskoi imperii (St Petersburg, 1866).

Materialy dlia torgovo-promyshlennoi statistiki. Svod dannykh o fabrichno-zavodskoi promyshlennosti v Rossii za 1897 g (St Petersburg, 1900).

Materialy k istorii Prokhorovskoi Trekhgornoi manufactury i torgovo-promyshlennoi deiatel'nosti sem'i Prokhorovykh. Gody 1799–1915 (Moscow, 1915).

Matissen, N., *Atlas manufacturnoi promyshlennosti Moskovskoi gubernii* (Moscow, 1872).

Memoir of the late Charles Baird, esq., of St Petersburg and and of his son, the late Francis Baird, 4, Queens Gate, London (London, 1867).

McKay, J. P., *Pioneers for Profit. Foreign Entrepreneurship and Russian Industrialization 1885–1913* (Chicago, IL, 1970).

Mendeleev, D., 'Vvedenie. Obzor fabrichno-zavodskoi promyshlennosti i torgovli Rossii', in *Fabrichno-zavodskaia promyshlennost' i torgovlia Rossii* (St Petersburg, 1893).

Metelercamp V.D., Niström K. *Kniga adressov stolitsy Moskvy* (Moscow, 1839).

Moskovskii Nekropol', 3 vols (St Petersburg: Tipografia S. Selivanovskogo, 1907–8).

Nevzorov, A. S. *Russkaia zhenshchina v deistvuiushchem zakonodatel'stve i v deistvitel'noi zhizni* (Revel, 1892).

Niström K., Niström, *Kniga adressov stolitsy Moskvy* (Moscow, 1839).

—, *Moskovskii adres-kalendar' dlia zhitelei Moskvy*, 4 vols (Moscow, 1842).

Obshchii svod po Imperii rezul'tatov razrabotki dannykh Pervoi vseobshchei perepisi naseleniia Rossiiskoi Imperii, proizvedennoi 28 ianvaria 1897 g, 2 vols (St Petersburg, 1905).

Ocherk deiatel'nosti Moskovskogo kupecheskogo obshchestva vzaimnogo kredita za dvadtsatipiatiletie (1869–1894) (Moscow, 1895).

Orekhovo-Zuevskii kalendar' i zapisnaia knizhka na 1903 g (Orekhovo, 1903).

Orlov, A., *Anna, kupecheskaia doch', ili barkhatnyi ridicul' iz Galantereinogo Riadu* (Moscow, 1832).

Orlov, P. A., *Ukazatel' fabrik i zavodov Evropeiskoi Rossii* (St Petersburg, 1881).

—, *Ukazatel' fabrik i zavodov Evropeiskoi Rossii i Tsarstva Pol'skogo* (St Petersburg, 1887).

—, and S. G. Budagov, *Ukazatel' fabrik i zavodov Evropeiskoi Rossii* (St Petersburg, 1894).

Otchiot dusheprikazchikov po dukhovnomu zaveshchaniiu Marii Fedorovny Morozovoi (Moscow, 1913).

Pamiatnaia knizhka Moskovskoi Gubernii na 1899 god (Moscow, 1899).

Pamiatnaia knizhka Sankt-Peterburgskoi gubernii na 1864 god (St Petersburg, 1864).

Perechen' fabrik i zavodov (St Petersburg, 1897).

Peterburgskii Nekropol', 4 vols (St Petersburg, 1912–13).

Polnoe sobranie zakonov Rossiiskoi Imperii (Complete Collection of Laws of the Russian Empire). PSZ. 1st series (1649-1825), 45 vols (St Petersburg, 1830–43); 2nd series (1826–81), 55 vols (St Petersburg, 1830–84).

Prilozheniia k trudam Redaktsionnykh komissii dlia sostavleniia Polozhenii o krest'ianakh, vykhodiashchikh iz krepostnoi zavisimosti. Svedeniia o pomeshchich'ikh imeniiakh, 6 vols (St Petersburg, 1860).

Proekt torgovogo ulozheniia Rossiiskoi imperii (St Petersburg, 1814).

Reinke, N., 'Dvizhenie zakonodatel'stva ob imushchestvennykh pravakh zamuzhnei zhenshchiny', *Zhurnal grazhdanskogo i ugolovnogo prava,* 3 (1884), pp. 69–70.

Radzig, A., *Khlopchatobumazhnaia promyshlennost' Rossii* (St Petersburg, 1891).

Reinke N. 'Dvizhenie zakonodatel'stva ob imushchestvennykh pravakh zamuzhnei zhenshchiny', *Zhurnal grazhdanskogo i ugolovnogo prava,* 3 (1884), pp. 69–70.

Rudolf M. *Ukazatel' mestnosti v Kremle i Kitae-gorode stolichnogo goroda Moskvy,* vol. 1, Kreml i Kitai-gorod (Moscow, 1846).

Samoilov, L., *Atlas promyshlennosti Moskovskoi gubernii* (Moscow, 1845).

Sbornik statisticheskikh svedenii o Rossii, izdavaemyi statisticheskim otdeleniem Imperatorskogo Russkogo Geograficheskogo obshchestva (St Petersburg, 1851).

Schulze-Gävernitz, G. von, *Krupnoe proizvodstvo v Rossii (Moskovsko-Vladimirskaia khlopchatobumazhnaia promyshlennost')* (Moscow, 1899).

Semevskii, V. I., *Krest'iane v tsarstvovanie Imperatritsy Ekateriny II,* 2 vols (St Petersburg, 1901–3).

Skal'kovskii, K., *Vserossiiskaia manufakturnaia vystavka v promyshlennom otnoshenii* (St Petersburg, 1870).

Smirnov, A. *Pavlovo i Vorsma, izvestnye stal'no-slesarnym proizvodstvom sela Nizhegorodskoi gubernii* (Moscow, 1864).

Smirnova-Rosset, A. O., *Vospominaniia, pis'ma* (Moscow: Pravda, 1990).

Spisok fabrik i zavodov (St Petersburg, 1903).

Spisok fabrikantam i zavodchikam Rossiiskoi imperii 1832 goda (St Petersburg, 1833).

Spisok kuptsov goroda Moskvy, ob'iavivshikh kapitaly na 1830 god, s pokazaniem imeiushchegosia pri nikh semeistva, chem torgovliu proizvodiat i gde zhitel'stvo imeiut. [Moscow, 1830].

Spravochnaia kniga o litsakh, poluchivshikh kupecheskie svidetelstva po 1 i 2 gil'diiam v Moskve na [1869-1898] god (Moscow, 1869–98).

Spravochnaia kniga o litsakh, poluchivshikh na [1867-1898] god kupecheskie svidetelstva po 1 i 2 gil'diiam (St Petersburg, 1867–98).

Statisticheskie svedeniia o fabrikakh i zavodakh v Sankt-Peterburge za 1862 god (St Petersburg, 1863).

Statisticheskie tablitsy Rossiiskoi imperi za 1856 godi, sostavlennye i izdannye po rasporiazheniiu ministra vnutrennikh del statisticheskim otdelom Tsentral'nogo statisticheskogo komiteta (St Petersburg, 1858).

Statisticheskie tablitsy Rossiiskoi imperii, izdavaemye po rasporiazheniiu ministra vnutrennikh del Tsentral'nym statisticheskim komitetom (St Petersburg, 1863), vol. 2. *Nalichnoe naselenie imperii za 1858 god.*

Statisticheskii vremennik Rossiiskoi Imperii (St Petersburg, 1866).

Statisticheskii vremennik Rossiiskoi Imperii, II, No 6 (St Petersburg, 1872).

Svedeniia o fabrikakh i zavodakh, deistvovavshikh v 1864 godu (St Petersburg, 1866).

Tabel'naia kniga nedvizhimykh imushchestv g. Sankt-Peterburga (St Petersburg, 1900).

Tarasov S. *Statisticheskoe obozrenie promyshlennosti Moskovskoi gubernii* (Moscow, 1856).

Timiriazev, D. A., *Razvitie glavneishikh otraslei fabrichno-zavodskoi promyshlennosti v Rossii s 1850 po 1879 god* (St Petersburg, 1881).

Tiutriumov, I. M., *Zakony grazhdanskie (Svod zakonov, t. X, ch. 1, izd. 1900 g.) s raz"iasneniami Pravitel'stvuiushchego Senata i s kommentariiami russkikh iuristov, izvlechennymi iz nauchnykh trudov po grazhdanskomu pravu* (St Petersburg, 1905).

M. Tugan-Baranovskii, *Russkaia fabrika v proshlom i nastoiashchem. Istoriko-ekonomicheskoe issledovanie* (St Petersburg, 1900).

Ukazatel' Vystavki rossiiskikh manufakturnykh izdelii, byvshei v St. Peterburge v 1839 godu (St Petersburg, 1839).

Ukazatel' V moskovskoi vystavki russkikh manufakturnykh proizvedenii. 1865 (Moscow, 1865).

Varadinov N. V., *Istoriia Ministerstva vnutrennikh del*, 3 vols (St Petersburg, 1862).

Varentsov, N., *Slyshannoe. Vidennoe. Peredumannoe. Perezhitoe. [Memoirs]* (Moscow, 1999).

Vedomost' o manufakturakh v Rossii za 1813 i 1814 gody (St Petersburg, 1816).

Vigel', F. F., 'Zapiski', in *Russkie memuary. Izbrannye stranitsy: 1800–1825* (Moscow, 1989).

Vinaver M. M., Grazhdanskaia khronika, *Vestnik grazhdanskogo prava* (1913).

Voenno-statisticheskii sbornik, vol. 4 (St Petersburg, 1871).

Vseobshchaia adresnaia kniga Sankt-Peterburga (St Petersburg 1867–8).

Yanson Yu. E. *Sravnitel'naia statistika Rossii i zapadnoevropeiskikh gosudarstv.* (St Petersburg, 1878).

Zhivopisnaia Rossiia, 19 vols (St Petersburg, 1879–1901).

Secondary Sources

Aksenov, A. I., *Genealogiia Moskovskogo kupechestva XVIII veka* (Moscow: Nauka, 1988).

Anan'ich B. V., *Bankirskie doma v Rossii, 1860–1914 gg. Ocherki istorii chastnogo predprinimatel'stva* (Leningrad: Nauka, 1991).

—, 'Novyi kurs. 'Narodnoe samoderzhavie' Aleksandra III i Nikolaia II', in Anan'ich B. (ed.), *Vlast' i reformy. Ot samoderzhavnoi k sovetskoi Rossii* (St Petersburg: Dmitry Bulanin, 1996), pp. 369–454.

Anfimov, A. M., 'Karlovskoe imenie Mecklenburg-Strelitskikh v kontse XIX-nachale XX v.', *Materialy po istorii sel'skogo khoziaistva i krest'ianstva SSSR* (Moscow: izdatel'stvo Akademii nauk SSSR, 1962), pp. 348–76.

—, *Krupnoe pomeshchich'e khoziaistvo Evropeiskoi Rossii, konets XIX-nachalo XX veka* (Moscow: Nauka, 1969).

Annenkova E., and Y. Golikov, *Printsy Ol'denburgskie v Peterburge* (St Petersburg: Rostok, 2004).

Arnoldus, D., *Family, Family Firm and Strategy: Six Dutch Family Firms in the Food Industry, 1880–1970* (Amsterdam: Aksant, 2002).

Atkinson, D., A. Dallin and G. Lapidus (eds), *Women in Russia* (Stanford, CA: Stanford University Press, 1977).

Bandhauer-Schöffmann, I., 'Businesswomen in Austria', in R. Beachy, B. Craig and A. Owens, *Women, Business, and Finance in Nineteenth-century Europe: Rethinking Separate Spheres* (Oxford and New York: Berg, 2005), pp. 110–25.

Barker H. *The Business of Women: Female Enterprise and Urban Development in Northern England 1760–1830 (New York: Oxford University Press, 2006)*.

Basch, N., *In the Eyes of the Law: Women, Marriage and Property in Nineteenth-Century New York* (Ithaca, NY: Cornell University Press, 1982).

Beachy, R., B. Craig and A. Owens (eds), *Women, Business, and Finance in Nineteenth-century Europe: Rethinking Separate Spheres* (Oxford and New York: Berg, 2005).

Berg M., Women's Property and the Industrial Revolution, *Journal of Interdisciplinary History*, 24:2 (1993).

Bernstein, L., *Sonia's Daughters: Prostitutes and their Regulations in Imperial Russia* (Berkeley, CA: University of California Press, 1995).

Boborykin P. *Kitai-Gorod* (Moscow: Moskovskii Rabochii, 1985).

Bogoslovsky M. M., 'Moskva v 1870-1890-kh godakh', in M. M. Bogoslovsky, *Istoriographia, memuaristika, epistoliaria* (Moscow: Nauka, 1987).

Bokhanov, A. N., *Krupnaia burzhuaziia Rossii, konets XIX v. – 1914 g.* (Moscow: Nauka, 1992).

Bovykin, V. I., 'Ekonomicheskaia politika tsarskogo pravitel'stva i industrial'noe razvitie Rossii, 1816-1900', *Ekonomicheskaia Istoriia. Ezhegodnik 2002* (Moscow: Rosspen, 2003).

Brownlee, E. W., and M. M. Brownlee, *Women in the American Economy: a Documentary History, 1675 to 1929* (New Haven, CT: Yale University Press, 1976).

Buryshkin, P. A., *Moskva kupecheskaia* (Moscow: Vysshaia shkola, 1991).

Busch, M., *Deutsche in St. Petersburg 1865-1914: Identität und Integration* (Essen: Klartext, 1995).

Catherine II's Charters of 1785 to the Nobility and the Towns, ed. by D. Griffiths and G. E. Munro, *The Laws of Russia Series II: vol. 289* (Bakersfield, CA: Schlacks Publishers, 1991).

Chapman, S., *Merchant Enterprise in Britain from the Industrial Revolution to World War I* (Cambridge: Cambridge University Press: 1992).

Chekhov A., 'Fragments of Moscow Life', in A. Chekhov, *Polnoe sobranie sochinenii i pisem*, 30 vols (Moscow, 1974–83); vol. 16 (1979).

Chereiskii L. A., *Pushkin i ego okruzhenie* (Leningrad: Nauka, 1988).

Chrimes, M., 'Baird, Charles', in *Biographical Dictionary of Civil Engineers in Great Britain and Ireland* (London: Thomas Telford, 2002), vol. 1, pp. 30–1.

Clements, B., *Bolshevik Women* (Cambridge: Cambridge University Press, 1997).

Clements, D. B., B. A. Engel and C. Worobec (eds), *Russia's Women. Accommodation, Resistance, Transformation* (Berkeley, CA: University of California Press, 1991).

Colli, A., *The History of Family Business, 1850-2000* (Cambridge: Cambridge University Press, 2003).

Davidoff, L., and C. Hall, *Family Fortunes: Men and Women of the English Middle Class, 1780–1850*, 2nd edn (Chicago, IL: University of Chicago Press, 1991).

Di Martino, P., 'Approaching Disaster: A Comparison between Personal Bankruptcy Legislation in Italy and England (*c.*1880–1939)', *Business History*, 47:1. (January 2005), pp. 23–43.

Dictionary of Russian Historical Terms from the Eleventh Century to 1917, comp. S. Pushkarev, ed. G. Vernadsky and R. T. Fisher Jr (New Haven, CT and London: Yale University Press, 1970).

Dostoevsky, F., *Podrostok*, in F. Dostoevsky, *Sobranie sochinenii*, 15 vols (Leningrad: Nauka, 1988–96), vol. 8 (1990).

Eimontova, R. G. 'Dvenadtsatyi god. Nashestvie', in *Istoriia Moskvy s drevneishikh vremen do nashikh dnei*, 3 vols (Moscow: Mosgorarchive, 1997–2000) vol. 2, pp. 24–42.

Engel, B. A., *Between the Fields and the City: Women. Work and Family in Russia, 1861–1914* (Cambridge: Cambridge University Press, 1994).

Mothers and Daughters. Women of the Intelligentsia in Nineteenth Century Russia (Ewanston, IL: Northwester University Press, 2000).

—, *Women in Russia, 1700–2000* (Cambridge: Cambridge University Press, 2004).

Erickson, A. L., 'The Marital Economy in Comparative Perspective' in M. Ågren and A. L. Erickson (eds), *The Marital Economy in Scandinavia and Britain 1400–1900* (Aldershot: Ashgate, 2005), pp. 3–20.

Evtuhov, C., and R. Stites, *A History of Russia: Peoples, Legends, Events, Forces, Since 1800* (Boston, MA and New York: Houghton Mifflin, 2004).

Farrow, L. A., *Between Clan and Crown: The Struggle to Define Noble Property Rights in Imperial Russia* (Newark, DE: University of Delaware Press, 2004).

Fedorchenko, K. G., *Rossiiskaia imperiia v litsakh. Entsiklopediia biografii*, 2 vols (Krasnoiarsk-Moscow: OLMA-Press, 2001).

Finn, M., 'Women, Consumption and Coverture in England, c.1760–1860', *Historical Journal*, 39:3 (1996), pp. 703–22.

Fomina, O. V., *Imushchestvenno-demograficheskaia kharacteristika moskovskoi kupecheskoi sem'i v poslednei treti XVIII v.* [Avtoreferat … kand. ist. nauk] (Moscow, 2003).

Freeze, G. L., 'The *Soslovie* (Estate) Paradigm and Russian Social History', *American Historical Review*, 91 (1986), pp. 1–36.

Gamber, 'Gendered Concerns: Thoughts on the History of Business and the History of Women', *Business and Economic History*, 23:1 (1994), pp. 129–40.

—, *The Female Economy: the Millinery and Dressmaking Trades, 1860–1930* (Urbana, IL: University of Illinois Press, 1997).

—, 'A Gendered Enterprise: Placing Nineteenth-Century Businesswomen in History', *Business History Review*, 72 (Summer 1998), pp. 188–217.

Gatrell, P., *The Tsarist Economy, 1850–1917* (London: B.T. Batsford Ltd, 1986).

Gavrilova, I. N., *Demograficheskaia istoriia Moskvy* (Moscow: Fast-Print, 1997).

Gershenkron, A., *Economic Backwardness in Historical Perspective* (New Haven, CT: Yale University Press, 1966).

Green, D. R., and A. Owens, 'Gentlewomanly Capitalism? Spinsters, Widows and Wealth Holding in England and Wales, c. 1800–1860', *Economic History Review*, 56:3 (2003), pp. 510–36.

Gregory, P., *Russian National Income 1885–1913* (London: Cambridge University Press, 1982).

Hautcoeur P.-C., and N. Levratto, 'Bankruptcy law and practice in 19th century France', *PSE (Paris School of Economics) Working Papers*, 2007–29.

Henderson, W. O., *The Industrial Revolution on the Continent: Germany, France, Russia, 1800–1914* (London: Frank Cass & Co., 1967).

Hildermeier, M., *Bürgertum und Stadt in Russland 1760–1870: Rechtliche Lage und Soziale Struktur* (Köln: Böhlau Verlag, 1986).

Holcombe, L., *Wives and Property: Reform of the Married Women's Property Law in Nineteenth-Century England* (Toronto, ON: University of Toronto Press, 1983).

Hudson, P., 'Capital and Credit in the West Riding Wool Textile Industry c. 1750–1850', in P. Hudson (ed.), *Regions and Industries: A Perspective on the Industrial Revolution in Britain* (Cambridge: Cambridge University Press, 1989), pp. 69–99.

Ivanov, A. E., *Vysshaia shkola Rossii v kontse XIX – nachale XX veka* (Moscow: Institut rossiiskoi istorii, 1991).

Joffe M., Lindenmeyr A., 'Daughter, Wives, and Partners: Women of the Moscow Merchant Elite', in J. L. West and I. Petrov (eds), *Merchant Moscow: Images of Russia's Vanished Bourgeoisie* (Princeton, NJ: Princeton University Press, 1997), pp. 95–108.

Kafengauz, L. B., *Evolutsia promyshlennogo proizvodstva Rossii (posledniaia tret' XIX v. – 30-t gg. XX v* (Moscow: Epifania, 1994).

Kahan, A., *Russian Economic History: the Nineteenth Century*, ed. R. Weiss (Chicago, IL and London: University of Chicago Press, 1989).

Kay, A., 'Small Business, Self-Employment and Women's Work-Life Choices in Nineteeth Century London', in D. Mitch, J. Brown and M. H. D. van Leeuwen, *Origins of the Modern Career* (Aldershot: Ashgate, 2004), pp. 191–206.

—, 'Retailing, Respectability and the Independent Woman in Nineteenth-century London', in R. Beachy, B. Craig and A. Owens (eds), *Women, Business, and Finance in Nineteenth-century Europe: Rethinking Separate Spheres* (Oxford and New York: Berg, 2005), pp. 152–66.

King, S., and G. Timmins, *Making Sense of the Industrial Revolution: English Economy and Society, 1700–1850* (Manchester: Manchester University Press, 2001).

Korelin, A. P., *Dvorianstvo v poreformennoi Rossii 1861–1900* (Moscow: Nauka, 1979).

Koval'chuk, A. V., *Manufakturnaia promyshlennost' Moskvy vo vtoroi polovine XVIII veka* (Moscow, 1999).

Kozlova, 'Khoziaistvennaia aktivnost' i predprinimatel'stvo kupecheskikh zhen i vdov Moskvy v XVIII v.', in *Torgovlia, kupechestvo i tamozhennoe delo v Rossii XVI-XVIII vekov* (St Petersburg, 2001), pp. 139–44.

—, 'Imushchestvennoe pravo i polozhenie zhenshchiny v kupecheskoi sem'e Moskvy XVIII v.', in *Stolichnye i periferiinye goroda Rusi i Rossii v srednie veka i rannee novoe vremia* (Moscow, 2003), pp. 259–75.

Krasko, A. V., *Eliseevy* (St Petersburg: VIRD, 1998).

Krivoshein, K.A., *Aleksandr Vasil'evich Krivoshein: sud'ba rossiiskogo reformatora* (Moscow: Moskovskii Rabochii, 1993).

Kliuchevsky, V. O., 'Kurs russkoi istorii', in V. O. Kliuchevsky, *Sochineniia*, 9 vols (Moscow: Mysl', 1987–90).

Kupecheskie dnevniki i memuary kontsa XVIII-pervoi poloviny XIX veka. Moscow, 2007.

Kuznets, S., *Modern Economic Growth* (New Haven, CT: Yale University Press, 1966).

Landes, D. S., *Dynasties: Fortunes and Misfortunes of the World's Great Family Business* (New York: Viking, 2006).

Lebedev, M., 'K istoriko-economicheskoi kharakteristike byvshei Nikol'skoi manufaktury', in *Istoriko-kraevedcheskii sbornik*, 2, (1959), pp. 5–19.

Lindenmeyr, A., *Poverty is not a Vice: Charity, Society, and the State in Imperial Russia* (Princeton, NJ: Princeton University Press, 1996).

—, 'Review on Marrese, A Woman's Kingdom', *Journal of Social History*, 38:2 (2004), p. 553–5.

Marrese, M. L., *A Woman's Kingdom: Noblewomen and the Control of Property in Russia, 1700–1861* (Ithaca, NY and London, 2002).

Mikhailov N. V., *Lakhta: piat' vekov istorii. 1500-2000* (Moscow: Ves'mir, 2001).

Mironov, B. N., *Sotsial'naia istoriia Rossii perioda Imperii (XVIII-nachalo XX v.). Genezis lichnosti, demokraticheskoi sem'i, grazhdanskogo obshchestva i pravovogo gosudarstva*, 2 vols. (St Petersburg: Dmitry Bulanin, 1999).

Morozova M. 'Moi vospominaniia', in *Moskovskii al'bom* (Moscow: Nashe Masledic, 1997).

Morozovy. Dinastiia fabrikantov i mezenatov. Opyt rodosloviia (Bogorodsk: Pechatnik, 1995).

Munting, R., 'Industrial Revolution in Russia', in M. Teich, R. Porter (eds) *The Industrial Revolution in national context: Europe and the USA* (Cambridge: Cambridge University Press), 1996.

Nathans, B., *Beyond the Pale: The Jewish Encounter with Late Imperial Russia* (Berkeley, CA and London: University of California Press, 2004).

Oppedisano, J. M., *Historical Encyclopedia of American Women Entrepreneurs: 1776 to the Present* (Westport, CT: Greenwood Press, 2000).

O'Rourke S., 'Women in a Warrior Society: Don Cossack Women, 1860–1914', in R. Marsh (ed.), *Women in Russia and Ukraine* (Cambridge: Cambridge University Press, 1996).

Otechestvennaia istoriia. Istoriia Rossii s drevneishikh vremen do 1917 goda. Entsiklopediia, 3 vols to date (Moscow: Bol'shaia Rossiiskaia entsiklopediia, 1994).

Owen T. C., *The Corporation under Russian Law, 1800–1917* (Cambridge: Cambridge University Press: 1992).

Owens, A., 'Property, Gender and the Life Course: Inheritance and Family Welfare Provision in Early Nineteenth-Century England', *Social History*, 26 (2001), pp. 297–315.

—, Schulte-Beerbühl M. (eds), *Women and Business Networks in the Early Industrialization* (Oxford, 2009, forthcoming).

Petersson, T., 'The Silent Partners; Women, Capital and the Development of the Financial System in Nineteenth-century Sweden', in Beachy, Craig, Owens (eds), *Women, Business, and Finance in Nineteenth-century Europe: Rethinking Separate Spheres* (Oxford and New York: Berg, 2005).

Petrov Y. A., 'Lichnye sostoianiia Morozovykh-'Timofeevichei', in *Trudy Pervykh Morozovskikh chtenii* (Moscow: Bogorodsk, 1995).

—, *Moskovskaia burzhuaziia v nachale XX v.: predprinimatel'stvo i politika* (Moscow: Mosgorarchive, 2002).

—, *Kommercheskie banki Moskvy. Konets XIX v.– 1914* (Moscow: Rosspen, 1998).

Phillips, N., *Women in Business, 1700–1850* (Woodbridge, Suffolk-Rochester, NY: Boydell Press, 2006)

Pietrow-Ennker B., *Russlands 'neue Menschen': Die Entwicklung der Frauenbewegung von den Anfaengen bis zur Oktoberrevolution* (Frankfurt-New York: Campus Verlag, 1999).

Pogrebinskii, A. P., 'Finansovaia politika tsarizma v 70-80-kh godakh XIX v.', *Istoricheskii arkhiv*, 2 (1960), pp. 130–44.

Potkina, I. V., *Na Olimpe delovogo uspekha; Nikol'skaia manufaktura Morozovykh. 1797-1917* (Moscow: Mosgorarchive, 2004).

Pushkareva, N., *Women in Russian History From the Tenth to the Twentieth Century* (Armonk, NY: M. E. Sharpe, 1997).

—, *Gendernaia teoriia i istoricheskoe znanie* (St Petersburg: Aleteia, 2007)

Raleigh, D. (ed.), *The Emperors and Empresses of Russia: Rediscovering the Romanovs* (Armonk, NY: M. E. Sharpe, 1996).

Ransel, D. L., *Mothers of Misery: Child Abandonment in Russia* (Princeton, NJ: Princeton University Press, 1988).

—, *Village Mothers: Three Generations of Change in Russian and Tataria* (Bloomington, IN: Indiana University Press, 2000).

Rieber, A. J., *Merchants and Entrepreneurs in Imperial Russia* (Chapel Hill, NC: University of North Carolina Press, 1982).

—, 'The Sedimentary Society', in E. W. Clowes, S. D. Kassow, J. L. West (eds), *Between Tsar and People: Educated Society and the Quest for Public Identity in Late Imperial Russia* (Princeton, NJ: Princeton University Press, 1991), pp. 343–66.

Rosslyn, W., *Deeds, Not Words. The Origins of Women's Philanthropy in the Russian Empire* (Birmingham: University of Birmingham Press, 2007).

Ruane, C., *Gender, Class, and the Professionalization of Russian City Teachers: 1860–1914* (Pittsburgh, PA: University of Pittsburgh Press, 1994).

Ruble, B. A., *Second Metropolis. Pragmatic Pluralism in Gilded Age Chicago, Silver Age Moscow, and Meiji Osaka* (Cambridge: Woodrow Wilson Center press & Cambridge University press, 2001).

Ruckman, J. A., *The Moscow Business Elite, A Social and Cultural Portrait of Two Generations, 1840–1905* (DeKalb, IL: Northern Illinois University Press, 1984).

Russian Women, 1698–1917: Experience and Expression, An Anthology of Sources, compiled by W. G. Wagner and others (Bloomington, IN: Indiana University Press, 2002).

Ryndziunsky, P. G., *Utverzhdenie kapitalizma v Rossii, 1850-1880 gg* (Moscow: Nauka, 1978).

Salmon, M., *Women and the Law of Property in early America* (Chapel Hill, NC: University of North Carolina Press, 1986).

Shanley, *Feminism, Marriage, and the Law in Victorian England* (Princeton, NJ: Princeton University Press, 1993).

Shcherbinin, P. P., *Voennyi faktor v povsednevnoi zhizni russkoi zhenshchiny v XVIII-nachale XIX vv.* (Tambov, 2004).

Shepelev, L. E., *Tsarism i burzhuaziia vo vtoroi polovine XIX veka* (Leningrad: Nauka, 1981).

Smail, J., The Culture of Credit in Eighteenth-Century Commerce: The English Textile Industry, *Enterprise and Society*, 4:2 (2003), pp. 299–325.

Solov'eva, A. M., *Promyshlennaia revoliutsia v Rossii v XIX v* (Moscow: Nauka, 1990).

Sparks, E., *Capital Intensions: Female Proprietors in San Francisco, 1850–1920* (Chapel Hill, NC: University of North Carolina Press, 2006).

Staves, S., *Married Women Separate Property in England, 1660–1833* (Cambridge, MA: Harvard University Press, 1990).

Stepanov, V., *N. Kh. Bunge: Sud'ba reformatora* (Moscow: Rosspen, 1998).

Stites R., *The Women's Liberation Movement in Russia: Feminism, Nihilism, and Bolshevism, 1860–1930* (Princeton, NJ: Princeton University Press, 1978).

Tairov N., *Akchuriny* (Kazan': Tatarskoeknizhnoe, 2002).

Thompstone, S., Russkoe Tekhnicheskoe obshchestvo i import britanskogo tekstil'nogo oborudovaniia, in S. Thompstone (ed.), *Rossiiskaia tekstil'naia promyshlennost'; tekhnologicheskii transfer, syr'e, finansy* (St Petersburg: Olearius Press, 2006).

Tikhomirova, M. N., 'Uchastie zhenshchin v promyshlennom proizvodstve Rossii v kontsa 60-kh-nachale 70-kh godov XIX veka (na materialakh Tverskoi Gubernii)', in *Zhenshchiny. Istoriia. Obshchestvo.* (Tver', 1999), pp. 34–46.

Tikhonov, Y. A., *Mir veshchei v moskovckikh i peterburgskikh domakh sanovnogo dvorianstva* (po novym istochnikam pervoi poloviny XVIII veka (Moscow: Kuchkovo pole, 2008).

Tishkin, G. A., *Zhenskii vopros v Rossii v 50–60 gg. XIX v.* (Leningrad: izdatel'stvo LGU, 1984).

Ulianova G. et al., *Two Centuries of Confectionery Industry in Russia.* Moscow, 2003, p. 20-6

—, *Blagotvoritel'nost' moskovskikh predprinimatelei, 1860–1914* (Moscow: Mosgorarchive, 1999).

—, 'Predprinimatel: tip lichnosti, dukhovnyi oblik, obraz zhizni', in *Istoriia predprinimatel'stva v Rossii*, 2 vols (Moscow: Rosspen, 1999), vol. 2, pp. 441–66.

—, 'Tuche, Schnaps und Farben; Unternehmerinnen aus Deutschen Familien in Russland im 19. Und zu Beginn des 20 Jahrhunderts', in D. Dahlmann, K. Heller, T. Igumnowa, J. Petrow, K. Reschke (eds), *«Eine Grosse Zukunft»*. *Deutsche in Russlands Wirtschaft* (Berlin-Moskau, 2000), pp. 90–7.

—, 'Die Unternehmerinnen als Wohltaeterinnen in Moskau. 1850-1914', in G. Hausmann (ed.), *Gesellschaft als lokale Veranstaltung. Selbstwervaltung, Assoziierung und Geselligkeit in den Städten des ausgehenden Zarenreiches* (Goettingen: Vanderhoeck & Ruprecht, 2002), pp. 405–32.

—, 'Merchant Women in Business in the Late Eighteenth and Early Nineteenth Centuries', in W. Rosslyn and A. Tosi (eds), *Women in Eighteenth-Century Russian Culture and Society* (London: Palgrave, 2007), pp. 144–67.

Vickery, A., 'Golden Age to Separate Spheres? A Review of the Categories and Chronology of English Women History', *Historical Journal*, 36:2 (1993), pp. 383–414.

—, *The Gentleman's Daughter: Women's Lives in Georgian England* (New Haven, CT and London: Yale University Press, 1998)

Vodarsky Ya. E., *Dvorianskoe zemlevladenie v Rossii v XVII - pervoi polovine XIX v.* (Moscow, 1988).

Viazemsky, P. A., *Staraia zapisnaia knizhka* (Leningrad: Izdatel'stvo pisatelei, 1929).

Wagner, W., *Marriage, Property, and Law in Late Imperial Russia* (Oxford: Clarendon Press, 1994; 2nd edn 2001).

West, J. L., and I. Petrov (eds), *Merchant Moscow: Images of Russia's Vanished Bourgeoisie* (Princeton, NJ: Princeton University Press, 1997).

Witte, S. Y., *Vospominaniia* , 3 vols (Moscow: Izdatel'stvo sotsial'no-ekonomicheskoi literatury, 1960).

Yukhneva, N. V., *Etnicheskii sostav i etnosotsial'naia struktura naseleniia Peterburga, vtoraia polovina XIX - nachalo XX v.: Statisticheskii analiz* (Leningrad: Nauka, 1984).

Yukina, I., *Russkii feminizm kak vyzov sovremennosti* (St Petersburg: Aleteia, 2007).

INDEX

Abdulova, Zuleikha, 22
acquired property, 193
Agafonova, Ksenia, 106
age stratification, 49–50, 94–6, 99–100, 107, 109
Akchurin family, 142
Akchurina, Fahri-Banu, 142
Aksenov, A. I., 5
Aksenova, Anna, 15
Akulova, Praskov'ia, 41
Albrecht, Anna, 22
Alekseev family, 57, 98, 169
Alekseev, N. A., 142
Alekseeva, Anis'ia, 80–2
Alekseeva, Tat'iana, 63
Alekseeva, Vera, 57
Alexander I, Emperor, 12, 43
Alexander II, Emperor, 73,119,137
Alexander III, Emperor, 177,196
Alexandra Fedorovna, Empress, 45
Anan'ich, B. V., 5
Andreanova, Agrippina, 106
Andreev family, 14
Androssov, V., 49
Apodiako, Polyxenia, 171
Apraksin family, 43
Apraksina, Maria, Countess, 118, 120
Arakelova, Elizaveta, 25
Arbat, Moscow, 53, 153, 157, 169, 183
artisans (tsekhovye), 34–5, 37, 40, 63, 78, 130

Babkina, Natal'ia, 4
Bade, Maria, 183
Baggovuth [Baggehufwudt], von Josephine, 171

Baidakova, Mar'ia, 82
Baird family, 96–7
Baird, Dorothea, née Holliday, 96, 98, 109
Bakhrushin family, 80–3
Bakhrushina, Natal'ia, 80–1, 108–9
Baklanov, Nikolai, 124, 127
Balk-Poleva, Varvara, 41
Baltic provinces, 171, 195
bankruptcy, 8, 36, 59, 67–9, 71, 78, 80, 111, 119, 127, 149, 155, 157–62, 164, 197–8
Bariatinskaia, Anna, 98
Bariatinskaia, Irina, 98
Bariatinskaia, Nadezhda, 98
Bariatinsky family, 43, 98
Barker, Hanna, 6
Barkov family, 67–9
Barkova, Mar'ia, 67–9
Bartel'ts, Elena, 26
Becker, Luise, 105
Belhert, Konstanzia, 78
Beliaeva, Aleksandra, 98
Belkina, 64, 73
Belousova, Anna, 191
Belova, Afim'ia, 101–2
Berg, Katharina, 178
Berg, Maxine, 6
Bezobrazov, V. P., 112
Bezobrazova, Nadezhda, 98
bill of exchange, 128, 159
Blokhina, Anis'ia, 25–6
Boborykin, P. D., *Kitai-Gorod*, 199
Bocharov, Mikhail, 160–2
Bogdanov family, 49, 51
Bogdanova, Ekaterina, 49, 51

Bogdanova, Maria, 92
Bogomazova, Elizaveta, 82
Bokhanov, A. N., 5
Bol'shaia (Bol'shova), Fedos'ia, 51–2
Bolotnova, Anna, 98
Borisova, Nadezhda, 63
Bostandzhoglo family, 142
Bouis, Hortensia, 78
Bovykin, V. I., 136
Branicka, Julia, 141
Branicka, Maria, Countess, 141, 170
Branitskaia [Branicka], Alexandra, Countess, née von Engelhardt, 38
Branitsky [Branicki] family, 43
Braun, Luzia-Nathalia, 178
Brodskaia, Sophia, 122
Brower, Daniel R., 76
Buksgevden [Buxhöwden], von Anna, 171
Bulgakova, 20
Bulochkina, Praskov'ia, 98
Bunge, N. Kh., 137
Burmakin family, 14
Bykovskaia, Elizaveta, 98–9
Bykovsky family, 84, 98–9

Campioni, Maria, 78
Canni, Giakomina, 105
Capitalism, 123
Catherine II, the Great, Empress, 10, 20, 39, 47
Catoire, Anne, 98
censuses (*revizii, perepisi*), 14, 23, 25, 33, 48–9, 74, 165
Chamov family, 66–7
Chamova, Ol'ga, 64, 66–7
Chario de, Maria, 78–80, 108
Charity, 60, 149, 155, 159
Chasovnikova, Marfa, 49
Chekhov, Anton Pavlovich, 80
Cherepakhina, Irina, 75
Chernysev family, 43
Chetverikov family, 48, 60
Chiuvaldina, Anna, 178
Chlodwig Hohenlohe-Schillingsfürst, Prince, 45
Clerks (*prikazchiki*), 51, 58–60, 65–7, 72, 131–2, 159, 186, 198–9

commercial (business) books, 54, 68, 128, 158–9
Commercial Court, 7, 68–9, 79, 111, 135, 152, 159–62, 198
Commercial Deputation (*torgovaia deputatsiia*), 38, 53–4, 62
Committee of Ministers, 124, 137
consumption, 23, 24, 30, 56, 104, 136, 164, 170, 173
Cossack women, 16–17, 22, 118, 120, 138
Craft, Anna, 180
credit, 1, 37, 67–9, 79, 84, 107–8, 119, 123, 126–8, 149, 152, 157–62, 164, 198
Crimean War (1853–6), 107, 113

Danilova, Anis'ia, 105
Davidoff, Leonore, 5–6
Davydova, Pelageia, 88, 94
Dediukhina, Glafira, née Sen'kov, 117
Dehn, von family, 171
Demidov family, 97, 177
Demography, 49–50, 74, 111, 184, 192
Dernova, Anna, 178
Deutsche Bank, 150
Dislen, Anna, 106
divorce cases, 184, 187, 190
Dmitrii Konstantinovich, Grand Duke, 93
Dobroliubov, N. A., 145
Dolgorukaia, Ol'ga, Princess, 118
Dolgorukov family, 20, 43
Dolgorukov, Vladimir, Prince, 151–4
Dolgorukova, Varvara, Princess, 20
domestic ideology, 164
domestic sphere, 3, 6, 84, 122
domesticity, 180
dowry, 3, 43, 66, 156, 163, 180, 185, 199
Dulout, Marie, 15
Dunasheva, Dar'ia, 49, 61
Dutfois family, 143
Dzhunkovskii, V. F., 150

economic crisis, 111–12, 126, 132, 138, 143, 157, 164, 135–6, 198
Edmondson, Linda, 4
education, 44–6, 163, 180, 184, 199
Efimova-Fomina, Avdot'ia, 49
Ekaterina Mikhailovna, Grand Duchess, 118
electricity, 149, 151, 181

Elena Pavlovna, Grand Duchess, 46
Eliseev, Grigorii, 93
Eliseeva, Tatiana, 93
Emancipation of the Serfs (1861), 2, 107, 196
Engel, Barbara Alpern, 3–4
England *see also* Great Britain, United Kingdom
Enners (Gehner), Anna-Katharina, 120, 178
Ermakova, Maria, 107
Ershova, Liubov', 105
Ershova, Tatiana, 105
estate management, 47
Eugenia, Princess of Oldenburg, née Duchess Eugenia of Leuchtenberg, 118–19
Evtuhov, Catherine, 198
exhibitions, 52, 65, 79, 83, 91, 119, 172

Factory Inspectorate (*fabrichaia inspektsiia*), 137
Falkenhagen, 118
family business strategies, 7, 47, 60, 71, 74, 81, 84, 86, 93, 105, 127, 145, 149–50, 157, 163, 173, 181, 181, 195, 197–8
family-name change, 129–32
Farrow, Lee, 3
Fedorova, Mar'ia, 63
Fedotova, Tat'iana, 22
Fedotova, Zinaida, 179, 191
Feodora of Hohenlohe-Langenburg, Princess, 45
Firsanov family, 185–6
Firsanova, Vera, 165–6, 185–90, 199
First All-Russian Population Census (1897), *see also,* censuses, 165, 174, 184, 192
Fomina O., 5
Forsbom, Laura-Maria, 142
Fürster, Katharina, 78

Gabai, Anna, 142
Gagarin family, 43
Gamber, Wendy, 6
Gatrell, Peter, 112
Gausch, Amalia-Luise-Leontina-Matilda, 176
Gavrilenko, Sofia, 106
Gehner, *see* Enners
Gel'tishchev, Ivan, 131–2

gender identity, 7, 108
gender ideology, 193–4
gender role(s), 3, 123, 156, 163, 180, 185, 196–7, 199
German businesswomen, 21–2, 58, 78, 88, 92, 94, 105, 120–2, 141–2, 158, 171, 174–6, 178, 196–7
Gershenkron, Alexander, 136
Getscher, Elisabeth, 78
Ginter, Emilia, 92
Girardin, de Delphine, [*pen name* Vicomte De Launay], 46
Giraud, Claude-Marie, 178
Gladkova, Natal'ia, 118
Glebova-Streshneva, Elizaveta, Princess, 21
Glushkova, Anna, 105
Golenishcheva, Anna, 91
Golitsyn family, 43, 46
Golitsyna, Natal'ia, Princess, née Countess Chernysheva, 21, 43–4
Golitsyna, Sophia, Princess, 118
Goneshina, Klavdia, 57–8, 61
Gonetskii, Aleksey, 187–90
Gorinevskaia, Anna-Maria, 183
Gornostaeva, Avdot'ia, 15
Gracheva, Varvara, 15
Great Britain, *see also,* United Kingdom, 26, 37, 43, 46, 70, 92, 97–8, 113–14, 136–7, 149, 155, 166, 170, 189
Gregory, Paul, 136
Griaznov family, 169
Gribov family, 51
Gribova, Avdot'ia, 51
Grigor'eva, Elena, 178
Guild (merchant) certificates, 23, 29, 54, 65, 67, 73, 75, 92, 94, 137, 144, 177, 191
Gurvich, Dina, 118
Gzhel'tsov family, 58

Hall, Catherine, 5–6
Hildermeier, Manfred, 5
Hopper family, 179
Hopper, Elizabeth, 179
Hübner, Albert, 158

Ignat'eva, Praskov'ia, 24
Ikskul, von Natalia, 171
Il'ina, Matrena, 106

Industrial Revolution, 7, 48, 70, 73, 81, 101, 108, 114, 127, 132, 136, 195
industry, 16–23, 33–47, 76–93, 114–122, 138–144, 167, 173
   braid production, 36, 56–7
   breweries, 116, 141, 143, 170
   button-making, 19
   calico printing, 23, 26, 29–30, 39, 63, 170
   carriage-making, 76, 90, 115, 139, 168
   chemical industry, 35, 48, 67, 75–7, 88–9, 92,3, 98, 103, 106, 112, 115, 139, 148, 168, 182
   China and pottery production, 19
   cosmetics (pomade) production, 35, 56, 60, 67, 103
   cotton textile industry, 15, 18, 22–3, 30–1, 34, 36–7, 39, 48–9, 51, 60–3, 70, 75–6, 78, 82, 85, 101, 112–14, 117, 125, 137, 144–50, 157–8, 169–70, 177
   distilleries, 116, 121–2, 141, 170–1
   earthenware and brick industry, 77, 89, 115, 139, 168
   fat and wax processing, 76, 88–9, 115, 139, 168
   flax and hemp industry, 35
   flour production, 76, 88–9, 112, 115–16, 139
   food industry, 112, 118, 120–2, 132, 138, 141, 166–8, 170–1, 177, 194–5
   glass and crystal industry, 16, 18, 26, 31, 35–6, 42,3, 45, 90, 106, 121
   iron and steel production, 16, 18, 35, 38–9, 96–7, 113, 136–7, 142, 176, 179
   leather industry, 21–2, 36–7, 83–4, 88–9, 92, 103, 108, 112–15, 122, 139, 168, 176, 178, 182
   linen industry, 17, 43, 112
   machine-building and metalworking, 97, 112–15, 139, 163, 166, 168
   matches making, 77, 115, 139, 168, 194
   paper making, 16, 18, 22, 31, 35–6, 39, 42, 56, 75–7, 90, 112, 115, 128–9, 139, 168, 179potash industry, 18, 35–6, 42, 44
   rope industry, 35

   soap-boiling, fat-rendering, candle-making, and wax-refining industries, 16, 22, 35–7, 141
   tanning, 16–17, 21–3, 35, 76–7, 83
   tobacco industry, 36, 55, 63, 76–8, 88–9, 91–2, 115, 122, 139, 142, 168, 180, 194
   vinegar production, 35
Innkeepers, 72, 104, 195
Iskakova, Zuleikha, 22
Ivoilova, Katerina, 22

Jablonowska, Ludgarda, Princess, née Tyszkiewicz, 121
Jews, *see also*, Pale of Settlement, 94, 121–2, 142, 174–6, 178–9, 192, 196–7
Joffe, Muriel, 4
Johansson, Elizaveta, 180
Joint stock companies, 87, 97, 123–4, 165, 177
Junget, Maria, 78

Kafengauz, L. B., 166
Kaidanova, Elizaveta, 75
Kalmykova, Alexandra, 181
Kanbina, Ekaterina, 91, 94, 96
Kandalintseva, Praskov'ia, 42
Kapobus, Philippina, 58
Karageorgievich, Arsen, Prince, 177
Karageorgievich, Aurora, née Demidova, Countess San-Donato, *see also* Demidov family, 176–7
Karneeva, Matrena, 58
Kaufman, Malka, 118
Kharitonenko, Natal'ia, 171
Khasbulatova, O. A., 4
Khludov family, 151–6, 163, 169
Khodateleva, Maria, 49
Khovanskaia, Elena, Princess, 41
Khovansky family, 43
Khoziaseitov family, 39
King, Steven, 127
Kirikova, Anna, 178
Kirilova, Matrena, 63
Kitaeva, Gadiba, 22
Kitai-Gorod, Moscow, 1, 38, 51–3, 56–70, 79, 85, 93, 99, 101, 125, 130–1, 147, 150, 157–60, 173, 186, 199

Kittary, M. Ya., 83, 91
Kleinmichel, Maria, Countess, 118
Kliuchevsky, Vasily Osipovich, 10
Knörzer, Alexandrina-Helena, née Fischer, 141
Kochubei, Prince, 79
Kondrat'eva, Feodora, 24
Konetskaia, Iroida, 178
Koniukhova, Aleksandra, 22
Kopteva, Maria, 22
Korff, Maria, 106
Kornilova, Paraskeva, 185
Kornoukhov family, 15
Koroliova, Anis'ia, 58
Korotkaia, Anna, 180
Korovin family, 21
Kosheverova, Glafira, 157–9, 164
Kotova, Fiona, 75
Kovan'ko, Pelageia, 106
Kovyliaev family, 39
Koz'micheva, Avdot'ia, 82
Kozlova, Anna, 24
Kozlova, N. V., 5
Krasil'shchikova, Anna, 117, 144
Krasulina, Matrena, 58
Kravtsova, Anna, 39
Krestovnikov, Grigorii, 150
Krivoshein, Aleksandr, 150
Kron, Augusta-Elisabete, 178
Kuchumova, Pelageia, 49
Kudriavtseva, Efimia, 81–2
Kulikova, Nastas'ia, née Pirogova, 133
Kumanina, Anna, 20
Kuniaeva, Praskov'ia, 63
Kurakina, Sophia, Princess, 118
Kushashnikova, Natal'ia, 57
Kutuzov, M. I., 24, 39
Kuvaev family, 169
Kuvaeva, Ekaterina, 117
Kuznets, Simon, 136
Kwolek-Folland, Angel, 6

Lanina, Ol'ga, 153
Laval' [la Valle] family, 43, 47
Laval' [la Valle], Aleksandra, Countess, née Kozitskaia, 43, 47

law on the admission of women to service at public and government institutions (1871), 111
Lawrence family, 92
Lawrence, Sophie, 92, 94
Leibrok, Julia, 106
Lenivova, Evdokiia, née Sen'kov, 117
Lenov family, 180–1
Lenova, Ekaterina, 180–1
Lepekhina, Matrena, 67
Lilienstadt, von Karoline, 171
Lindenmeyr, Adele, 2, 4
Linkiewicz, Agata, 20
Loginova, Agaf'ia, 63
Luk'ianchikova, Pelageia, 63

Maksheev, A., 73
Maksimova, Dar'ia, 63
Maksimovich, Evdokia, 144, 176, 184
Mamatova, Sagida, 22
Mardonini, Elena, 105
Maria Fedorovna, Empress, widow of Paul I, 45
Marrese, Michelle Lamarche, 2–3, 5, 47
Married women, 3, 10–11, 37, 39, 73, 88, 99, 106, 175, 180, 184, 194, 197
Maslennikov family, 39
Maslovskaia, Anna, 118
Mass consumption, *see* consumption
Matveev family, 14
Matveeva, Anna, 82
Matveeva, Maria, née Babkina, 80, 117, 123–9, 132
Medvedeva, Avdot'ia, 23, 49
Meliard, Marguerite, 78
Meshchanstvo, meshchanki, 2, 12, 17–18, 21, 31, 33–5, 37, 40, 42, 49, 50, 54, 60, 63, 70, 78, 85, 118, 120, 130, 138, 159, 196
Meshchersky family, 43
Miasnikov-Tverdyshev family, 47
Miatlev family, 4, 44
Miatleva, Praskov'ia, née Countess Saltykova, 44
Mill, John Stuart, *The Subjection of Women,* 111
Miller, Sophia-Ernestina, 105
Modern economic growth, 136, 191
Monigetti, Francesca, 78

Monoszon, Tsyva, 178
Morelle, Catherine, 78
Morozov, S. T. (Savva), 147, 149–151
Morozov, T. S., 145–9
Morozova, Maria, 135, 145–151, 163, 167
Morozova, Varvara, née Khludova, 153, 169
Morskova, Anna, 118
Moshnina Nadezhda, 75
Munting, Roger, 137
Murav'iova, Klavdia, 173
Murina, Alevtina, 183
Musina-Pushkina, Liubov', Countess, 118

Nadezhina-Cherkasova, Maria, 173
Nalbandova, Persane, 171
Napoléon Bonaparte, 24, 39, 65
Nemilova, Evdokiia, 117
Nevezhin family, 130
Nevezhina, Ekaterina, 130
Nicholas I, Emperor, 43, 45–6, 118
Nicholas II, Emperor, 189–90
Noble female entrepreneurs, 2, 4, 20, 31,
    42–7, 70–1, 79–80, 91, 96, 109, 116,
    118, 120, 132, 138, 176–7, 195–6
Nomikos, Kolimira, 170
Nosov family, 85–7
Nosova, Natal'ia, 81–2, 857, 109
Nussbaum, Elizabeth, 143

Okhotnikova, Sofia, 106
Old Believers, 14, 37, 145, 199
Opochinina, Dar'ia, 39
Orlov family, 43
Orlov, Aleksandr, 1–2
Ostrovskii A. N., 145
Owen, Thomas, 5, 123

Pale of Settlement, 122, 142, 176, 192
Panina, Maria, 135, 157, 159–62, 164
Panova, Anna, 21
Paul I, Emperor, 45
Pechkovskaia, Natal'ia, 183
Peter I, the Great, Emperor, 11, 43–4
petite bourgeoisie, see, *meshchanstvo*
Petrov Yu. A. (Iu. A.), 5
Petrova, Matrena, 51
Petrovskaia, Alexandra, 178
philanthropy, *see*, charity

Phillips, Nicola, 6
Piazzo, Amalia, 105
Pigot, Julia, 78
Pimenova, Dar'ia, 63
Plevako, F. N., 189
Pogozheva, Sofia, 183
Poliakova, Praskov'ia, 52–3
Polish female entrepreneurs, 43–45, 116,
    121, 141, 170, 174, 197
Polovtsova, Nadezhda, 176–7, 196
Poltoratskaia, Anna, 22
Ponomariov family, 39
Popova, Olimpiada, 75, 82
Potemkina, Praskov'ia, Countess, 20
Potkina, I. V., 5, 149
Potocka, Alexandra, 141
Potocka, Maria, Countess, 118, 120, 141
Pototsky [Potocki] family, 43, 121
Power of attorneys, 68, 71–2, 148, 158,
    160–2, 186–7, 199
Pribytkova, Ekaterina, 75
Prokhorov family, 61–2
Prokhorova, Ekaterina, 61–2
Protas'eva, Maria, 75
Protopopova, Matrena, 27–9
Purgusova, Elizaveta, 24
Pushkareva, N. L., 4
Pushkin, Aleksandr Sergeevich, 43, 47
Pushkina, Elena, 41

Radzig, Anton, 113
Radziwill family, 43–5
Ragoza, Vera, 117
Rakhmanova, Avdot'ia, 9
Ramm, von Elena, 171
Ransel, David, 4–5
Rasteriaev family, 92–4
Rasteriaeva, Agraphena, 75, 92–4, 96, 109
Razumovskaia, Maria, Countess, née Prin-
    cess Viazemskaia, 26, 46
Razumovsky family, 43, 46
remarriage of widows 62, 120, 129, 197
Remizova, Glafira, 117
Rennenkampf, von Luise, 171
Repnins family, 43
Reshetnikova, Agraphena, 75
Restaurant keepers, 55, 56, 58, 103–5, 109,
    182, 186

Riabinin family, 37–8
Riabinina, Anna, 37–8
Rieber, Alfred, 5, 183
Rosslyn, Wendy, 4
Rozanova, Natalia, 49
Ruane, Christine, 4
Ruckman, Jo Ann, 5, 60

Sabimova, Vakhrama, 22
Saltykov family, 21, 24, 43–4
Sangushko, Roman, Prince, 120
Savicheva, Maria, 183
Savostina, 75
Sayn-Wittgenstein-Sayn, Stephanie, née
    Radziwill, 43–5
Schulze-Gävernitz, von Gerhart, 170
Selezneva, Avdot'ia, 63
Semenova, Praskov'ia, 92
Serebrennikova, Pelageia, 175
Sergei Aleksandrovich, Grand Duke, 190
Services sector, *see* Innkeepers, Restaurant
    keepers
Shakhovskaia, Varvara, Princess, 20
Shaposhnikova (Shomova), Avdot'ia, 62–3
Shchekin family, 135, 151–5, 163–4
Shchekina, Nadezhda, née Khludova,
    151–5, 163–4, 199
Shchenkov, Vladimir, 158
Shelepova, Varvara, 27, 49
Sheremetev family, 15, 42–3, 55, 63, 66,
    172–3
Shirabardina, Praskov'ia, 22
Shirokova, Avdot'ia, 63
Shmakov family, 39
Shomov, Savva, 63
Shostakova, 21
Shukhova, Fedos'ia, 82
Shuvalova, Sophia, Countess, 118
Sichkova, Nastas'ia, 23
Simirenko family, 119
Simirenko, Sophia, 119
Simon, Julie, 142
Simonov family, 145–7
single women, 3, 37, 172, 184, 197
Skorobogatova, Anna, 63
Smith family, 143–4
Smith, Janet, 143–5
Soboleva, Avdot'ia, 50

Sokolova, Alexandra, 63
Soldatenkov family, 145
Soldatenkov, K. T., 145
Solov'eva, A. M., 81
Southern provinces (Ukrainian, Little-
    Russian) 39, 41–2, 74, 195
Stanislavsky, Constantine, 57
Stenbok-Fermor, Nadezhda, Countess,
    96–8, 109, 176–7
Stepanova, Avdot'ia, 24
Stepanova, Marfa, 63
Stieglitz, Alexander, 177
Stites, Richard, 4
Stolypin, P. A., 150, 190
Stolz, Theresa, 143
Striziver, Vera, 178
Stroemfeld, Sophie, 117
Strukova, Akulina, 27
Suchkova, Tat'iana, 82
Sukhanova, Anna, 64–6
Svechina, Fedos'ia, 41
Sviderskaia, Franziska, 107
Syreishchikov family, 59–60

Tatar businesswomen, 21–2, 94, 121, 142,
    196
Tatishchev family, 177
Tereshchenko, Nadezhda, 171
Tiesenhausen, von Alexandra, 171
Tikhomirova, M. N., 5
Tikhonova, Anna, 157
Timiriazev, D. A., 112
Timmins, Geoffrey, 127
Tishkin G. A., 4
Tiuliaeva, Maria, 75
Tolokonnikova, Pelageia, 50
Tolstaia (Tolstoy), Anna, Countess, 118
Tolstaia (Tolstoy), Stepanida, Countess, 20
Tolstoy family, 43
trade, 102–7, 181–185
    bookshops, 183
    chandleries, 44, 48, 75, 80, 88, 91, 98,
        112
    chemicals and cosmetics selling, 56, 66,
        93, 183
    coffee and tea selling, 54, 56, 64, 67,
        98–9, 107, 179
    colonial goods retail, 93

food and drink retail, 55–6, 72, 98,
    102–4, 109, 179, 181–2
haberdashery, 1, 56, 66, 92, 103, 182
tobacco retail, 56, 64, 67, 102–4, 109,
    179, 181–2
Tret'iakova, Ul'iana, 75
Tret'iakova, Praskov'ia, 64–5, 67
Trikha, Aleksandra, 98
Trubetskaia, Ekaterina, 47
Trustees 93, 128
Trusteeship 152–4, 164
Tsurikova, Anna, 117
Tsyganov family, 130
Tsyganova, Avdot'ia, 130
Tubenthal, Elena, 183
Tyzskiewicz, Helena, 141

Ukraine, *see* Southern provinces
Ukrainian female entrepreneurs, 121, 141,
    170–4, 196–7
United Kingdom (UK), *see also* Great
    Britain, England, 26, 37, 43, 46, 70, 92,
    97–8, 113–14, 136–7, 149, 155, 166,
    170, 189
United States 3, 15, 136, 137
Utkina, Irina, 63
Uvarov family, 43

Varentsov, N., 156
Verevkina, Alexandra, 75
Viazemsky family, 43
Viazemsky, P. A., Prince, 46
Vickery, Amanda, 5
Victoria, Queen of the United Kingdom, 46
Vigel, F., 44
Vinaver, M. M., 186
Vinogradova, Maria, 118

Vitova, Praskov'ia, 117
Vitztum, Leonia, Countess, 118
Vlas'eva, Avdot'ia, 23, 26, 28–30
Voitekhova, F., 118
Volkonskaia, Aleksandra, Princess, 20
Volkonsky family, 43
Vürgang, Anna, 78
Vyzhilov family, 123, 128–9
Vyzhilova, Anna, 129, 132

Wagner, William G., 3
Weil, Frada, 191
Weisbrem, Anna, 178
Widows, 3, 8, 10–12, 21, 30, 33, 37, 50–57,
    62, 71, 77, 80, 88, 91, 98–9, 156, 167,
    180, 184, 192, 197
Witte, S. Yu., Count, 177–8
Worobec, Christine, 4
Wrangel, von Justina, 171
Wrede, von Maria, 171

Yakovlev, Savva, 97
Yusupov, Nikolai, Prince, 124
Yusupova, Princess, 4

Zakrevsky family, 43
Zav'ialov family, 172, 199
Zavadovsky, Count, 47
Zernova, Anna, 98
Zezina, Matrena, 26, 28, 30
Zherebtsova, Paraskeva, 185
Zhukova, Aleksandra, 88, 94
Zindel [Zündel], Emilia, 78, 81–2
Zubov family, 43
Zubova, Natal'ia, Countess, 20, 42
Zvezdina, Taisiia, 106, 175

For Product Safety Concerns and Information please contact our EU
representative GPSR@taylorandfrancis.com
Taylor & Francis Verlag GmbH, Kaufingerstraße 24, 80331 München, Germany